PATHOLOGY AND THE POSTMODERN

Mental Illness as Discourse and Experience

EDITED BY
DWIGHT FEE

SAGE Publications
London • Thousand Oaks • New Delhi

First published 2000

SAGE Publications Ltd
6 Bonhill Street
London EC2A 4PU

SAGE Publications Inc
2455 Teller Road
Thousand Oaks, California 91320

SAGE Publications India Pvt Ltd
32, M-Block Market
Greater Kailash – I
New Delhi 110 048

British Library Cataloguing in Publication data

A catalogue record for this book is available from the British Library

ISBN 0–7619–5252–7
ISBN 0–7619–5253–5 (pbk)

Library of Congress catalog card number 99-72926

Typeset by Photoprint, Torquay, Devon

Contents

IV TOWARD NEW APPROACHES: EPISTEMOLOGY, RESEARCH, POLITICS

Notes on Contributors

LeslieBeth Berger received her doctorate at the University of Massachusetts at Amherst, and is a developmental psychologist now working as a consultant in Sarasota, Florida. She is author of *Incest, Work, and Women: Understanding the Consequences of Incest on Women's Careers, Work and Dreams* (Charles C Thomas, 1998)

Vivien Burr is Principal Lecturer in Psychology at the University of Huddersfield. She teaches and publishes in the areas of social constructionism, gender, and personal construct psychology, and is the author of *An Introduction to Social Contructionism* (Routledge, 1995), *Invitation to Personal Construct Psychology* with Trevor Butt (Whurr, 1992), and *Gender and Social Psychology.*

Trevor Butt trained as a clinical psychologist and is now Principal Lecturer in the Department of Behavioural Sciences at the University of Huddersfield. He is the author, with Vivien Burr, of *Invitation to Personal Construct Psychology* (Whurr, 1992), and has published in the fields of personal and social constructionism. He has a particular interest in the psychology of George Kelly and the phenomenology of Merleau-Ponty.

Dwight Fee is currently Visiting Assistant Professor of Sociology at Middlebury College in Middlebury, Vermont. In addition to his interest in mental illness, he teaches and publishes in the areas of contemporary social theory and epistemology, interpretive social psychology, and sexuality and gender studies. Having received his doctorate in 1996 from University of California, Santa Barbara, he is now working on a book that explores heterosexuality and friendship, to be published by the University of Chicago Press.

Michael R. Fraser wrote his doctoral dissertation in sociology at the University of Massachusetts, Amherst, on the role of informal social support in the lives of individuals living with HIV. He is Senior Research Associate with the Data and Community Assessment Division at the National Association of County and City Health Officials (NACCHO), currently designing a nationwide study of public health infrastructure as well as developing information technology programs for local health departments. His articles have appeared in such journals as *Demography, Evaluation Review, Contemporary Sociology*, and *Social Problems.*

Mark Freeman is Professor of Psychology at the College of the Holy Cross, where he also serves as Associate Dean of the College. He is the author of *Rewriting the Self: History, Memory, Narrative* (Routledge, 1993), *Finding the Muse: A Sociopsychological Inquiry into the Conditions of Artistic Creativity* (Cambridge University Press, 1993), and numerous articles on the self, autobiographical narrative, and the psychology of art.

Kenneth J. Gergen is the Mustin Professor of Psychology, Swarthmore College, and Chair of the Program in Interpretation Theory. He is a co-founder of the Taos Institute, working at the interface between social constructionist theory and social practice, and the author of *The Saturated Self* (Basic Books, 1991) and *Realities and Relationships* (Harvard University Press, 1994).

Simon Gottschalk is Associate Professor of Sociology at the University of Nevada, Las Vegas. His main areas of interest revolve around postmodernism, sociology of mental disorders, ecopsychology, and cultural studies. He received his BA from the University of Haifa (Israel), his MA from the University of Houston, and his PhD from the University of California, Santa Barbara. He is the author of several articles that have been published in *Symbolic Interaction*, *Journal of Contemporary Ethnography*, *Studies in Symbolic Interaction*, as well as several book chapters.

Rom Harré graduated in mathematics and physics and then in philosophy and anthropology. He did his postgraduate work in Oxford under J. Austin. His published work includes studies of both natural and human sciences, such as *Varieties of Realism* (Blackwell, 1986), and the trilogy *Social Being* (Blackwell, 1993), *Personal Being* (Harvard, 1984) and *Physical Being* (Blackwell, 1991). His current research interests concern the ways that language enters into all aspects of human life, including the sense of self (discussed in *Pronouns and People* (Sage), with P. Muhlhausler) and the emotions. His most recent book is *The Singular Self* (Sage, 1998). He has also been involved in theoretical studies of the computational model of the mind popularized as Artificial Intelligence. He is currently Professor of Psychology at Georgetown University, Washington, DC, in addition to his affiliation with Linacre College, Oxford University.

John P. Hewitt is Professor of Sociology at the University of Massachusetts at Amherst, where he has taught since 1970. He is the author of *Self and Society: A Symbolic Interactionist Social Psychology* (7th edition, Allyn & Bacon, 1997), and of *Dilemmas of the American Self* (Temple University Press, 1989). The latter won the 1990 Charles H. Cooley Award of the Society for the Study of Symbolic Interaction. His most recent book is *The Myth of Self-Esteem: Finding Happiness and Solving Problems in America* (St Martin's Press, 1998). His current interests include English real ale, the American West, especially the Sonoran Desert, and his grandchildren.

Fred Newman received his doctoral training in philosophy of science at Stanford University. A psychotherapist and a playwright, he is currently director of training, East Side Institute for Short Term Psychotherapy, and artistic director of the Castillo Theatre, both in New York City. He is author of *Performance of a Lifetime* (Castillo International, 1996), *Let's Develop! A Guide to Continuous Personal Growth* (Castillo International, 1994), and *The Myth of Psychology* (Castillo International, 1991). With co-author Lois Holzman, he has published *The End of Knowing* (Routledge, 1997), *Unscientific Psychology: A Cultural-Performatory Approach to Understanding Human Life* (Praeger, 1996) and *Lev Vygotsky: Revolutionary Scientist* (Routledge, 1993). An edited collection of Newman's plays, *Still on the Corner and Other Postmodern Political Plays*, was published in 1998.

Jackie Orr is Assistant Professor of Sociology at Syracuse University. She has published work on women, panic, and postmodernity, and on the techno-poetics of Black-urban rap music. She received her PhD from the University of California, Berkeley in 1999. Her dissertation, *Panic Diaries: Psychiatry, Cybernetics, Psychiatry, and the Technoscientific Control of Social Dis-Ease*, examines the genealogy of collective and individual 'panic' in the Cold War crucible of atomic culture, cybernetic science, and normalizing psycho-power. She also experiments with multimedia performance as a method for exploring connections between bodies, memory, power, and communications media.

Steven R. Sabat has been at Georgetown University since earning his doctorate at the City University of New York, where he specialized in neuropsychology. The main focus of his research has been on the remaining intact abilities of Alzheimer's Disease sufferers, the experience of having the disease from the sufferer's point of view, and the ways in which communication between the afflicted and their caregivers may be enhanced. In addition, his interests include the epistemological basis of our understanding of the effects of brain injuries on human beings.

Jane Ussher is currently Associate Professor of Critical Psychology in the Centre for Critical Psychology, University of Western Sydney, Nepean. She also practices as a clinical psychologist, part-time. Her publications include: *The Psychology of the Female Body* (Routledge, 1989), *Women's Madness: Misogyny or Mental Illness?* (Harvester Wheatsheaf [and the University of Massachusetts Press], 1991), *Gender Issues in Clinical Psychology* (Routledge, 1992), *The Psychology of Women's Health and Health Care* (Macmillan, 1992), *Psychological Perspectives on Sexual Problems* (Routledge, 1993), *Body Talk: A Material-Discursive Analysis of Madness, Sexuality and Reproduction* (Routledge, 1997), and *Fantasies of Femininity: Reframing the Boundaries of Sex* (Penguin 1997).

Janet Wirth-Cauchon is Assistant Professor of Sociology at Drake University. In addition to gender and mental illness, her research and teaching interests include feminist theory, identity and culture, and the intersections between psychoanalysis, the body, and technology. She is currently working on a book, *Borderlines: Gender, Madness, and Psychiatric Narrative.*

Preface

It may seem reckless for someone with no direct training or clinical experience in psychiatry, psychopathology, or abnormal psychology to embark on a project which critically confronts much of the dominant thinking in those very areas. But the situation is hardly new. Sociologists have made significant contributions to the conceptual, empirical, and policy-oriented problems within mental health research, and it was developments in feminist theory, deviance studies, and symbolic interactionism, broadly conceived, that defined the sociological legacy in the area primarily in terms of external critique and reform advocacy. However, in the 1960s and '70s, when more explicit lines were being drawn within debates about psychiatric diagnosis, stigma, and institutionalization, it was often those in the psychological sciences and in mental health work who themselves became most noticeable in their opposition to developments within their own fields. This volume reflects contemporary developments in both of these realms of inquiry.

It is my sense that there is a renewed and widespread desire to explore and question established positivist approaches to mental disorder and its contemporary expositions. This claim might seem questionable when considering the recent influx of psychopharmacology and other technologies that are, in some sense, attempting to 'conquer inner space,' as Jackie Orr discusses in her chapter here. However, despite these developments – and perhaps, ironically, in part because of them – an implicit part of the old critiques is haunting many of those currently invested in the field of mental health, whether they be therapists, researchers, activists, or, frequently now, patients – namely that mental illness, in addition to whatever else it may be, is a problem of *knowledge*. Put simply, it is now more often assumed or suspected that we can no longer simply describe what is 'out there' in terms of the 'problem of mental illness,' nor what is 'in there' with respect to 'aberrant' subjectivities and behaviors, without considering epistemological issues. Therefore, the recent expansion of the biomedical revolution has, partly through its own force alone, placed matters of context and legitimacy at the center of scientific claims. Whether 'for' or 'against' psychiatry (and unqualified, immutable positions seem harder to assume), the problem of knowledge obligates us to consider on what basis we make claims to truth, with what authority, and with what consequences. It also requires a new critical reflexivity about the 'truth' of our own suffering. Now often radically invested in our own mental states, we cannot escape the unsettling question of how far the discourses of disorder practically extend. In hypermediated and increasingly medicalized social worlds, can we even trust our own pain?

New historical, epistemological, and, indeed, bodily struggles, of course, require new accountings of the empirical conditions that seem to be behind them. While sections of the book locate institutional changes and track shifts in expert knowledges, many of the chapters present explicit or implicit strategies for change – in theory, method, and research. Some of the authors also address potential ways to reconfigure persons as historical subjects within the changes we are only beginning to understand. Beyond theoretical debates about the status of 'the subject,' the concern here is about working toward more creative and critical engagements with an environment characterized by expanding and increasingly refined systems of psychotherapeutic expertise, ongoing reconstruction of the boundaries of the pathological (and therefore the 'normal'), and more stark, often market-driven, efforts to codify and colonize the intrapsychic realm – all movements with durable histories that now forge on, relatively unimpeded. But again, this book is a product of its time: an era that affords the opportunity to realize the full significance and possibility that comes with aggressively positioning the knowledges that were once virtually position*less* within the guise of an innocuous, free-floating objectivity that guaranteed relative immunity from both 'internal' or 'external' inquests. The only certainty, of course, is that this is a portentous moment, and it requires new and sometimes unpopular commitments.

I would like to thank the many people who offered assistance and encouragement throughout the duration of this project. The editorial staff at Sage, London, have my sincere appreciation for their efforts and flexibility throughout. Ziyad Marar provided early encouragement at the proposal stage, and was chiefly responsible for giving this project a chance. I can imagine no better publishing editor than Naomi Meredith, whose practical help and patience made the process a smooth one for me, a first-time editor with lots of questions. I would also like to thank Rosemary Campbell and Kate Scott for their help in the latter stages of the manuscript preparation, and to Lucy Robinson, my first contact with Sage, for her editorial assistance as well.

In preparing the manuscript, my assistant Christy E. Gell provided invaluable assistance with proofreading, but her insights also helped me to consider larger editorial and conceptual issues about the project as a whole. The assistantship was partially funded by a small grant from the Faculty Professional Development Fund at Middlebury College. More generally, the College quickly provided the support and facilities necessary to finish the project during my recent move to Vermont.

I would like to acknowledge the influence of David D. Franks, Thomas J. Scheff, Jackie Orr, and, more recently, Gerald C. Davison, for his comments on the Introduction and for his overall encouragement. Thank you to Houghton Mifflin for permission to reproduce extracts from *Prozac Nation*.

Kenneth J. Gergen has been an intellectual inspiration, and his support helped the book to find this fortunate place in the Inquiries in Social Construction Series. I would also like to thank students in my 'sociology of mental illness' courses over the past several years who have pushed my thinking and helped me to originally formulate this project. My friends at Vassar, Andrew Davison and William Hoynes, offered regular incentives and motivation, as did my family. My greatest appreciation goes to Eve H. Davison for her uncompromising assurance and loving support, to which I am continually indebted. Finally, I would like to express my appreciation to the authors themselves for their creative efforts, but also for their patience and conscientiousness throughout the course of the project.

Dwight Fee

PART I INTRODUCTION

1

The Broken Dialogue: Mental Illness as Discourse and Experience

Dwight Fee

A recent pamphlet published by the National Alliance for the Mentally Ill (NAMI) states on its opening page that 'mental illnesses are disorders of the brain that disrupt a person's thinking, feeling, moods, and ability to relate to others. Just as diabetes is a disorder of the pancreas, mental illnesses are brain disorders. . . . [They] are not a result of personal weakness, lack of character, or poor upbringing.' On the next page, we see the words 'Open Your Mind: mental illnesses are brain disorders.' Flipping the pamphlet over, one notices in small print: 'This material made possible by an educational grant from Lilly Neuroscience: improving lives, restoring hope.'

Clearly, this is a time when biomedical and otherwise reductionist explanations and understandings of mental disorder are dominant in scholarly, scientific, and psychotherapeutic worldviews and practices. The pervasive viewpoint is that the only way that mental illnesses can be recognized as 'real' – and hence worthy of funded research, insurance coverage, rigorous study, and, in the case above, coalition-building – is when they are anchored in the language of bio-physiology or possibly some other deep-seated individual factor. Furthermore, expert narratives surrounding psychiatric illness are reproduced through isolating ostensibly 'natural' elements from 'social' ones. As with any large area of study, exceptions abound, but the biology-versus-society logic remains central in most debates surrounding the origins and phenomenology of mental illness, and indeed is one force driving the most recent efforts to 'ground' major psychiatric syndromes within medical and psychobiological confines.

This volume was put together in an effort to expand and invigorate the dialogue about the history, phenomenology, and contemporary experience of mental illness in a sociohistorical context that is in several respects increasingly hostile to the tenets of 'social constructionism' – a perspective fundamental to such discussions. However, while we have inherited the legacy of the eighteenth century when madness became an 'object,' a thing-in-itself, discoverable by dispassionate positivist inquiry (Foucault, 1965), there is now a subtle but noticeable desire on the part of many theorists, clinicians, and students to engage the complexity of human pathology in ways that recognize the contingency of psycho-scientific knowledge and its political, cultural, and technological embodiments. This desire has the potential to initiate dialogue and debate across academic disciplines and professional divides that go beyond simple critique.

The anti-psychiatry movement of the 1960s and '70s was a well-known voice of opposition to psychiatric authority, and there have been many other attempts at reform that have been connected to, for example, feminist, prisoner, and human rights movements. While indebted to and derived from these efforts, more recent approaches are beginning to call attention to the discursive or textual underpinnings of mental life and its role in the study of psychopathology (e.g. Levin, 1987; Parker et al., 1995; Rose, 1989; Shotter, 1992; Smith 1990). Following a linguistic or 'interpretive turn' in the social sciences and humanities, work in this area – heterogeneous as it is – seeks to contest the meanings that inform mental health theory and practice, and often emphasizes how the life of the self is implicated in this knowledge-centered struggle.

Perhaps as one segment of a larger 'gathering storm' of movements confronting expert knowledge in the mental and medical sciences (McNamee and Gergen, 1992), the accounts presented in this book view 'mental illness' as a social object, the significance of which is an ongoing accomplishment within institutions, language, and interaction. The book questions the taken-for-granted assumption that mental disorders are simply 'out (or in) there.' Recent theoretical developments in constructionist and postmodern thought are invoked to recast the opposition between the pathological and the normal, and the social and discursive forces that reproduce these domains and the dichotomy between them.

While the project attempts to place 'mental illness' within the realms of history, culture, and politics, as a whole it also emphasizes how discourse is appropriated and lived out at intimate levels, how the deepest realms of somatic sensation and psychological suffering are intertwined with the technologies, knowledges, and stories of culture. Avoiding a fall back into 'environmental' arguments, the aim is to push against the 'nature–society' dualism without rigidly denying physiological and intrapsychic processes in pathological experience. Rather, the emphasis here is placed upon how bodies and minds are immersed within economic, political, and scientific struggles. Thus, in bringing symbolic and material frameworks to the forefront, 'mental disease' readily becomes destabilized as a trans-historical and intrapsychic essence. However, is it possible to bring these elements up from secondary status without erasing illness phenomenology? More specifically, is it tenable to discuss mental pathology as a socio-historical and linguistic construction *and* as a 'true' debilitating condition? Can we really have it both ways? This volume hopes to provide one touchstone in which to address these questions and to contribute to such an interpretive undertaking.

There is a pressing and often practical need for regarding mental disorder as entangled with social life and language, as well as a palpable, felt condition which damages mental functioning, interpersonal relationships, and other aspects of thought and behavior. In a changing landscape of mental health policy, capitalist expansion, and profound cultural divergences, knowledge systems about mental disorder are attempting to keep pace with rapidly transforming worlds of subjective turmoil, worlds that do not necessarily reflect the cleanliness of rational diagnostic division. Furthermore, as the empirical and epistemological assumptions internal to these knowledge systems are viewed with more skepticism (often from within), it is worth considering whether or not refurbishing inherited positivist protocol – developing 'better science' – is now the best or only response.

Confronting illness ontology from an interpretive framework is one way that we can begin to discuss mental disorder without reifying its metaphysical status (Ingleby, 1980); however, doing so does not have to mean ignoring or minimizing the real effects of 'madness.' Clearly (or not so clearly) a *non*-objectified orientation to mental illness is difficult even to imagine. Our modern understanding of mental disorder, an Enlightenment product, was created through the understanding that disorders were 'alien' – external and irrational maladies to be fathomed and hopefully rectified by the scientific expert, imbued with mysterious powers of *moral* adjudication. Consequently, there is no discernible dialogue *between* 'mental illness' and human experience. Just as the confined lunatic first became a spectacle to look at as 'other' – a stable contrast to bourgeois standards of reason (Foucault, 1965) – the alienated and disjoined framework through which we still view mental pathology remains a hermeneutic dead-end and political problematic. As Foucault puts it:

> The constitution of madness as a mental illness, at the end of the eighteenth century, affords the evidence of a broken dialogue. . . . The language of psychiatry, which is a monologue of reason *about* madness, has been established only on the basis of such a silence. (1965: x–xi)

It is an important and encouraging time to reconnect the pathological to the rapidly shifting material, cultural, and psychosocial realms of life, and to likewise alter our theoretical and methodological frameworks to better understand such connections. We now have a unique opportunity to bring mental illness into a new world of contingency, flux, and thus of profound possibility. An important aim here, then, is to present ways in which mental illness can be, in a sense, 'unmastered,' removed from its objective and oppositional status and reintroduced into languages of relationship and recognition, a turnabout which has implications for all areas of theory and practice. While taking personal experience seriously, the constructionist perspective allows us to 'direct our gaze not at the mad but at the culture, institutions, and language which makes madness matter so much' (Parker et al., 1995: 14).

Pathology and 'the Postmodern'

New suspicions and critiques of positivism and empiricism, including the chapters here, may not be explicitly 'constructionist.' Some may be feminist, critical, deconstructionist, poststructuralist, or belong to no clear orientation at all. Social constructionism is not a field *per se*, and certainly not a discipline; as an area it is still murky, although this indeterminacy is part of its deconstructionist and reconstructive potential. The conceptual strength of social constructionism is precisely its postmodern-allied anti-foundational approach to meaning and linguistic boundaries, which allows modes of interpretation and renderings of knowledge that collapse naturalized dichotomies between subject and object and knower and known.

The boundaries of postmodernism, too, are somewhat amorphous and continually contested. While many reject the term because of perceived obscurity or empty faddism, postmodern thinking has become increasingly institutionalized in recent years (perhaps to many people's dismay) at the same time that constructionist studies are readily acknowledged and mainstreamed. Postmodern studies have brought new kinds of analyses and critiques to bear on questions of self and subjectivity, particularly as new media and technological forces radically mediate experience in daily life (e.g. Grodin and Lindlof, 1996). Postmodern thought is now recognizable to many with its characteristic attention to the relationship between power, knowledge, and the self (Foucault, 1977, 1980), its suspicion of self-justified meta-narratives, particularly those deemed scientific (Lyotard, 1984), and in its unstable, partial, and anti-metaphysical view of language (Derrida, 1974). Overlapping with articulated constructionist assumptions, it is generally held that 'the degree to which a given account of world or self is sustained across time is not dependent on the objective validity of the account but on the vicissitudes of social process' (Gergen, 1994: 51). Accordingly, a main postmodern strategy is the undermining of 'totalizing' knowledges which, like the *Diagnostic and Statistical Manual of Mental Disorders* (*DSM*) – the central diagnostic text for psychiatric illness classification in the US (American Psychiatric Association, 1994) – stand in isolation from socio-political context. The inference is that objective validity always entails discursive and political positioning. Therefore, the intersection of postmodern and constructionist approaches has a particular utility in our environment of medical and otherwise causal and determinist models of mental disorder.

But there is also the matter of what new situations and conditions we now confront. 'Mental hygiene' movements in the early twentieth century, based on more holistic and preventative approaches, were phased out in the US as the revolution in biological psychiatry took hold after World War II (Grob,

1994). Now, we see the radicalization of this movement to the extent that a new revolution in illness technology is coming into sharp focus. It is no longer just drug therapy that is at issue, but the entire corporate enterprise that has followed the almost complete demise of community and publicly funded mental health care. While the increasing privatization of mental health establishments in Britain and America leaves a serious ambiguity about the future of care delivery and about the future of psychiatry itself (Samson, 1995), it does not necessarily translate into a widespread abandonment of biomedical concepts and treatments, as Samson suggests (1995: 83). While based more on happenings in the US – but surely relevant to Britain and Europe as well – it is difficult to escape the conclusion that we are seeing only the beginnings of biomedical intervention, this time in business and entrepreneurial garb.

This new merger of scientific, commercial, and corporate interests has taken the suffering subject into a new 'technocratic' system of inert diagnostics and global business and market communications. As bio-technological and psychopharmacological machineries propagate, bodies and subjective life (disproportionately women's) become new sites of economic interchange and pharmaceutical investment, creating new relationships between 'symptomology' and the flows of electronic and capitalist exchange vested in that very distress (Orr, 1990). Beyond Prozac and new antidepressant drug controversies, this metamorphosis of psychoscientific determinism threatens to make earlier therapies, policies, and programs, and all of their humanistic import, almost unrecognizable.

Here in Chapter 3, Jackie Orr again confronts the interface of psychiatric, scientific, and pharmaceutical realms, this time addressing the historical construction of hysteria, and specifically how this syndrome was important in establishing the legitimacy of somatically based and therefore 'true' diagnostic categories. She infiltrates the methods through which panic disorder, one of hysteria's conceptual offspring, became 'validated' through a self-fulfilling 'methodological drama' of sorts, where the effectiveness of drug treatments on isolated clusters of panicked symptoms led to the syndrome's presumed internal 'reality.' Her discussion of the implications of this kind of scientific 'performance' takes on a certain immediacy as quests intensify to 'conquer inner space.'

In terms of the postmodern social climate, there is also the broad issue about the present dimensions of psychological, interpersonal, and existential struggles. First, the stripping or reworking of many modern institutions and formations – gender, family, sexuality, work, intimacy – is surely bringing about new reality dilemmas, existential anguish, and accordant methods of coping. Within the last few generations, expectations in these realms, once embedded in presupposed custom, have become drastically contested and altered. Persons must contend with an environment with less and less discursive and institutional foundations for living, requiring active interpretation of 'local,' situated meanings (Giddens, 1990, 1991). It amounts to having a self that is always one step outside of things, and, in the relative absence of sustaining traditions, being forced to engage meaning on relatively unpredictable terms.

Alongside this 'detraditionalization' are the all-embracing material forces associated with new technologies and media, and the 'acceleration' and destabilization they bring to everyday life. 'Sanity' becomes a harshly relative term when interaction is no longer grounded in techniques of communication which rely on shared narrative structures, discernible collectivities, and on the predictable intentions of institutions and actors. Amidst the flows of electronic and visual significations, positioning one's self as a stable unit with rational grounding in the world becomes difficult and perhaps purposeless. In Chapter 2, Simon Gottschalk ventures into this dizzying terrain, and utilizes diagnostic vocabularies to comprehend the hyper-mediated, screen-filled environment of the postmodern. 'Diagnosing' the self in these conditions, Gottschalk finds fear, anxiety, and paranoia, as well as (and no less subtle) chronic numbness and ambivalence. Dismantling the normative languages of individual pathology, he discusses these as sociocultural 'symptoms' of an increasingly unhinged post/modernity, and raises important epistemological implications of his analysis of this expanding milieu.

Similarly, there could be a growing sense of 'incommensurability' to life (Lyotard, 1984) derived from new problems of self-identity given this scenario of institutional fragmentation and cultural-technological acceleration. Some argue that our perceptions and viewpoints are now more 'simulated' than 'original' (Baudrillard, 1993) and thus no longer emanate from a priori singular self-center. Presently we must contend with chronic uncertainty and radical choice for life-style and identity construction (Giddens, 1991), and it is now more likely that our own self-definition becomes progressively more elusive as subjectivity becomes 'populated' with multiple and often discordant voices (Gergen, 1991). These forces challenge the roles and normative frameworks supporting the modernist project of systematizing and allocating identities in rational frameworks. Since Erikson, psychiatrists and psychologists have been warned about 'identity diffusion' as a clinical syndrome – a condition of 'contradictory character traits,' 'temporal discontinuity,' 'lack of authenticity,' and, most remarkably in one description, 'gender dysphoria' and 'moral and ethnic relativism' (Akhtar, 1984). While extreme cases of self-fragmentation are surely detrimental, 'identity immutability,' say, is perhaps now more of a psychic liability.

Kenneth Gergen, in Chapter 5, expands upon his work on postmodern selfhood, arguing that technological developments in this century are working against the grain of modernist views and ideals of self, where consciousness, character, and morality have all been integrally grounded within the individual. This process does not reflect a loss or dissolution of self, but a broad, disparate transformation away from division and binaries, and toward 'polyvocal' identities that are ushering in rife but undetermined 'relational imaginaries.' Inspired by Gergen's work in this area, Mark Freeman's subsequent chapter explores the complex association between postmodern discourse of aesthetics and identity, and the lived realities of artists who have experienced various kinds of 'breakdowns' in regard to their work and subjective life. Freeman explores how the artists, with a radical awareness of construction and conventionality, have developed various life strategies and views that often run *against* relational stances, suggesting that postmodern sensibilities sometimes end up in modernist isolation or pragmatic reprieves. Freeman has provided needed study of lived experience within ostensibly postmodern realities, and has urged us to consider that, perhaps ironically, some specifically modernist tenets of identity may be necessary to maintain commitments beyond the inner self.

These four interrelated themes – in brief, corporate-scientific 'technocracy,' institutional fragmentation, new media technologies, and the disruption and multiplication of self – all reflect new historical shifts but also signify predicaments within modern discourses, particularly with respect to science, truth, and self – the main underpinnings of Enlightenment-based ideals of progress and freedom. The essential connection between these elements, where the encapsulated person is the centerpiece in a rational design of scientific mastery, has been basic to mental and behavioral science. Some have hence foreshadowed their dissolution, asserting that effective accounts of postmodern life are impossible through modern, rationalized means (Kvale, 1992). Whether or not this is the case, new approaches are needed that engage these tangible changes along with their conceptual implications. In Chapter 9, Vivien Burr and Trevor Butt confront the implications of postmodern perspectives for psychology, and in particular for therapy and counseling. Invoking the work of Foucault, Rorty, and contemporary social constructionism, they point to the disciplinary underpinnings of psychotherapy, its normalizing effects, and how dimensions of a 'postmodern psychology' may provide a way out of the regulatory, truth-seeking mechanisms built into its modernist epistemology. Established constructivist and pragmatic approaches are also discussed as having a distinct value in mental health professions.

As Burr and Butt explain, narrative approaches in theory and therapy, which recast subject–object binaries and deconstruct positivist therapeutic frameworks, are becoming further established and respected (see McNamee and Gergen, 1992; White and Epston, 1990). Fred Newman, in Chapter 12, delves specifically into this area, but with an eye toward frequently overlooked philosophical issues. Newman argues that much of postmodern-inspired narrative therapy, as divergent as it is from rationalist, deductive models, remains entangled with scientifically based explanatory frameworks, and thus runs the risk of becoming as dogmatic and stultifying as the old externalizing, categoric models. Drawing from the work of Wittengenstein, Vygotsky, and his own work, often in collaboration with Lois Holzman, Newman argues against the necessity of having to choose between old or 'new' fictions or constructions. Rather, he calls for therapeutic approaches and understandings that would continually expose the constraints of the old meanings and stories – reflecting an unqualified recognition of the 'human authorship' of consciousness.

Toward 'Postparadigmatics'

Considering the innovations taking place within and across clinical, scientific, and interpretive-theoretical worlds, the situation is not always one of complete ideological contrast and polemics between 'established science' and those embracing epistemological changes. Remarkably to some, those developing constructionist or postmodern approaches to consciousness and language sometimes make contributions to scientific endeavors. In Chapter 11, Steven Sabat and Rom Harré address the assumption that those with Alzheimer's Condition undergo a 'loss of self.' Establishing links between Alzheimer-related brain research and the grammar of personal pronouns used by 'AC' sufferers in their own case studies, Sabat and Harré explore how those with AC express a sense of singularity, intention, as well as a specific awareness of their contextual situations and statuses. While pointing out common, problematic assumptions about AC experience, the authors, through their sociolinguistic expertise, also highlight implications for understanding the relationship between brain functioning and self-understanding.

Of course, the larger stirrings are on the other side of the epistemological divide, where formerly impervious systems of thought are increasingly cognizant about the embedded quality of natural and social scientific knowledge. While psychology, relatively speaking, has had the most difficulty with postmodernism, there is some renewed vocal opposition to the *DSM* and to the clinical and diagnostic approaches it indirectly fosters (see Kirk and Kutchins, 1992), often among counselors and clinicians themselves (e.g. Caplan, 1995). Further, issues of power and language are being incorporated into new perspectives on specific illness syndromes (e.g. Capps and Ochs, 1995; Glass, 1993). The fact that some popular textbooks in abnormal psychology emphasize the role of paradigms and subjectivity in mental illness research and theory should also not be overlooked (e.g. Davison and Neale, 1998).[1] But going further than scientific and professional enclaves, misgivings about disembodied, objectified knowledge runs deep into broad shifts and sensibilities:

> Modernity ends, since it is, in part, a question of culturally shared consciousness, as people begin to realize that there is a critical distance that separates them from the thinking and living they have inherited. . . . But postmodern thinking also begins with a strong sense – articulated, however, only with difficulty – that we are living in a time of transition, a moment between two epochs: the known and the unknown. Postmodern thinking begins with a sense that the foundations of the world we inherited are crumbling, and that we are being called upon to build a very different world for the future. Postmodern thinking problematizes what was once unquestionable: the paradigm of knowledge, truth, and reality that has dominated the whole of modern history. (Levin, 1987: 3)

Thus, 'the postmodern' is a set of historical and social conditions that encourages a sense of the 'postparadigmatic' – 'an obligatory sense of the provisional' (Simon, 1996: 27). This idea has an extensive history, but has become radicalized through a widespread discernment that 'efforts at framing the "facts" of a specific time and place in the language of the timeless and the universal serves neither science nor society' (1996: 27). Assuming a postparadigmatic *stance*, then, is one that attempts to reveal the intersections of knowledge, language, and action in particular locales with a prescience about the intersubjective venture required for understanding such an intersection. Departing from a neutral zone of unaccountable objectivity, the very condition that breeds the most oppressive traits of biological or psychological stricture, the movement is toward reflexive confrontations with the meanings of madness – those we assume, criticize, and re/create, along with the taken-for-granted practices inextricable from those meanings. The path necessarily leads to the transformative and political dimensions of knowledge: 'what we are willing to accept in our world, to accept, to refuse and to change, both in ourselves and in our circumstances' (Foucault, 1997: 79).

Mental Illness, Historical Process, and Self-Experience

Like any group, those engaging constructionist and postmodern thought differ in their etiological views of mental illness, and this project reflects that variability. Most in the area hold that biological and psychological substrata – *if* we can, depending on the perspective, readily assume any at the outset – become salient for particular social and ideological reasons. Even schizophrenia, a benchmark biological syndrome, has broad and inconsonant criteria, and exemplifies a profound struggle with the meanings of malfunction and subjective experience that extends into modernity at large (Sass, 1992). Others, of course, refuse to ground or causally link clinical syndromes to any notion of biochemical or physiological grounding. The general bearing advocated here is that no system of thought or perspective can claim categorical legitimacy, and that this anti-dogmatism must apply to new accounts that seek to discharge the phantoms of the past. Predictably, the challenge for anti-positivist approaches to pathology is to have sufficient flexibility to consider all relevant factors that are part of the intersection of language and lived experience that define and re/produce 'mental illness' – including those ostensibly intra-individual. At the same time, there is a pressing need for critiques and imaginative reworkings of the excesses of 'illness metaphysics' and psychological and biological reductionism.

An initial step in this direction involves recasting some humanistic conceptions of experience and mental life that support preponderant attitudes about psychological ailment and health. Many have argued that subjectivity can no longer be viewed as something stable and enclosed, 'carried' by the individual from context to context. The self is not a transcendental essence or entity that is transparently accessible by the subject, but is rather a part of historically delimited systems of knowledge and meaning (Flax, 1993; Parker, 1992; Weedon, 1987). In contrast to an axiomatic substance, emphasis in most postmodernist frameworks is placed on the continual and shifting creation of self-experience through systematizing and regulative knowledge-power networks. In the modern era, psychiatric discourse is one of the scientific networks that has contrived its view of mental disorder through opposites and contrasts – health/pathology, normal/abnormal, rational/irrational – which serve to justify conceptual binaries and real-world exclusions.

In addition to reproducing specific kinds of experts and organizations that oversee these divisions (Flax, 1993: 96; Foucault, 1965), it is crucial to recognize that various categories and strategies become the intellective currency circulating across personal and social realities. In other words, discourse is inhabited and authenticated by acting subjects, who attach – though not in a completely determined way – societal meanings to their distress. While not all syndromes involve reflexive appropriation of illness narratives, they all implicate the encompassing meanings and social structures that give recognizable form to our experiences of well-being and affliction. Just as no scientific story can sit in conceptual or historical isolation, neither can the actual experiences we deem pathological.

Janet Wirth-Cauchon provides a poignant illustration of this approach in Chapter 7. Concerned with the interface of psychiatric knowledge and women's experience, she examines 'borderline personality disorder' both as a reflection of the contradictory and marginalized status of women, and as a troublesome, pathologizing stigmatization. Through case narratives and close examination of the psychotherapeutic encounter, Wirth-Cauchon reveals that, beyond inner pathology, the medical construction of the borderline category reproduces gendered notions of self. Women's perceived 'liquidity' and 'boundlessness,' while being meaningful responses to the ubiquitous contradictions they face, are nevertheless constructed as 'dangerous' (yet sometimes seductive) through objectified, patriarchal discourse.

Raising issues about the construction of disorders, then, does not deny 'real' forms of pathogenic experience in the world, but it does suggest more multidimensional modes of conceptualizing and representing that experience. If the self can not be disjoined from discourse, the phenomenology of pain and desolation are closely tied to the shifts of bodies and selves within structures of power and knowledge. This evokes a move away from the 'essentials' of mental illness where madness is 'a fact concerning the human soul, its guilt, its freedom . . . inscribed within the dimensions of interiority' (Foucault, 1987: 72), and toward more explicit elaborations on the relationship between interior states and external forces. Much research in psychology and psychiatry is of course directed at contemporary pathologies – who experiences what disorder, how often, under what circumstances, and so on – but there is little in the way of explorations of the historicized crossings of discourse and experience.

Beyond Labeling Theory and Anti-Psychiatry

The idea that mental disorder is closely tied to problems of meaning and to institutional dynamics was first visibly explored within the realm of the anti-psychiatry movement (Becker, 1964; Cooper, 1967; Laing, 1967, 1969;

Szasz, 1970, 1972). Psychiatrists were often the most radical in critiquing their own discipline: mental illnesses were 'false substantives' concocted by modern psychiatry, in Szasz's view; in Laing's case they were existential predicaments often characterized by insights and perceptual realms unavailable to those judged 'sane' (Laing, 1969; Parker et al., 1995: 24). Defining illness experience as 'problems in living,' Szasz was particularly adamant about the need to 'abandon the entire physicalistic-medical approach to mental illness and to substitute novel theoretical viewpoints and models, appropriate to psychological, social, and ethical problems' (1972: 95).

Szasz and others found themselves allied with (mostly) sociological thinkers who emphasized the labeling process involved in psychiatric practice, arguing that it was societal reaction to those labeled ill – and not intrinsic properties of the individual – that was the crux for understanding the phenomenology of mental disorder (esp. Scheff, 1974, 1975). Reflecting trends in the sociology of deviance (Becker, 1973; Lemert, 1951), related ethnographic scholarship emphasized how social structures turned labels into self-fulfilling prophecies, thereby ensuring the reproduction and prosperity of the institutions invested in illness classification (Goffman, 1961; Rosenhan, 1973).

As stated, the present volume is beholden to these studies and writings. The early work in this area is perhaps best represented by the classic, symbolic interactionist-inspired anthology *The Mental Patient: Studies in the Sociology of Deviance* (Spitzer and Denzin, 1968), and it is plausible that *Pathology and the Postmodern* is in some respects a theoretical 'update' of that invaluable book. The two texts share an emphasis on power in the diagnostic enterprise; they also have a common suspicion of the role of institutions, and social and material structures that are implicated in the conceptualization and treatment of mental disorder; and both projects highlight the psychodynamic, subjective effects of these forces. There are, however, some important points where extensions and revisions of the venerable sociological accounts become salient in this project.

First, it is apparent that there is more pointed attention paid to the sociolinguistic and therefore fluid quality of psychoscientific knowledge. Consequently, in several chapters there is a shift toward the reciprocal nature of discourses of health and pathology. A helpful concept to understand this change is 'institutional reflexivity' (Giddens, 1991), a condition where 'abstract systems' of knowledges about self and living are continually incorporated into local environments of thinking and behavior, which in turn feed back upon those permeating systems. Giddens argues that systems of expertise – say, in this case, psychotherapy and psychopharmacology – are becoming increasingly specialized and more closely attuned to developing their own effectiveness, being 'reflexively highly mobilized' (1991: 30–1). While our actions take place inside of these systems or discourses, an overall reflexive context allows the actions of individuals (not always distinguishable from 'expert systems' themselves) to work back upon and reconstitute these realms.

With respect to drug intervention, in Chapter 8 John Hewitt, Michael Fraser, and LeslieBeth Berger analyze the effects of antidepressants, Prozac specifically, on conceptions of self, and how psychopharmacology is being implicated in the social meanings of well-being and depression. Through a symbolic interactionist orientation, the authors describe how Prozac functions in role-taking processes as well as in self-definition more generally. While acknowledging the importance of physiological and biochemical elements, the authors hold that the effects of Prozac on mood cannot be easily disentangled from a mediating discourse of 'self-esteem.' This construct, especially crucial in American contexts, helps to shape the quality and significance of internal states like 'depression.' An implication here is that the 'medicated self,' now increasingly common, reinforces and reproduces specific meanings of mood, adjustment, and psychological health.

In this context, the phenomenology of disordered experience cannot be easily divorced from the tactics and technologies we use to comprehend, systematize, and address even severe cognitive and behavioral problems. Pathological experience does not stop 'in the person'; it feeds back into cultural meaning systems of illness, as well as into treatment technologies such as psychopharmacology and psychotherapy that continually help make that suffering ascertainable. The dissemination of expert knowledge predictably brings more intense efforts to refine the understanding of the condition by both the subject and the expert, expanding both the professionalized and personalized discourses of illness and their intimate reciprocity. The cyclical process only heightens our attention – institutionally *and* personally – to our selves, our moods, our bodies. Illness identities proliferate; psychotherapeutic and psychotropic treatments intervene; the knowledge base of mental disorder transforms – all in no particular order.

Anti-psychiatric and traditional sociological thought utilize humanistic or 'liberal' frameworks of the subject to make their case against psychiatric authority. For many, however, the scenario just described elicits more post-structural or postmodern views that do not assume a solely repressive view of power, as one is always immersed in power/knowledge systems and must invoke strategies within them. As described, the self, in more recent work, is conceptualized as something produced within discourses – often within technologies of health – and is not presumed a priori. In other words, we become certain kinds of 'subjects' through institutions, and, capable of reflexive agency, are not merely coerced by them in a purely external and determined fashion.[2] Often positing one-way causal processes of labeling, preceding models did not afford much agency to those labeled 'mad,' and, because of a difference in historical situations, did not explore how lives are intertwined with psychological languages that make us incessantly attuned to our own psychosocial dispositions.

In Chapter 4, I attempt to sketch out how the experience of 'depression' can involve a 'discursive project' where socially meaningful identities are produced through a new reflexive engagement with clinical understandings of depression. Recent memoirs and autobiographies that make depression their central focus, such as *Prozac Nation* (Wurtzel, 1995), reveal that depression now often involves detailed story-telling and confession, a process which in turn constructs the cultural narratives which make depression a certain kind of comprehensible condition, and, now, a cultural reference point. Of course, depression is a 'genuine' experience and involves many factors, but in a situation where illnesses, knowledges, and identities intermingle, purely externally based and causal models of the disorder become, in many instances, more difficult to sustain.

In a hyper-reflexive context, it is also more plausible to connect mental illness to various cultural struggles and changes, which can be seen as an effort to get beyond positivist and traditionally humanistic approaches. For anti-psychiatry, there was not much to say about specific syndromes, as they were completely arbitrary designations. Laing felt that there were certain existential 'truths' found within schizophrenic experience, and others held similar views. However, most argued as if illnesses were only myths dreamed up by experts, perhaps to control certain kinds of objectionable behavior. Even since labeling theory, there is still often little weight placed on how specific clusters of conduct become intelligible as aspects of historical rupture and social struggle, although many historical studies attempt to make some of these linkages (e.g. Foucault, 1965; Porter, 1987; Scull, 1989). As one dimension of the broken dialogue, of course, as a society we refuse to recognize ourselves in the mentally ill person. In social science, the same process has only been more visible, with implications beyond the realm of theory: 'The analyses of our psychologists and sociologists, which turn the patient into a deviant and which seek the origin of the morbid in the abnormal, are, therefore, above all a projection of cultural themes' (Foucault, 1987: 63). Closely connected is the problem of how meanings of madness have historically been used as tools of oppression along lines of gender, as well as sexuality and race (see Gilman, 1985).[3] It is hoped that this volume will prompt studies that address these connections and their consequences.

Relatedly, the realistic and observable suffering of persons has also not been part of the narratives of critics and theorists emphasizing the social and linguistic dimensions of mental disorder. It is little wonder why many practitioners and others in close quarters with those diagnosed mentally ill, such as Glass (1993), have such disdain for those who glorify and almost sanctify pathological states. Glass rightfully 'deconstructs the deconstructionists' such as Deleuze and Guattari (1977) in their efforts to make the schizophrenic a cultural and political hero, and he convincingly castigates those who minimize the role of power in the making of psychotic worlds (Glass, 1993, 1995). Through psychoanalytic reasoning he explores how his patients' sufferings – mostly women with dissociative identity disorder – are intertwined with interpersonal abuse and the encompassing power within the patriarchal and phallocentric order (Glass, 1993). However, unmoved by any questioning of modernist or structural views of the self, Glass heaps postmodernism into one insouciant movement, often exaggerating its supposed shared 'celebration' of fragmentation.[4]

Still, Glass's message is worth serious consideration: at what point in illness theorizing is the actual person lost? With the best intentions, labeling theory, as well as some more recent and often qualitatively different perspectives, have made ideological critique insular from the perseverance of indisputable pain and impairment. Glass is also helpful in pointing to the one area that has *not* made that inexcusable oversight, namely feminist theory. While Glass finds psychoanalytically oriented feminism the most illuminating (esp. Irigaray, 1985; Kristeva, 1986), it is a part of an entire benefaction of work that has revolutionized the phenomenological as well as the gendered dimensions of mental illness (Busfield, 1996; Chesler, 1972; Showalter, 1985; Smith, 1990; Ussher, 1991).

Many feminist theorists explicitly confront the impact of institutionalized knowledge and its role in self-construction, a standpoint that was a motivating factor behind this volume. In contrast to the underlying conservatism or naïveté in much of anti-psychiatry – as those with even the most severe difficulties are, by implication, left to fend for themselves (Sedgwick, 1982) – feminist theory has been instrumental in discussing how women's subjectivities have been caught up and negotiated within psychiatric discourse. At the same time, through genealogical studies of hysteria through contemporary debates about the pathologizing of women in *DSM-IV*, this praxis-centered research has brought attention to tangible worlds of domination and distress, as well as to the practical action required for the general democratizing of mental health systems.

One such example is Jane Ussher's discussion in Chapter 10. Extending her prior work, she critiques the 'positivist/realist' tradition in conceptualizing and treating 'women's madness' in order to develop a perspective which stays true to the tangible experiences of women, but refuses to anchor those experiences in static frameworks that neglect situational and structural contexts, and issues of power. Instead, she delineates a fluid, interrelated model which incorporates material, discursive, and intrapsychic processes. This model fundamentally relies upon the multidimensional relationship between knowledge, structural oppressions, and person-centered phenomenology.

The chapters in this book, then, take important themes from the anti-psychiatric and labeling theory approaches, but each in its own way, drawing from diverse areas, engages mental disorder as an existent force in the lives of real people. The authors may not all agree about its derivations or about, given our historical moment, exactly how it should be conceptualized and addressed. However, in an attempt to re-create a dialogue with mental illness, all incorporate previously minimized dimensions – epistemological, material, political – into new accounts of mental pathology that will, hopefully, lead to further engagements with the constructed complexity of human suffering. The aim is to perhaps reach a point where, as Ernest Becker wrote in his dedication in *The Revolution in Psychiatry* thirty-five years ago, 'psychiatry' – and, we should now add, mental science in general – 'will be an agent of social change, rather than a shelter from social confusion.'

Notes

1. The changes in psychology and in the field of psychopathology, however, are limited and should not be exaggerated. One renowned psychologist wrote me the following about *DSM* controversies:

> The way most people look at things is the deification of the DSM, which, I believe, takes a very 'naive realism' stance vis-a-vis mental disorders. The DSM is for most mental health professionals analogous to the two tablets Moses brought down from Mt. Sinai. While the writing on the tablets changes from time to time . . . the basic categorical and 'externalizing' framework remains.

2. I do not mean to simplify or exaggerate the differences between these types of perspectives. There is often much overlap between them, and much, of course, is a matter of one's substantive focus. Goffman and Foucault are in some ways markedly different in their theoretical standpoint and focus. As Foucault himself once put it, 'Goffman's problem is the institution. My problem is the rationalization of the management of the individual' (1989: 299). There are, however, many connections between them in terms of their concerns about twentieth-century psychiatric power and its effects upon the person.

3. Gilman's text (1985) is an exemplary analysis of how ethnic, racial, and sexual stereotypes have intertwined with the meanings of mental disorder in a range of historical contexts. On ethnicity, also see Littlewood and Lipsedge (1982).

4. Glass certainly raises valid criticisms of some postmodern quests to abandon all unitary concepts of meaning, structure, and self. But in his often repetitive diatribe, one senses a 'middle ground' that is overlooked, except in occasional remarks such as 'one can be sympathetic to the postmodern criticism of truth . . . without rejecting conceptions of psychological reality and structure' (1993: 77). As said, an important task here is to understand how that psychic structure is implicitly connected to larger realms of meaning and power – an undertaking Glass would seem to support.

References

Akhtar, S. (1984) 'The Syndrome of Identity Diffusion.' *American Journal of Psychiatry*, 14: 1381–85.

American Psychiatric Association (1994) *Diagnostic and Statistical Manual of Mental Disorders*. 4th edn. Washington, DC: American Psychiatric Association.

Baudrillard, J. (1993) *Simulations*. New York: Semiotext(e).

Becker, E. (1964) *The Revolution in Psychiatry*. New York: Free Press.

Becker, H. (1973) *Outsiders: Studies in the Sociology of Deviance*. New York: Free Press.

Busfield, J. (1996) *Men, Women, and Madness*. New York: New York University Press.

Caplan, P.J. (1995) *They Say You're Crazy: How the World's Most Powerful Psychiatrists Decide Who's Normal*. New York: Addison-Wesley.

Capps, L. and Ochs, E. (1995) *Constructing Panic: The Discourse of Agoraphobia*. London and Cambridge, MA: Harvard University Press.

Chesler, P. (1972) *Women and Madness*. New York: Avon.

Cooper, D. (1967) *Psychiatry and Antipsychiatry*. London: Tavistock.

Davison, G.C. and Neale, J.M. (1998) *Abnormal Psychology*. 7th edn. New York: Wiley. (1st edn, 1974.)

Deleuze, G. and Guattari, F. (1977) *Anti-Oedipus: Capitalism and Schizophrenia*. New York: Viking.

Derrida, J. (1974) *Of Grammatology*. Baltimore: Johns Hopkins University Press.

Flax, J. (1993) *Disputed Subjects: Essays on Psychoanalysis, Politics and Philosophy*. London and New York: Routledge.
Foucault, M. (1987) *Mental Illness and Psychology*. Berkeley: University of California Press. (First English translation published by Harper & Row, 1976.)
Foucault, M. (1965) *Madness and Civilization: A History of Insanity in the Age of Reason*. New York: Vintage.
Foucault, M. (1977) *Discipline and Punish*. New York: Vintage.
Foucault, M. (1980) *Power/Knowledge: Selected Interviews and Other Writings 1972–1977* (C. Gordon, ed.). New York: Pantheon.
Foucault, M. (1989) 'Truth is in the Future,' in S. Lotringer (ed.), *Foucault Live: Collected Interviews, 1961–1984*. New York: Semiotext(e). pp. 298–301.
Foucault, M. (1997) *The Politics of Truth*. New York: Semiotext(e).
Gergen, K.J. (1991) *The Saturated Self: Dilemmas of Identity in Contemporary Life*. New York: Basic Books.
Gergen, K.J. (1994) *Realities and Relationships: Soundings in Social Construction*. London and Cambridge, MA: Harvard University Press.
Giddens, A. (1990) *The Consequences of Modernity*. Stanford, CA: Stanford University Press.
Giddens, A. (1991) *Modernity and Self-Identity: Self and Society in the Late Modern Age*. Stanford, CA: Stanford University Press.
Gilman, S.L. (1985) *Difference and Pathology: Stereotypes of Sexuality, Race, and Madness*. Ithaca, NY: Cornell University Press.
Glass, J. (1993) *Shattered Selves: Multiple Personality in a Postmodern World*. Ithaca, NY: Cornell University Press.
Glass, J. (1995) *Psychosis and Power: Threats to Democracy in the Self and the Group*. Ithaca, NY: Cornell University Press.
Goffman, E. (1961) *Asylums: Essays on the Social Situation of Mental Patients and Other Inmates*. New York: Anchor.
Grob, G. (1994) *The Mad Among Us: A History of the America's Mentally Ill*. New York: Free Press.
Grodin, D. and Lindlof, T. (eds) (1996) *Constructing the Self in a Mediated World*. London and Thousand Oaks, CA: Sage.
Ingleby, D. (ed.) (1980) *Critical Psychiatry: The Politics of Mental Health*. New York: Pantheon.
Irigaray, L. (1985) *This Sex Which Is Not One*. Ithaca, NY: Cornell University Press.
Kirk, S.A. and Kutchins, H. (1992) *The Selling of DSM: The Rhetoric of Science in Psychiatry*. New York: Aldine de Gruyter.
Kristeva, J. (1986) 'The True/Real,' in T. Moi (ed.), *The Kristeva Reader*. New York: Columbia University Press. pp. 214–37.
Kvale, S. (ed.) (1992) *Psychology and Postmodernism*. London and Thousand Oaks, CA: Sage.
Laing, R.D. (1967) *The Politics of Experience*. New York: Ballantine.
Laing, R.D. (1969) *The Divided Self*. New York: Pantheon.
Lemert, E. (1951) *Social Pathology*. New York: McGraw-Hill.
Levin, D. (ed.) (1987) *Pathologies of the Modern Self: Postmodern Studies on Narcissism, Schizophrenia, and Depression*. New York: New York University Press.
Littlewood, R. and Lipsedge, M. (1982) *Aliens and Alienists: Ethnic Minorities and Psychiatry*. Harmondsworth: Penguin.
Lyotard, J.-F. (1984) *The Postmodern Condition: A Report on Knowledge*. Minneapolis: University of Minnesota Press.
McNamee, S. and Gergen, K.J. (eds) (1992) *Therapy as Social Construction*. London and Thousand Oaks, CA: Sage.
Orr, J. (1990) 'Theory on the Market: Panic, Incorporating,' *Social Problems*, 37 (4): 460–84.

Parker, I. (1992) *Discourse Dynamics: Critical Analysis for Social and Personal Psychology*. London and New York: Routledge.
Parker, I., Georgaca, E., Harper, D., McLaughlin, T. and Stowell-Smith, M. (1995) *Deconstructing Psychopathology*. London and Thousand Oaks, CA: Sage.
Porter, R. (1987) *A Social History of Madness*. New York: Weidenfeld & Nicolson.
Rose, N. (1989) *Governing the Soul: The Shaping of the Private Self*. London and New York: Routledge.
Rosenhan, D. (1973) 'On Being Sane in Insane Places,' *Science*, 179: 250–8.
Samson, C. (1995) 'Madness and Psychiatry,' in B.S. Turner (ed.), *Medical Power and Social Knowledge*. 2nd edn. London and Thousand Oaks, CA: Sage. (1st edn, 1987.) pp. 55–83.
Sass, L.A. (1992) *Madness and Modernism: Insanity in the Light of Modern Art, Literature, and Thought*. New York: Basic Books.
Scheff, T. (1974) 'The Labeling Theory of Mental Illness,' *American Sociological Review*, 39: 444–52.
Scheff, T. (1975) *Labeling Madness*. Englewood Cliffs, NJ: Prentice Hall.
Scull, A. (1989) *Social Order/Mental Disorder: Anglo-American Psychiatry in Historical Perspective*. Berkeley: University of California Press.
Sedgwick, P. (1982) *Psycho Politics*. New York: Harper & Row.
Shotter, J. (1992) ' "Getting in Touch": The Meta-Methodology of a Postmodern Science of Mental Life,' in S. Kvale (ed.), *Psychology and Postmodernism*. London and Thousand Oaks, CA: Sage. pp. 58–73.
Showalter, E. (1985) *The Female Malady: Women, Madness, and English Culture, 1830–1980*. New York: Pantheon.
Simon, W. (1996) *Postmodern Sexualities*. London and New York: Routledge.
Smith, D. (1990) *The Conceptual Practice of Power: A Feminist Sociology of Knowledge*. Boston: Northeastern University Press.
Spitzer, S.P. and Denzin, N.K. (eds) (1968) *The Mental Patient: Studies in the Sociology of Deviance*. New York: McGraw-Hill.
Szasz, T. (1970) *The Manufacture of Madness*. New York: Dell.
Szasz, T. (1972) *The Myth of Mental Illness*. London: Paladin.
Ussher, J. (1991) *Women's Madness: Misogyny or Mental Illness?* Amherst: University of Massachusetts Press.
Weedon, C. (1987) *Feminist Practice and Poststructualist Theory*. Oxford and Cambridge, MA: Blackwell.
White, M. and Epston, D. (1990) *Narrative Means to Therapeutic Ends*. New York: Norton.
Wurtzel, E. (1995) *Prozac Nation: Young and Depressed in America*. New York: Riverhead. (First published by Houghton Mifflin 1994.)

PART II PSYCHIATRIC DISCOURSE AND MENTAL LIFE IN POSTMODERN SPACES

2

Escape from Insanity: 'Mental Disorder' in the Postmodern Moment

Simon Gottschalk

Modern Diagnoses and Postmodern Crises

> The only sanity worth having is one which, in a deep sense, is a re-cognition of the madness of contemporary society.
>
> (Maguire, 1996: 171)

> The self-inflicted psychotic pollution by a culture will not respond to any psychiatric treatment as long as its main symptoms (regression, dissociation, de-individualization) are systematically nurtured and encouraged by surrounding cultural milieux. . . . Those of us who live today in Europe and the US suffer from a chronic psychosis whose intensity is still mild. If the manifestly paranoid and schizoid characteristics of our daily behaviors are not experienced for what they really are, it is simply because we all share them.
>
> (Laplantine, 1973: 112)

I'll start with a premise and a question. The premise suggests that different epochs and societies foster distinct types of mental disorder in its members.[1] The question is: which types of mental disorder are most likely to characterize individuals living in the contemporary (postmodern) moment? Consulting the relevant literature, I am uncertain as the list of the various diagnoses suggested by this literature sketches an annoyingly imprecise clinical picture. I note that the postmodern self is diagnosed as *anxious* (Massumi, 1993), *schizophrenic* (Jameson, 1983, 1988; Levin, 1987) *multiphrenic* and *fragmented* (Gergen, 1991), *paranoid* (Burgin, 1990; Frank, 1992), *depressed* and *nihilistic* (Levin, 1987), *self-possessed* (Kroker, 1992), *postnomic* (Frank, 1992) and *anti-social* (Gottschalk, 1989). Suffering from *narcissistic pathology* (Frosh, 1991; Langman, 1992) and *schizoid dichotomy* (Kellner, 1992), s/he oscillates between *terror* and *chronic boredom* (Grossberg, 1988; Petro, 1993), *panic* and *envy* (Kroker and Cook, 1986; Langman, 1992), *strained casualness* and *ecstatic violence* (MacCannell, 1992), among other conditions.

How to make sense of all this? Stretched across a variety of psychiatric categories and torn by several diagnostic axes, this self could be afflicted by none of these disorders and by every one of them at the same time. But, perhaps, that is precisely the point. Perhaps one way of resolving this confusion is to consider that the disagreements between these various diagnoses partly result from utilizing a self-contradictory approach which relies on *modern* assumptions about the self in order to understand the psychological characteristics of individuals living in the *postmodern* moment. In the following section, I attempt to explain this contradiction and suggest a different approach.

From the Modern Self to Postmodern Selfhood

> What would it be like to have never had these commercialized images in my head? What if I had grown up in the past or in a nonmedia culture? Would I still be 'me'? Would my 'personality' be different? I think the unspoken agreement between us as a culture is that we're not supposed to consider the commercialized memories in our head as real, that real life consists of time spent away from TVs, magazines, and theaters. But soon the planet will be entirely populated by people who have only known a world with TVs and computers. When this point arrives, will we still continue with pre-TV notions of identity? Probably not.
>
> (Coupland, 1996: 112)

> Memories are made of Aunt Jemima mornings.
>
> (advertisement)

The idea that 'every age develops its own peculiar forms of pathology, which express in exaggerated form its underlying character structure' (Lasch, 1978, quoted in Frosh, 1991: 63), introduces difficult problems when one decides to approach the contemporary moment from a postmodern perspective. Over the last two decades or so, the 'postmodern' has become one of the most controversial concepts in the human and other sciences, and the topic of a growing number of articles, books, conferences, seminars, and intellectual skirmishes.[2] Characteristically, the postmodern means different things to different people, and it is rare to find two authors who define it similarly. Whereas many dismiss this concept as the faddish articulation of a crisis among Western intellectuals or worse (Callinicos, 1990; Faberman, 1991; Huber, 1995; Morin and Kern, 1993; Rosenau, 1992), others approach it with more intellectual curiosity and tolerance (Agger, 1992; Denzin, 1996;

Dickens, 1995; Dickens and Fontana, 1994, 1996; Hall, 1996; Seidman, 1994a, 1994b, 1996). For the purpose of this essay, I will simplify the definition of the postmodern, and use it to refer to three interrelated phenomena: a particular historical moment; the psychological expressions of this moment; and its cultural articulations.

The postmodern refers first to a particular period in the history of Western society and the planet (post-World War II). Traumatized at birth by the horrors of Auschwitz and Hiroshima, this period has been characterized by increasingly accelerating and disorganized change in all social institutions (see Crook et al., 1992; Dickens, 1995; Harvey, 1989). Although often uncomfortable with the concept of the postmodern, many sociologists and others still accept that these momentous changes do distinguish the present moment from a previous 'modern' one, and thus warrant the coining of a new term that denotes their uncertain and ongoing effects.

Second, the postmodern concept also refers to the psychological correlates or expressions of such changes (see, e.g., Connor, 1989; Gitlin 1989a, 1989b; Jameson, 1983, 1984b; MacCannell, 1992). The accelerating transformations located in the abstract economic, political, religious, military, techno-scientific, and other institutions are inevitably experienced in our everyday life. Changes in the external macro-social landscape are accompanied by changes in the internal psychological one, and the postmodern thus also points to a 'mood,' 'spirit,' 'zeitgeist' (Gitlin, 1989a), or collective psychological dispositions which are assumed to characterize contemporary individuals.

Third, these macro- and micro-transformations are also interrelated with changes occurring in those institutions directly concerned with cultural production (academia, art, mass media). In academia, the postmodern term refers to a wide range of intellectual positions that advance a radical criticism of modern approaches, while also developing different ones that, they hope, will be more attuned to the contemporary moment (see Denzin, 1996).

Believing that everyday life in post-World War II society is constantly and *qualitatively* transformed by an exponentially accelerating pace of change which we do not really comprehend, and which traditional models cannot seem to adequately explain (Baudrillard, 1983a; Denzin, 1994; Lyotard, 1984; Marcus, 1994; Seidman, 1994a, 1994b, 1996), postmodern social scientists have proceeded to explore this perceived gap between the traditional models of thought and the contemporary everyday we experience. For some, such explorations have resulted in proclamations such as (among others): the end of the social and sociology (Baudrillard, 1983a), of meaning and Man (Baudrillard, 1983b), of philosophy and culture (Kaplan, 1988), of referentiality (Poster, 1988), of the modern self (Gergen, 1991), of time, space, methods, truth (Rosenau, 1992), of history, ideology, art, social class (Jameson, 1984a), of citizenship (Wexler, 1991), and of 'the rule of the Enlightenment and its Trinity of Father, Science, and State' (see Gitlin, 1989a). Reframing these foundational terms as obsolete yet ideologically powerful modern constructs, scholars following the postmodern turn have thus called for the 'abandonment of previous social theory' (Kroker and Cook, 1986). Reactions to such a call have been predictably mixed (Kaplan, 1988; Rosenau, 1992; Ross, 1989), and, as Dickens and Fontana (1996) note, often emotional.

This questioning of pivotal modern constructs necessarily affects post-modern approaches to the slippery concept of the 'self.' As Gergen (1991) observes, the dominant modern view specified that the self was a finite, rational, self-motivated and predictable entity which displayed consistency with itself and others across contexts and time (see also Anderson and Schoening, 1996; Bauman, 1996; Geertz, 1983; Gubrium and Holstein, 1994; Hall, 1996). As modern theorists saw it, this self could be healthy or pathological, self-fulfilled or alienated, but it could be isolated, observed, diagnosed, and preferably 'improved.' In postmodern theory, however, this assumption is rejected as obsolete and ideological (Erickson, 1995; Flax, 1990; Frosh, 1991; Gergen, 1996; Grodin and Lindlof, 1996; Jameson, 1984b; Kellner, 1992, 1995; Langman, 1992; Lather, 1991; Mouffe, 1989; Sass, 1992; Stephanson, 1988; Weedon, 1987). Destabilized by poststructuralist arguments positing the 'self' as a constraining cultural imperative, a 'conversational resource,' or *story* we tell ourselves and each other (Gubrium and Holstein, 1994; McNamee, 1996), the solid and stable modern self loses its footing and becomes fluid, liminal and protean self*hood* (Gergen, 1991; Kvale, 1992). In postmodern thought, this selfhood is a continuous *process* that is constituted through the multiple and sometimes self-contradictory relationships in which one participates. These processes and relationships – and their verbal articulations – are now given priority over the self-propelled, self-contained, and atomized entity posited by modern discourses (Gergen, 1996). As I'll also elaborate below, these processes and relationships are increasingly *mediated* by new technologies of simulation and telepresence, and such mediation constitutes an essential dimension for the understanding of postmodern selfhood.

Taken together, these ideas now hopefully explain the argument advanced above. More specifically, if we posit postmodern selfhood as a mutable, liminal, multiple, interdependent, and interactive process, then relying on *DSM-IV*[3] diagnoses will prevent us from understanding it, since *DSM*-type diagnoses rest on – and reproduce – the idea of a stable, self-contained, and isolated modern self. If the *modern self* is an obsolete construct (see Jameson, 1984a), and if the *DSM* is the most authoritative tool which evaluates such a construct for its 'deficiencies,' then, logically, this tool is inappropriate to develop an understanding of *postmodern selfhood*. Additionally, such a tool also reproduces modern positivist assumptions about a macro-social order and a consciousness that continues to exist mainly in nostalgic discourses. A postmodern approach to 'mental disorders' should thus proceed according to a different logic than the ones guiding modern psychiatry, psychology, and sociology.

Psychosocial Paths Across the Postmodern Landscape

> Pathology is always metaphorical.
>
> (Levin, 1987: 4)

> Psychotizing cultures are those which exact a psychic tension and energy which is absolutely unbearable by the majority of group members. . . . But at the same time, in order to reduce the pathological effects resulting from their own development, such societies increasingly allow compensatory regressive mechanisms whose role is to buffer the perception of a nightmarish real.
>
> (Laplantine, 1973: 112)

Before I proceed, I must briefly mention three interrelated steps that guide this essay. The first one is inspired by critical theory, and questions the ideological biases of modern 'mind' sciences. Psychological discourses traditionally seek to locate the causes of mental disorder in restricted family dynamics, and psychiatry typically attempts to trace its roots in individual biology. But such reductions are ideologically motivated and are thus neither neutral nor innocent. Explanations of mental disorders as restricted individual troubles tend to reproduce a certain worldview about the psyche, about society, and about their interrelationships. Such explanations are, needless to say, also immensely consequential for the kinds of therapeutic intervention likely to be utilized, and thus, ultimately, will significantly influence whatever counts as a desirable prognosis. Additionally, by failing to critically address the broad sociocultural environment in which individuals live, such explanations tacitly endorse the idea that the existing social order is indeed sane, and that 'normal' (i.e. accepted, socially desirable, conforming) social psychological dispositions are indeed healthy. My first critical step thus consists in questioning these ideas. At the same time I want to point to the destabilizing macro- and micro-social forces, now driving individuals into a 'normal' madness that positivist psychiatry and psychology cannot (or do not attempt to) fathom. In other words, given the possibility of a pathological sociocultural environment (see Fromm, 1956), what distinguishes the psychiatric patient from 'normal' citizens cannot be reduced to fundamentally different psychological, genetic, or biochemical attributes.

Therefore, informed by both the critical approach outlined above and the idea of postmodern selfhood, I discuss 'mental disorders' as *psychosocial paths*. From this position, these conditions called 'mental disorders' by the *DSM-IV* become dynamic, interrelated, interpersonal and even sequential strategies (ways of feeling, perceiving, thinking, and acting) we develop in our attempts to proceed across the landscape – or through the labyrinth – of everyday life, called the postmodern. This second step – positing mental disorders as interpersonal strategies – has a long tradition in critical psychiatry, and has been substantially developed in the works of Delacampagne (1974), Laing (1967, 1969, 1985), and Lasch (1978), among others. In their extensive research, ethnopsychiatrists such as Al-Issa (1982), Devereux (1980), Fourasté (1985), Laplantine (1973), Linton (1956), and Opler (1959,

1967) have convincingly documented that such strategies are inevitably informed by the patient's culture. Enriching this understanding, scholars such as Laing, Bateson (Bateson et al., 1956), Lemert (1962), and others associated with the Palo Alto School (Winkin, 1981) have also suggested that these strategies constitute responses to incapacitating communication patterns between 'disturbed' individuals and their – often no less disturbed – significant others.[4]

Informed by postmodern theory, the third step guiding this work insists that the exponentially accelerating pace of change spinning the postmodern landscape is risk-laden, anxiety-provoking, and often all too painful.[5] Writing this, I am fully aware that many sociologists and other human scientists will convincingly contend that the *modern* landscape could be similarly characterized (Berger et al., 1974; Callinicos, 1990; Giddens, 1990, 1991; Hoggett, 1989; Kahler, 1967; Sass, 1992; Van den Berg, 1961, 1974). Yet, I believe that there are important differences between the two. One condition which already distinguishes the postmodern landscape (both external and internal) from a modern one is its constant saturation by multiple electronic screens which simulate emotions, interactions, events, desires, and thus a certain 'reality.' From TV screens to computer terminals, from surveillance cameras to cell phones, we increasingly experience everyday life, reality, and Others via technologies of spectacle, simulation, and 'telepresence.' By comparison to individuals living in previous periods, postmodern individuals must now proceed across this hallucinatory landscape, and, perhaps more interestingly, may very well *experience* it through a consciousness which is inevitably contaminated – encoded – by these new technologies and the logic they promote. As I'll discuss below, when increasing aspects of our daily lives are orchestrated and mediated by these technologies, new social psychological reactions must necessarily follow. Accordingly, whereas the classical sociological literature contains a wealth of compelling insights elucidating the social psychological changes fostered by the shift from a premodern to a modern moment, this literature could neither anticipate the incomprehensible saturation of everyday life by the multimedia, nor assess the effects of such a saturation on postmodern selfhood – whether consciously felt or not.

Of course, the postmodern 'turn' in the social sciences hinges on much more than just this claim of multimedia saturation. The long list of modern 'ends' mentioned earlier, the palpable economic and cultural globalization of everyday life, the rise of brutal fundamentalisms, the now blasé return of genocides, the awareness of ecocides, the chronic 'crisis of legitimacy' extending to an increasing number of institutions, and the new forms of warfare (see Bauman, 1995) constitute some other important interacting trends supporting the claim that the postmodern is indeed a new moment and, to quote philosopher Bernard Henry Lévy (1994), a particularly vicious one. Yet, while the media saturation of everyday life constitutes but one term in the postmodern equation, it is, I believe, a significant one precisely because such a saturation invariably *mediates* our very experiencing of these other alarming trends characterizing the present moment. We not only visually absorb electronic simulations that claim to represent reality, but perhaps increasingly are adopting these simulations as the very templates *against which* we evaluate reality and *through which* we understand it.

Following these three steps, I attempt to reach a tentative and always incomplete synthesis of the various postmodern 'mental disorders' suggested by the literature. A few cautionary notes are necessary before I proceed. First, I do not seek to 'prove' that these postmodern 'disorders' are *caused* by contemporary sociocultural trends. Following Sass's (1992) extensive study of schizophrenia and modernity, I want to discuss the *affinities* these strategies share with these trends. Second, I intend neither to offer a comprehensive analysis of postmodern selfhood, nor to provide a definitive diagnosis of what it suffers from, or even to arbitrate between different theories of this or that diagnosis. I am more interested in striking a resonating chord in readers, and in asking different kinds of questions.

Thus, if we can agree that many of those conditions we call 'mental disorders' are individual expressions of sociocultural trends, then a critical approach to 'mental disorders' will shift the focus away from the *individual* and toward these *trends* he or she reacts to, internalizes, and reproduces. It will apprehend such disorders as *sociocultural* rather than as *individual* conditions. Additionally, if we can accept the notion of a mutable postmodern selfhood rather than a stable modern self, then mental 'disorders' should be similarly apprehended as changing interpersonal *strategies* individuals develop rather than as fixed and internal 'diseases' they fall prey to. Finally, when we question, rather than tacitly accept, the *sanity* of the sociocultural environment we live in, the ideological dimensions of established concepts such as 'normality,' 'sanity,' and 'mental disorder' should become increasingly visible and untenable.

Assessing the Climate: Low-Level Fear

> The threats of death, insanity and – somehow even more fearsome – cancer lurk in all we eat or touch.
>
> (Rabinowitch in Giddens, 1991: 123)

> We may now be entering the era of a continuous and silent holocaust.
>
> (Bauman, 1995: 159)

> We inhabit/inhibit huge wells of fear and incoherence. If we could utter and express this disturbing richness, then present structures of hierarchy could not endure. I do not try to convince you of the existence or extent of this fear: *it is here*. I feel it and suppress it; I feel it and repress it in others.
>
> (Maguire, 1996: 169)

Feeling anxious? Research conducted by government agencies report that the diagnostic category psychiatrists most often assign their patients is anxiety disorder (Gallagher, 1995: 252), and conservative estimates suggest that more than 12 percent of the population is so diagnosed. Acknowledging the endless list of problems plaguing the collection and analysis of epidemiological data,[6] it is still the case that most people who become psychiatric statistics approach mental health workers with complaints about states of body, mind, heart, or relations which they (and others) define as problematic, and for which they seek quick solutions – preferably in the psychopharmacological form.

While Freud (1961) argued in *Civilization and Its Discontents* that a heightened anxiety was the unavoidable price of an advanced civilization feeding off members' instinctual repression, Frankfurt School theorists (Fromm, 1956; Marcuse, 1955, 1968) added a critical-historical twist to this interpretation. As they suggested, in order to perpetuate domination, different sociohistorical conditions – or 'stages' of civilization – imposed different quotas of repression. Further, anxiety was manipulated into particular forms and channeled through culturally and historically distinct coping strategies or 'escape mechanisms.' Accordingly, it seems reasonable to suggest that individuals living in a postmodern moment – characterized by the lack of compelling cultural truths, parameters, center, or horizon – must experience this anxiety in significantly different ways than citizens living in more repressive yet seemingly more organized periods. As Baudrillard aptly put it, 'the revolution of our time is the *uncertainty* revolution – an uncertainty which covers all aspects of everyday life, including especially the sense of identity' (1993: 42–3, my italics).

In the postmodern moment, then, the fate of Freud's 'normal' anxiety of civilization (i.e. growing instinctual repression) remains uncertain, but it does not seem far-fetched to suggest that its intensities must be considerably amplified by this growing sense of radical uncertainty. As Maguire insists, 'fear is the unspoken but crucial subtext of our social normality . . . in most of us and in much of our culture there are reservoirs of hurt, anger and fear without which the strange "decorum" of our everyday being cannot be properly understood' (1996: 172). Similarly, it does not seem unreasonable to suggest that the dynamics of this already heightened anxiety of civilization must also be significantly transformed among the increasing number of individuals who did not, and will not, grow up in the kinds of family modern psychologists had in mind while assessing the extent to which a modest form of mental health was possible at all in societies such as our own (Elliott, 1994; Frosh, 1991; Giddens, 1991; Silverstone, 1993). In effect, not only must a large number of contemporary individuals proceed across a vertiginously anxiety-provoking, risk-laden, and unfamiliar sociocultural terrain, but they must also do so *without* the assistance of a variety of stabilizing psychological mechanisms which – it is assumed – can only be appropriately developed through a long process requiring the enduring presence of stable and consistent parental figures. As Langman notes:

> Freud treated Guilty Man tormented by unacceptable desires; today's patient is Tragic Man, an empty façade seeking ever more problematic confirmation of a fragmented selfhood that anxiously experiences itself without cohesion either

> from within as legacies of infancy or from without in the pluralistic life worlds. (1972: 73–4)

To add insult to injury, Freud's 'normal' anxiety of civilization is not only exacerbated early on by parental disappearance, unpredictable presence, replacement and confusion, but is also substantiated *ad nauseum* on screens which obsessively repeat stories of random catastrophe, anonymous brutality, and insatiable desire. Accordingly, the strategies one deploys to better deflect this constant experience of insecurity, vulnerability, and lack may coalesce into psychosocial dispositions that blur once-distinct psychiatric diagnoses. Massumi, for example, observes a condition of anxiety that

> is vague by nature. It is nothing as sharp as panic. Not as localized as hysteria. It does not have a particular object, so it's not a phobia. But it's not exactly an anxiety either, it is even fuzzier than that. It is *low-level fear*. A kind of background radiation saturating existence. . . (1993: 24)

This permanent and insidious low-level fear is the given, the very *climate* of the postmodern landscape. It is in this climate (both internal and external) that postmodern selfhood unfolds, breathes, and engages the everyday. The 'diagnoses' assigned postmodern individuals thus constitute psychosocial strategies that are deployed in response to this condition of permanent low-level fear. These strategies are grounded in it, informed by it, and, with varying degrees of success, manage it.

Assessing the Landscape: Telephrenic Maps

> The screen that provides with information about the world's realities, is also a screen against the shock of seeing and knowing about those realities. . . . A certain reality is perceived but its significance is de-realized. . . . The weightlessness of the image induces a sense of detachment and remoteness from what is seen . . . .
>
> (Robbins, 1994: 460)

> Roseanne Greco, 52, of West Islip, was charged with second-degree murder for killing her husband, Felix, in their driveway in 1985. She insisted at the time that the cartoon character [Felix the Cat] had taken over her husband's body. Roseanne Greco was found mentally competent to stand trial.
>
> (Massumi, 1993: 17)

Ethnopsychiatrists and critical theorists have long suggested that knowing a patient's culture is essential to understand the mental disorders she or he suffers from. Applying this ethnopsychiatric recommendation to ourselves, it seems clear that any discussion of our own postmodern culture must assign a central place to telecommunication media. Altheide expressed this point well when he remarked, that 'we regard the mass media as major factors in contemporary social life . . . culture is not only mediated through mass media; rather, culture in both form and content is constituted and embodied in mass media' (1995: 59).

While Fromm (1956) suggested that the routine economic and cultural dynamics of a society could encourage socially patterned neurotic disorders, ethnopsychiatrists Laplantine (1973) and Devereux (1980) argue that contemporary Western society systematically cultivates psychotic ones through the circulation of collective electronic hallucinations that are *real*ized and authenticated on media screens (see also Chen, 1987). Elaborating on such claims, theorists of the postmodern (Baudrillard, 1983c; Frosh, 1991; Jameson, 1984b; Kaplan, 1987; Kellner, 1995; Levin, 1987; MacCannell, 1992) advance that the media saturation of everyday life has radically destabilized central social and psychological experiences such as time and space, the real and the simulated, the serious and the entertaining (see also Meyrowitz, 1985). According to them, such a destabilization promotes a fragmented and disoriented consciousness which displays interesting similarities with schizophrenia or even multiphrenia (Gergen, 1991). Frosh, for example, notes that

> the dominant psychological experience of all people is that of psychosis: the messages surrounding us really are meaningful only in a persecutory sense, as capitalism grinds into its final gear. Everyone struggles to find their own place to stand in this maelstrom, their own imaginary self to stave off the deconstructing forces all around. Those that succeed relatively well stay 'sane', but their deeper experiences are still those of madness which is acted out in the more concrete and obvious symptomatology of schizophrenics. (1991: 146–7)

Yet, while the schizophrenic diagnosis might at first sound appropriate to describe a person's confusion between intersubjective and idiosyncratic reality (Sass, 1992), the tentative concept of *telephrenia* emphasizes that *both* intersubjective *and* idiosyncratic reality, the very experiences of perception and (self-)reflection, have already been affected by the multimedia.[7] As Guy Debord argued, 'the spectacle is not a collection of images, but *a social relation among people* mediated by images' (1977: 1, my italics). For Langman also,

> the intrusion of television into the socialization process, the relation of self to Other has taken on a new quality. . . . In the age of television, we learn to see Others as if our eyes were a camera . . . [and] self-presentations are increasingly intertwined with popular imagery, at times becoming parodies of media images and celebrities . . . the Other may be present and within view or what has been called the 'Other of the Imaginary,' the anonymous viewers that inhabit malldom or all those folks out there in the television audience. (1992: 56, 63)

In the telephrenic mind then, this media presence is not just 'more powerful than the reality principle' (Fiske and Glynn, 1995: 509), but *displaces* the reality principle and posits itself as the absolute referent. Here, ego defense mechanisms, fantasies, and repressed memories incorporate past media scenarios or anticipated ones. Replacing the more traditional Freudian slips, unconscious media flashbacks or 'moments' randomly discharge into an already disoriented conscious. By comparison to the psychiatric description of the schizophrenic patient, therefore, the *telephrenic* individual suffers neither from an inability to function in intersubjective reality, nor from an exacerbated 'self-reflexivity to the point of dissolution' (Sass, 1992).[8] As the schizophrenia of the electronic age, telephrenia points to a radically altered way of perceiving self, Others, and reality. But then, does the reoccurring delusion(?) among Western modern schizophrenics of being controlled and deadened by an omnipotent and omniscient 'machine' (see Sass, 1992) sound all that unreasonable in postmodern telephrenics? Further, if 'delusions, hallucinations, incoherence, grossly disorganized or catatonic behavior, and flat or inappropriate affect' constitute the major symptoms of schizophrenia listed by *DSM-IV* (American Psychiatric Association, 1994: 295), it seems that such tendencies are systematically nurtured by the televisual logic and the psychosocial dispositions it invites spectators to internalize. Burgin writes:

> We are in turn bombarded by pictures not only of hopelessly unattainable images of idealized identities, but also images of past and present suffering, images of destruction, of bodies quite literally in pieces. We are ourselves 'torn' in the process, not only emotionally and morally but in the fragmentary structure of the act of looking itself. In an image-saturated environment which increasingly resembles the interior space of subjective fantasy turned inside out, the very subject–object distinction begins to break down, and the subject comes apart in the space of its own making. (1990: 63)

Beyond televisual screens, the multiple sockets linking consciousness to virtual sites of entertainment, communication, and consumption bring the blurring between mind and electronic screen to a *fait accompli* whose consequences cannot be presently imagined (Gottschalk, 1997). Paradoxically then, by comparison to schizophrenic symptoms usually described as dramatically visible and audible,[9] the telephrenic ones appear quite unremarkable in the society of the spectacle. As always, it is a matter of degree.

Having suggested low-level fear as the *climate* of the postmodern moment and mind, I now add telephrenia – this internalized bizarre media logic – as the constantly shifting *cultural and psychological maps* we unconsciously activate while engaging the everyday. Because such maps were absent in previous historical moments and minds, I believe that they must be included in any discussion of the 'diagnoses' attributed to postmodern selfhood.

Choosing an Itinerary: Tense Ambivalence

> Not only am I unable to decide whether something is beautiful or not, original or not, but the biological organism itself is at a loss to know what is good for it and what is not. In such circumstances, everything becomes a bad object, and the only primitive defense is abreaction and rejection.
>
> (Baudrillard, 1993: 74)

How to manage this permanent anxiety? The postmodern climate and maps outlined above may nurture a variety of responses that are not satisfactorily explained by *DSM* diagnoses. For example, Grossberg (1988), Jameson (in Stephanson, 1989), Petro (1993), and others have suggested that postmodern selfhood is characterized by rapidly shifting intensities which oscillate between complete indifference and passionate involvement, between intense idealization and devaluation, between terror and chronic boredom. Of course, *DSM-IV* provides a label for such rapid emotional shifts; it organizes such dispositions and others with the diagnosis of a 'borderline personality disorder' (American Psychiatric Association, 1994: 301.83). Awaiting the discovery of biological 'causes,' such a disorder is usually traced to a problematic childhood (e.g. Schwartz-Salant, 1987; Weaver and Clum, 1993).

Located in a wider sociocultural environment, however, it seems that those 'borderline' dispositions are reasonably synchronized to a very disturbing everyday existence. When yesterday's celebrated products, ideas, styles, and desires are today ridiculed in favor of their improved tomorrow, when 'spouses are being traded as cheaply and easily as used cars' (Derber, 1996: 111), when continual uprootedness is normal, when our immediate physical space is constantly being altered, and when expert knowledge is instantly obsolete, to remain passionately committed to anything is to obsess. In such a situation, relationships and self-presentation are orchestrated with the single purpose of achieving what Bauman calls 'maximum impact and instant obsolescence' (1995: 90). Following Gergen's (1991) notion of 'microwave relationships,' intense emotional heat quickly turns into cold indifference, and commitment binds individuals only until further notice, if at all. Perhaps the most enduring form of commitment postmodern individuals are increasingly encouraged to develop is the *serial* kind dedicated to commercial brands whose names and logos are proudly displayed on T-shirts, baseball caps, and bumper stickers:

> And so here the snag is no longer how to discover, invent, construct, assemble (even buy) identity, but how to prevent it from sticking. Well-constructed and durable identity turns from an asset into a liability. The hub of postmodern life strategy is not identity building, but avoidance of fixation. . . . The main identity-bound anxiety of modern times was the worry about durability; it is the concern with commitment-avoidance today. Modernity built in steel and concrete; postmodernity, in bio-degradable plastic. (Bauman, 1996: 19–24)

This normalized assault on any sense of constancy is also complicated by the increasingly common experience of virtual interaction which collapses time and space, reorganizes one's experiences of Others, selfhood, and communication, and thus necessarily transforms their very meaning (see Altheide, 1995; Turkle, 1995; Weigert, 1997). Considering such types of virtual interaction, Virilio, for example, warns that 'the fact that one can be closer to another who is far away than to the one who is close by constitutes the political dissolution of the human species. . . . We confront here a considerable menace, the loss of the other' (1996: 45–6). Increasingly immersed in technologically mediated and decontextualized interactions with virtual others, chronically ambivalent engagements and widely shifting intensities become 'normal,' expected, and then easily cross over from the screens into an already compromised 'real.'

Those 'borderline' tendencies also constitute psychosocial strategies that are quite attuned to a 'normal' but demented televisual logic. When the experience of selfhood is increasingly guided by the glorification of a 'throw-away society' – promoting constant change as its axial cultural principle, chronic anxiety *cum* discontent as its reigning psychological mood, and instant obsolescence as its ruling economic imperative – it would seem that one almost needs to become 'borderline' in order to stay 'with it.' In a situation where obsolescence has become a major sin and source of anxiety, the psychiatric criteria of constancy, stability, and continuity (which the borderline assumedly lacks) seem increasingly dubious.

Traffic Rules: Reasonable Suspicion

> Paranoia is the normal state of affairs in the postmodern world, paranoia well-founded on the activities of eavesdroppers, information-manipulators, liars. Nothing and no-one can be trusted; they may know us better than we know ourselves, and will always put this knowledge to their own use.
>
> (Frosh, 1991: 132)

> In the morning I walked to the bank. I went to the automated teller machine to check my balance. . . . The figure on the screen roughly corresponded to my independent estimate, feebly arrived at after long searches though documents, tormented arithmetic. Waves of relief and gratitude flowed over me. The system had blessed my life. I felt its support and approval. . . . What a pleasing interaction. I sensed that something of deep personal value, but not money, not that at all, had been authenticated and confirmed.
>
> (DeLillo, 1986: 46)

> Today, the surveillance screen tends to replace the window.
>
> (Virilio, 1996: 66)

Whom do you really trust? The conditions discussed above might also encourage 'normal' yet deeply problematic rules of engagement while interacting with Others in the postmodern landscape. Gumpert and Drucker (1992: 90) note that 'transactions' increasingly eclipse 'interactions,' and Bauman (1995: 90) adds that such transactions are essentially narcissistic, mutually exploitative, partial, and fragmented. Here, one squeezes out as much pleasure or novel sensation as possible from the Other, and severs up the bond once the supply has dried out, when sensations fail to live up to their promised intensity, or when the Other starts voicing irritating expectations concerning nurturing responsibility and enduring commitment. As narcissistic recognition by Others becomes an (if not *the*) obsessive quest in the society of the spectacle (Langman, 1972), the diffuse suspiciousness ('paranoia') often attributed to postmodern individuals does not, at first, revolve so much around the fear of the physical harm Others might inflict, but perhaps around the fear of the emotional needs they might hide, impose, awaken, and predictably frustrate.

But such transactions also unfold between highly mobile, threatened, and fiercely competitive individuals. As we are routinely reminded, life in the postmodern moment is a struggle for diminishing resources – a struggle fought in societies which are technologically unstable, bureaucratically terrorizing, politically delegitimized, and decidedly punitive toward those unfortunate ones whose usefulness has ceased to fulfill the needs of a 'flexible' capitalism gone global, supersonic, and increasingly ruthless (see Lévy, 1994; Morin and Kern, 1993). Painting a seemingly realistic picture of the contemporary moment, the media portray the everyday as 'a jungle deprived even of jungle laws' (Bauman, 1995: 36), and normalize – if not openly celebrate – a reality where most people die young, violently, and victims of another's ill will, negligence, or incompetence. According to social analyst Behr, citizens 'have abdicated to violence in the same way as they abdicate to natural disasters such as hurricanes, thunderstorms and floods' (1995: 17). As Behr also remarks, such overall dispositions are well expressed in recent Hollywood trends depicting a world where the rich and the excluded underclass live in close proximity but never actually meet face-to-face, except to murder each other (1995: 220).

While an individual verbalizing such permanent distrust and fears of victimization would undoubtedly earn a paranoid diagnosis, Burgin reminds us that 'to whatever extreme the paranoid process may appear to take the subject, it is never far from "normal" psychology' (1990: 64). Ironically, if basic trust undoubtedly remains the healthiest position to engage every-day life (Frosh, 1991; Giddens, 1991; Silverstone, 1993), such a position requires an increasing psychological investment in those processes Freud identified as denial, splitting, and magical thinking. Massumi's 'low-level fear' thus also interacts with – and enables – suspicious dispositions, which, although diffuse, are routinely concretized on media screens as a variety of threatening Others – from mutant viruses to demented family members, from aliens to techno-catastrophes.

It might also be interesting to explore whether postmodern 'paranoids' (Burgin, 1990; Frank, 1992; Gitlin, 1989b) delude about similar types of villains or predicaments. Although prediction is always a risky business, I anticipate that 'delusions of surveillance' might increasingly appear as a common diagnostic subtype in the psychiatric evaluation of such individuals. Yet, such delusions would only caricature an increasingly bizarre everyday, requiring that we willingly subject ourselves to electronic surveillance whenever we step into the public realm – the private one being next. From airports to offices, from parking lots to malls, from banks to campus, we are increasingly becoming the preys of real and simulated monitoring devices (Altheide, 1995; Bogard, 1996). As the subjects of constant observation, we are increasingly playing our role in an anonymous voyeur's perverted fantasy demanding that every act we perform in public spaces should now become captured on tape, made available for reproduction, analysis, communication, and – in the near future – even morphing. Visits to the doctor's office, cyberspace, or the mall generate instant flows of electronic traces in virtual data banks we'll probably never access. At the same time, we also know that these traces *could*, in nanoseconds, be retrieved, organized, and combined in any way judged appropriate by the computer logic and its technicians (see Lyon, 1994). To some extent, the practice of 'cocooning' (Ansay, 1994; Derber, 1996) – the noticeable withdrawal from public life, the privatization of leisure, the flight behind the walls of gated communities – normalizes such a condition through paranoid architectural forms (see Davis, 1992).

Lemert's (1962) classical research on individuals labeled paranoid is also instructive in this respect. As he remarked, those rather unremarkable people had often 'become paranoid' following a period marked by disturbing interaction dynamics involving exclusion and surveillance by real and known others. Within the postmodern, however, constant surveillance and the circulation of information about private matters have become normalized and predictable. Such practices are legitimized 'for your own security,' enacted in an increasing number of life-spheres, and deployed by anonymous and invisible others for unfathomable reasons. Accordingly, in his or her firm conviction of being constantly monitored and investigated by invisible and overall not benevolent others, the postmodern 'paranoid' may be only carelessly verbalizing what 'normal' citizens experience mostly as a nagging apprehension. As Levin suggests:

> Paranoid fantasies of panoptical and acoustic surveillance, thought control and attacks of demonic possession should not be immediately dismissed as symptoms of private madness: it could be argued that they manifest an awareness that may be in touch with a normally concealed reality . . . . (1987, quoted in Frosh, 1991: 135)

Worse yet, whereas Lemert's 'paranoids' could sense problematic changes in interaction and directly attempt to engage others and clarify misunderstandings, the invisible and technological mediation of postmodern surveillance is increasingly prohibiting such interventions. To complicate matters, this technologically induced and inconspicuous 'paranoia' must be further intensified by the increasingly normalized experience of interacting with bureaucrats who casually delegate decisions about complex human situations to computer programs which – as we are routinely reminded – crash, err, are broken into by genius hackers, or are contaminated by viral infections (Ross, 1991).

Taking all these conditions together, the kinds of psychosocial disposition that can reasonably be expected to develop under the double imperative of electronic monitoring and investigation as *sine qua non* conditions of citizenship/consumption have remained largely unexplored. Paranoid? Perhaps. But when everyday life increasingly unfolds in institutions which are obsessed by the need to observe, by a fetish for more information, and by the tacit assumption that everyone is suspect, we should perhaps accept the notion that entire social systems can be paranoid. In such a situation, individual diagnoses become farcical.

Traveling Conditions: So Fast, So Numb[10]

> Just as an excess of pain causes you to fall into a faint or unconsciousness, and just as extreme danger plunges us into a state of physical and mental indifference which corresponds to the brutal indifference of the world towards ourselves, isn't the disintensification of affects (or 'movements of the spirit') in an artificially animated world a ruse of the species while awaiting a better world?
>
> (Baudrillard, 1990: 170)

> Note that in thirty brief years, violence and slaughter had increased at geometric ratio, while the human reaction to it had altered inversely.
>
> (Mumford, 1954: 170)

Characterized by *DSM-IV* (American Psychiatric Association, 1994) as lack of desire for close relationships, inability to experience pleasure, indifference to praise or criticism, and emotional coldness and detachment, the schizoid diagnosis often assigned to postmodern selfhood is usually linked to problematic childhood dynamics. In R.D. Laing's (1969) important work, for example, the schizoid disorder is a developing process in which a child essentially reacts to – and perpetuates – family dynamics that incapacitate and invalidate his or her emerging sense of self. Both seeking and fearing Others' validation, the schizoid develops a protective 'false self-system' – psychological processes which neutralize the emotional impact of what one perceives, feels, and does. These processes tend to *objectify* both Others and self, a disposition Laing already observed in the 'normal' conduct of everyday life:

> A partial depersonalization of others is extensively practised in everyday life and is regarded as normal if not highly desirable. Most relationships are based on some partial depersonalizing tendency in so far as one treats the other not in terms of any awareness of who or what he might be in himself but as virtually an android robot playing a role or part in a large machine in which one too may be acting yet another part. (1969: 47)

However, Laing's assumption of a true 'inner self' the schizoid is trying to maintain, and the fundamental distinction he draws between this inner self and a 'false self-system' are, as we have seen above, problematic in post-modern theory. Also lacking in his account is the probable influence of the multimedia logic on the schizoid's perceptions and experiences. More explicitly, as a central contributor to the Palo Alto School's distinctive approach to mental illness, Laing (1961) paid particular attention to repetitive 'schizogenic' communication patterns through which parents were believed to promote schizoid disorders in their offsprings.[11] Among these six schizogenic forms people can use to drive others crazy, four seem especially relevant for a postmodern approach to the 'schizoid' process:

> (1) *p* repeatedly calls *o*'s attention to areas of personality of which *o* is dimly aware, areas quite at variance with the kind of person *o* considers himself to be. (2) *p* simultaneously exposes *o* to stimulation and frustration or to rapidly

> alternating simulation and frustration. (3) *p* switches from one emotional wavelength to another while on the same topic (being 'serious' and then being 'funny' about the same thing). (4) *p* switches from one topic to the next while maintaining the same emotional wavelength (e.g. a matter of life and death is discussed in the same manner as the most trivial happening). (Searles in Laing, 1961: 121)

Replacing '*p*' with a variety of TV programs or *the televisual logic* itself, and '*o*' with the audience, the case could be made that repetitive schizogenic communicative patterns also circulate in 'normal' households, under the guise of entertainment or – more alarmingly – information. For example, the pervasive numbness and detachment characterizing the postmodern 'schizoid' might also narcotize a media-engineered 'pain of inadequacy' (Bauman, 1995: 157; Sass, 1992: 79) (see points 1 and 2 above). Alongside the list of childhood dynamics that might have nurtured it, this pain is constantly irritated by televisual voices calling attention to, and demeaning, every body part or function that has not yet been connected to its appropriate object – preferably a designer brand. Routinely evoked for commercial purposes, this pain of inadequacy is predictably resolved, on-screen, by an alter(ed) ego who finds psychological salvation through compulsive consumption. Accordingly, remarks Langman (1972: 71), this seemingly 'schizoid' indifference might actually serve to control a more volatile *envy*. As he adds, 'postmodern envy is not so much in wanting your neighbor's spouse or even wanting his/her various possessions. . . . Envy is a comparison of one's own subjectivity to that of the Other. This creates what might be called a "relative deprivation of selfhood".' Such envy is also fueled by 'narcissistic pathology . . . the extreme expression of normalcy in amusement society where recognition from others has become problematic and often frustrated.' Approaching Laing's insights with postmodern questions, therefore, we can deduce that if it is Others' validation the schizoid is really seeking, the sources of this need, its expression, the identity of these Others, what they expect, and the relationships one can establish with them, have all been transformed beyond recognition in the society of the spectacle.

Other affinities also exist between 'schizoid' dispositions and the varieties of 'schizogenic' communication patterns routinely found on TV and other screens (see points 3 and 4 above). As Baudrillard's quote cited at the beginning of this section suggests, the 'schizoid' strategy might very well also constitute a 'ruse' individuals develop as they become increasingly attuned to a 'necrophilic television' (Robbins, 1994: 457) which peddles a sleazy 'pornography of the dying' (Burgin, 1990: 53), while simultaneously encouraging autistic responses to such material. Switching effortlessly between Bosnia's ethnic cleansing and professional ice-skating, 'the catastrophic and the banal are rendered homogeneous and consumed with equal commitment' (Robbins, 1994: 460; and especially Postman, 1985). Do these televisual communication patterns devitalize emotional centers – a little like electroconvulsive therapy at a distance? Do they require that we do indeed deploy these self-protective mechanisms in order to neutralize the full emotional impact of a delirious 'real,' and to prevent terminal paralysis or breakdown? Here also, those 'schizoid' dispositions deplored at the individual level constitute but pale and benign articulations of schizogenic communication patterns that we accept as 'normal' because they appear on media screens.

Beyond these 'normal' and routine schizogenic forms, the 'schizoid' strategy should finally be assessed in terms of the inhuman speed catapulting everyday life in the present moment. Whereas the 1960s slogan warned amphetamine users that 'speed kills,' the *sociocultural* speed at which we are increasingly required to engage Others and everyday life might also induce addiction, disorientation, inappropriate emotional responses, exhaustion, and accidental death (Ansay, 1994; Bertman, 1998; Ferrarotti, 1990; Morin and Kern, 1993, Virilio, 1986, 1990, 1996). As a relatively unexplored dimension which is increasingly guiding everyday life, speed's invisible and debilitating force could very well constitute an essential element for the development of a more critical understanding of postmodern 'schizoid' tendencies as well as other 'disorders.' If paleness, nausea, and vomiting accompany motion sickness, a constricting of the heart, a chronic decrease in emotional temperature, and a sullen detachment from Others may be at least partly symptomatic of a toxic speed sickness.

Taken together – daily invalidations by moronic mantras constantly calling attention to and criticizing every aspect of one's very beingness, seeking Others' validation, secretly envious of their subjectivity, being confused by a media logic which casually obliterates the difference between the abominable and the trivial, and being constantly hurled about by the sheer velocity of everyday life – one relatively accessible solution is to go blank, to develop emotional anesthesia. Following this strategy, the postmodern shrug replaces the modern shriek, emotional cruise control kicks in, and radical indifference is mobilized to better ensure performance or, at least, some stability. To put it in a characteristic 1990s slogan: *Whatever*.

Yet, while this numbing strategy or 'adiaphorization' (Bauman, 1995: 149) might be psychologically adaptive in the short run, its long-range impacts remain dubious. MacCannell, for example, warns that such a strategy is not fail-proof, and that postmodern selfhood can be characterized by a 'kind of intense, strained casualness that sometimes fails to hold and is overturned by euphoric frenzy and ecstatic violence' (1992: 220). As Bauman also remarks, 'an admixture of violence is now suspected and expected to appear in the most intimate relationships, where love and mutual well-wishing were supposed to rule supreme' (1995: 156). Accordingly, if emotional flatness traces a relatively comfortable path through the psychosocial war zone of everyday life, it can also lead to an emotional minefield which, to the surprise of all concerned, seems to increasingly detonate in the private sphere. More disturbingly perhaps, the radical indifference, the objectification of Others, the chronic coldness and lack of empathy characterizing the 'schizoid' move might also lead to a psychosocial zone which is both more disciplined and more ruthless.

Final Destination: The Socio(path)

> In sociopathic societies, the clinical effort to dissect the sociopathic personality cannot be separated from an analysis of national character and ideology.
>
> (Derber, 1996: 24)

> But then, when you've just come to the point when your reaction to the times is one of total and sheer acceptance, when your body has become somehow tuned into the insanity, and you reach that point where it all makes sense, when it clicks . . . .
>
> (Ellis, 1991: 6–7)

> Whatever It Takes.
>
> (TV advertisement for Digital™)

The various psychosocial strategies outlined above might also lure post-modern selfhood to settle in a psychosocial region which is alarmingly similar to the condition catalogued by *DSM-IV* as antisocial personality disorder (Derber, 1996; Gottschalk, 1989; Sanchez, 1986).[12] Driven by a fierce individualism which is neither restrained by social bonds nor capable of empathy, the anti social personality disorder (or sociopath) is characterized by 'ruthless manipulation, impulsivity, deceitfulness, irritability, aggressiveness, reckless disregard for the rights of others, consistent irresponsibility, lack of remorse, skillful role-playing, and a high tolerance for excitement' (American Psychiatric Association, 1994: 647–9). Of course, most individuals living in the postmodern moment cannot be labeled as sociopaths, whatever this label means. Again, I am referring here to *tendencies* that, in more diluted combinations, may be systematically encouraged and more readily accessible in the current moment.

More precisely, in a situation where anything can become – in short succession – an object of desire, rejection, irrelevance, and danger; in a situation where distrust guides the normal everyday, where emotional interactions are fragmentary, exploitative, and in any case nonbinding, and where immediate pleasure, excitement, and attention are the only remaining and much celebrated games, the sociopathic move might become increasingly seductive. In its clear and simple rules, all Others are essentially worthless beyond their immediate purpose. All ambiguities are resolved by the single-minded logic of the omnipotent self (Reid, 1978; Reid et al., 1986; Sanchez, 1986; Smith, 1978). While Others' social validation was a primary concern for the schizoid, it has become, for the sociopath, largely irrelevant. *Whatever it takes*, warns Digital™. Besides, if *DSM-IV* lists 'compulsive lying,' 'manipulation,' and 'deceitfulness' as characteristic of the sociopathic *modus operandi*, I can think of very few commercial ads which do not engage audiences according to these exact same principles.

By comparison to Deleuze and Guattari (1977), who posited the schizophrenic process as an extreme metaphor of, and reaction to, the social disorganization unleashed by advanced capitalism, I suggest that the 'sociopathic' process symbolizes a different reaction to this disorganization. Both the schizophrenic and the sociopath retreat from the social, but the latter controls this departure, keeps his (usually his) bearings, and acts with cold rage, impeccable control, superior intelligence, and merciless strategic skills. Granted, most individuals living in the postmodern moment are certainly not those 'classic' sociopaths who perpetrate the gory massacres so hypocritically deplored on media screens. At the same time, as Laing (1961, 1967, 1969) and other Palo Alto School researchers remind us, coercion, abuse, humiliation, and mutilation are more likely to be perpetrated as verbal and emotional interactions between 'normal' individuals than as dramatic physical assaults between an ax-wielding monster and his victim.

Finally, while the sociopath directly and physically victimizes Others in order to achieve certain psychosocial pleasures, Bauman suggests that our fascination for necrophilic television might fulfill similar gruesome functions. As he notes, 'we live through the deaths of others, and their death gives meaning to our success: we have not died, *we* are *still* alive' (quoted in Robbins, 1994: 458). If this is indeed the case, these dispositions supposedly setting the *DSM* 'sociopath' apart from the 'normal' have become much less compelling than we used to believe.

Psychosocial Journey in the Postmodern Terrain: A Tentative Synthesis:

> In truth, what we are calling individual 'psychopathology,' and are treating as such, are only the more extreme cases of a collective suffering in which we all take part in accordance with our individual constitution and character.
>
> (Levin, 1987: 482)

I have approached various suggested diagnoses of postmodern selfhood as dynamic and intersecting psychosocial strategies individuals develop as they engage an increasingly pathogenic everyday world. As I have emphasized throughout this essay, these strategies cannot be explained by advancing individualizing theories of biochemical, genetic, or psychological dysfunctions. They are private and perhaps exaggerated articulations of, and reactions to, collective trends that are systematically normalized, albeit in more diluted forms, in the present moment.

To recapitulate, postmodern selfhood proceeds across a landscape constantly radiating with 'low-level fear' and saturated by compelling media voices which obsessively recite stories of permanent catastrophe, random brutality, and constant dissatisfaction. Increasingly encoding both conscious and unconscious processes, television and other technologies of telecommunication also cultivate a radical ambivalence and disorientation *vis-à-vis* Others, selfhood, and reality ('telephrenia'). Accordingly, any object can – often unexpectedly – become a 'bad object,' a source or target of violence, fear, hostility, or abandonment ('borderline personality disorder'). Informing relationships between fiercely competitive and permanently threatened individuals, such a volatile orientation is also modulated by a diffuse suspiciousness and distrust ('paranoia'), which is exacerbated by the experience of constant and anonymous surveillance. While a radical detachment ('schizoid personality disorder') manages to maintain some control and allows for a 'modicum of pseudo-functioning' (Kovel, 1988, quoted in Frosh, 1991), it sometimes fails to hold, and explodes in unpredictable violent outbursts among otherwise seemingly well-adjusted individuals. In others ('sociopaths'), this violence is more successfully controlled, more strategically deployed, and released from all anxiety or guilt.

Viewed in isolation, each of the suggested *DSM* syndromes tells only a part of the story – a particular strategy or 'moment' in this selfhood process. In some ways, if Gergen (1991) suggests that the postmodern self is 'multiphrenic' and 'fragmented,' I have gathered here some of these fragments and have tentatively organized them as an unfolding process. This proposed process does not claim to comprehensively explain postmodern selfhood and its 'pathologies' but seeks instead to promote an alternative approach. The strategies discussed here are neither exhaustive nor mutually exclusive. They combine with each other, lead to other ones, and coalesce, if only for a while, into clinical pictures that the *DSM-IV* freezes as static diagnoses. In so doing, the psychiatric discourse reaffirms its fundamental assumptions positing the self as an isolated entity, mental illness as a private trouble located 'within' this entity, and the 'normal' as equivalent to the 'sane.'

Finally, I realize I have granted the multimedia quite a bit of importance in my discussion of postmodern 'diagnoses,' and I fear that readers might interpret this attention as suggesting a simple causal link between multimedia and mental disorders. This is not my intention. The multimedia do not 'cause' people to develop mental disorders. Rather, they normalize, celebrate, and make acceptable psychosocial dispositions that, although normalized, are fundamentally unhealthy. The argument that such dispositions are, to various degrees, activated in our everyday life with real Others opens up an entire new range of questions pertaining to the reciprocal relationships between multimedia, the everyday, and mental disorders. This is partly what I have attempted to do here.

Conclusions: The Greening of Postmodern Selfhood

> Thus, the metropolitan type of man – which of course, exists in a thousand individual variants – develops an organ protecting him against the threatening currents and discrepancies of his external environment which would uproot him. He reacts with his head instead of his heart.
>
> (Simmel, 1965: 411)

> When you think about the incredible neurotic complexities of millions of individuals and about the cumulative effects of all those problems, you

> realize that the psychic pollution of the planet is much worse than the biological or technological one.
>
> (Baudrillard, 1995: 47)

> Precisely because we have acquired the power to work our will upon the environment, the planet has become like that blank psychiatric screen on which the neurotic unconscious projects its fantasies.
>
> (Roszak, 1995: 5)

Scholars associated with ecopsychology, ecofeminism, deep ecology, and related discourses have long suggested that the pathologies psychiatry locates in individual minds – and those that psychology trace to family processes – originate elsewhere. More precisely, they argue that our pathologies may actually express the problematic reactions humans will unavoidably develop upon finding themselves uprooted from their natural environment that they then proceed to destroy. In the deep ecology view (Conn, 1995; Devall, 1988; Devall and Session, 1985; Dickens, 1992; Maines, 1990; Merchant, 1989, 1994; Metzner, 1995; Shepard, 1992), this uprooting constitutes a painful physical, emotional, and cognitive exile; and this exile in turn distorts human consciousness, dispositions, and relations. Unfortunately, psychologists and therapists have typically ignored this critical fact. They have rarely questioned the larger urban context framing their research endeavors and therapeutic practices. Pushing this point a bit further, the taken-for-granted belief that mental health and sane psychosocial processes can indeed flourish in an everyday which is so ostensibly dissociated from – and destructive of – its natural habitat *is itself delusional and symptomatic of this very dissociation*. Such a belief attests to a collective autism, to chronic impairment in reality-perception, and, as Shepard (1992) proposes in his brilliant *Nature and Madness*, to a collective developmental disorder which leads to grossly inappropriate and (self-)destructive behaviors.

Despite accusations of essentialism (see Zimmerman, 1994) and epistemological impurity (see Maines, 1990), ecopsychologists maintain that 'de-naturation' dehumanizes, devitalizes, and extinguishes fundamental understandings – ways of knowing – which may not be socially constructed (Searles, 1960; Spretnak, 1991; see also Marcuse, 1972; Roszak, 1995). As many thinkers associated with these perspectives also argue, the recovery of such understandings is a vital means *and* end both of digging out the psychosocial roots of our demented assault on the environment, and of mending our collective psyche. Both projects are intimately interconnected.

Synthesizing findings generated through a variety of experiments, therapeutic encounters, theoretical developments, and pedagogical practices, several ecopsychologists argue that ecologically informed shifts in the definition and experience of selfhood can radically transform how individuals re-cognize their relationships with human and non-human Others (Cahalan, 1995; Fox, 1990; Greenway, 1995; Harper, 1995; Sewall, 1995; Thomashow, 1995). Although the precise temperament of such a selfhood is not altogether clear, scholars interested in the topic agree that some of its distinctive traits include: mutuality, reciprocity, cooperation, a nurturing ethic, complementarity, empathy, the experience of permeable boundaries between inner and outer processes, and an all-inclusive identification with both human and non-human Others (Naess, 1989).[13]

In a postmodern moment characterized by a lack of direction, horizon, center, anchor, or empathy, an ecological turn in social psychology is long overdue. Although the liberation of human beings from social and psychological oppression has always constituted the essential thrust of the critical project, this time there is much more at stake. It is now increasingly clear that such a project cannot proceed without both sound ecological ethics and radically new understandings of the psyche–ecology link. An ecologically grounded approach to selfhood should thus constitute the new path and destination of a critical, but hopeful, postmodern social psychology.

Notes

This chapter is a modified version of an article which appeared in *Studies in Symbolic Interaction*, 21, 1998.

1. I want to specify here that by 'mental disorders' I am referring to those behavioral, emotional, and cognitive patterns which (a) are judged abnormal, bizarre, undesirable, and odd by either the individual experiencing them and/or by those around him/her, and (b) which are not demonstrably caused by organic dysfunctions. This definition thus excludes all those mental conditions judged abnormal but attributed to causes squarely located in the individual's organism. Thus, although discourses about the latter category are no less socially constructed than discourses about the former, there is, until further notice, little controversy between psychiatrists and social scientists about their etiology. Beyond this distinction, critical theorists have also called our attention to the important difference between 'normality' and 'sanity.' Thus, cognitive, emotional, and behavioral conditions considered as 'abnormal' by members of a society may in fact be 'sane,' and conditions considered as 'normal' may in fact be pathological.

2. See Agger (1992), Anderson (1990), Bauman (1995, 1988), Best and Kellner (1991), Connor (1989), Crook et al. (1992), Denzin (1991, 1993, 1994), Denzin and Lincoln (1994), Dickens and Fontana (1994), Featherstone (1991, 1988), Flax (1990), Foster (1983), Gane (1991), Gergen (1991), Gitlin (1989a), Gottschalk (1993, 1995a, 1995b, 1997), Grossberg (1988), Harvey (1989), Hassan (1983, 1987), Hebdige (1988a, 1988b), Hollinger (1994), Huyssen (1986, 1990), Jameson (1983, 1984a, 1984b, 1988), Kaplan (1987, 1988), Kellner (1992, 1995), Kroker (1992), Kroker and Cook (1986), Kvale (1992), Lyotard (1984), MacCannell (1992), Marcus (1994), Pfohl (1990, 1992), Poster (1988, 1990, 1995), Rosenau (1992), Ross (1991), Seidman (1994a, 1994b, 1996), Smart (1990), Tyler (1986), Vattimo (1992), Venturi et al. (1977), Wolin (1984). Of course, this list is but a minuscule sample of an exponentially growing body of texts that address a multiplicity of postmodern topics from a wide variety of angles.

3. *DSM-IV* refers to the *Diagnostic and Statistical Manual of Mental Disorders* (4th edn) (American Psychiatric Association, 1994). For a better appreciation of the psychiatric definitions of paranoid, anxiety, anti-social, borderline, schizoid, and schizophrenic disorders, the reader is encouraged to consult the original version.

4. Bateson et al. (1956), Laing (1969), and Watzlawick (1971), for example, have specifically focused on 'schizogenic' communication patterns within the family such as: disconfirmation/tangentiality, mystification, and double bind. In these respective cases, parents communicate in ways which invalidate the child, which deny the child's perceptions and

experience of reality, and which effectively paralyze the child by emitting two contradictory messages at different levels of communication while forcing the child to respond.

5. As Freud argued, 'the avoidance of unpleasure may be a more significant motivating force in human behavior than the obtaining of pleasure' (Robbins, 1994: 454). Support for the assumption of a painful everyday abounds in a growing variety of sources. See, for example, Bauman (1995), Burgin (1990), Frosh (1991), Maguire (1996).

6. Here also, the list of works criticizing psychiatric assumptions, ideology, biases, and methods is too long to enumerate. See, for example, Banton (1985), Broverman et al. (1970), Brown (1984, 1986), Chesler (1972), Conrad (1980), Costrich et al. (1975), Delacampagne (1974), Foucault (1965), Ingleby (1980), Laing (1967, 1969, 1985), Rosenhan (1973), Scheff (1975, 1984), Sedgwick (1982), Showalter (1985), and Szasz (1970, 1972, 1987).

7. Postmodern works discussing the influence of television in everyday life, consciousness, and even sociological theory can be especially found in Agger (1992), Baudrillard (1983a, 1990, 1993), Chen (1987), Clough (1992, 1997), Denzin (1992), Gergen (1991), Gottschalk (1995a, 1997), Hartley (1992), Kellner (1995), Langman (1992), Meyrowitz (1985), Mitroff and Bennis (1989), Morley (1992), Poster (1990), Postman (1985), Silverstone (1989, 1993, 1994). Note also that this literature focuses only on television. More recent works also address the possible effect of other technologies of telecommunication and simulation such as videos (Gottschalk, 1995b), computers (Poster, 1995, 1990; Turkle, 1995), and virtual reality (Chayko, 1993; Robbins, 1994; Virilio, 1996).

8. Even though Sass compellingly argues that schizophrenia exacerbates the modern cultural trend toward self-reflexivity, today it seems impossible to talk about self-reflexivity without, again, asking oneself about the influence of media texts in such an activity.

9. Scheff's (1975, 1984) work is especially relevant in this respect since he approaches schizophrenia and other mental disorders as effects of 'residual deviance' – visible, audible, and quasi-palpable violations of unwritten norms of interaction.

10. R.E.M. (1996) 'So Fast, So Numb.' *New Adventures in Hi-Fi*. Warner Brothers.

11. See note 4 above.

12. The terms 'sociopath,' 'psychopath,' and 'anti-social personality disorder' are used interchangeably in the literature and esentially point to the same diagnostic picture.

13. Simmons (1993: 134) summarizes Naess's deep ecological view as follows:

1. The value of non-human life is independent of the usefulness of the non-human world as resources.
2. The diversity of life-forms has a value in itself and humans may reduce this variety only to satisfy vital needs.
3. The flourishing of non-human life requires a diminution of the size of the human population.
4. The increasing manipulation of the non-human world must be reversed by the adoption of different economic, technological and ideological structures.
5. The aim of such changes would be a greater experience of the connectedness of all things, and enhancement of the quality of life rather than an attachment to material standards of living.
6. Those who agree with this have an obligation to join in the attempt to bring about the necessary changes.

References

Agger, B. (1992) *Cultural Studies as Critical Theory*. London: Falmer Press.

Al-Issa, I. (ed.) (1982) *Culture and Psychopathology*. Baltimore: University Park Press.

Altheide, D. (1995) *An Ecology of Communication: Cultural Formats of Control*. New York: Aldine De Gruyter.

American Psychiatric Association (1994) *Diagnostic and Statistical Manual of Mental Disorders*. 4th edn. Washington, DC: American Psychiatric Association.

Anderson, J.A. and Schoening, G.T. (1996) 'The Nature of the Individual in Communication Research,' in D. Grodin and T.R. Lindlof (eds), *Constructing the Self in a Mediated World*. London and Thousand Oaks, CA: Sage. pp. 206–25.

Anderson, W.T. (1990) *Reality Isn't What It Used To Be*. San Franciso: Harper & Row.

Ansay, P. (1994) *Le Capitalisme dans la vie quotidienne*. Brussels: Éditions Vie Ouvrière.

Banton, R. (1985) *The Politics of Mental Health*. Oxford: Macmillan.

Bateson, G., Jackson, D., Haley, J., and Weakland, J.H. (1956) 'Toward a Theory of Schizophrenia,' *Behavioral Science*, 1(4): 251–64.

Baudrillard, J. (1983a) 'The Ecstasy of Communication,' in H. Foster (ed.), *The Anti-Aesthetic: Essays on Postmodern Culture*. Port Townsend, WA: Bay Press. pp. 111–59.

Baudrillard, J. (1983b) *In the Shadow of the Silent Majorities*. New York: Semiotext(e).

Baudrillard, J. (1983c) *Simulations*. New York: Semiotext(e).

Baudrillard, J. (1990) *Cool Memories*. New York: Verso.

Baudrillard, J. (1993) *The Transparency of Evil*. New York: Verso.

Baudrillard, J. (1995) *Fragments*. Paris: Galilée.

Bauman, Z. (1988) 'Is There a Postmodern Sociology?,' *Theory, Culture & Society*, 5: 217–37.

Bauman, Z. (1995) *Life in Fragments*. Oxford: Basil Blackwell.

Bauman, Z. (1996) 'From Pilgrim to Tourist – or a Short History of Identity,' in S. Hall and P. du Gay (eds), *Questions of Cultural Identity*. London and Thousand Oaks, CA: Sage. pp. 18–38.

Behr, E. (1995) *Une Amerique qui fait peur*. Paris: Plon.

Berger, P., Berger, B., and Kellner, H. (1974) *The Homeless Mind: Modernization and Consciousness*. New York: Vintage.

Bertman, P. (1998) *Hyperculture: The Human Cost of Speed*. Westport, CT: Praeger.

Best, S. and Kellner, D. (1991) *Postmodern Theory*. New York: Guilford Press.

Bogard, W. (1996) *The Simulation of Surveillance: Hypercontrol in Telematic Societies*. New York: Oxford University Press.

Broverman, I.K., Broverman, D., Clarkson, F., Rosenkraitz, P., and Vogel, S. (1970) 'Sex-Role Stereotypes and Clinical Judgments of Mental Health,' *Journal of Consulting and Clinical Psychology*, 34: 1–7.

Brown, P. (1984) 'Marxism, Social Psychology, and the Sociology of Mental Health,' *International Journal of Health Services*, 14: 237–64.

Brown, P. (1986) 'Diagnostic Conflict and Contradiction in Psychiatry,' *Journal of Health and Social Behavior*, 28: 37–51.

Burgin, V. (1990) 'Paranoiac Space,' *New Formations*, 12: 61–75.

Cahalan, W. (1995) 'Ecological Groundedness in Gestalt Therapy,' in T. Roszak, M.E. Gomes, and A.D. Kanner (eds), *Ecopsychology: Restoring the Earth, Healing the Mind*. San Francisco: Sierra Club Books. pp. 216–23.

Callinicos, A. (1990) *Against Postmodernism: A Marxist Critique*. New York: St Martin's Press.

Chayko, M. (1993) 'What is Real in the Age of Virtual Reality? "Reframing" Frame Analysis for a Technological World,' *Symbolic Interaction*, 16 (2): 171–81.

Chen, K.H. (1987) 'The Masses and the Media: Baudrillard's Implosive Postmodernism,' *Theory, Culture & Society*, 4: 71–88.

Chesler, P. (1972) *Women and Madness*. New York: Doubleday.

Clough, P. (1992) *The End(s) of Ethnography: From Realism to Social Criticism*. London and Thousand Oaks, CA: Sage.

Clough, P. (1997) 'Autotelecommunication and Autoethnography: A Reading of Carolyn Ellis's *Final Negotiations*,' *The Sociological Quarterly*, 38 (1): 95–110.

Conn, S.A. (1995) 'When the Earth Hurts Who Responds?,' in T. Roszak, M.E. Gomes, and A.D. Kanner (eds), *Ecopsychology: Restoring the Earth, Healing the Mind*. San Francisco: Sierra Club Books. pp. 156–71.

Connor, S. (1989) *Postmodernist Culture: An Introduction to Theories of the Contemporary*. New York: Basil Blackwell.

Conrad, P. (1980) 'On the Medicalization of Deviance and Social Control,' in D. Ingleby (ed.), *Critical Psychiatry*. New York: Pantheon. pp. 102–20.

Costrich, N., Feinstein, J., Kidder, L., Marecek, J., and Pascale, L. (1975) 'When Stereotypes Hurt: Three Studies of Penalties for Sex-Role Reversals,' *Journal of Experimental and Social Psychology*, 11: 520–30.

Coupland, D. (1996) *Polaroids from the Dead*. New York: HarperCollins.

Crook, S., Pakulski, J., and Waters, M. (1992) *Postmodernization*. London and Thousand Oaks, CA: Sage.

Davis, M. (1992) *City of Quartz: Excavating the Future in Los Angeles*. New York: Vintage.

Debord, G. (1977) *The Society of the Spectacle*. Detroit: Black & Red.

Delacampagne, C. (1974) *Antipsychiatrie: Les Voies du sacré*. Paris: Bernard Grasset.

Deleuze, G. and Guattari, F. (1977) *Anti-Oedipus: Capitalism and Schizophrenia*. London: Athlone Press.

DeLillo, D. (1986) *White Noise*. New York: Penguin.

Denzin, N.K. (1991) *Images of Postmodern Society*. London and Thousand Oaks, CA: Sage.

Denzin, N.K. (1992) *Symbolic Interactionism and Cultural Studies: The Politics of Interpretation*. Cambridge, MA: Basil Blackwell.

Denzin, N.K. (1993) '*Rain Man* in Las Vegas: Where is the Action for the Postmodern Self?,' *Symbolic Interaction*, 16 (1): 65–77.

Denzin, N.K. (1994) 'Postmodernism and Deconstructionism,' in D.R. Dickens and A. Fontana (eds), *Postmodernism and Social Inquiry*. New York: Guilford Press. pp. 182–202.

Denzin, N.K. (1996) 'Sociology at the End of the Century,' *The Sociological Quarterly*, 37 (4): 743–52.

Denzin, N.K. and Lincoln, Y.S. (eds) (1994) 'The Fifth Moment,' in N.K. Denzin and Y.S. Lincoln (eds), *Handbook of Qualitative Research*. London and Thousand Oaks, CA: Sage. pp. 575–86.

Derber, C. (1996) *The Wilding of America: How Greed and Violence Are Eroding our Nation's Character*. New York: St Martin's Press.

Devall, B. (1988) 'The Ecological Self,' in B. Devall (ed.), *Simple in Means, Rich in Ends: Practicing Deep Ecology*. Salt Lake City, UT: Peregrine Smith Books. pp. 39–72.

Devall, B. and Session, G. (1985) *Deep Ecology*. Salt Lake City, UT: Peregrine Smith.

Devereux, G. (1980) *Basic Problems of Ethnopsychiatry*. Chicago: University of Chicago Press.

Dickens, D. (1995) 'The Ethical Horizons of Postmodernity,' *Symbolic Interaction*, 18 (4): 535–41.

Dickens, D. and Fontana, A. (1994) *Postmodernism and Social Inquiry*. New York: Guilford Press.

Dickens, D. and Fontana, A. (1996) 'On Nostalgic Reconstruction in Interactionist Thought – Or Realism as the Last Refuge of a Scoundrel,' *Studies in Symbolic Interaction*, 20: 181–92.

Dickens, P. (1992) *Society and Nature: Toward a Green Social Theory*. Philadelphia: Temple University Press.

Elliott, A. (1994) *Psychoanalytic Theory*. Oxford: Basil Blackwell.

Ellis, B.E. (1991) *American Psycho*. New York: Vintage.

Erickson, R.J. (1995) 'The Importance of Authenticity for Self and Society,' *Symbolic Interaction*, 18 (12): 121–44.

Faberman, H.A. (1991) 'Symbolic Interactionism and Postmodernism: Close Encounters of a Dubious Kind,' *Symbolic Interaction*, 14: 471–88.

Featherstone, M. (1988) 'In Pursuit of the Postmodern: An Introduction,' *Theory, Culture & Society*, 5: 195–215.

Featherstone, M. (1991) *Consumer Culture and Postmodernism*. London and Thousand Oaks, CA: Sage.

Ferrarotti, F. (1990) *Time, Memory, and Society*. New York: Greenwood Press.

Fiske, J. and Glynn, K. (1995) 'Trials of the Postmodern,' *Cultural Studies*, 9 (3): 502–21.
Flax, J. (1990) *Thinking Fragments*. Berkeley: University of California Press.
Foster, H. (ed.) (1983) *The Anti-Aesthetic: Essays on Postmodern Culture*. Port Townsend, WA: Bay Press.
Foucault, M. (1965) *Madness and Civilization: A History of Insanity in the Age of Reason*. New York: Vintage.
Fourasté, R. (1985) *Introduction à l'ethnopsychiatrie*. Paris: Mesope.
Fox, W. (1990) *Toward a Transpersonal Ecology: Developing New Foundations for Environmentalism*. Boston and London: Shambala.
Frank, A.W. (1992) 'Cyberpunk Bodies and Postmodern Times,' *Studies in Symbolic Interaction*, 13: 39–50.
Freud, S. (1961) *Civilization and Its Discontents*. New York: Norton.
Fromm, E. (1956) *The Sane Society*. New York: Doubleday.
Frosh, S. (1991) *Identity Crisis: Modernity, Psychoanalysis and the Self*. New York and London: Routledge.
Gallagher, B. (1995) *Sociology of Mental Illness*. 3rd edn. Englewood Cliffs, NJ: Prentice Hall.
Gane, M. (1991) *Baudrillard: Critical and Fatal Theory*. New York and London: Routledge.
Geertz, C. (1983) *Local Knowledge*. New York: Basic Books.
Gergen, K.J. (1991) *The Saturated Self: Dilemmas of Identity in Contemporary Life*. New York: Basic Books.
Gergen, K.J. (1996) 'Technology and the Self: From the Essential to the Sublime,' in D. Grodin and T.R. Lindlof (eds) *Constructing the Self in a Mediated World*. London and Thousand Oaks: Sage. pp. 127–40.
Giddens, A. (1990) *The Consequences of Modernity*. Stanford, CA: Stanford University Press.
Giddens, A. (1991) *Modernity and Self-Identity: Self and Society in the Late Modern Age*. Stanford, CA: Stanford University Press.
Gitlin, T. (1989a) 'Postmodernism Defined, at Last!,' *Utne Reader*, July–August: 52–63.
Gitlin, T. (1989b) 'Post-Modernism: Roots and Politics,' *Dissent*, Winter: 110–18.
Gottschalk, S. (1989) 'From the Cheerful Robot to the Charming Manipulator: A Millsian approach to the Sociopath.' Paper presented at the American Sociological Association Annual Conference, San Francisco.
Gottschalk, S. (1993) 'Uncomfortably Numb: Countercultural Impulses in the Postmodern Era,' *Symbolic Interaction*, 16 (4): 351–78.
Gottschalk, S. (1995a) 'Ethnographic Fragments in Postmodern Spaces,' *Journal of Contemporary Ethnography*, 24 (2): 195–238.
Gottschalk, S. (1995b) 'Videology: Video Games as Postmodern Sights/Sites of Ideological Reproduction,' *Symbolic Interaction*, 18: 1–18.
Gottschalk, S. (1997) 'Between the Screen and the Everyday: Ethnography in/of the Interface,' in J. Epstein (ed.), *Wilderness of Mirrors: Symbolic Interaction and the Postmodern Terrain*. New York: Garland.
Greenway, R. (1995) 'The Wilderness Effect and Ecopsychology,' in T. Roszak, M.E. Gomes, and A.D. Kanner (eds), *Ecopsychology: Restoring the Earth, Healing the Mind*. San Francisco: Sierra Club Books. pp. 122–35.
Grodin, D. and Lindlof, T.R. (eds) (1996) *Constructing the Self in a Mediated World*. London and Thousand Oaks, CA: Sage.
Grossberg, L. (1988) 'Putting the Pop Back into Postmodernism,' in A. Ross (ed.), *Universal Abandon? The Politics of Postmodernism*. Minneapolis: University of Minnesota Press. pp. 167–90.
Gubrium, J.F. and Holstein, J.A. (1994) 'Grounding the Postmodern Self,' *The Sociological Quarterly*, 35 (4): 685–703.
Gumpert, G. and Drucker, S. (1992) 'From the Agora to the Electronic Shopping Mall,' *Critical Studies in Mass Communication*, 9: 189–200.

Hall, S. (1996) 'On Postmodernism and Articulation: An Interview with Stuart Hall,' in D. Morley and K.H. Chen (eds), *Stuart Hall: Critical Dialogues in Cultural Studies*. New York and London: Routledge. pp. 131–50.

Harper, S. (1995) 'The Way of Wilderness,' in T. Roszak, M.E. Gomes, and A.D. Kanner (eds), *Ecopsychology: Restoring the Earth, Healing the Mind*. San Francisco: Sierra Club Books. pp. 183–200.

Hartley, J. (1992) *Tele-Ology*. New York: Routledge.

Harvey, D. (1989) *The Condition of Postmodernity*. Oxford: Basil Blackwell.

Hassan, I. (1983) 'Desire and Dissent in the Postmodern Age,' *Kenyon Review*, 5 (1) (Winter): 1–18.

Hassan, I. (1987) *The Postmodern Turn: Essays in Postmodern Theory and Culture*. Columbus: Ohio State University Press.

Hebdige, D. (1988a) *Hiding in the Light*. New York and London: Routledge.

Hebdige, D. (1988b) 'Postmodernism and the "The Other Side",' in A. Ross (ed.), *Universal Abandon? The Politics of Postmodernism*. Minneapolis: University of Minnesota Press. pp. x–xi.

Hoggett, P. (1989) 'The Culture of Uncertainty,' in B. Richards (ed.), *Crises of the Self*. London: Free Association Books. pp. 27–39.

Hollinger, R. (1994) *Postmodernism and the Social Sciences: A Thematic Approach*. London and Thousand Oaks, CA: Sage.

Huber, J. (1995) 'Centenial Essay: Institutional Perspectives on Sociology,' *American Journal of Sociology*, 101: 194–216.

Huyssen, A. (1986) *After the Great Divide: Modernism, Mass Culture, Postmodernism*. Bloomington: Indiana University Press.

Huyssen, A. (1990) 'Mapping the Postmodern,' in J.C. Alexander (ed.), *Culture and Society: Contemporary Debates*. Cambridge: Cambridge University Press. pp. 355–75.

Ingleby, D. (ed.) (1980) *Critical Psychiatry*. New York: Pantheon.

Jameson, F. (1983) 'Postmodernism and Consumer Society,' in H. Foster (ed.), *The Anti-Aesthetic: Essays on Postmodern Culture*. Port Townsend, WA: Bay Press. pp. 111–25.

Jameson, F. (1984a) 'The Politics of Theory: Ideological Positions in the Postmodernism Debate,' *New German Critique*, 33: 53–66.

Jameson, F. (1984b) 'Postmodernism, or, the Cultural Logic of Late Capitalism,' *New Left Review*, 146: 53–92.

Jameson, F. (1988) 'Cognitive Mapping,' in C. Nelson and L. Grossberg (eds), *Marxism and the Interpretation of Culture*. Urbana: University of Illinois Press. pp. 347–57.

Kahler, E. (1967) *The Tower and the Abyss: An Inquiry into the Transformation of Man*. New York: Viking.

Kaplan, E.A. (1987) *Rockin' Round the Clock: Consumption and Postmodern Culture in Music Television*. London: Methuen.

Kaplan, E.A. (ed.) (1988) *Postmodernism and its Discontents*. London: Verso.

Kellner, D. (1992) 'Popular Culture and the Construction of Postmodern Identities,' in S. Lash and J. Friedman (eds), *Modernity and Identity*. Oxford: Basil Blackwell. pp. 41–177.

Kellner, D. (1995) *Media Culture*. New York and London: Routledge.

Kovel, J. (1988) *The Radical Spirit: Essays in Psychoanalysis and Society*. London: Free Association Books.

Kroker, A. (1992) *The Possessed Individual: Technology and the French Postmodern*. New York: St Martin's Press.

Kroker, A. and Cook, D. (eds) (1986) *The Postmodern Scene: Excremental Culture and Hyper Aesthetics*. New York: St Martin's Press.

Kvale, S. (ed.) (1992) *Psychology and Postmodernism*. London and Thousand Oaks, CA: Sage.

Laing, R.D. (1961) *Self and Others*. New York: Pantheon.

Laing, R.D. (1967) *The Politics of Experience*. New York: Pantheon.

Laing, R.D. (1969) *The Divided Self*. London: Pelican.

Laing, R.D. (1985) *Wisdom, Madness and Folly: The Making of a Psychiatrist*. New York: McGraw-Hill.
Langman, L. (1972) 'Neon Cages: Shopping for Subjectivity,' in R. Shields (ed.), *Lifestyle Shopping: The Subject of Consumption*. New York and London: Routledge. pp. 40–82.
Laplantine, F. (1973) *L'Ethnopsychiatrie*. Paris: Éditions Universitaires.
Lasch, C. (1978) *The Culture of Narcissism: American Life in an Age of Diminishing Expectations*. London: Abacus.
Lather, P. (1991) *Getting Smart*. New York and London: Routledge.
Lemert, E. (1962) 'Paranoia and the Dynamics of Exclusion,' *Sociometry*, 25: 2–20.
Levin, M.D. (1987) 'Clinical Stories: A Modern Self in the Fury of Being,' in M.D. Levin (ed.), *Pathologies of the Modern Self: Postmodern Studies on Narcissism, Schizophrenia and Depression*. New York: New York University Press. pp. 479–530.
Lévy, B.H. (1994) *La Pureté dangereuse*. Paris: Éditions Grasset.
Linton, R. (1956) *Culture and Mental Disorder*. Springfield, IL: C.C. Thomas.
Lyon, D. (1994) *The Electronic Eye: The Rise of Surveillance Society*. Minneapolis: University of Minnesota Press.
Lyotard, J.-F. (1984) *The Postmodern Condition: A Report on Knowledge*. Minneapolis: University of Minnesota Press.
MacCannell, D. (1992) *Empty Meeting Grounds*. New York and London: Routledge.
McNamee, S. (1996) 'Therapy and Identity Construction in a Postmodern World,' in D. Grodin and T.R. Lindlof (eds), *Constructing the Self in a Mediated World*. London and Thousand Oaks, CA: Sage. pp. 141–53.
Maguire, J. (1996) 'The Tears Inside the Stone,' in S. Lasch, B. Szerszynski, and B. Wynne (eds), *Risk, Environment and Modernity: Towards a New Ecology*. London and Thousand Oaks, CA: Sage. pp. 169–88.
Maines, C. (1990) *Green Rage: Radical Environmentalism and the Unmaking of Civilization*. Boston: Little Brown & Co.
Marcus, G. (1994) 'What Comes (Just) After "Post"? The Case of Ethnography,' in N.K. Denzin and Y.S. Lincoln (eds), *Handbook of Qualitative Research*. London and Thousand Oaks, CA: Sage. pp. 563–74.
Marcuse, H. (1955) *Eros and Civilization*. Boston: Beacon.
Marcuse, H. (1968) *One-Dimensional Man*. Boston: Beacon.
Marcuse, H. (1972) *Counterrevolution and Revolt*. Boston: Beacon.
Massumi, B. (1993) 'Everywhere You Want To Be: Introduction to Fear,' in B. Massumi (ed.), *The Politics of Everyday Fear*. Minneapolis: University of Minnesota Press. pp. 3–37.
Merchant, C. (1989) *The Death of Nature: Women, Ecology and the Scientific Revolution*. New York: HarperCollins.
Merchant, C. (ed.) (1994) *Ecology*. Atlantic Highlands, NJ: Humanities Press.
Metzner, R. (1995) 'The Psychopathology of the Human–Nature Relationship,' in T. Roszak, M.E. Gomes, and A.D. Kanner (eds), *Ecopsychology: Restoring the Earth, Healing the Mind*. San Francisco: Sierra Club Books. pp. 55–67.
Meyrowitz, J. (1985) *No Sense of Place*. New York: Oxford University Press.
Mitroff, I. and Bennis, W. (1989) *The Unreality Industry*. New York: Birch Lane.
Morely, D. (1992) *Television, Audience, and Cultural Studies*. New York: Routledge.
Morin, E. and Kern, B. (1993) *Terre–Patrie*. Paris: Éditions du Seuil.
Mouffe, C. (1989) 'Radical Democracy: Modern or Postmodern?,' in A. Ross (ed.), *Universal Abandon? The Politics of Postmodernism*. Minneapolis: University of Minnesota Press. pp. 31–45.
Mumford, L. (1954) *In the Name of Sanity*. New York: Harcourt, Brace and Co.
Naess, A. (1989) *Ecology, Community and Lifestyle: Outline of an Ecosophy*. Cambridge: Cambridge University Press.
Opler, M.K. (1959) *Culture and Mental Health: Cross-Cultural Studies*. London: Macmillan.
Opler, M.K. (1967) *Culture and Social Psychiatry*. New York: Atherton.
Petro, P. (1993) 'AfterShock/Between Boredom and History,' *Discourse*, 16 (2): 77–100.

Pfohl, S. (1990) 'Welcome to the Parasite Café: Postmodernity as a Social Problem,' *Social Problems*, 37 (4): 421–42.

Pfohl, S. (1992) *Death at the Parasite Café: Social Science (Fictions) and the Postmodern*. New York: St Martin's Press.

Poster, M. (ed.) (1988) *Jean Baudrillard: Selected Writings*. Stanford, CA: Stanford University Press.

Poster, M. (1990) *The Mode of Information*. Chicago: University of Chicago Press.

Poster, M. (1995) *The Second Media Age*. Cambridge: Polity Press.

Postman, N. (1985) *Amusing Ourselves to Death*. New York: Viking.

Reid, W. (1978) *The Psychopath*. New York: Brunner/Mazel.

Reid, W., Dorr, D., Walker, J., and Bonner, J. (eds) (1986) *Unmasking the Psychopath*. New York: Norton.

Richards, B. (ed.) (1989) *Crises of the Self: Further Essays on Psychoanalysis and Politics*. London: Free Association Books.

Robbins, K. (1994) 'Forces of Consumption: From the Symbolic to the Psychotic,' *Media, Culture & Society*, 16: 449–68.

Rosenau, P. (1992) *Postmodernism and the Social Sciences: Insights, Inroads, and Intrusions*. Princeton: Princeton University Press.

Rosenhan, D.L. (1973) 'On Being Sane in Insane Places,' *Science*, 179–258.

Ross, A. (ed.) (1989) *Universal Abandon: The Politics of Postmodernism*. Minneapolis, PA: University of Minneapolis Press.

Ross, A. (1991) *Strange Weather: Culture, Science and Technology in the Age of Limits*. London: Verso.

Roszak, T. (1995) 'Where Psyche Meets Gaia,' in T. Roszak, M.E. Gomes and A.D. Kanner (eds), *Ecopsychology: Restoring the Earth, Healing the Mind*. San Francisco: Sierra Club Books. pp. 1–20.

Sanchez, J. (1986) 'Social Crises and Psychopathy: Toward a Sociology of the Psychopath,' in W. Reid, D. Dorr, J. Walker, and J. Bonner (eds), *Unmasking the Psychopath*. New York: Norton. pp. 78–97.

Sass, L.A. (1992) *Madness and Modernism: Insanity in the Light of Modern Art, Literature, and Thought*. New York: Basic Books.

Scheff, T.J. (ed.) (1975) *Labeling Madness*. Englewood Cliffs, NJ: Prentice Hall.

Scheff, T.J. (1984) *Being Mentally Ill: A Sociological Theory*. New York: Aldine.

Schwartz-Salant, N. (1987) 'The Dead Self in Borderline Personality Disorders,' in M.D. Levin (ed.), *Pathologies of the Modern Self*. New York: New York University Press. pp. 115–62.

Searles, H.F. (1960) *The Nonhuman Environment*. New York: International Universities Press.

Sedgwick, P. (1982) *Psycho Politics: Laing, Foucault, Goffman, Szasz and the Future of Mass Psychiatry*. New York: Harper & Row.

Seidman, S. (1994a) *Contested Knowledge: Social Theory in the Postmodern Era*. Oxford: Basil Blackwell.

Seidman, S. (ed.) (1994b) *The Postmodern Turn: New Perspectives on Social Theory*. Cambridge and New York: Cambridge University Press.

Seidman, S. (1996) 'The Political Unconscious of the Human Sciences,' *The Sociological Quarterly*, 37 (4): 699–719.

Sewall, L. (1995) 'The Skill of Ecological Perception,' in T. Roszak, M.E. Gomes, and A.D. Kanner (eds), *Ecopsychology: Restoring the Earth, Healing the Mind*. San Francisco: Sierra Club Books. pp. 201–15.

Shepard, P. (1992) *Nature and Madness*. San Francisco: Sierra Club Books.

Showalter, E. (1985) *The Female Malady*. New York: Pantheon.

Silverstone, R. (1989) 'Let Us Then Return to the Murmuring of Everyday Practices: A Note on Michel de Certeau, Television and Everyday Life,' *Theory Culture & Society*, 6: 77–94.

Silverstone, R. (1993) 'Television, Ontological Security and the Transitional Object,' *Media. Culture & Society*, 15: 573–98.
Silverstone, R. (1994) *Television and Everyday Life*. New York and London: Routledge.
Simmel, G. (1965) 'The Metropolis and Mental Life,' in K.H. Wolffin (ed.), *The Sociology of Georg Simmel*. New York: Free Press. pp. 409–24.
Simmons, I.G. (1993) *Interpreting Nature: Cultural Constructions of the Environment*. New York and London: Routledge.
Smart, B. (1990) 'Modernity, Postmodernity and the Present,' in B.S. Turner (ed.), *Theories of Modernity and Postmodernity*. London and Thousand Oaks, CA: Sage. pp. 14–30.
Smith, R.J. (1978) *The Psychopath in Society*. New York: Academic Press.
Spretnak, C. (1991) *States of Grace: The Recovery of Meaning in the Postmodern Age*. San Francisco: HarperCollins.
Stephanson, A. (1988) 'Regarding Postmodernism – A Conversation with Frederic Jameson,' in A. Ross (ed.), *Universal Abandon? The Politics of Postmodernism*. Minneapolis: University of Minnesota Press. pp. 3–30.
Szasz, T. (1970) *The Manufacture of Madness*. New York: Harper & Row.
Szasz, T. (1972) *The Myth of Mental Illness*. London: Paladin.
Szasz, T. (1987) *Insanity*. New York: Wiley.
Thomashow, M. (1995) *Ecological Identity*. Cambridge, MA: MIT Press.
Turkle, S. (1995) *Life on the Screen*. New York: Simon & Schuster.
Tyler, S. (1986) 'Postmodern Ethnography: From Document of the Occult to Occult Document,' in J. Clifford and G.E. Marcus (eds), *Writing Culture: The Poetics and Politics of Ethnography*. Berkeley: University of California Press. pp. 122–40.
Van den Berg, J.H. (1961) *The Changing Nature of Man: Introduction to a Historical Psychology*. New York: Norton.
Van den Berg, J.H. (1974) *Divided Existence and Complex Society*. Pittsburgh: Duquesne University Press.
Vattimo, G. (1992) *The Transparent Society*. Baltimore: John Hopkins University Press.
Venturi, R., Brown, S., and Izenour, S. (1977) *Learning from Las Vegas: The Forgotten Symbolism of Architectural Form*. Cambridge, MA: MIT Press.
Virilio, P. (1986) *Speed and Politics*. New York: Semiotext(e).
Virilio, P. (1990) *Popular Defenses and Ecological Struggles*. New York: Semiotext(e).
Virilio, P. (1996) *Cybermonde: La Politique du pire*. Paris: Textuel.
Watzlawick, P. (1971) 'Patterns of Psychotic Communication,' in P. Doucet and C. Laurin (eds), *Problems of Psychosis*. Amsterdam: Excerpta Medica. pp. 44–53.
Weaver, T.L. and Clum, G.A. (1993) 'Early Family Environment and Traumatic Experiences Associated with Borderline Personality Disorder,' *Journal of Consulting and Clinical Psychology*, 61 (6): 1068.
Weedon, C. (1987) *Feminist Practice and Poststructuralist Theory*. Oxford: Basil Blackwell.
Weigert, A. (1997) *Self, Interaction, and Natural Environment: Refocusing our Eyesight*. Albany, NY: State University of New York Press.
Wexler, P. (1991) 'Citizenship in the Semiotic Society,' in M. Featherstone (ed.), *Consumer Culture and Postmodernism*. London and Thousand Oaks, CA: Sage. pp. 164–75.
Winkin, Y. (1981) *La Nouvelle Communication*. Paris: Éditions du Seuil.
Wolin, R. (1984) 'Modernism vs. Postmodernism,' *Telos*, 62 (Winter): 9–29.
Zimmerman, M.M. (1994) *Contesting Earth's Future: Radical Ecology and Postmodernity*. Berkeley: University of California Press.

3

Performing Methods: History, Hysteria, and the New Science of Psychiatry

Jackie Orr

> The ways in which she struggles in the trap, the disjointed sentences in which she has begun to think herself through from where she is, the tentative experiments with a direction – these come themselves to be described as 'symptoms'. Lacking adequate formulation, they can have no direction, no outcome, no progressive movement. They abort at the outset. They become merely 'expressive', merely a motion or a gesture, a raving, a hysteria, an attack on the dark in the dark . . . .
>
> (Smith, 1975: 6)

> 'I' is not an interior affair.
>
> (Acker, 1993: 211)

'I' begin with three scenes and a bad dream. A few stories set circulating within a theoretical moment more attentive now to its own textual stagings, more curious about its methodological dramas and 'material-semiotic actors,' creatively provoked by the claim that theoretical productions are, inescapably, performative.[1] This is one way to describe the contemporary scene in(to) which I write.

A different description of the same scene might be: There's an actor onstage, everything around him is red, white, and blue. He's in a wheelchair and nothing moves except his mouth, his eyes, the lump in his throat rising up, then down. It's the 1996 US Democratic National Convention and the opening speaker used to be Superman but now he's a quadriplegic. Addressing the United States of America through a television screen, the actor says, 'If we can conquer outer space, we can conquer inner space. And that's the region of the brain, and the central nervous system . . . .'[2] The audience applauds.

She says, again, ' "I" is not an interior affair' – and never far from the symptomatic scene of writing, or this consequential theater of performing methods.

Scene One: Acute Grief

On a late autumn night in November 1942, 114 bodies are delivered to the emergency room of Massachusetts General Hospital, victims of one of the most famous and fatal episodes of urban panic: Boston's Coconut Grove Club fire, in which 491 people die. A *Newsweek* description of the scene at the popular nightclub reads:

> Every available table was taken . . . a girl, her hair ablaze, hurtled across the floor screaming 'Fire!' That shriek heralded catastrophe. Some 800 guests, insane with panic, lunged in a wild scramble to get out. . . . Flames flashed with incredible swiftness. . . . The revolving doors jammed as the terror-stricken mob pushed them in both directions at the same time. (1942: 43–4)

At Mass. General, as part of an integrated emergency response, the psychiatric staff arrive quickly on the scene.

The psychiatry department first opens at Mass. General in 1934 under the directorship of Stanley Cobb, marking an early experiment in the incorporation of psychiatry into general medicine: within the architecture of this large, private teaching hospital for Harvard Medical School, psychiatry is organizationally and conceptually structured as a support service for other medical specialties in the hospital (White, 1984: 220). Patients in the general hospital are transferred to psychiatric services when no organic problem can be found to account for their symptoms. From its beginning, the psychiatric ward at Mass. General is deeply connected to the emergence of psychosomatic medicine as a new field. Under the directorship of Cobb, a neuropsychiatrist interested in hypnosis and psychoanalysis, as well as neurotransmission and brain anatomy, the psychiatry department probes the uncertain terrain of 'mind–body' connections, attempting to chart the intimate entanglements of psyche and soma.

In a report detailing the aftermath of the Coconut Grove Club disaster, Stanley Cobb writes that in monitoring the survivors for 'problems of psychiatric study and management,' the psychiatric staff were particularly interested to observe the 'physiological features of grief' amongst those survivors who had lost friends and family in the fire (Cobb and Lindemann, 1943: 818, 822). 'Since acute grief is one of the most frequent psychogenic factors found in patients with psychosomatic disorders,' Cobb explains, the Coconut Grove Club victims offered an important opportunity for systematic observation and research. The psychiatric staff found evidence of pupil dilation, heat waves to the head, flushing, sweating, and sighing as one possible 'nucleus of a physiologic disturbance . . . form[ing] the background for . . . "emotional distress".' Within the tangled circuits of psychic and somatic disturbance, the empirical outline of observable physiological patterns is becoming, just barely, intelligible.

Scene Two: Agoraphobia (or, Fear of the Marketplace)

The Hypnosis and Psychosomatic Medicine Clinic at Mass. General Hospital grows out of an overflow of outpatients being treated with hypnosis for psychosomatic disorders. All the patients have been referred from other medical specialties within the hospital for intractable problems, presumably of psychic origin. Dr David Sheehan is one of two young psychiatrists who organizes the small clinic in the early 1970s (Sheehan, 1996). In 1974, using patients from the Psychosomatic Medicine Clinic, Sheehan begins a controlled experimental study comparing the effects of two different pharmaceutical drugs in the treatment of agoraphobia (Sheehan et al., 1980). The central feature of agoraphobia – which means, literally, 'fear of the marketplace' – is the inability to leave one's home unaccompanied without experiencing acute levels of anxiety.

By 1981, the Psychosomatic Medicine Clinic at Mass. General Hospital becomes the site for a clinical trial comparing two drugs in the treatment of panic disorder, a new psychiatric diagnosis for people suffering from frequent episodes of floating terror, called panic attacks (Sheehan, 1996).[3] The diagnostic label 'panic disorder' first appears one year earlier, in 1980, in the third edition of the *Diagnostic and Statistical Manual of Mental Disorders* (*DSM-III*), American psychiatry's official diagnostic classification system (American Psychiatric Association, 1980). The 1980 handbook claims to be the first US psychiatric classification system that relies on empirical data and observable criteria, rather than theoretical speculation, to identify discrete mental disorders. The criteria-specific definition of 'panic disorder' includes heart palpitations, dizziness, hot and cold flashes, sweating, fear of dying, fear of going crazy, or of doing something uncontrolled.

A subsequent clinical study directed by Sheehan in the Psychosomatic Medicine Clinic, comparing Xanax, imipramine (Tofranil), and placebo for the treatment of panic, becomes the prototype for worldwide clinical drug trials of Xanax conducted from 1983 to 1987 in fourteen countries with 1,700 research subjects (Sheehan, 1996).[4] The international clinical trials are organized and funded solely by the Upjohn Company, pharmaceutical manufacturer of Xanax. Findings from the 'Worldwide Panic Project' demonstrate Xanax's effectiveness in easing panic symptoms around the globe. By the late 1980s, Xanax becomes the most popularly prescribed drug in the United States for the treatment of panic and anxiety.

Scene Three: Histrionic Behavior

You stand before the sun not blinking and your eyes go fire you rise burning you become black you become bird you rise blackbird just below orange sun circle rising – only dawn and already you are flamed. She stands before the framed image hanging in the Irene G. and Philip F. Faneuil Art Gallery on the first floor of the ambulatory-care wing of Massachusetts General Hospital. Joan Mirò, *Woman and Birds in Front of the Sun*, she'll have to remember to write that down. *At her back, acute grief, for all the burning girls who once yelled 'Fire!'* . . . She blinks.

She takes the elevator to the seventh floor. 'Room 717, Psychosomatic Medicine Clinic' says the sign on the door. *In front of her, fear of this marketplace, in which so many anxieties are exchanged . . .*

She is a researcher researching a site of research. A site already multiple, thick with possible descriptions she cannot yet inscribe. A field already scattered with symptomatic scenes she does not yet diagnose.

So each week for four months, 'I' enter through the door of the Psychosomatic Medicine Clinic at Mass. General Hospital. I have been accepted as a research subject in a clinical trial comparing Xanax and another drug for the treatment of panic disorder and depression. The Upjohn Company sponsors the study. The 'Sheehan Patient-Rated Anxiety Scale,' with Upjohn's name printed in the upper corner, is one of several questionnaires filled out each week. I meet briefly each time with a psychiatrist, then for a longer interview and check-up with the young research assistant.

Week #6. The Psychiatrist's Office. *What is this map we're on? My locations are primarily monosyllabic and multiple choice: 1 2 3 4 5 6 7 (How bad was the panic attack?). Yes No (Did you experience sexual interest or a change in sexual interest?). Worse No Improvement Some Improvement Better Much Better Very Much Better (How was your anxiety this week compared to last week?). In miles (How far would you go away from home, alone?). How close do you think you are to your baseline experience, before you started having problems?*

Research subject: *Well, I'm pretty far away because now I have to take drugs to get near my baseline.*
Psychiatrist: [smiling] *I know what you mean. But putting aside the drugs, how far away are you from your normal experience?*
Research subject: *Well, not far. But I think sometimes with these drugs I'm* more *calm than I ever was before.*

The doctor smiles and makes a note.

Later, she writes it all down. Everything she can remember. What she wore, what he wore, the pictures on the wall, the color of her blood, the contents of her dreams, the answers to questions they ask, the possibility of questions they never broach, the stories she tells, the stories they don't even begin to want to hear, the needles, the jokes, the straps around her wrists for the EKG. And the day when, while the research assistant was out of the room, she picks up the *DSM-III* psychiatric diagnostic manual on the desk to look up 'hysteria.' It had disappeared, replaced by the new classification 'Histrionic Personality Disorder.' She reads: 'Individuals with this disorder are lively and dramatic and are always drawing attention to themselves. They are prone to exaggeration and often act out a role . . . in both sexes overt behavior often is a caricature of femininity. . . . Usually these individuals show little interest in intellectual achievement and careful, analytical thinking . . .' (American Psychiatric Association, 1980: 313–15). Carefully, dramatically, she writes it all down, recording the entangled text(ure)s of her field.

And a Bad Dream

Once upon a time I watched this movie, Total Recall. *Arnold Schwarzenegger plays an ordinary guy who goes to get his dreams programmed so he can have a real vacation. Things get crazy, 'cause instead of getting his dreams programmed Arnold learns that his entire mind's been programmed, all his memories erased, and he's not really an ordinary guy but a secret agent from Mars who works for a Big Corporation that's trying to crush the rebellion of masses of mutants and poor people.*

A few days after I see Total Recall *I have a dream. It's a pretty nice dream in the woods, in a big two-story house, with a family and all that. Until I look in a mirror and see all my teeth crumbling in my mouth. I get scared and run downstairs and all of a sudden there's a TV camera crew in the kitchen. The people who were in the dream are all taking off their make-up and costumes and getting ready to tape the next scene. One woman – she'd been my friend in the dream – says to me, 'That was really funny, the part when you got afraid of the feminine.' I start to panic 'cause I had thought that I was someplace real or at least in a dream and instead everybody's just actors, performing scripted scenes, then analyzing my dream. I lie down on the floor, fetal-like and terrified. Another woman with a headset and clipboard comes over to me and says quickly into the microphone, 'WZBC-TV. . . . We need to send this one back.' She spins me around and I wake up. I was afraid to dream, afraid to be awake. The difference between these two states was very unclear.*

Performing Methods

> **per • form** (pər-fôrm´) v. **1.** To begin and carry through to completion; do: *perform an appendectomy.* **2.** To take action in accordance with the requirements of; fulfill (a promise or duty, for example). **3.a.** To enact (a feat or role) before an audience. **b.** To give a public presentation of.

> **meth • od** (mĕth´əd) n. **1.** A means or manner of procedure; especially, a regular and systematic way of accomplishing anything. **2.** Orderly and systematic arrangement; orderliness; regularity . . . **3.** The procedures and techniques characteristic of a particular discipline or field of knowledge. **-the Method.** A system of acting in which the actor recalls emotion and reactions from his past experience and utilizes them in the role he is playing.

On December 31, 1899, a young woman patient of Sigmund Freud terminates the psychoanalysis in which they have been engaged for three months. In the first weeks of the new year, of this new century, Freud writes a now-famous case history of the patient he calls 'Dora,' demonstrating his application to her case of hysteria the techniques of dream analysis outlined in his recent master work *The Interpretation of Dreams* (1900). Out of this therapeutic failure – for Dora, according to the young psychoanalyst, left his office as much a hysteric as when she entered – Freud mines sufficient material for a theoretical success. Fashioned from the woman's dreams, her symptomatic complaints as well as her dramatic departure, Freud constructs a compelling clinical portrait of the hysterical figure (Freud, 1963).

The significance of his patient's termination of the analysis is for Freud tied to the knot of memory, resistance, and repetition that binds the hysteric to the often highly theatrical scene of her symptoms. '*Hysterics suffer mainly from reminiscences*,' explains Freud in his earliest case studies, published in 1893 before the technique of psychoanalytic dream interpretation has been imagined (Breuer and Freud, 1957: 7). Indeed, it is through their early attempts to use hypnosis to treat hysterical symptoms that Freud and his colleague Joseph Breuer first observe the repression of past trauma beneath the repetitious expression of symptoms, and note the curative effects of memory in cathartically releasing the somatic trace of a repressed psychic event. For Freud, faced in 1899 with the evident failure of his new technique to promote a therapeutic 'total recall,' the explanation rests in the hysteric's stubborn insistence on *performing*, and not simply recalling, her memory of a past trauma. 'Thus she *acted* an essential part of her recollections and phantasies instead of reproducing it in the treatment,' the jilted doctor writes (Freud, 1963: 141). Since one of Dora's past traumas provoked a fantasy of revenge, it is the performance of that revenge in an abrupt leave-taking of the unsuspecting analyst that prevents the new technique from achieving a successful cure.

Live on screen, a young white girl in braids and braces sits on the couch next to her mother. She describes to the TV talk show host and today's live studio audience her first attacks of panic. The sudden terror, sweaty palms, a pounding heart – the same dramatic symptoms her mother experienced in her twelve-year battle with panic disorder. The camera swings to a grey-suited man in a swivel chair: Dr Jerrold Rosenbaum, a psychiatrist in the Psychopharmacology Unit at Massachusetts General Hospital. He describes panic disorder as a biochemically based disease, perhaps genetically passed from parent to child. Before the commercial break, a 1–800 number which TV viewers may call for more information flashes on the bottom of the screen.

Or so the doctor's story goes.

A few weeks later, I phone the 1–800 number and enter the screening process for research subjects in Mass. General's clinical research on panic disorder. I am not currently suffering from panic. I was diagnosed with panic disorder over a year ago, took Xanax for several months, and then found other practices of treatment and cure: breath, dream, memory, writing. During four months of ethnographic fieldwork at Mass. General, drawing on my own past experiences of this psychic dis-ease, I perform the role of a woman suffering from panic.

Some seventy-five years after Freud analyzes in print his productive failure to cure the young hysteric with the new method of dream interpretation, a proliferation of feminist writings reinscribe the historical figure of the hysteric with many of the subversive desires, imaginary resistances, collective eroticisms, and material(ist) longings also characterizing a creative decade of women's political and theoretical movements (Cixous and Clément, 1986; Gallop, 1982; Irigaray, 1985; Moi, 1981; Rose, 1978; Showalter, 1985). The hysteric, whose body, writes Catherine Clément, 'is transformed into a theater for forgotten scenes' (1986: 5), becomes something of a contemporary theater of transferential memory for a mostly white and middle-class cohort of women intellectuals.[5] What is remembered and reinscribed in these recent feminist theories of hysteria circles incessantly around the question of the meaning, a reading, an (im/possible?) re-writing of the symptomatic scene of the hysterical body. From out of the frame of Freud's sighting as a feminine disease in need of a psychoanalytic cure, the hysteric is taken in this feminist re-vision as the contradictory site of a reaction – in turn resistive and resigned – to a symptomatic social, embodied in the psychic evidence of women's dis-ease. 'In fact it is the very notion of *mental illness*,' Clément goes on, quoting from Claude Lévi-Strauss, 'which is in question. For if . . . the mental and the social are one and the same, it would be absurd, in the cases where the social and the physiological come into direct contact, to apply to one of those two orders a notion (such as illness) which has no meaning except within the other order' (1986: 21). Within a social order where 'becoming a woman' can make you sick, and can secure your exile from the very language in which your cure is to be staged, the flight of a woman hysteric from Freud's analysis becomes readable as a different story: a story telling not of a specific and surmountable failure of technique, but of *the limits of the method itself* in transforming (as against blindly, earnestly repeating) the socially structured scene out of which the symptoms of dis-ease emerge.

Room 717, Psychosomatic Medicine Clinic. *I sign in, showing the blue plastic registration card with my identity impressed in raised white letters. A name not precisely mine, composed, like the stories I will report, out of a knowledge intensely personal and collective. The research assistant introduces himself and leads me down a white hallway into the exam room, where I sign a patient consent form agreeing to be a subject of research. He explains the two research goals of the project: to determine which drug (Xanax, Tofranil, or placebo) is more effective for treating panic; and to explore the history of anxiety disorders. Participation in the program is free. I 'pay' for the treatment by giving them information that will help them achieve their research goals. I then follow him down another hallway – 'Hollywood – is it real or is it fiction?' asks a silver-framed poster on the wall – and into the psychiatrist's office. The psychiatrist has sandy hair and a moustache, a gold wedding ring on his finger. He is friendly, casual. He* *asks me a series of questions which he reads off xeroxed sheets of paper in his lap. When he's finished, he asks if I have any questions for him.*

Research subject: *Um . . .* [Her only real question is whether or not he believes she has panic disorder. She doesn't ask this.] *Wow, so many questions coming my way for the last hour – I'm not sure I can think of any for you –*
Psychiatrist: [chuckling to himself] *Yes, now you get to be the aggressor for awhile.*

When I decided to conduct research in a clinical research setting by performing the dis-orderly role of a panicked woman, I was flying through the literature that retold the history of hysteria in a feminist register, in an excessive and experimental language that compelled me to remember differently the story of my 'own' dis-ease. 'Sorties: Out and Out: Attacks/ Ways Out/Forays' was Cixous's ascendant title for her poetic, theoretical conjuring of the feminine hysterical body as the body that flies – 'voler,' the French word she uses, meaning both 'to fly' and 'to steal.' Playing in and against the limits of a language that expresses such telling duplicities, analyzing the social structuring of that language through the gendered traces of hysterical symptoms, such texts had a contagious effect on my imagination of possible methods for sociological research. If my methods seemed somewhat hysterical, somewhat mad from the viewpoint of reason, so much the better.

I could even recognize, however perversely and perhaps patho*logically*, the conceptual resources provided by the strange inter-discipline of US sociology to rationalize my methodological theater of the irrational. The 'sick role' was and remains a popular notion in US social science, culled from the theoretical writings of Talcott Parsons, whose functionalist concept of 'the social system' imprinted itself deeply over two decades in the dominant sociological imagination. Mental health and illness, medical science, psychoanalysis – Parsons theorized this complex of practices within the parameters of social systems functioning, and the built-in imperatives of social control (Parsons, 1951: 428–79; 1960a, 1960b). Defining mental illness as the impairment of the capacity to perform social roles within the social system, Parsons conceptualizes the 'sick role' as the equilibrating force that prevents such incapacity from spinning out of control (1960b: 258–9). Sickness, one form that social deviance and resistance to social role performance can take, actually serves to function as a form of social control through the channeling of that potential deviance into the performative obligations of the 'sick role.' Most importantly, the 'sick role' obliges the sick person to remain isolated from others who are sick like her; and, relatedly, to seek professional, expert help for her illness and cooperate with the therapeutic treatments as prescribed (1960b: 275–6). '[M]otivationally as well as bacteriologically, illness may well be "contagious",' Parsons explains. The sick role effectively contains the possible social contagion of deviant dis-ease.

The revenge of the sick role, then? A deviant desire to disrupt the professional efficiencies of dominant mental (and social?) orders not by resisting that assigned role, but rehearsing it with a studied vengeance, staging it against its own rituals of containment, gaining healthy access to that theater of medicalized, individualized cure (and social control?) through the proper performance of a dis-eased submission. The sick role deployed not to dissuade the contagion of social dis-ease but to incite it?

Within the field of sociology, Parsons's 'sick role' remains a well-known notion. Less known or at least less noticed is Parsons's ethnographic fieldwork, conducted early in his career as a young sociology professor at Harvard, in which, 'equipped with a white coat and the (albeit nonmedical) legitimate title of doctor,' he performed the role of a physician, 'making ward rounds, observing operations, going on the home visit service' (Parsons, 1970: 835). Massachusetts General Hospital was one of the locations for his research. Parsons was particularly interested in the emergence of 'psychosomatic medicine' as a new field, and the work being conducted in the psychiatry department at Mass. General under the directorship of Stanley Cobb. Although he considered it a 'major failure of my career' to have never written up a study of medical practice based on his early research, Parsons did draw extensively on his fieldwork experience in conceptualizing both the 'sick role' and the 'doctor role' as a transferential relation, played out in a dense field of social interaction involving the complex interplay of unconscious motives and social structure (1970: 837–8).

Week #9. *Once each month during the clinical research, they take a sample of my blood. The day before this visit, I swallow four blue plastic capsules from the white plastic jar they give me each week. The first week, after my acceptance into the clinical trial, I open the blue capsule, pour out the powder, and find the smooth white pill tucked into one end. Each month when they draw the sample, I know I need to have some of this pill in my bloodstream. From its effects – the sedation and heavy calm that suffuses me within thirty minutes of taking it – I recognize the drug is Xanax. When I go in for the visit where they will draw my blood, I am groggy, deeply tranquilized as I roll up my sleeve and extend my bare arm. The research assistant puts on white plastic gloves that snap as he pulls them up around his wrist. With one gloved finger he strokes the raised, thick, slightly blue stream of my vein. Inserting the silver-thin needle, he draws four vials of blood. It is deep red and beautiful. As he labels the vials he says, 'You're a trooper,' explaining that most women – 'biological destiny, I guess' – are smaller than men and sometimes their veins are too. So the veins can be hard to find. 'You have great veins,' he tells me, turning to take off his gloves and wash his hands in the white porcelain sink. That night I dream. I'm on an island. A group of women engaged in play, a game of singing and tossing the word-song from body to body. Dora. Anne. Emmy. Ida. For a moment, the game becomes ping-pong and I play, dancing little wild jazz steps each time I hear the ball bounce across the table. I wake, still groggy and sleep-heavy, incanting out of dream and without meaning until the word-song which has* *become my lips finally shapes into conscious sense: 'What other Eve stories do you know? . . . What other Eve stories do you know?'*

At the time I performed my fieldwork at Mass. General, I had not yet read Judith Butler's (1990a) work on the performative, repetitive corporeal acts constituting the gendered body. '[T]he acts by which gender is constituted bear similarities to performative acts within theatrical contexts. . . . The body is not a . . . merely factic materiality; it is a materiality that bears meaning, if nothing else, and the manner of this bearing is fundamentally dramatic' (Butler, 1990b: 272). Later, her writings would give theoretical grounding to my somewhat improvised ethnographic impulse to theatricalize the panicked body. Gender is not the only – perhaps not even the most transgressive – social identity to engage in 'cross-dressing.' The healthy body in 'drag,' impersonating the drama of embodied dis-ease, has been historically perceived as a subterranean threat to both the epistemology of medicine and the social ethic of productivity. My own intentions were more modest. But certainly a provocative finding of my fieldwork was, simply, that it is possible to successfully impersonate panic disorder within a medical-scientific clinic where research and treatment is premised on a biochemical model of disorder. Biochemical research on panic, like the psychoanalytic healer with whom it professes no relation, remains curiously beholden to the symptomatic story-tellings of those who say (how) they suffer.[6]

My central desire in re-enacting panic was to have access, differently, to the role of being a sick woman and a subject of research. 'If the ground of . . . identity is the stylized repetition of acts through time . . . then the possibilities of . . . transformation are to be found . . . in a different sort of repeating, in the breaking or subversive repetition of that style' (Butler, 1990b: 271). I wanted access to this social field, the medical clinic, where, as one historian once wrote, 'sickness, which had come to seek a cure, [is] turned into a spectacle' (Foucault, 1975: 85). I wanted to enter this charged historical field differently, from the position of a woman sickened not by her 'own' individualized symptoms, but by my growing sense that psychiatric discourse has confidently, and with great consequence, abandoned the difficult task of cure for the fascinated pursuit of pharmaceutical effects.

Week # 16. *I enter for the last visit to the Psychosomatic Unit at Mass. General. I am late. I wait, staring hard in front of me at* Haystacks in Provence. *Reflected in Van Gogh's framing is a red fire alarm, hanging on the wall opposite, just above my head. I wait staring hard at the fire alarm reflecting still red among gold haystacks.*

The Psychiatrist's Office. *I am feeling good, I say. Floating some from the Xanax, I try to participate as we discuss my future. The research is ending. I express my desire to get off the drug, even though it's had a good effect. We complete the usual forms quickly. When I leave his office, he shakes my hand, wishes me luck, and says I've done well.*

The Exam Room. *The research assistant calls in the psychiatrist to help him figure out how much of the drug to give me to take home. They decide*

140 pills are sufficient. The psychiatrist then asks the assistant to open up the blue capsule – there is some hesitation, the assistant seems unsure of this friendly command, but with me and the psychiatrist watching, he opens the blue capsule, pours out the white powder and the small white round pill. I say nothing. The psychiatrist is trying to see whether or not I can break the pill in half. Looking at it, he recommends that I break it up and decrease my dosage by only half a pill at a time. The moment is awkward. We are in a controlled, double-blind clinical experiment. Neither the patient nor the researchers are to know what treatment, if any, I'm swallowing. After the psychiatrist leaves, I ask the assistant if I can know for sure what drug I've been taking. He leaves the room. I stare at the 'Norpramin Word-a-Day Calendar' provided by Merrell Dow, Inc. Today's word is 'entre nous *(ahn truh noo) (Fr.) between ourselves; confidentially.' He returns, and confirms it is Xanax. 'Even though I'm not supposed to know that. So I'm forgetting it right now.' A double-blinding: not knowing, then learning, then forgetting again. A curious method. He asks me general questions about the final two months of research. I say I've learned a lot and feel much better but I really have a lot of questions about panic. Perhaps drugs aren't the best treatment? The assistant eagerly begins to talk about neurons misfiring. Drugs can stop the neurons from misfiring. Sometimes psychoanalysis can use talking to stop the neurons from misfiring. They're both valid. I talk about panic being a cultural thing – all these people panicking for no good reason in the last half of the twentieth century. He asks if I've read Thomas Szasz's,* The Myth of Mental Illness*? I say I have. 'Szasz says that mental illness is a rational response to an insane situation,' he goes on. I nod my head. My foot is swinging, one leg crossed over the other. 'But Szasz was a radical. It's a lot easier to change an individual than to change the world. But enough philosophy,' and he goes back to counting out my 140 pills. I nod my head; I swing my foot. Between us, confidentially, just* entre nous, *this* is *double-blind research. Neither you nor I know the cure, and we couldn't even really diagnose the dis-ease. It's still blind, baby, even though you and I know the name of that little round pill stuck tight in the end of that sky-blue capsule. It's still doubly blind. I don't know precisely how to speak my dis-ease but I seek without certainty within this crazy staging some steps toward its cure.*

'A house was on fire,' Dora told the doctor. 'My father was standing beside my bed and woke me up. I dressed myself quickly. Mother wanted to stop and save her jewel-case; but Father said: "I refuse to let myself and my two children be burnt for the sake of your jewel-case." We hurried downstairs, and as soon as I was outside I woke up' (Freud, 1963: 81). Freud's interpretation of his hysterical patient's dreamwork constructs an elaborate edifice bringing together the repressed fragments of infantile experience, wishes from the unconscious, childhood bedwetting and masturbation, the fear of syphilis, love for the father, disgust at the secretions of female genitals, a daydreamed desire for a kiss from Freud – to build a compulsively intricate case study. But it does not cure. One hundred years after she takes her leave of the earnest doctor, the hysteric, as yet unrelieved of her symptoms, operates still as a theater for forgotten social scenes.

And what really to make of such dreams, the ones that leave you startled out of sleep, the family house on fire, and you again a child, and burning? How to interpret, wide-awake and reeling, this dramatic refusal of the dream's primary function: to be, according to Freud, the guarantor of sleep (Freud, 1965: 267–8) ?

'One cannot yet say of the following history "it's just a story." It's a tale still true today,' writes Cixous in the opening to her history of hysteria. 'Most women who have been awakened remember having slept, *having been put to sleep*' (Cixous and Clément, 1986: 66). But might the truth of the hysteric's history today, twenty-five years after her French feminist renaissance, lie elsewhere? I, too, remember waking. Out of a different sleep. Startled out of a bad and different dream. In the family house – on the floor, *fetal-lie and terrified* – trapped in the unconscious trace of prime-time TV – *'that was really funny, the part where you got afraid of the feminine'* – panicked, performing – *'we need to send this one back'* – spinning crazy out beyond the cure of *Total Recall*. Awakening from such a troubled sleep, today, I wonder if the figure of the hysteric has not functioned somewhat, for feminists like me, as a 'screen memory'?[7] The theater of forgotten scenes we have projected onto her figure itself a deceptive 'screen' for other memories, other forgotten histories, even more unsettling? Secrets even more suppressed. How to interpret today the memories knotted into dream when our screens fragment and multiply, becoming the crowded site of reception for filmic projections, digitalized ghosts, televisual dreams? How to begin again to tell a gendered history of dis-ease when – in psychiatric fact if not in feminist theory – the hysteric has, again, so symptomatically performed a departure from the scene?

We begin between ourselves. Standing before woman and birds in front of the sun. We and the birds. We and women. Begin. This time she looks only black-edged, a sketch of an outline of her body surrounded and filled in by background. And around woman's black edges outlined – clear white space, static on both sides of her edges. Inside and out. A white static aura inside and out along the black edges standing before her standing in front of the sun. I blink. The scene passes. I take my leave. Exiting round through the revolving glass door at Massachusetts General Hospital.

Re-presenting Symptoms

> Every science must constitute its object of study; indeed, that is its most fundamental achievement.
>
> (Haraway, 1983: 135)

In the 1980 US psychiatric classification for mental disorders (*DSM-III*), hysteria disappears from the diagnostic nomenclature. Hysteria and its celebrated array of florid symptoms – including the communicative style of hysterics themselves, their 'imprecise, vague, exaggerated, colorful and dramatic' way of describing their symptoms, and their reputed propensity to change the subject when asked to detail their complaints (Purtell et al., 1951: 904) – are disassembled into a multiplicity of other diagnostic categories. According to Steven Hyler and Robert Spitzer, chair of the American Psychiatric Association Task Force charged with overseeing the new design of *DSM-III*, it is hoped this redistribution and re-presenting of hysterical symptoms will 'result in more reliable and valid diagnostic categories' (Hyler and Spitzer, 1978: 1500).

'Reliability' and 'validity' are the key watchwords and rallying cries of the authors of the 1980 *DSM-III*. Marking the radical transformations in both the content and form of the new classification system from its predecessor *DSM-II* (American Psychiatric Association, 1968) as a 'signal achievement for psychiatry,' Spitzer applauds the advancement of psychiatry and its diagnostic language, as embodied by *DSM-III*, toward a fulfillment of the 'scientific aspirations of the profession' (Bayer and Spitzer, 1985: 187). The science of psychiatry, its pursuit of a mirror relation with medical diagnosis and procedure founded on a common immersion in the rules and rhetoric of scientific method, depends upon the ability of the profession to establish a rational language of diagnosis secured by the proven 'reliability' and 'validity' of the classificatory order it assigns to its peculiarly disturbed field of dis-orderly objects (Kirk and Kutchins, 1992; Spitzer and Fleiss, 1974; Spitzer et al., 1978).

Previous to *DSM-III*'s rationalizing achievement, the language of US psychiatric diagnosis shared, less anxiously, a certain affinity with the language of hysteria: vague, imprecise, not given to descriptive detail so much as to a dramatic propensity for speculative elaboration. That is to say, psychiatry, like hysteria, was deeply beholden to the language and narrative genre of psychoanalysis (American Psychiatric Association, 1952, 1968). Within the psychoanalytically oriented psychiatry which dominated institutional and theoretical practice throughout the 1950 and '60s, reliable and valid diagnostic categories were neither desired nor missed by clinicians. In 1972, when a group of research psychiatrists based at Washington University School of Medicine in St Louis published what became known as the 'Feighner criteria,' together with an argument for the expediency of specific diagnostic criteria in the definition and validation of mental disease, they were not responding to a widespread dissatisfaction with the diagnostic system among practicing clinical psychiatrists (Feighner et al., 1972). Their primary aim in suggesting detailed, empirically observable diagnostic criteria for fourteen psychiatric illnesses, along with the validity evidence for each, was to 'expedite psychiatric investigation' and provide a common language and framework for research psychiatrists to compare data at different research sites (1972: 57).

Curiously, one of the fourteen valid and reliable mental diseases for which the Feighner group describes diagnostic criteria is hysteria. For a patient to be diagnosed with hysteria, the authors report, she must experience at least twenty-five symptoms (for a 'definite' diagnosis), or between twenty and twenty-four symptoms (for a 'probable' diagnosis), in nine out of ten clusters of symptom-categories in which a total of sixty specific symptom-criteria is listed (1972: 59–60).

Indeed, among the small group of research psychiatrists that publishes the influential 'Feighner criteria,' arguments for the possibility of stabilizing and specifying the diagnosis of hysteria through the identification of explicit, observable criteria have been made since the early 1960s (Guze, 1967; Guze and Perley, 1963; Perley and Guze, 1962; Woodruff et al., 1969). In 'The Diagnosis of Hysteria: What Are We Trying to Do?,' Samuel Guze, a psychiatrist with the St Louis Group, suggests that hysteria – given the controversy and ambiguity surrounding its definition over the past 2,500 years – is an exemplary diagnosis with which to test the power of explicit criteria in reliably establishing the existence of a uniform, homogeneous psychiatric disease whose validity can be empirically confirmed (Guze, 1967: 491). Concluding with the remark that studies to date 'strongly suggest that the syndrome [of hysteria] we have been describing and studying is a valid and recognizable disorder,' Guze urges the development of systematic diagnostic criteria as a general goal for psychiatric knowledge (1967: 497).

In the intervening years between the St Louis Group's attempts to use hysteria as the empirical stage on which to perform the scientific powers of a reliable and valid diagnostic method, and the publication of *DSM-III* (among whose authors members of the St Louis Group figure significantly) with its 'revolution' in psychiatric classification through the inclusion of specific diagnostic criteria for each clinical syndrome, an interesting drama has been enacted. Most importantly, perhaps, the professional and practical interests represented by research psychiatry, with its predominantly biological and medicalized approach to mental disorders, become a persuasive hegemonic force; the medicalization of US psychiatry places the diagnostic system squarely at the center of psychiatric knowledge, as research investigators replace clinicians as the dominant voice in psychiatry (Wilson, 1993). The introduction of explicit, specific symptom-criteria as the key to successfully standardizing the method and outcome of psychiatric diagnosis is heralded as a 'common language' in which clinicians and research investigators can speak of, and together manage, 'the disorders for which they have professional responsibility' (American Psychiatric Association, 1980: 1). Released from its reliance on unsubstantiated theories (i.e. psychoanalytic accounts of unconscious conflicts) and, at best, untested clinical evidence, the new language of diagnosis will be grounded in the objective, descriptive features of disease, and driven by the demands of empirical data and research (1980: 6–8).

How interesting, then, that one of the earliest objects of mental disorder established by the new methodological procedures should be excluded as a valid and reliable diagnosis in the classificatory system built up partly on the early 'evidence' of its existence. Is hysteria's absence from *DSM-III* simply the effect of the long (here, short) march of scientific progress that could disprove by 1978 what was enthusiastically validated just ten years earlier? Or is its disappearance from the diagnostic scene a symptom of something more complex going on in this 'revolution' of psychiatric science? What exactly is the status of the 'empiricity' ushered in by the performance of new methods of descriptive diagnosis? What social theater is operating to produce the persuasive drama of reliable 'data' on which to base the symptomatic profile of dis-ease? What psychic and social realities are materializing on US psychiatry's new empirical stage?

Of particular historical interest to me are the somewhat hysterical features of the 'real,' empirically based disease entities named by the new science of psychiatry and its data-driven methods. From the point of view of diagnosis and medical science, hysterical symptoms always presented the difficult problem of telling the difference between 'real' (organic, somatically based) and 'simulated' or 'fake' (psychically, non-physiologically based) disease (Hyler and Spitzer, 1978: 1503). In its role as the great pretender, the 'ubiquitous mimic' of authentic medical disorders, hysteria became the diagnostic category *par excellence* for marking the difference between true organic dysfunction and its impersonation (Sheehan et al., 1980: 51). In what ways do the new methods of scientific psychiatry perform a somewhat hysterical elision between establishing the 'real' existence of mental disorder, and enacting its simulation? Whereas the hysterical symptom confounds the diagnostic distinction between a somatically versus psychically based disorder, the hysterical psychiatric diagnosis, I suggest, may confound the distinction between an empirically based 'real' object and one that is 'performed' by the very methods establishing its empiricity.

How might a medicalized and scientifically fortified psychiatry enact such a theatrical feat? The door to this methodological drama is opened by the thorny epistemological issue of 'validity.' Scientific validity is intended as a measure of the closeness or looseness of fit between a concept and that which it purports to represent; it always involves claims about the nature of the reality of the object represented. A 'valid' construct is understood to touch upon the 'reality' of that which it attempts to name; a construct with low or no validity is understood to have missed its mark. As psychiatry bootstraps its way toward enunciating 'reliable' and 'valid' classifications of mental disease, the problem of operationalizing a measure of construct 'validity' looms large (Kirk and Kutchins, 1992: 28–30). The most common solution to the validity problem – apart from simply ignoring it and focusing exclusively on 'reliability' (a more manageable methodological problem), or vaguely operationalizing it as the 'utility' or 'usefulness' of the construct (e.g. Fleiss et al., 1972: 168; Spitzer and Fleiss, 1974: 341) – is to measure validity by reference to the power of the diagnostic classification to either predict the course of the disorder, or predict the most effective treatment outcome (Guze, 1967: 491–2).

And it is here, in this tentative measure of validity-as-prediction, that the door opens on a strange teleological spectacle: the use of that most systematic of psychiatric treatments, pharmaceutical drugs, first to give visibility to a particular cluster of symptoms which disappear after pharmaceutical treatment, and then to confirm the validity of a diagnostic category (based on the explicit criteria describing that symptom-cluster) by 'predicting' the effectiveness of that drug in treating that diagnosis.

But let us leave the realm of hypothetical speculation, and return to the historical stage to see this spectacle unfolding in the strange materiality of new psychiatric research methods.

In the 1980 *DSM-III*, from which hysteria has disappeared, the new diagnostic entity 'panic disorder' makes its psychiatric debut. Defined primarily as the experience of attacks of floating terror, or 'panic attacks,' the diagnostic criteria for panic disorder include a list of twelve specific symptoms; at least four of the symptoms must appear in at least three attacks occurring within a three-week period for the patient to be diagnosed with panic (American Psychiatric Association, 1980: 231–2). The empirical foundations for this new disease category rest in the early work of Donald Klein, a research psychiatrist and current director of research and development at the New York State Psychiatric Institute, an internationally renowned center for psychiatric research. Klein was also a senior member of the nineteen-person Task Force which oversaw the development of *DSM-III*.

In the late 1950s, Klein designed and implemented a series of psychopharmacological experiments at Hillside Hospital, a private New York State mental institution. At that time, research psychiatrists at Hillside had complete control over pharmaceutical prescriptions for all patients (Klein, 1996). They were allowed to perform, as Klein describes it, systematic 'human experimentation,' including the now-famous studies he published in the early 1960s on the effects of imipramine, an early antidepressant (Klein, 1964, 1967; Klein and Fink, 1962). Klein administered a single, standardized dosage of imipramine to 80 percent of all patients institutionalized at Hillside, not to treat any specific mental disorder, but to conduct research on the 'various patterns of behavioral response' among different subgroups of patients (Klein, 1996: 432). To Klein's surprise, the drug appeared to calm a heterogeneous group of patients who all suffered from severe anxiety symptoms, or anxiety attacks.

On the basis of this empirical evidence Klein argued, unsuccessfully, for over a decade of the existence of a clinically significant anxiety syndrome defined by spontaneous panic attacks that could be effectively treated with an antidepressant drug. Not until the mid-1970s, when these findings were replicated in the Psychosomatic Medicine Clinic at Massachusetts General Hospital with a group of patients variously diagnosed with hysteria, anxiety neurosis, or agoraphobia, did the concept of what would become 'panic disorder' begin to take hold (Sheehan et al., 1980). Dr David Sheehan, who conducted the research at Mass. General's Psychosomatic Medicine Clinic, never embraced Klein's diagnostic distinction or its inclusion in *DSM-III*, arguing to this day that panic disorder should be understood – along with its genealogical predecessor, hysteria – as part of a broader complex of symptoms (Sheehan, 1996; Sheehan and Sheehan, 1982).

Klein explicitly formulated his experimental method as 'pharmaceutical dissection,' proposing it as a valid, reliable way to identify and classify the existence of mental disorder. 'Pharmaceutical dissection' operates as a kind of inductionism in reverse: working backward from drug effect to syndrome, it reveals discrete psychiatric syndromes as a function of drug response (Klein, 1967). Panic disorder 'exists' as a distinct and real mental disorder because, in response to imipramine, a specific cluster of symptoms disappears. That cluster constitutes a distinct diagnostic category by virtue of its observable relation to pharmaceutical intervention. Klein explained how the increasing effectiveness and proliferation of pharmaceutical agents confronted psychiatry with the inadequacy of its diagnostic classification system, and argued for the 'utility of psychiatric diagnosis when appropriately modified for prediction of treatment outcome' (1967: 118).

It is not difficult to see the logic by which an experimentally oriented and pharmaceutically well-supplied research psychiatry could benefit from an intimate relation between the diagnostic boundaries of mental disorder and the observable effects of pharmaceutical treatment. If pharmacy could 'dissect' mental disorders into discrete objects and diagnostic categories, then pharmacy would be well positioned, and predictably so, to treat such objects with standardized, systematic efficacy: the same pharmaceutical effects that create the empirical boundaries of disease classification could construct the empirical evidence of its cure. But the 'reality' of the diagnostic categories so constructed is a far reach from the valid and reliable criteria of a scientific method. The method of pharmaceutical dissection performs its objects with a perhaps enviable precision, but the diagnostic language that results is as much a theater of constructed effects and selectively staged symptoms as the psychoanalytic discourse it attempts to displace.

This does not stop pharmaceutical dissection (or psychoanalysis) from being a powerful method. But it suggests, I hope, some of the profound ways that contemporary methods for naming and treating psychic dis-ease are themselves carved out of intensely historical stories, created from complexly knotted desires for scientific certainty *and* slippery methodological stagings, for 'real' objects *and* simulated stand-ins. While the case of panic disorder is not representative of the 'empirical' methods used to construct all or even most of the diagnostic categories in *DSM-III*, it is symptomatic of the epistemological tendencies and psychiatric practices made possible by re-presenting symptoms in the seductive language of scientific data.

One final historical thread in this hysterical weave of psychiatry and science should be noted. The principle of pharmaceutical dissection and the pursuit of the 'reality' of mental dis-order in the actions of and reactions to pharmaceuticals are not without their attempt at scientific foundation. Although today every prescription drug is still accompanied by a thin white sheet of typed information that mentions, in very small print, that the exact pharmacological action of the drug remains unknown, there is no absence of theoretical speculation. Donald Klein is the author of one of the more widely disseminated theories first published in *Diagnosis and Drug Treatment of*

Psychiatric Disorders, which today, in its second edition (Klein et al., 1980), is the most influential textbook on clinical psychopharmacology in the US.

Klein proposes a cybernetic model of drug–central nervous system interaction in which psychotropic drugs operate to normalize defective self-regulatory 'control mechanisms' in the human brain (Klein et al., 1980: 814). From its earliest emergence in state-sponsored research efforts during World War II to help improve the effectiveness of anti-artillery aircraft, cybernetics has conceptually remodeled an interdisciplinary range of objects – from animal societies to computers to human behavior and the brain – as communications or information-processing devices (Haraway, 1983; Heims, 1991; Wiener, 1948). In particular, cybernetics' productive analogy between the electrical operations of early computing machines and the electrical 'switching' operations of neuronal activity in the human brain opened up whole new imaginary and technological fields for rethinking the human central nervous system as a vast communications network. Control of the network was relayed through the communication of biochemical 'messages'; dysfunction or breakdown in the network was conceived as the relay of deviant messages through abnormal neurotransmissions in the brain.

This circuiting of analogies between the behavior of computers and of the human central nervous system is fundamental to cybernetics' founding desire to define the essential 'unity of a set of problems' organized around 'communication, control, and statistical mechanics, whether in the machine or living tissue' (Wiener, 1948: 19). For those psychiatrists, like Stanley Cobb at Mass. General, pursuing the promise of psychosomatic medicine through a translation of the Freudian neurosis into the dysfunction of the physiological neuron, cybernetics offered a rich conceptual technology for revisioning the 'immateriality' of psychic disturbance as the material flows of electrochemical communication in the brain. Cybernetics promised an integration of the old mind/body dualism through the materialist metaphors of communications theory (Bowker, 1993). Talcott Parsons, in an invited address to the American Psychosomatic Society in 1960, asserted the 'basic conception' that ' "behavior" is subject to a graded hierarchical system of control mechanisms in the cybernetic-information theory sense,' and that 'basic processes of control' which we ordinarily think of as 'processes of communication' are operating at all levels in the system: from the social and cultural level, to the organic level, to the subsystems of cells, organs, and tissue (Parsons, 1960a: 114).

While the cybernetic image of the brain as a complex communication center, controlled and self-regulated through the processing of information, is more a productive science fiction than a proven scientific fact, it nonetheless operates today to 'naturalize' the use of pharmaceuticals in the treatment of psychic dis-ease. Klein's cybernetic model of drug–central nervous system interaction can be found in many popularized images of the workings of pharmaceutical drugs. In its 1984 corporate annual report, the Upjohn Company, manufacturer of Xanax, reports this story:

> Information passed along a nerve cell's axon is assimilated by the . . . receiving cell through synaptic connections. Neurotransmitters (chemicals) . . . diffuse across this space and bind to receptors on the receiving cell, and the message has been delivered. Contemporary neuropharmacology seeks to modify aberrant messages that occur in certain disease states. (Upjohn Company, 1985: 21)

Panic disorder, in this cyber-scene of scientific story-tellings, can be cast in the role of an 'aberrant message'; Xanax scripted as communicating its normalizing cure.

The contemporary re-presentation of the symptoms of mental disease as the effects of a biological, interior theater of communication dis/orders gives the history of hysteria, today, a curious spin. If once upon a time the hysterical symptom was the great confounder of the difference between a physiologically and a psychically based disease, today it is the stories a medicalized and scientific psychiatry tells itself that perform that same confusion. In the introduction to the fourth and most recent edition of the *DSM*, the authors introduce the latest psychiatric classification system for mental disorders with a pronouncement against the unfortunate term *mental disorder*, which 'implies a distinction between "mental" disorders and "physical" disorders that is a reductionistic anachronism of mind/body dualism' (American Psychiatric Association, 1994: xxi). But if the desire of the hysterical symptom was to speak in the language of 'real' physical disorders so as to symptomatically express the existence of a memory forgotten at great psychic cost, the desire of a biologically based theory of mental disease as physical dysfunction communicates something quite different: an impulse, perhaps, to forget the psychic reality of a symptom, and affect its 'real' modification through largely biochemical methods of control. It became the peculiar fate of hysteria as a diagnostic construct in the US to come under the speculative gaze of this biologically reoriented psychiatry, just as hysteria was (symptomatically?) disappearing from the scene (Flor-Henry et al., 1981; Ludwig, 1972). In his attempt in the early 1970s to hypothesize a neurobiological theory of hysteria, Arnold Ludwig states: 'If the mysterious leap from mind to body is ever to be understood, then what is needed is a theoretical model which is biologically based, relates clinical symptoms to known central nervous system functions, and which permits theory-related predictions capable of scientific validation' (1972: 771). Hysteria, having made the leap from mind to body in its own theatricalizing terms, leaves the diagnostic scene at just the moment that psychiatry, in a language radically different though perhaps no less symptomatic, performs its own dramatic crossing of that 'mysterious' divide.

Restaging the Symptomatic Subject

> Symptoms ignored, however, do not disappear, and . . . [that which] we would deny only appears elsewhere, perhaps in more virulent forms.
>
> (Romanyshyn, 1989: 29)

When I began my performative fieldwork at Mass. General Hospital as a research subject in a clinical drug trial for Xanax, I wanted to keep panic and its disorders close to their symptomatic theater, to work against their digitalized translation into computerized data and their smooth suppression by pharmaceutical drugs. My fieldnotes were the antidote, the excessive and dramatic elaboration of everything that was systematically made invisible, rendered unspeakable, aggressively managed by the language and practices producing me as a clinical subject. By the time the fieldwork ended, my project had shifted. From desiring to keep the symptom close to its story, I began to imagine how I could bring its techno-corporate cure (this pill called Xanax) back to *its* symptomatic scene, to challenge its identity as an objective scientific technology and re-present it as the condensation of a quite historical, perhaps somewhat hysterical, story (Orr, 1990, 1993).

I began to try to write within and against the limits of ethnographic practice, compelled by the insistent question, 'In what fields does field work occur'? (Gordon, 1990: 491). You walk through the door of the Psychosomatic Medicine Clinic one day and you find xeroxed questionnaires digitalizing your stories, a bottle of blue pills heading for your bloodstream: years later, you discover behind that same door the accumulated effects of post-World War II restructurings of psychiatric discourse into the pursuit of empirical correlates between brain biochemistry and human behavior: fieldwork occurs in the field of history. You enter the Psychosomatic Medicine Clinic thinking you desire to destroy the discursive straitjacket which forces psychic dis-ease to speak itself in the grammar of individualized, biologized disorder; you leave that clinic and spend years studying the straitjacket, wanting to learn its pattern, tying and untying its game until you too and what you have to speak are somewhat cut from its same cloth: fieldwork never occurs outside the fields of desire, dream, phantasmatic perceptions, compulsed repetitions, the imaginary.

Taking seriously the sign over the entrance to my field was helpful: Psychosomatic Medicine Clinic. Tracing the institutionalized emergence of psychosomatic medicine in the US and its close association with the post-World War II interdisciplinings of cybernetics – which brought together not only engineering, mathematics, and information theory, but all three with psychiatry, neurology, and medicine – offered some historical clues to the symptomatic scene of power and desire enacted each time I visited the clinic. The peculiar 'wholism' pursued by the psychosomatic interest in the connections between mind and body became further elaborated in cybernetics' founding analogy between the electrical operations of the computing machine and the human central nervous system – early computer design was conceptually sparked by perceiving the function and processes of the computer as an 'ideal means for realizing in the metal the equivalents of . . . neuronic circuits and systems' (Wiener, 1948: 22).

This dream of understanding and materializing – in the metal, not the flesh, and with a powerful desire for their abstract equivalence – a certain perception of mind–body connection grounded in the image of mind as a command–control–communication center and body as its systems parameters is repeated, perhaps compulsively, in the conceptual framing of the action of psychotropic drugs as a reconfiguration of the neurotransmissions, or the message centers, in the brain to correct for the deviant signals which constitute mental disorder. The imperative for the clinical subject to function within the research site as herself a node in a vast network of information flows, from her speech and her bloodstream to a coded information byte into a computer database through a relay of algorithms into a set of quantified statistical findings to the corporate research and development division to the marketing department and perhaps, if all goes well, to the Food and Drug Administration – this imperative flows from a Cold War imaginary of cybernetic and systems thinking making possible, both technologically and conceptually, today's 'revolution' in the pharmaceutical treatment of mental disorders and distress.

My intent here is not to position pharmaceutical drugs on the psychoanalytic couch. Quite the contrary. I much prefer to pull psychoanalysis, and its theoretical origins in Freud's *Project for a Scientific Psychology* (1962), into genealogical relation with the technoscientific emergence of psychopharmaceutical drugs as a promising treatment technology for mental dis-ease.[8] Nathan Kline, a research psychiatrist and the 'father' of US psychopharmacology in the 1950s, was fond of quoting Freud's observation: 'Behind every psychoanalyst stands the man with the syringe.' And behind every man with the syringe, I would suggest, stands a historical symptom. What precisely that is, and how to analyze and cure it without repeating the Oedipal il/logics and gendered phantasms of psychoanalytic discourse, I am not sure. But I am quite certain that Christopher Reeve's spectacular call – from within the confines of an almost complete paralysis, amongst the nationalist paraphernalia of prime-time democratic capitalism – to conquer inner space, the region of the brain and the central nervous system, is a telling symptom. The battle for the command–control–communication–information centers of behavior, memory, and desire is on. We are living through the Decade of the Brain, and entering the Decade of Behavior.[9] How to navigate the political imaginary and power networks of such a fantastic voyage is a panicky question that saturates my field.

Notes

1. I am referring broadly to a focus on the metaphors and materiality of 'performativity' and 'performance' coming out of recent work in queer studies, feminist theory, technoscience studies, experimental ethnography, and post-structuralist thought, including Butler (1990a) and Case (1990); see Haraway (1991) for a discussion of 'material-semiotic actors.' This contemporary insistence on 'the performative' resonates in interesting, if largely unexplored, ways with the influential language of functionalism and symbolic interactionism in US sociology, in which concepts of 'social actor,' 'social role,' 'self-presentation,' and 'role

performance' were elaborated. For those who might care, this text may be read as the revenge of the 'sick role,' a notion proposed by Talcott Parsons over forty years ago which still circulates today within medical sociology. Central to Parsons's definition of the 'sick role' is its successful channeling of potential social deviance into an individualized role

> so that the two most dangerous potentialities, namely, group formation and successful establishment of the claim to legitimacy are avoided. The sick are tied up, not with other deviants to form a 'sub-culture' of the sick, but each with a group of non-sick . . . and, above all, physicians. The sick thus become a statistical status class and are deprived of the possibility of forming a solidary collective

– and, one might add, deprived of the possibility of re-presenting their symptoms as a collective social performance. See Parsons (1951: 477).

2. Christopher Reeve, speech broadcast on NBC-TV from the Democratic National Convention, Monday, August 26, 1996.

3. See Sheehan, 1996. The drug study compared motrin and alprazolam (Xanax) – both pharmaceuticals owned by the Upjohn Company – in the treatment of panic disorder. Results of the study showed alprazolam to be remarkably effective in easing the symptoms of panic disorder. Although the study's findings have never been published, they were the springboard to conducting controlled clinical trials of alprazolam and the first indication to the Upjohn Company that Xanax could indeed be a 'blockbuster' best-selling drug for the treatment of anxiety and panic.

4. See Sheehan, 1996. For a more complete description of Upjohn's international clinical trials, see Klerman (1988). For a critique of the studies' claim of efficacy with Xanax, see Marks (1989); and discussion by Breggin (1991: 350–2).

5. 'Transference' is the central psychoanalytic concept Freud used to name the powerful intersubjective relation between analyst and analysand. It is a 'chaotic field of energy in which, by virtue of the savage force of that field, memories are remembered and forgotten, desires are forged and re-forged' (Gordon, 1990: 494).

6. The decision to enter a field under what some may want to call 'false' pretenses is fraught with methodological, political, and ethical questions. It is not my purpose in this essay to raise these questions in their complexity. But I would remind readers of the possibility that the investigation of certain institutional settings and ethnographic situations becomes impossible *without* the use of what I am here calling 'impersonation.' The fact that I entered, as a researcher, a research setting as an 'impersonator' may be particularly disturbing to some readers/researchers. I admit to a fantasy that social and scientific research would be far more useful and accurate if more research 'objects' were also taking notes and publishing their findings. Fantasies, of course, are always entangled with fields of power. For an excellent analysis of the power relations structuring US government protocols for the protection of human subjects see Duster et al. (1979).

7. I am drawing here on Freud's notion of 'screen memory,' whereby the figures or events in a childhood memory, as in dreamwork, operate as a cover or alibi for more unrepresentable, repressed, and significant psychic material. See Freud (1962).

8. For an interesting historical and theoretical consideration of Freud's *Project for a Scientific Psychology* in relation to both contemporary neuroscience and French post-structuralism, see Wilson, (1996). For the biological underpinnings of Freud's theoretical career, and commentary on his life-long belief that the physio-chemical bases of neuroses would someday be found, see Sulloway, (1979); and James Strachey's Introduction to Breuer and Freud, (1957).

9. The 'Decade of the Brain' (1990–1999) is a National Institute of Mental Health initiative to promote research, public education, and funding for brain research connected to mental

disorders. The 'Decade of Behavior' (2000–2009) is a related initiative to promote basic research in the behavioral sciences.

References

Acker, K. (1993) *My Mother: Demonology*. New York: Grove Press.

American Psychiatric Association (1952) *Diagnostic and Statistical Manual of Mental Disorders*. 1st edn. Washington, DC: American Psychiatric Association.

American Psychiatric Association (1968) *Diagnostic and Statistical Manual of Mental Disorders*. 2nd edn. Washington, DC: American Psychiatric Association.

American Psychiatric Association (1980) *Diagnostic and Statistical Manual of Mental Disorders*. 3rd edn. Washington, DC: American Psychiatric Association.

American Psychiatric Association (1994) *Diagnostic and Statistical Manual of Mental Disorders*. 4th edn. Washington, DC: American Psychiatric Association.

Bayer, R. and Spitzer, R.L. (1985) 'Neurosis, Psychodynamics, and *DSM-III*: A history of the controversy,' *Archives of General Psychiatry*, 42: 187–95.

Bowker, G. (1993) 'How to be Universal: Some Cybernetic Strategies, 1943–70,' *Social Studies of Science*, 23: 105–27.

Breggin, P.R. (1991) *Toxic Psychiatry*. New York: St Martin's Press.

Breuer, J. and Freud, S. (1957) *Studies on Hysteria*. New York: Basic Books.

Butler, J. (1990a) *Gender Trouble: Feminism and the Subversion of Identity*. New York: Routledge.

Butler, J. (1990b) 'Performative Acts and Gender Constitution: An Essay in Phenomenology and Feminist Theory,' in S.-E. Case (ed.), *Performing Feminisms: Feminist Critical Theory and Theatre*. Baltimore, MD: Johns Hopkins University Press. pp. 270–82.

Case, S.-E. (1990) *Performing Feminisms: Feminist Critical Theory and Theatre*. Baltimore, MD: Johns Hopkins University Press.

Cixous, H. and Clément, C. (1986) *The Newly Born Woman*. Minneapolis: University of Minnesota Press.

Clément, C. (1986) 'The Guilty One,' in H. Cixous and C. Clément, *The Newly Born Woman*. Minneapolis: University of Minnesota Press. pp. 3–59.

Cobb, S. and Lindemann, E. (1943) 'Neuropsychiatric Observations,' *Annals of Surgery*, 117: 814–24.

Duster, T., Matza, D., and Wellman, D. (1979) 'Fieldwork and the Protection of Human Subjects,' *The American Sociologist*, 14: 136–42.

Feighner, J.P., Robins, E., Guze, S.B., Woodruff, R.A., Winokur, G., and Munoz, R. (1972) 'Diagnostic Criteria for Use in Psychiatric Research,' *Archives of General Psychiatry*, 26: 57–63.

Fleiss, J.L., Spitzer, R.L., Endicott, J., and Cohen, J. (1972) 'Quantification of Agreement in Multiple Psychiatric Diagnosis,' *Archives of General Psychiatry*, 26: 168–71.

Flor-Henry, P., Fromm-Auch, D., Tapper, M., and Schopflocher, D. (1981) 'A Neuropsychological Study of the Stable Syndrome of Hysteria,' *Biological Psychiatry*, 16 (7): 601–26.

Foucault, M. (1975) *The Birth of the Clinic: An Archaeology of Medical Perception*. New York: Vintage Books.

Freud, S. (1962) 'Screen Memories,' in *The Standard Edition of the Complete Psychological Works of Sigmund Freud, Vol. III*. London: Hogarth Press. pp. 303–22.

Freud, S. (1962) 'Project for a Scientific Psychology', in *The Standard Edition of the Complete Psychological Works of Sigmund Freud*, Vol. 1. London: Hogarth Press. pp. 295–397.

Freud, S. (1963) *Dora: An Analysis of a Case of Hysteria*. New York: Macmillan.

Freud, S. (1965) *The Interpretation of Dreams*. New York: Avon Books.

Gallop, J. (1982) *The Daughter's Seduction: Feminism and Psychoanalysis*. Ithaca, NY: Cornell University Press.

Gordon, A. (1990) 'Feminism, Writing, and Ghosts,' *Social Problems*, 31 (4): 485–500.

Guze, S.B. (1967) 'The Diagnosis of Hysteria: What Are We Trying to Do?,' *American Journal of Psychiatry*, 124 (4): 491–8.

Guze, S.B. and Perley, M.J. (1963) 'Observations in the Natural History of Hysteria,' *American Journal of Psychiatry*, 119: 960–5.

Haraway, D. (1983) 'Signs of Dominance: From a Physiology to a Cybernetics of Primate Society, C.R. Carpenter, 1930–1970,' in W. Coleman and C. Limoges (eds), *Studies in History of Biology*. Baltimore, MD: Johns Hopkins University Press. pp. 130–219.

Haraway, D. (1991) 'Biopolitics of Postmodern Bodies,' in *Simians, Cyborgs and Women. The Reinvention of Nature*. New York: Routledge. pp. 203–30.

Heims, S.J. (1991) *The Cybernetics Group*. Cambridge, MA: MIT Press.

Hyler, S.E. and Spitzer, R.L. (1978) 'Hysteria Split Asunder,' *American Journal of Psychiatry*, 135 (12): 1500–4.

Irigaray, L. (1985) *Speculum of the Other Woman*. Ithaca, NY: Cornell University Press.

Kirk, S.A. and Kutchins, H. (1992) *The Selling of DSM: The Rhetoric of Science in Psychiatry*. New York: Aldine de Gruyter.

Klein, D.F. (1964) 'Delineation of Two Drug-Responsive Anxiety Syndromes,' *Psychopharmacologia*, 5: 397–408.

Klein D.F. (1967) 'Importance of Psychiatric Diagnosis in Prediction of Clinical Drug Effects,' *Archives of General Psychiatry*, 16: 118–26.

Klein, D.F. (1996) Interview conducted at the New York State Psychiatric Institute, March 26.

Klein, D.F. and Fink, M. (1962) 'Psychiatric Reaction Patterns to Imipramine,' *American Journal of Psychiatry*, 119: 432–8.

Klein, D.F., Gittelman, R., Quitkin, F., and Rifkin, A. (1980) *Diagnosis and Drug Treatment of Psychiatric Disorders: Adults and Children*. 2nd edn. Baltimore, MD: William & Wilkins.

Klerman, G.L. (1988) 'Overview of the Cross-National Collaborative Panic Study,' *Archives of General Psychiatry*, 45: 407–12.

Ludwig, A.M. (1972) 'Hysteria: A Neurobiological Theory,' *Archives of General Psychiatry*, 27: 771–7.

Marks, I.M. (1989) 'Letter to the Editor,' *Archives of General Psychiatry*, 46 (7): 668–70.

Moi, T. (1981) 'Representation of Patriarchy: Sexuality and Epistemology of Freud's Dora,' *Feminist Review*, 9: 60–73.

Newsweek (1942) December 7, pp. 43–4.

Orr, J. (1990) 'Theory on the Market: Panic, Incorporating,' *Social Problems*, 37 (4): 460–84.

Orr, J. (1993) 'Panic Diary: (Re)constructing a Partial Politics and Poetics of Disease,' in J. Holstein and G. Miller (eds), *Reconsidering Social Constructionism: Debates in Social Problems Theory*. New York: Aldine de Gruyter. pp. 441–82.

Parsons, T. (1951) *The Social System*. New York: Free Press.

Parsons, T. (1960a) 'Some Reflections on the Problem of Psychosomatic Relationships in Health and Illness,' in *Social Structure and Personality*. New York: Free Press. pp. 112–26.

Parsons, T. (1960b) 'Definitions of Health and Illness in the Light of American Values and Social Structure,' in *Social Structure and Personality*. New York: Free Press. pp. 257–91.

Parsons, T. (1970) 'On Building Social Systems Theory: A Personal History,' *Daedalus: Journal of the American Academy of Arts and Sciences*, 99 (4): 826–81.

Perley, M.J. and Guze, S.B. (1962) 'Hysteria – The Stability and Usefulness of Clinical Criteria,' *New England Journal of Medicine*, 9 (March 1): 421–6.

Purtell, J.J., Robins, E., and Cohen, M.E. (1951) 'Observations on Clinical Aspects of Hysteria: A Quantitative Study of 50 Hysteria Patients and 156 Control Subjects,' *Journal of the American Medical Association*, 146 (10): 902–9.

Romanyshyn, R. (1989) *Technology as Symptom and Dream*. New York and London: Routledge.

Rose, J. (1978) 'Dora: Fragment of an Analysis,' *m/f*, 2: 5–21.

Sheehan, D.V. (1996) Interview conducted at the University of South Florida Psychiatry Center, April 19.

Sheehan, D.V. and Sheehan, K.H. (1982) 'The Classification of Anxiety and Hysterical States. Part I. Historical Review and Empirical Delineation,' *Journal of Clinical Psychopharmacology*, 2 (4): 235–43.

Sheehan, D.V., Ballenger, J., and Jacobsen, G. (1980) 'Treatment of Endogenous Anxiety With Phobic, Hysterical, and Hypochondriacal Symptoms,' *Archives of General Psychiatry*, 37: 51–9.

Showalter, E. (1985) *The Female Malady: Women, Madness, and English Culture, 1830–1980*. New York: Pantheon.

Smith, D. (1975) 'Women and Psychiatry,' in D. Smith and S. David (eds), *Women Look at Psychiatry*. Vancouver: Press Gang Publishers. pp. 1–19.

Spitzer, R.L. and Fleiss, J.L. (1974) 'A Re-analysis of the Reliability of Psychiatric Diagnosis,' *British Journal of Psychiatry*, 125: 341–7.

Spitzer, R.L., Endicott, J. and Robins, E. (1978) 'Research Diagnostic Criteria: Rationale and Reliability,' *Archives of General Psychiatry*, 35: 773–82.

Sulloway, F.J. (1979) *Freud: Biologist of the Mind*. New York: Basic Books.

Upjohn Company (1985) *The Upjohn Company Annual Report 1984*. Kalamazoo, MI: Upjohn Company.

White, B.V. (1984) *Stanley Cobb: A Builder of the Modern Neurosciences*. Boston: Francis A. Countway Library of Medicine.

Wiener, N. (1948) *Cybernetics: or Control and Communication in the Animal and the Machine*. New York: Technology Press.

Wilson, E.A. (1996) 'Projects for a Scientific Psychology: Freud, Derrida, and Connectionist Theories of Cognition,' *Differences: A Journal of Feminist Cultural Studies*, 8 (5): 21–52.

Wilson, M. (1993) '*DSM-III* and the Transformation of American Psychiatry: A History,' *American Journal of Psychiatry*, 150 (3): 399–410.

Woodruff, R.A., Clayton, P.J., and Guze, S.B. (1969) 'Hysteria: An Evaluation of Specific Diagnostic Criteria by the Study of Randomly Selected Psychiatric Clinic Patients,' *British Journal of Psychiatry*, 115: 1243–8.

4

The Project of Pathology: Reflexivity and Depression in Elizabeth Wurtzel's *Prozac Nation*

Dwight Fee

> Nothing could be more false than the myth of madness as an illness that is unaware of itself as such. . . . The way in which a subject accepts or rejects his illness, the way in which he interprets it and gives signification to its most absurd forms, constitutes one of the essential dilemmas of the illness.
>
> (Foucault, 1987: 46–7)

> I am incoherent and know it.
>
> (Wurtzel, 1995: 115)

'The Thin Red Line' was the cover story not long ago in the *New York Times Magazine* (Egan, 1997). The article discusses a new rise in 'cutting' and other similar self-mutilating behaviors among young people, particularly women, that involve the deliberate but not usually life-threatening destruction of one's own body tissue – for instance, slicing an arm with a razor or burning a leg with a lighter. Many experts view the behavior as a compulsion directed toward obfuscating 'a deeper, more intolerable psychic pain associated with feelings of anger, sadness or abandonment' (1997: 3). Cutting seems to be something done to engage or relieve this internal suffering and feeling of emptiness – to 'feel alive' and perhaps more in control.

According to the author's interviews, there is reason to think the phenomenon of cutting may involve other factors as well, such as a culturally based antagonism between women and their bodies, or the fact that women more often 'turn their anger inward.' Whatever the case, the condition is now apparently on the increase, and thus clinicians are wondering whether it should be considered an independent syndrome, given that self-mutilation is presently one of many criteria now used to delimit and diagnose 'borderline personality disorder.' Whether or not self-mutilation or 'cutting' should constitute a self-existing diagnostic entity, the assumption about the condition is that is it is precipitated by things outside of itself – things cause 'it.' These things might be psychological, cultural, and perhaps even historical.

However, it is worth asking whether or not this all-too-real phenomenon can be implicated *in its own* pathogenesis. Simply put, can the cultural production and reproduction of the *idea* – 'cutting' – play a role in how it becomes a possible action? Perhaps at some level cutting involves what it *means* to cut, and is not a simple or determined outcome of only exterior forces or variables.

Reflexivity as 'Reality'

I would like to briefly explore this issue, but in reference to the more ubiquitous syndrome of 'depression.' In discussing the limits of purely 'external' and causal approaches to depression, I hope to illustrate how reflexivity is increasingly crucial for conceptualizing this and by implication, perhaps other syndromes and pathologies. Aspects of this argument have been stated before through a variety of theories and accounts[1] but have not been systematically discussed with respect to a historical context of 'institutional reflexivity' (Giddens, 1990, 1991). Indeed, this may already seem a reiteration of the basic idea of a 'self-fulfilling prophecy,' or of a new trend in the medicalization or 'pathologization' of behavior, or, in a general way, a simple depiction of the contemporary power of psychiatric labels. While these issues are surely implicated, I hope to extend beyond these perspectives while making some provisional observations about new tendencies at work between self-understanding, psychiatric illness, and knowledge systems of mental health.

What is new, for one, is that some clinical syndromes, like depression, are becoming increasingly mediated. That is, they are aspects of self that can inform processes of self-construction and self-definition much more readily than they did in the past. In other words, languages of depression no longer exist solely within the discourse of psychiatry or within the mental health profession more generally. Rather, depression and other diagnostic categories are now *social objects* – points of personal and collective significance. Thus, 'depression' is something that increasing numbers of people know about – often in some degree of sophistication – and hence might invoke in a variety of ways to make sense of the trajectory of their lives. This does not deny the reality of depression, but it complicates dominant assumptions that entities like depression are completely external – that is, outside agents that unidirectionally invade the (otherwise healthy, unmitigated) self.

In addition to whatever else it may be, depression is now often a *discursive project* – a reflexive process of self-definition and identity construction. 'Depression,' then, is rarely just that; it is often an active, interpretive process of culturally informed self-communication. This self-dialogue, radicalized in recent years, intervenes between the supposedly direct, one-way association between an underlying state and its direct, observable indicators. Whatever biological or purely psychological substrata might exist, it still holds that the more we discuss what depression *is* and how it affects our lives – in effort to understand 'it,' to develop a relationship to 'it,' to combat 'it' – the more we add to its discursive life and, as will be illustrated, confound normative medicalized, intrapsychic, and clinical understandings. Depression, then, as a powerful *story*, must be taken as seriously as other aspects or dimensions of the condition. After all, 'stories are maps for action – they look into the future, tell us how we are motivated, guide us gently into who we will be. They make certain worlds more plausible. They signpost directions to be taken' (Plummer, 1995: 173).

It would be erroneous to argue that there is no such thing as depression (or, indeed, to warn against deliberating about it). I only wish to underscore the power of narration and self-interpretation, and to argue that the newly hyper-reflexive embodiments of depression bring matters of language and social construction into the heart of felt experience. To illustrate, I will examine the best-selling memoir, *Prozac Nation: Young and Depressed in America* (Wurtzel, 1995), a text that is a part of a new influx of published autobiographies organized around the experience of mental disorder, which is itself emblematic of a reflexive revolution.[2] However, let me first provide a quick review of the dominant thinking about depression.

'Depression' in Expert Realms

Despite the fact that it may be the most common psychiatric illness that clinicians are likely to encounter (Andreasen and Black, 1995), there are many different approaches to understanding depression and its variants. It is fair to say, though, that the most accepted perspective in psychiatric circles, arguably the most influential, are basically somatic, pointing toward biological, physiological, and genetic factors at base, with 'environmental' conditions existing as mediating factors or external pressures or triggers. As the psychiatrists Klein and Wender state: 'The majority of cases of depressive and manic-depressive illness appear to be genetically transmitted and chemically produced. Stated differently, the disorders seem to be hereditary, and what is inherited is a tendency toward abnormal chemical functioning (sometimes called a "chemical imbalance") in the brain' (1993: 87). The authors discuss several studies to support this view, including twin studies which conclude that identical twins – those who share identical genes – also share depression 33 to 70 percent of the time. From this perspective, situational or environmental factors implicated in depression reflect the relative effectiveness of a kind of underlying 'immune system.' 'Some people show a decreased psychological resilience, an inability to cope with stresses that most people can overcome' (1993: 94). Thus, any 'social' processes are reduced down to elements or variables within an overall biomedical problem. And of course, treatment follows in kind. Antidepressants are often used to correct perceived 'vulnerabilities,' generally targeting deficits or imbalances of neurotransmitters (see Hewitt, Fraser, and Berger, Chapter 8, this volume).

The term 'medical model' might be more useful than 'psychiatric' to describe this overall approach because many psychiatrists hold to other theories and understandings of depression, sometimes used in conjunction with organic and bio-reductionist models. The psychoanalytic orientation, for example, has remained a viable stance and method of treatment throughout the establishment of the biomedical paradigm during the last forty years or so. The classic Freudian-analytic theory, crudely put, involves a psychodynamic process implicitly connected with the activity of mourning. Here, following the loss of a love-object – most often a person – feelings of helplessness and dependence are repressed and transformed into self-directed anger or rage (Freud, 1968; Klein and Wender, 1993: 95), hence the popularized idea of depression as 'anger turned inward.' Originally published in 1917, Freud's 'Mourning and Melancholia' argued that through a denial of, or compensation for, the loss, the lost person or 'object' is 'introjected' by the mourner along with feelings of anger about abandonment and guilt over past wrong-doings against the deceased (Freud, 1968; see also Davison and Neale, 1998: 231). Clearly, the loss of someone close is only one of many circumstances that could give rise to 'melancholia.' Freud stated the lost object could be lost love in one form or another and could be experienced consciously or unconsciously. Regardless, the loss of the object and the resulting toll on the ego become one and the same. 'The analogy with mourning led us to conclude that [the patient] had suffered a loss in regard to an object; what he tells us points to a loss in regard to his ego' (Freud, 1968: 55). Others after Freud have attempted to make the theory more amenable to include the importance of self-esteem within everyday transactions with the object world. For example, Gaylin argued that depression is mourning over a lost sense of self-worth in a general sense, so that 'any loss of self-esteem or any symbol of it should produce a depression' (1968: 16–17).

One of the more popular accounts of depression, especially in more recent years, is cognitive, or 'cognitive-behavioral' most recognizably. Here, Freudian depth models are replaced with observable symptoms, thus allowing clearer distinctions between normal sadness and a clinical notion of abnormal depression (Radden, 1987). More central, though, is the notion that one's thoughts and beliefs are central in causing or influencing depressive experience – and that these often 'irrational beliefs' (Ellis, 1962) or distorted or 'negative schemata' (Beck, 1967; Sacco and Beck, 1995), especially when mediated by stressful life events, can 'bias' one toward a pattern of pessimistic cognitions that lead the way to depression (see Goldfried and Davison, 1994). In this sense, one might become socialized into 'learned helplessness' (Seligman, 1974) – 'giving up' in a sense – adopting a passive stance toward life events that require normative coping skills.

There are, of course, many other common perspectives. The existentialist approach – the European contribution to an otherwise healthy-minded 'third force' psychology in the US – emphasizes the tangible experience of persons in an uncertain and repressive historical context, calling forth recognition of the tragic and perhaps absurd dimensions of human experience. The ambiguities and anxieties of 'being in the world' challenge one to find a way to live with insight, 'authentically,' in the present, and to courageously work toward future possibilities (see May, 1983).

But as different as these approaches are, they share basic criteria about the expression and quality of depression, even if the experience of depression cannot be easily divorced from basic problems of human meaning and selfhood, as is the case with existentialism (and some psychoanalytic thought). In other words, there is not too much disagreement on what depression looks like, and these qualities are reflected in the *Diagnostic and Statistical Manual of Mental Disorders*. The fourth edition of the *DSM* (American Psychiatric Association, 1994) indicates nine criteria for a major depressive episode (five of which must be present for a continuous two-week period). Abbreviated, these are: depressed mood; loss of interest in activities; significant weight loss or weight gain; insomnia or hypersomnia; restlessness or psychomotor slow-down; fatigue; feelings of worthlessness or guilt; relative inability to concentrate; and recurrent thought of death, sometimes including suicidal thoughts or behavior.

Most of the dominant approaches to depression require something at the outset – an external (or sometimes intrapsychic) origin, a starting point, an 'aversive event.' While depression is thought to work backward, affecting one's definition of those events and circumstances deemed 'aversive,' might this interpretive feedback process include the *perception* and *identification* that (true or not) 'one is depressed'?

Wurtzel and the Depressive Identity

Prozac Nation is a detailed and rich chronicle of a young woman's experience with depression. Meticulous and thoughtfully written, it is difficult to do justice to the book's depth and intricacies in a few short pages. However, I would like to provide a brief overview of Wurtzel's life-story in order to convey how depression, as an acute experience *and* as an interpretive lens, fuse to become a central part of Wurtzel's identity. This occurs with respect to the real, tangible events in her life, where she learned to adopt the language of depression, as well as in the process of recounting that very experience in book form – perhaps an example of a new influx of 'autopathographies' (see Udovitch, 1994).

Wurtzel opens the story with a description of her in college at Harvard, curled up fetal-like on a bathroom floor, unable to stop crying. She has stopped taking her lithium – one of the medications she took during her early years at Harvard – and begins describing her already too-long battle with her feelings of misery. She recalls how hopeless she felt and how she was doomed to a certain existence, one shared by certain well-known others:

> I know that into every sunny life a little rain must fall and all that, but in my case the crisis-level hysteria is an all-too-recurring theme. The voices in my head, which I used to think were just passing through, seem to have taken up residence. And I've been on these goddamn pills for years. At first, the idea was to get me going so I could respond to talk therapy, but now it seems clear that my condition is chronic, that I'm going to be on drugs forever if I just want to be barely functional. . . . And I'm starting to wonder if I might not be one of those people like Anne Sexton or Sylvia Plath who are just better off dead, who may live in that bare, minimal sort of way for a certain number of years, may even marry, have kids, create an artistic legacy of sorts, may even be beautiful and enchanting at moments, as both of them supposedly were. But in the end, none of the good was any match for the aching, enduring, suicidal pain. Perhaps I, too, will die young and sad, a corpse with her head in the oven. Scrunched up and crying here on a Saturday night, I can see no other way. (1995: 8)

Throughout the book are general remarks and observations about depression: what it feels like, how it manifests itself, its consequences, and so on. However, in the first chapter, Wurtzel attempts to communicate the full gravity of depressive episodes:

> One morning you wake up afraid you are going to live. . . . [Depression has] got nothing at all to do with life. In the course of life, there is sadness and pain and sorrow, all of which, in their right time and season, are normal – unpleasant, but normal. Depression is in an altogether different zone because it involves a complete absence: absence of affect, absence of feeling, absence of response, absence of interest. The pain you feel in the course of a major depression is an attempt on nature's part (nature, after all, abhors a vacuum) to fill up the empty space. But for all intents and purposes, the deeply depressed are just the walking, waking dead.
>
> And the scariest part is that if you ask anyone in the throes of depression how he got there, to pin down the turning point, he'll never know. There is a classic moment in *The Sun Also Rises* when someone asks Mike Campbell how he went bankrupt, and all he can say in response is, 'Gradually and then suddenly.' When someone asks how I lost my mind, that is all I can say too. (1995: 22)

In terms of her accounts of the sources and causes of her depression, Wurtzel touches upon a variety of factors – family dynamics, genetics, personality traits, and even cultural and historical themes. Raised during the late 1960s and 1970s, she regularly discusses the generational issues associated with a shift in historical eras. As she puts it, 'I hate to think that personal development, with its template of idiosyncrasies, can be reduced to explanations as simple as "it was the times," but the sixties counterculture – along with its alter ego, eighties greed – has imprinted itself all over me' (1995: 23). But more than this, Wurtzel's regular elaborations about her family relationships and upbringing suggest that she views these elements as the major factors underlying her depression. In brief, she tells about how her father was a pill-popping depressive himself, and, while in continual conflict with her mother, slept most of the time. Wurtzel describes the household as extremely dysfunctional and 'paranoid,' before and after her parents' divorce when she was very young. Her parents 'were constantly at odds with each other, and all they gave me was an empty foundation that split down the middle of my empty, anguished self' (1995: 29). Expectedly, her parents' relationship was a major part of her extensive therapy, beginning in childhood, with several different psychiatrists and psychologists. Her father, however, continually failed to pay the therapy bills, often landing them in legal trouble.

> So I mention the family history of depression to every new therapist when it finally occurs to me, and they always feel obligated to point out the genetic component of mental illness. But then I'll tell them a little about my immediate family background and sooner or later, as the narrative continues, they're sure to say something like, *No wonder you're so depressed*, like it's the most obvious response. (1995: 33)

During the first three chapters or so, a salient theme emerges, namely Wurtzel's own reflexive battles with her pain and 'illness' – that is, 'what this all means' with respect to who she is and perhaps who she has become. Wurtzel describes how even in early adolescence she had developed a gloomy and sullen disposition. On several occasions she wonders about the relationship and connection between her depressed personality – a 'shtick,' as she once refers to it – and the 'real thing':

> The trouble was, I thought this alternative persona that I had adopted was just that: a put-on, a way of getting attention, a way of being different. And maybe when I first started walking around talking about plastic and death, maybe then it was an experiment. But after a while, the alternative me really just was me. (1995: 45)

This is also when Wurtzel begins to describe the need for a concrete understanding of her condition. Through her youth and even into her college years she desperately wanted clear dimensions to her experience, ways to understand her profound unhappiness and instability that would provide personal and social legitimation. Regularly referring to one of her favorite musicians, Bruce Springsteen, she remarks how much easier things would be if she could simply get in touch with her 'blue-collar blues,' that is, feel as though she could connect her internal torment to something outside herself. 'That is all I want in life: for this pain to seem purposeful.' She could even be a 'fucked-up Marxian worker person, alienated from the fruits of my labor. My misery will begin to make sense' (1995: 50). She further remarks:

> Here was this thing called depression that was not definable in any sort of concrete way . . . that had simply taken up residence in my mind – a mirage, a vision, a hallucination – and yet it was creeping into the lives of everyone who was close to me, ruining them all as I was ruined myself. . . . My parents could argue until late into the night about what to do about *this* – this thing – but they were basically bickering about something that in measurable terms did not exist. I found myself *wishing* for a real ailment, found myself longing to be a junkie or a coke-head or something – something real. . . . What does getting help with depression mean? Learning to keep away from your own mind? (1995: 67–8)

Looking back at her adolescence in the 1980s, when those around her described her as so 'full of promise,' Wurtzel begins to accept the fact that she is a changed person – someone with a chronic condition that sets her apart from others. However, at least now she can be relatively contented with a more tangible way to define herself:

> I realized, rather painfully, that the girl I had once been, the one who bossed everyone around, the one who could hold sway over any situation, was simply not coming back. No matter if I ever got out of this depression alive, it made no difference because it had already fundamentally changed me. There had been permanent damage. My morose character would not ever go away because depression was everything about me. It colored every aspect of me so thoroughly, and I became resigned to that. And in a strange way, this resignation allowed me to stabilize. (1995: 96)

True recovery would not be possible, then, even if she were no longer depressed. But, at least she is able to forge a new kind of self-definition through an almost comfortable seating in her condition.

At this point, now in college, Wurtzel views herself as basically normal, but 'not right' either. Doing better at Harvard, enjoying life slightly more, she is, in her words, 'like a recovering alcoholic who gives up drinking but still longs, daily if not hourly, for just another sip of Glenfiddich. . . . I could be a depressive who wasn't actively depressed, an asymptomatic drone for the cause' (1995: 97). She is also now in therapy at the college's counseling center, initially with a therapist who refused to help her get on medication.

After describing her experiences with a summer job as an arts reporter in Texas, including such problems as failed romantic relationships, she returns to Harvard with a renewed resolve to 'beat' her depression, even though the condition as such still remains elusive to her. At this time, she has a miscarriage, not realizing she is pregnant. The event makes her extremely upset, touching upon many of her existential and interpersonal dilemmas. She spends a night in the college infirmary, crying uncontrollably, and is given the anti-anxiety drug Xanax, then Valium, and finally Thorazine, an anti-psychotic. The curious effect of the episode, according to Wurtzel, is that now she has more of an 'actual' basis on which to interpret her suffering, and she has found others around her more sympathetic: 'Suddenly my problems seemed to have a physical cause and I was more satisfied with somatic explanations than the usual psychic ones . . . [friends] seemed to have more sympathy than when it was all just depression and all so ineffable' (1995: 191).

Around this same time, Wurtzel begins seeing a psychiatrist in private practice, Diana Sterling. While continuing to struggle with the meaning and tangibility of her condition, often 'feeling bad about feeling bad,' it is Dr Sterling more than any other person who helps her to recognize that she is depressed, and regularly reminds her of the difficulty involved in recovery: ' "You don't need an excuse to be depressed," Dr Sterling told me in one of our sessions. "You just are" ' (1995: 192).

Sprinkled throughout *Prozac Nation* are allusions to suicide, and references to it at this point in the book now become more noticeable. In response to Dr Sterling's plea for Elizabeth to accept herself as depressed, and not to feel as though she needs concrete reasons to feel lousy, Wurtzel tells her therapist:

> That's the reason a suicide try has always appealed to me. I mean, since I've been such a cosmic failure in my numerous attempts to get addicted to drugs and alcohol, the only terrible thing I can see happening would be if I were to overdose or something. Then people would think I was really sick and not just kind of depressed, which is what they think now. (1995: 193)

After a quick development of a serious romantic relationship with a man and its subsequent painful dissolution, Wurtzel takes another turn downward, and Dr Sterling arranges a long-term stay for her at the Harvard infirmary. After describing the new situation, Wurtzel comments on new confusions about her relationship to depression:

> It seems that I have spent so much time trying to convince people that I really am depressed, that I really can't cope – but now that it's finally true, I don't want to admit it. . . . It seems not so long ago, maybe only a decade ago, I was a little girl trying out a new persona, trying on morbid depression as some kind of punk rock statement, and now here I am, the real thing. (1995: 232)

During this crisis, Wurtzel makes desperate calls to her therapist, 'crying like a rainstorm.' She tells Dr Sterling that if she ends her life, 'there will be blood on her hands' (1995: 233). Deciding to treat her acute anxiety and agitation, Dr Sterling prescribes Xanax until a psychopharmacologist at McLean Hospital can further evaluate her. The decision to try Xanax, according to Wurtzel, was based on Sterling's opinion that 'even worse than the depression itself is the fear I seem to have about never escaping from it' (1995: 234). The Xanax does little to help, as Wurtzel endures an intense panic attack when venturing outside the infirmary. Dr Sterling then decides to put Wurtzel on Mellaril, another anti-psychotic drug. Although taking it for some time, it too proves basically ineffective.

Moving toward the end of the book, after a trip to Britain, Wurtzel is back at Harvard. She makes her way back to the infirmary, where Dr Sterling asks her to consider beginning taking Prozac, which, although fairly new at the time, is recommended on the basis of the consultation Wurtzel has in the meantime with psychiatrists at McLean Hospital:

> The McLean people recommend fluoxetine because they have diagnosed me with *atypical depression.* This diagnosis was not easy for them, or for Dr Sterling, to come by, as the occasional appearance of manic-like episodes . . . might indicate that I suffer from either manic-depressive illness or cyclothymia, a milder type of mood-swing disease. But in the end, the diagnosticians conclude that I've been too persistently down and not florid enough in my manic periods to be bipolar. Atypical depression is long-term and chronic, but the sufferer's mood can occasionally be elevated in response to outside stimulus. . . . The atypically depressed are more likely to be the walking-wounded, people like me who are quite functional, whose lives proceed almost as usual, except that they're depressed *all* the time. . . . The trouble is that as the years pass, if untreated, atypical depression gets worse and worse, and its sufferers are likely to commit suicide out of sheer frustration with living a life that is simultaneously productive *and* clouded by constant despair. (1995: 298–9)

After reading further about atypical depression – learning from psychiatric texts that the condition is also characterized by 'rejection sensitivity' (particularly romantic) – she remarks how 'those symptoms perfectly delineate my symptoms. I feel suddenly so much less lonely' (1995: 300).

As days pass while Wurtzel waits miserably to see if Prozac will work, she learns her mother has been mugged – badly hurt – and is now in hospital. The episode helps to initiate an emotional discussion between the two where Wurtzel confesses her guilt about her continuing unhappiness, as well as her regrets about the inability to be fully supportive to her mother.

> 'But, Elizabeth,' she says, in the most reasonable voice I've heard from her in years, 'there is something wrong with you: You're depressed. That's a real problem. That's not imaginary. Of course you can't deal with anything. You're depressed.' . . . And it's strange, but when she said those words to me, when she said, *You're Depressed*, it became a reality for me for the first time in a long, long time. Not that I wasn't aware that I felt like shit all the time – there was no avoiding that – but I had ceased to think of it as a legitimate condition, as a real disease, even if it had a fancy diagnosis like *atypical depression.* (1995: 311–12)

Thus, according to Wurtzel, it takes her mother's words – assumedly within the context of Dr Sterling's influence – to allow her to (again) fully recognize herself as depressed, as someone with a real condition.

In the last chapter of the book, Wurtzel's scattered commentaries on suicide seem to come together into a logical but still surprising scenario. Although Prozac begins to have beneficial effects, it perhaps gives her the energy to initiate an action she has long considered. As she puts it: 'my improved affect did not in any way sway me from the basic philosophical conviction that life, at its height and at its depth, basically sucks' (1995: 315). Now, 'hell-bent' on suicide, she fantasizes how she would ideally follow through with a suicide attempt. During a therapy session with Dr Sterling, Wurtzel describes how she would cut her arteries in the bath, but with the lights off, as she had heard that many people attempting suicide this way get frightened at the first sight of blood and abort the attempt. She then imagines out loud to Dr Sterling what the perfect music would be for the event: Janis Joplin and Billie Holliday. Wurtzel writes how, during this narration to Dr Sterling, she becomes 'rhapsodic, like a reformed coke addict going gaga over the thought of doing some blow' (1995: 318); consequently, Sterling refuses to let her go home. Invoking Anne Sexton's poem 'Wanting to Die,' Wurtzel concludes that 'there is no logic to the suicide imperative, it is just something that I must do, and something I must do now' (1995: 319). She excuses herself to the bathroom and takes what is left in the bottle of Mellaril that she had been carrying. Wurtzel's description of the event implies that in the moment she knows at some level that it was 'probably not a lethal dose' and that she was in fact making a 'wimpy attempt' that was bound to fail. When Dr Sterling pounds on the door, Wurtzel, lying on the floor, reaches up and unlocks the door. Whisked to the emergency room by Dr Sterling, Wurtzel is able to vomit much of what she had ingested, and, in a euphoric state, thinks: '*I have survived an attempt on my life*' (1995: 321 original emphasis).

The book ends with Wurtzel, after having recovered from this trauma, describing the significant improvement she now feels with Prozac. Her mood change is so dramatic that it makes her almost fearful of getting better. She concludes:

> In a strange way, I had fallen in love with my depression. Dr Sterling was right about that. I loved it because I thought it was all I had. I thought depression was the part of my character that made me worthwhile. I thought so little of myself, felt that I had such scant offering to give the world, that the one thing that justified my existence at all was my agony . . . .
>
> But depression gave me more than just a brooding introspection. It gave me humor, it gave me a certain what-a-fuck-up-I-am schtick to play with when the worst was over. . . . I had developed a persona that could be extremely melodramatic and entertaining. It had, at times, all the selling points of madness, all the aspects of performance art.
>
> But . . . I was so scared to give up my depression, fearing that somehow the worst part of me was actually all of me. The idea of throwing away my depression, of having to create a whole new personality, a whole way of living and being that didn't contain misery as its leitmotif, was daunting. . . . How would I ever survive as my normal self? And after all these years, who was that person anyway? (1995: 326–7)

The Interweaving of Discourse and Experience

Wurtzel's book presents layer upon layer of textual interpretation. The act of reconstructing the past – any past – involves reading back into the world with the ever-shifting conceptual frameworks of the present (Plummer, 1995: 40–1). Here, the situation is particularly complex, as 'depression' is the major interpretive frame through which the story of the past is told. The problem is that the purpose of the narrative itself – its reason for being, in large part – is to demonstrate the fluidity of the frame ('depression'). That is, a major theme of *Prozac Nation* is the problem involved in defining an identity as someone depressed. The story is told through – and is at the same time directed at – the mercurial domain of depression.

The fear expressed at the end of the book – that she might not be able to recognize herself as 'not depressed' (1995: 327), and the earlier observation that 'no matter if I got out of this depression alive, it made no difference because it had already fundamentally changed me' (1995: 96) – would seem to suggest that Wurtzel could not easily separate completely 'depressed' from 'not depressed' locations in her life. While this could be one interesting thematic to be taken from her story – depression as transmuting entity, and thus not exactly a fixed entity at all – her conclusions run the other way. Throughout most of the book, 'depression' is a fragmented, uneven experience, bouncing from situation to situation, from paradox to paradox, refusing a stable phenomenological grounding. However, Wurtzel's movement through the therapeutic and psychopharmacological realms slowly but persistently turns the story almost into a straightforward recovery tale, now a culturally dominant mode of story-telling (Plummer, 1995). In her epilogue, Wurtzel discusses how she does not pretend to know what causes depression, but in pointing to her success with Prozac she concludes that the essence of severe depression, or at least its central mechanisms, can be captured within biochemical terms: '[A]fter an accumulation of life events made my head such an ugly thing to be stuck in, my brain chemistry started to agree' (1995: 345).

Wurtzel may be right; she knows quite a lot about depression, perhaps as much as some experts, given how much she has explored, studied, and written. But this itself is crucial to what we now understand as depressive experience: lay people know what it is, know how to talk and argue about it, and, consequently, know how to use it to construct biographies. We now thrust our own subjectivity into a diagnostic, and now rhetorical, category – which, historically, has been the chattel of experts. In other words, these knowledges, once confined to particular discursive locales, have spilled over into what we commonly recognize and perhaps feel *as* depression. But it is the experts themselves who, presumably from the story, help Wurtzel to place her depression outside of mediating forces; the bouncing ball of depression simply needed adequate pinpointing, articulation, and acceptance.[3]

Again, I am not suggesting that depression is a state of false-consciousness or that it is a psychosomatic illness. Rather, understanding depression requires, in addition to a host of things, an account of the mediating process of self-interpretation *vis-à-vis* the now ubiquitous concept (or social object) of 'depression' and its intricate feedback into the realm of experience. This idea is somewhat similar to Parsons's concept of the 'sick role' (1951, 1964; see also Siegler and Osmond, 1974): a learned role that introduces those defined as ill to a system of codes and expectations – most notably, the obligation to 'get well' through proper medicalized channels and relationships. For Parsons, the sick role was one aspect of an encompassing structural system that functioned to control deviance through institutionalized constraint. The sick role, however, does not provide a sense for how meanings of sickness are formed and inhabited outside of, or prior to, formal medical or mental health institutions. Similarly, the concept of a sick role does not convey the complex, fluid quality of illness identification that seems to characterize our context – a perspective that runs in contrast to accounts that have posited only the 'internalizing' of static, constraining roles. This applies to Goffman's (1961) classic work on confined psychiatric patients' obligation to play out the scripts of madness, as well as Scheff's important work in labeling theory (1975): are we only subjected *to* ideological regimes, passively adopting predetermined languages of illness through external coercion?

Beyond something external and constraining, depression seems to be a site of self-*production*, a hermaneutic location, used to construct meaning and build personal significance. This problem reflects Foucault's view that power 'traverses and produces things,' and is a 'productive network which runs through the whole of the social body, much more than a negative instance whose function is repression' (1980: 119). But there is also the question of why this kind of self-production, in a general way, is problematic yet at the same time so necessary.

'Institutional Reflexivity' and Discourses of Health

Anthony Giddens (1991) argues that the 'detraditionalizing' influences of modernity have changed the relationship between knowledge, institutions, and 'self-identity.' In recent years, central traditions around personal, social, and political life have become pluralized, relativized, and reworked at many levels – which, by definition, challenges their status as traditions. In this situation, living with uncertainty becomes normative, as persons must address the question, 'how should I live my life?' through reflexive encounters with contingent 'abstract systems,' which are the culturally produced and often discrepant systems of knowledge and expertise used to address this continually emerging question. In a detraditionalizing 'late-modernity,' Giddens explains, 'forms of traditional authority become "authorities" among others, part of an infinite pluralism of expertise' (1991: 195).

'Institutional reflexivity' refers to the broad and pervasive condition whereby information and knowledge are continually incorporated into social life and activity, consequently reshaping them; however, at the same time, those 'reconstituted' environments are also transformative and work back into abstract systems of knowledge and expertise. At a personal level, living in a historical context of institutional reflexivity means to actively engage the filtering back of expert knowledge into daily life and predicaments, as the habitual reappropriation of knowledge is the 'very condition of the "authenticity" of everyday life' (Giddens, 1994: 91).

A main challenge for individuals in late-modern life is to sustain a coherent and relatively continuous 'narrative of the self' amidst the incessant refashioning and uprooting of the cultural milieu. Without a central sense-making foundation for action and understanding, the 'project' of maintaining self-continuity is characterized by risky ventures into this reflexive climate where one must rely on mediated information (that depends on other forms of mediated information) in order to negotiate life-style options and construct self-identity:

> In the post-traditional order of modernity, and against the backdrop of new forms of mediated experience, self-identity becomes a reflexively organized endeavor. The reflexive project of the self, which consists in the sustaining of coherent, yet continuously revised, biographical narratives, takes place in the context of multiple choice as filtered through abstract systems. (Giddens, 1991: 5).

Utilizing this approach, it may be increasingly difficult now to 'have' depression, as a purely externally derived condition. That is, depression's meaning is chiefly derived from engagements with intermixing elements of abstract systems – mass media, therapy, psychopharmacology, *DSM-IV* (on shelves at all major bookstores), (other) popular health references, and, perhaps portentously now, autobiographies (and even further, analyses of autobiographies?). *Prozac Nation* – as Wurtzel's story – describes this engagement; but as an information source, it is now itself *constitutive*, however subtly, of the very abstract system it thematically addresses. Thus, critical concerns of sociologists should now reach somewhat further than whether or not a person accepts the 'psychiatric line' in understanding his or her situation (Denzin, 1968; Goffman, 1961, 1968). Someone seeking therapy for depression, which is itself an important historical development in reflexive encounters with mental illness, has often *already* been immersed within the discourse of the syndrome.

Therefore, within a context of institutional reflexivity, people are thrust into processes of signification and identity-work as soon as they feel the condition could somehow pertain to them, and maybe even before. For growing numbers of people, especially in the US, it is basically impossible to be 'outside' of the discourses of mental health. Therefore, it is equally difficult for persons to escape at least entertaining the idea that, at some junctures, they might be 'depressed.' And maybe they are. The point is that 'reflexively organizing life-planning, which normally presumes consideration of risks as filtered through contact with expert knowledge, becomes a central feature of the structuring of self-identity' (Giddens, 1991: 5). In this sense, depression is, again, not a circumscribed label or a preset sick role as much as it is an increasingly pervasive yet fluctuating point of cultural and personal awareness – a mutable conceptual framework used to read into self and experience.

Giddens also argues that continual engagement with abstract systems requires regular 'reskilling' – that is, the subjective reworking of knowledge and skills so that they have practical relevance within localized and personal life. Of course, this process, too, is fraught with difficulties, as knowledge continually shifts due to the constant reflexive reordering of abstract systems through scientific as well as cultural transitions, perhaps diminishing our basic trust in those systems. But the point here is that while reflexive 'reskilling' does not have to involve 'educating' one's self about, in this case, depression, it does mean that it is increasingly difficult to sit back, insulated, able to locate the 'raw' inner state of depression without implicit reference to narratives about it. When Wurtzel gave her depression a name through the help of others (and that is what she desired most as a very unhappy young adult, an anchoring relationship to her condition), the discourse of depression allowed her to reorganize her personal biography, but in a way that did not flow directly from the 'untouched' experience of someone psychologically sick. What is crucial here is that reskilling around knowledges of depression, especially when utilized in reference to expert opinion of whatever variety, can obviously become a consequential point of self-construction.

One other related and useful theme in Giddens's work is the 'commodification of experience' – the capitalist-based, standardized manufacture and, in a sense, distribution, of life-styles and life-choices in easy-to-use form. Here, 'not just lifestyles, but self-actualization is packaged and distributed according to market criteria' (1991: 198). Self-help materials or TV soap operas are clear examples, as they often address life predicaments – problems often linked to detraditionalization – in a 'prepackaged' or formulaic manner. However, Giddens points out that the commodification of self-experience is not to be equated with passive adoption of information or images; rather, persons 'react creatively to processes of commodification which impinge on their lives. . . . Individuals actively discriminate among types of available information and interpret it on their own terms' (1991: 199).

It seems that depression, at some level, is one of many 'psychological commodities' now available for reflexive consumption. While not exactly a life-style or life-choice (one would hope), depression *is* something taken up as an object of self-understanding and decision-making. It also has certain narratives attached – implicit programs almost – that provide a means for understanding the dimensions of depressive experience and anchoring it in the self. And it is certainly indirectly 'marketed' in a number of respects. *Prozac Nation* is one such example, a point that Wurtzel indirectly discusses in her epilogue. That is, perhaps Wurtzel 'reskilled' to some extent through the act of writing her public biography, and we, as readers, can perhaps reskill by reorganizing our own biographies through consuming hers. Depression, then, as a commodified experience, also comes with its own various built-in 'self-help' manuals of sorts.

Thus, it is the larger context of radical, institutionalized reflexivity in everyday life that impels us to incessantly monitor our moods, minds, and bodies through culturally produced languages. With narratives of pathology and sickness being routinely incorporated into self-dialogue, even minor mental, emotional, or physical changes can mean trouble and uncertainty.[4] For Giddens, the body, in fact, is a main site of reflexivity, as it is 'less and less an extrinsic "given", functioning outside the internally referential systems of modernity, but becomes itself reflexively mobilized' (1991: 7).

Just by its title, Peter Kramer's influential book *Listening to Prozac* (1993) assumes that psychiatric drugs like Prozac directly change dispositions and create versions of self without a self there to apprehend and mediate the process. In other words, the drug does not create an alter or 'personality' in isolation from the larger interpretive project of understanding and constructing one's self 'as ill' or 'as medicated' or both. So the emphasis is not just on being drugged, but, within and a part of that, the ongoing and contingent realization of what it *means* to be drugged in effort to treat depression (see Karp, 1996). And Kramer's best-seller itself, perhaps more than Wurtzel's, has surely contributed in some measure to popular definitions of that meaning. In its print advertising, Eli Lilly, Prozac's manufacturer, makes it clear to potential consumers that the drug will not change one's personality ('only depression can do that,' the advertisement reads). Commercial and scientific struggles over what it means to be depressed are thus also important elements that influence how we choose to treat it.

Knowledge, Illness Narratives, and Identity

There are two studies that further clarify the implications of a reflexive orientation to depression. These works are David Karp's important phenomenological perspective on depression in *Speaking of Sadness* (1996), and Dorothy Smith's discussion of women and madness in the renowned feminist treatise *The Conceptual Practices of Power* (1990). Both books emphasize the interconnections between self-experience and mental illness, as well as how the circulation of knowledge implicates both.

Karp interviewed an extensive number of people diagnosed with depression in an attempt to understand the subjective experience and problems of meaning that are a part of living with the condition. One important dimension of his research was to understand how identities are constructed through the illness. Sensitive to issues about the social construction of the depressive self, Karp found that all of the people he interviewed endured similar identity turning points through their 'careers' of depression (1996: 55–6). First, there was a period of 'inchoate feelings' that lacked an identifiable label, but were conceived of as linked to situations and concrete events. Second, there was a period when the idea that 'something is really wrong with me' came to the center of awareness, and persons began to see their problems existing within themselves and not within situations at hand. The third stage was characterized by an acute crisis of some sort related to depression that brought people into the therapeutic world of (usually) medical-psychiatric authorities. Obviously, this is when a classification was formally given to their experience, one that allowed them to 'redefine their past, present, and future in illness terms' (Karp, 1996: 63). One man with a chronic back problem told Karp that, while he knew his back pain would eventually diminish, depression 'had a life of its own. And what I saw basically recast my whole life until that moment' (1996: 64). During the crisis period, Karp describes an ambivalent situation where the person often found profound relief in receiving the diagnosis – very similar to Wurtzel's experience – but also realized that this meant that they now exist inside the domain of 'mental illness.' Thus, the fourth stage was 'coming to grips with an illness identity.' As complex as this situation was, as people looked for causes, developed theories, and generally 'reskilled' we might say, most people 'wanted simultaneously to embrace the definition of their problem as biomedical in nature while rejecting the notion that they suffer from "mental" illness' (Karp, 1996: 72).

Wurtzel clearly experienced a progression of illness identification that closely reflected the four phases Karp uncovered. In making conclusions about the relationship between depression and identity, Karp writes that 'depression often involves a life centered on a nearly continuous process of construction, deconstruction, and reconstruction of identities in the face of repeated problems' (1996: 75), which again reflects the tribulations of Wurzel, as she herself repeatedly notes within the pages of *Prozac Nation*. However, Wurtzel's project itself – the writing of those pages and the shaping of the narrative – involves an additional layer of interpretation 'after the fact' as she moves back through lived experiences as an author – further reskilled, an expert to an extent – out to explain depression. It can be assumed that within her experience depression gradually becomes a salient location through which she can recognize and differentiate herself in immediate situations; later, looking back through the discourse of depression when writing, she is able to apply a sense of linear and contextual coherence to those situations.

Reports from Karp's interviews – for example, 'well, I knew I was different from other children,' in the first 'inchoate feelings' stage – are representative of this kind of reconstruction. The feelings and perceptions are real, and so too are the patterns and phases Karp notices; however, they arise and become real because they are derived to a significant extent from someone named depressed, and thus from someone occupying a *socio-cultural* position. Karp states that 'most of those reporting bad feelings from an early age could not conclude something was "abnormal" because they had no baseline of normalcy for comparison' (1996: 58). It is reasonable to ask, though, whether at that time there was something 'there' at all. This is perhaps unanswerable, but there can not be an unambiguous, self-existing stage one or two without a stage four, where identities become reflexively organized and one learns how to construct a depressed biography through crises or turning points. Depression, like many aspects of identity, speaks from within itself as it reconstructs its past.[5]

Karp's predominant view seems to be that depression, as we recognize it in our society, is 'there,' mostly because of cultural and socioeconomic dis-connection, and gradually comes to express itself through social and medical understandings, as slippery as these might be. This is surely reasonable. Furthermore, Karp makes it clear that he is not concerned with debating what depression 'is'; his focus is almost solely on the meanings attributed to it by sufferers. However, there seem to be more radical implications of one of his subtly stated conclusions: that in an increasingly medicalized society, there is a 'culturally induced readiness to interpret pain as illness' (1996: 178). We might further add that pain is not always prior to a discourse of illness, as the two can go hand in hand or relate dialectically. Depression can be a realization continually achieved through reflexive encounters with its *own* pain – suffering already recognized as depression.

Dorothy Smith further implies how experience and discourse fuse at the nexus of depression. In her critique of the epistemology of psychiatric practice, she works against the conception that 'the individual can be separated from what is happening to that individual in the psychiatric context,' and further argues that when 'counting people becoming mentally ill you are also counting what psychiatric agencies do' (Smith, 1990: 117). One specific aspect of her in-depth analysis applies here to the problem of the reciprocity between what Giddens calls 'abstract systems' (e.g. medical, psychiatric, and psychological knowledges) and the production of subjective experience.

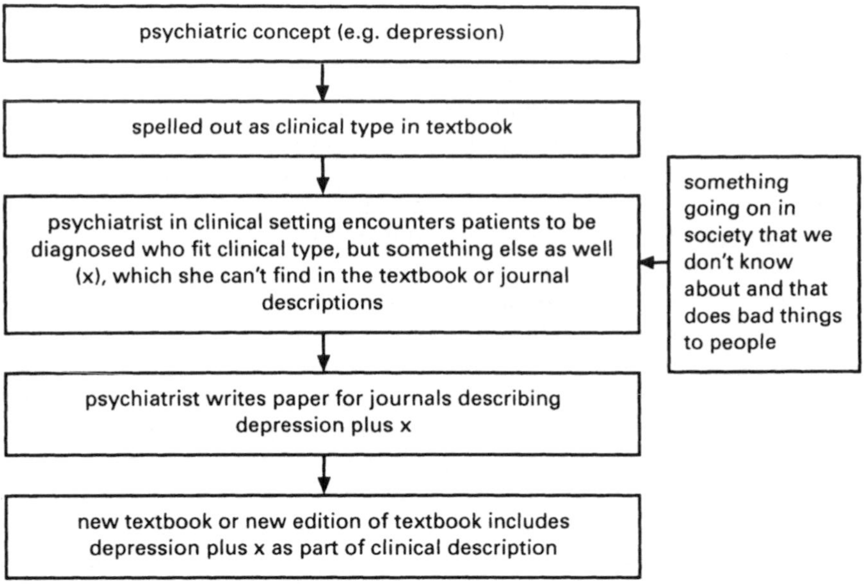

Figure 4.1 *Smith's 'Repairing the ideological circle' (1990: 131)*
Source: From The Conceptual Practices of Power: A Feminist Sociology of Knowledge by Dorothy E. Smith. Copyright 1990 by Dorothy E. Smith. Reprinted with the permission of Northeastern University Press.

Smith asserts that 'the clinical entities of mental illness are formalizations of types originating in the interrelation between clinical experience and the theories and systematic investigations of psychiatric discourse' (1990: 128). In its relationship to the evolving forms of human problems and suffering, psychiatry, in lieu of directly engaging underlying conditions in actual conditions of people's lives, regularly tries to conceptually keep up by revising its clinical vocabulary. As Smith puts it: 'Psychiatric responses to changes learned in actual local situations appear as new clinical insights, the description of variant clinical entities, [and] the evolution of new methods of treatment' (1990: 130). Figure 4.1 is Smith's diagram depicting this process. This creation and re-creation of knowledge and practice – the 'recycled reality' of mental illness (Smith, 1990: 130) – is not confined to mental health experts, as already discussed. Smith similarly discusses how the discourse seats itself within a variety of cultural, educational, and media-driven locales.

What is most important for Smith is that while mental health statistics tell us something important about people's lives,

> These operations make over, tidy up, sort out, and shape what is actually happening to people into properly recognizable forms. If you are dealing with a 'well-educated' population, much of the shaping will have already taken place before the patient gets to the agency. (1990: 130)

This is obviously very close to what has already been discussed as a consequence of reflexivity. In her book, though, Smith implies some idea of a prior and uncontaminated dimension of people's struggles before they are subject to clinical discourse and practice, before the 'actuality' of suffering is processed through a kind of epistemological 'meat grinder,' as she puts it. Of course, this is a valid assumption, but perhaps not the whole story. Smith theorizes how women become 'psychiatrized' through a discourse which encroaches upon their interpretations and dispositions, but she is 'not doing away with the actualities of people's experiences that underlie diagnoses of mental illness' (1990: 129). In fact, she makes it clear that in her critique of the connection between psychiatric ideology and practice, she wants to 'set aside' the issue of mental illness in terms of the 'minds and feelings and bodies of women' (1990: 132). From a viewpoint that fully incorporates reflexive processes, this is virtually impossible to conceptualize.

Figure 4.2 illustrates Smith's diagram, but adds institutional reflexivity as the condition that allows a more interrelated sense for how 'experience' – localized, individual, even bodily – is also implicated at some level. Specifically, Figure 4.2 does not allow for tangible experience (Smith's 'something going on . . . that's bad') to be completely divorced, at least entirely, from the transmuting discourse. The broken arrows in Figure 4.2 indicate that revised expert knowledge can never complete the ideological circle without spilling over into the realm of experience to some degree, as institutional reflexivity obligates one out of necessity to systematically infiltrate expert-

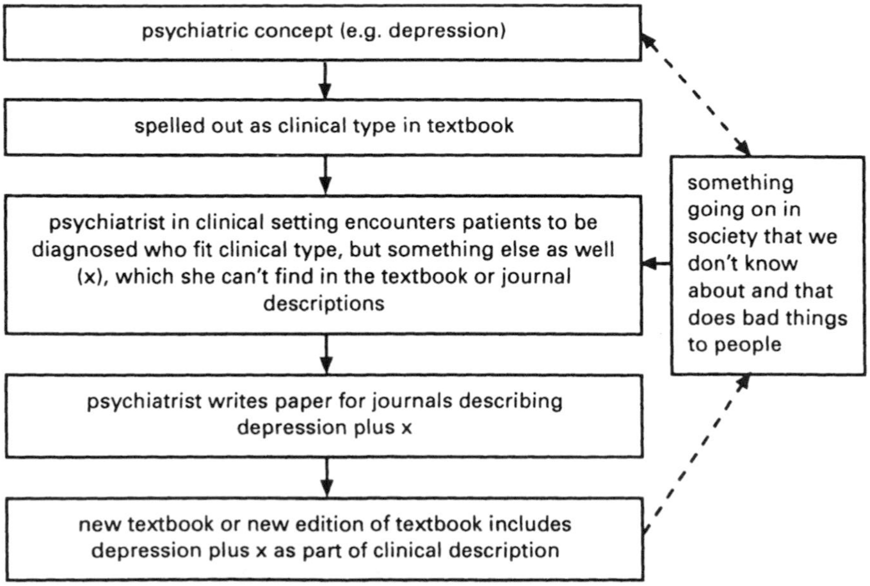

Figure 4.2 *Adding institutional reflexivity to Smith's 'Repairing the ideological circle' (1990: 131)*

ise. Consequently, conceptions of depression are often in mutual dialogue and entangled with what we recognize as 'our experience.' Those conceptions do not necessarily cause the 'bad things,' but they are part of the apparatus that can, in an undetermined sense, make them recognizable and meaningful as such.

Depression: Disorder, Discipline, Drama

Moving toward final assessments, consider again Wurtzel's suicide attempt near the end of the book, which, in a sense, is the emotional pinnacle of the story. The phrase 'suicide attempt' almost belongs in quotation marks, because, as Wurtzel herself describes, it was (fortunately) a less than an unequivocal and arrant effort to take her life. As readers, making sense of this episode requires creative and somewhat problematic interpretation, as does the reconstruction of *Prozac Nation* as a whole. Nevertheless, without doubting for a moment her feelings of intense despair and all-out desperation that day in Dr Sterling's office, there is room to make informed speculations about how the coming together of certain dilemmas may have contributed to her (spontaneous?) decision to overdose.

In terms of Wurtzel's own sequencing, several things had recently happened prior to the event. First, depression had finally become a kind of 'truth' for her: she had recently been formally diagnosed with 'atypical depression,' which helped her to feel 'less lonely,' and Prozac was immediately prescribed. Also, in attending to her mother after the mugging, Wurtzel confessed guilt over being 'absorbed' in her depression, and her mother explicitly validated her daughter's depressive condition, which had dramatic implications for Wurtzel; before this, 'I never felt I had a right be to depressed' (1995: 312). It may have been that Wurtzel's pain had, in an ironic sense, finally become purposeful; it was not simply that an underlying depression had gotten 'worse.'

Her vivid, almost obsessive, reflexivity about suicide was connected to her desire to confirm her own depression, and in the same way to have others believe that she was 'really' ill. The overdose, then, may have been the clichéd 'cry for help,' but it was also perhaps anticipated through Wurtzel's own desperate attempts to dramatize that which she thinks she has, and, through the act itself, to confirm it. She knows about the connections between depression and suicide; she may have even known at some level that, statistically speaking, some depressed patients are more likely to attempt suicide when on an upswing, often after starting antidepressant therapy. Of course, we don't know. But Wurtzel's reflexive, 'meta-depression' as she puts it herself (1995: 234), seemed to have its own emotional and behavioral climax. Furthermore, the overdose as later narrated in *Prozac Nation* – placed within an exhilarating conclusion – became her literary climax; and now, here it has unwittingly become the focus of *my own* analytic climax. Within or ostensibly outside the experience, depression's story, its narrative life, seems virtually inescapable.[6]

Defending the view that the 'essential nature' of suicide is psychological, Shneidman writes that 'psychache,' a term he coins for psychological pain, 'stems from thwarted or distorted psychological needs. In other words, suicide is chiefly a drama in the mind' (1997: 23). Shneidman argues that his view translates into the direct study of 'human emotions described in plain English in the words of the suicidal person' (1997: 24). But it is clear that 'the terms and forms by which we achieve understanding of the world and ourselves are social artifacts, products of historically and culturally situated interchanges among people' (Gergen, 1994: 49) – and these emergent terms and forms are intrinsic to who we are and what we *do*.

A specific, reflexivity-focused constructionism would further quality Wurtzel's final claim that once somebody becomes a depressed 'clinical case,' one's story 'is absolutely and completely his own' (1995: 351). Wurtzel's story needed others, it needed experts, it needed narrative form, and, even within the throws of a suicidal euphoria, it needed the backdrop of her own reflexive efforts that defined what depression did to her. Here, Durkheim's (1951) account of the external, structurally independent causes of suicide are obviously inapplicable; we must actively inhabit meaning and make it belong to us, yet, in somewhat of a Durkheimian sense, that is more of a social process than an intrapsychic one. Furthermore, it seems that when we claim stories as exclusively 'ours,' we do so at our own risk.

Prozac Nation is an invaluable illustration of the disaggregated, unpredictable, and tortuous quality of depression. It seemed to be all of these things (and more) all at once, and in this sense is not fully concordant with popular and simplified conceptualizations. Depression had Wurtzel curled up on the bathroom floor, it severely damaged her relationships with others, and it even almost ended her life. At the same time, and just as central, depression allowed her – *compelled* her – to develop a relationship to 'it,' as she explained so eloquently. It was obviously a love–hate relationship, but one that became internal to her tragic exigency. As a reskilled recoverer, within parts of the book and certainly in writing it, she was able to reduce this complex drama to a one-dimensional story about the wake and aftermath of an illness invasion. Through her own reflexivity she almost managed, in the final analysis, to remove reflexivity from the experience of depression.

My point has been that reflexivity around this mental illness has become intensely radicalized, and is part of a larger trend of self-objectification and identity-building through reflexive confrontations with/in expert knowledges and technologies. If *Prozac Nation* shows that an important source of Wurtzel's depression was figuring out her depression, it also reveals the chronic uncertainty and the immense emotional expenditure that this involves. The point is not that depression became a self-fulfilling prophecy. Rather, the discourse of depression was something Wurtzel could not simply unreflectively 'take on' nor choose to ignore; it was manifest simultaneously an unstable individual experience, a shifting social location, and a perspective that more often than not was never quite sure of itself.

The danger comes when a *disciplined* relationship emerges within this tumultuous context. Without venturing into an overview of Foucault's thinking here (see Burr and Butt, Chapter 9, this volume), self-monitoring and self-regulation must be considered as a potential aspect or outcome of reflexivity around depression. Historically, as a form of large-scale social administration and surveillance, discipline was crucial in the building and implementation of categories and typologies of human beings and their behavior (Foucault, 1977). As a technique of regulation, discipline helped to designate and thus re/create 'deviant' populations as subjects came to monitor themselves through the process of absorbing and internalizing external moral scutinization. In the early asylums, precursors to our modern psychiatric regime, Foucault theorized that the patient was compelled to participate in the recognition, confession, and nullification of his or her aberrance. Thus, madness became fixed within individuals – 'talked into being' in a sense – in the name of therapeutic strategy (Foucault, 1965; see Cushman, 1995). Patients, however, lost their own subjective footing and agency as they came to apprehend themselves through a mirror of their own pathology: 'the patient finds himself . . . already alienated in the doctor' (1965: 274). Foucault further writes:

> This, then, is the phase of abasement: presumptuously identified with the object of his delirium, the madman recognizes himself as in a mirror in this madness whose absurd pretensions he has denounced; his solid sovereignty as a subject dissolves in this object he has demystified by accepting it. He is now pitilessly observed by himself. (1965: 264)

While the institutional relationships Foucault described have obviously changed, the technologies of illness categorization, confession, and *apprehension* – that is, ways of re-creating ourselves through them – have only become finer and more widespread. In a progressively more medicalized and 'psychiatrized' milieu, we no longer need to have the doctor sitting across from us; forms of mediation can be found while perusing a bookstore, being prescribed a pill (or simply exploring whether or not one needs a pill), or reading an autobiography. In this situation, reflexivity does not directly usher in discipline, but it is one possible trajectory (see Rose, 1990).

Once more, this argument could be read as a suspicion of the 'authenticity' of depression as a serious or dangerous state, or, say, phenomenologically as 'complete absence,' as Wurtzel described it. Clearly, reflexivity may not apply in all instances; life is sufficiently tragic by itself. There are surfeits of moments that bring on abject despair and desolation without being significantly bound up within reflexive reworking. The point is that reflexive processes are now more present, visible (thus marketable), and consequential aspects of what we simultaneously see, construct, and endure within a larger existential plight.

Therefore, no instance of depression, reflexive or non-reflexive, is any more or less 'real' than another. Reflexivity around depression is something increasingly salient and is turning many depressions – in all of their constituted elaborateness – *also* into discursive projects that work back into experience. *Reflexivity, in short, is part of the essence*; it does not necessarily lessen or trivialize depression's 'legitimacy.' The purpose is to add to a complexity that, although mostly denied under positivism, is always there. But there is a specific implication here about strict biomedical and psychologically confined approaches. Reflexivity *does* qualify and loosen positivism's supposed objective grasp of the underlying essence of depression. A reflexive reality to depression entails a certain 'denaturalization' of its objective status as a purely external affliction. This approach does not require a rejection of organic processes, but 'it does require the effort of going beyond that and examining what can be understood in terms of individuals situated in specific points of time and space: individuals *with* and *within* history' (Simon, 1996: 30, my emphasis).

Depression can thus be seen as a constructed but 'true' story within a larger historical drama that puts human agency in a new role within a previous circumscribed and mystified arena of individual mental pathology. Foucault wrote that 'there is a very good reason why psychology can never master madness; it is because psychology became possible in our world only when madness had already been mastered and excluded from the drama' (1987: 87). In other words, we – and not just psychology – do not know how to talk about disorders like depression without reference to the discourse of diagnostic classification and abnormality which guarantees a kind of non-communication, even to one's self, in a period of such intense and ubiquitous verbalization.

Notes

1. See Foucault (1987), Keyes (1985), Miller (1983), Sontag (1979), and Wiener and Marcus (1994).

2. For other popular examples of a 'reflexive revolution' around depression and related problems, see Jamison (1995), Manning (1995), Slater (1996), and Styron (1990).

3. It is worth considering, too, whether or not depression – 'atypical' or not – is even the best pathological locus for the story. From my own amateur, clinically untrained perspective, *Prozac Nation* works equally well, or even better, as an illustration of 'borderline personality' organization. (For more on the borderline condition, see Wirth-Cauchon, Chapter 7, this volume.)

4. One illustration of this can be found recently on the front-page headline of the *Monitor* (June 1998), published by the American Psychological Association, which warns about growing anxiety among older adults over Alzheimer's. As knowledge about the condition widens, 'anxiety about the disease is likely to increase . . . as thousands of sensitized but otherwise normal elders cringe inwardly with every forgotten phone number.'

5. Goffman alludes to this process even within the experience of those confined to psychiatric hospitals:

> An important aspect of every career is the view the person constructs when he looks backward over his progress; in a sense, however, the whole of the prepatient career derives from this reconstitution. The fact of having had a prepatient career, starting with an effective

complaint, becomes an important part of the mental patient's orientation, but this part can begin to be played out only after hospitalization proves what he has been having, but no longer has, is a career as a prepatient. (1968: 234)

6. It would seem that this kind of attention to reflexivity would have implications for both sociologically and psychologically reductionist approaches to suicide. Since Durkheim's classic causal, social-structural approach (1951), most accepted thinking now on suicide is clinically and psychologically oriented, but there are clear efforts to incorporate a variety of mental, cultural, and structural factors (see Maris, 1997). The use of suicide notes has obviously demonstrated that, historically, suicide became used as a mode of self-expression, and the tone, form, and language of the notes tended to reproduce each other as they become chronicled and publicized (Etkind, 1997). Suicidal 'contagion,' of course, is a long-recognized problem (see Velting and Gould, 1997) but does not address reflexive processes *per se*. One problem with theorizing reflexivity, as illustrated below, is the dualistic language that essentially makes it invisible.

References

American Psychiatric Association (1994) *Diagnostic and Statistical Manual of Mental Disorders*. 4th edn. Washington, DC: American Psychiatric Association.

Andreasen, N.C. and Black, D.W. (1995) *Introductory Textbook of Psychiatry*. 2nd edn. Washington, DC and London: American Psychiatric Press.

Beck, A. (1967) *Depression: Clinical, Experimental and Theoretical Aspects*. New York: Harper & Row.

Cushman, P. (1995) *Constructing the Self, Constructing America: A Cultural History of Psychotherapy*. New York: Addison-Wesley.

Davison, G.C. and Neal, J.M. (1998) *Abnormal Psychology*. 7th edn. New York: Wiley. (1st edn, 1974.)

Denzin, N.K. (1968) 'The Self-Fulfilling Prophecy and the Patient–Therapist Interaction,' in S. Spitzer and N.K. Denzin (eds), *The Mental Patient: Studies in the Sociology of Deviance*. New York: McGraw-Hill. pp. 349–57.

Durkheim, É. (1951) *Suicide: A Study in Sociology*. New York: Free Press.

Egan, J. (1997) 'The Thin Red Line,' *The New York Times Magazine*, July 27. p. 20.

Ellis, A. (1962) *Reason and Emotion in Psychotherapy*. New York: Lyle Stuart.

Etkind, M. (1997) . . . *Or Not to Be: A Collection of Suicide Notes*. New York: Riverhead.

Foucault, M. (1965) *Madness and Civilization: A History of Insanity in the Age of Reason*. New York: Vintage.

Foucault, M. (1977) *Discipline and Punish*. New York: Vintage.

Foucault, M. (1980) *Power/Knowledge: Selected Interviews and Other Writings 1972–1977* (C. Gordon, ed.). New York: Pantheon.

Foucault, M. (1987) *Mental Illness and Psychology*. Berkeley: University of California Press. (First English translation published by Harper & Row, 1976.)

Freud, S. (1968) 'Mourning and Melancholia,' in W. Gaylin (ed.), *The Meaning of Despair*. New York: Science House. pp. 50–69.

Gaylin, W. (1968) 'The Meaning of Despair,' in W. Gaylin (ed.), *The Meaning of Despair*. New York: Science House. pp. 3–25.

Gergen, K.J. (1994) *Realities and Relationships: Soundings in Social Construction*. London and Cambridge, MA: Harvard University Press.

Giddens, A. (1990) *The Consequences of Modernity*. Stanford, CA: Stanford University Press.

Giddens A. (1991) *Modernity and Self-Identity: Self and Society in the Late Modern Age*. Stanford, CA: Stanford University Press.

Giddens, A. (1994) 'Living in a Post-Traditional Society,' in U. Beck, A. Giddens, and S. Lash, *Reflexive Modernization*. Stanford, CA: Stanford University Press. pp. 56–109.
Goffman, E. (1961) *Asylums: Essays on the Social Situation of Mental Patients and Other Inmates*. New York: Anchor.
Goffman, E. (1968) 'The Moral Career of the Mental Patient,' in S. Spitzer and N.K. Denzin (eds), *The Mental Patient: Studies in the Sociology of Deviance*. New York: McGraw-Hill. pp. 226–34.
Goldfried, M.R. and Davison, G.C. (1994) *Clinical Behavior Therapy*. Expanded edn. New York: Wiley-Interscience.
Jamison, K.R. (1995) *An Unquiet Mind: A Memoir of Moods and Madness*. New York: Vintage.
Karp, D.A. (1996) *Speaking of Sadness: Depression, Disconnection, and the Meanings of Illness*. Oxford and New York: Oxford University Press.
Keyes, C. (1985) 'The Interpretive Basis of Depression,' in A. Kleinman and B. Good (eds), *Culture and Depression*. Berkeley: University of California Press. pp. 153–74.
Klein, D.F. and Wender, P.H. (1993) *Understanding Depression*. Oxford and New York: Oxford University Press.
Kramer, P.D. (1993) *Listening to Prozac*. New York and London: Penguin.
Manning, M. (1995) *Undercurrents: A Therapist's Reckoning with Depression*. New York: HarperCollins.
Maris, R. (1997) 'Social Forces in Suicide: A Life Review, 1965–1995,' in R. Maris, M. Silverman, and S. Canetto (eds), *Review of Suicidology, 1997*. New York and London: Guilford Press. pp. 42–60.
May, R. (1983) *The Discovery of Being*. New York and London: W.W. Norton.
Miller, D.R. (1983) 'Self, Symptom, and Social Control,' in T. Sarbin and K. Scheibe (eds), *Studies in Social Identity*. New York: Praeger. pp. 319–38.
Parsons, T. (1951) *The Social System*. New York: Free Press.
Parsons, T. (1964) *Social Structure and Personality*. New York: Free Press.
Plummer, K. (1995) *Telling Sexual Stories: Power, Change, and Social Worlds*. London and New York: Routledge.
Radden, J. (1987) 'Melancholy and Melancholia,' in D. Levin (ed.), *Pathologies of the Modern Self*. New York: New York University Press. pp. 231–50.
Rose, N. (1990) *Governing the Soul: The Shaping of the Private Self*. London and New York: Routledge.
Sacco, W. and Beck, A. (1995) 'Cognitive Theory and Therapy,' in E.E. Beckham and W. Leber (eds), *Handbook of Depression*. 2nd edn. New York: Guilford Press. pp. 329–51.
Scheff, T. (1975) *Labeling Madness*. Englewood Cliffs, NJ: Prentice Hall.
Schneidman, E. (1997) 'The Suicidal Mind,' in R. Maris, M. Silverman, and S. Canetto (eds), *Review of Suicidology, 1997*. New York and London: Guilford Press. pp. 22–41.
Seligman, M.E.P. (1974) 'Depression and Learned Helplessness,' in R. Friedman and M. Katz (eds), *The Psychology of Depression: Contemporary Theory and Research*. Washington, DC: Winston-Wiley.
Siegler, M. and Osmond, H. (1974) *Models of Madness, Models of Medicine*. New York: Harper & Row.
Simon, W. (1996) *Postmodern Sexualities*. London and New York: Routledge.
Slater, L. (1996) *Welcome to My Country: A Therapist's Memoir of Madness*. New York: Anchor.
Smith, D. (1990) *The Conceptual Practice of Power: A Feminist Sociology of Knowledge*. Boston: Northeastern University Press.
Sontag, S. (1979) *Illness as Metaphor*. New York: Vintage.
Styron, W. (1990) *Darkness Visible: A Memoir of Madness*. New York: Randon House.
Udovitch, M. (1994) 'Endless Bummer,' *The Village Voice*, September 27.
Velting, D. and Gould, M. (1997) 'Suicide Contagion,' in R. Maris, M. Silverman, and S. Canetto (eds), *Review of Suicidology, 1997*. New York and London: Guilford Press. pp. 96–137.

Wiener, M. and Marcus, D. (1994) 'A Sociocultural Construction of "Depression",' in T. Sarbin and J. Kitsuse (eds), *Constructing the Social*. London and Thousand Oaks, CA: Sage. pp. 213–31.

Wurtzel, E. (1995) *Prozac Nation: Young and Depressed in America*. New York: Riverhead. (First published by Houghton Mifflin, 1994).

PART III PATHOLOGY AND SELFHOOD: NEW AND CONTESTED SUBJECTIVITIES

5

The Self: Transfiguration by Technology

Kenneth J. Gergen

> To know who you are is to be oriented in moral space, a space in which questions arise about what is good or bad, what is worth doing and what is not, what has meaning and importance for you and what is trivial and secondary.
>
> (Taylor, 1989)

The conception of persons as integral and internal selves serves a keystone function within the configuration of beliefs typically equated with cultural modernism. Modernist institutions, as nurtured within the Enlightenment, and fulgently flowering within the present century, are importantly premised on the assumption of persons as quintessentially interior, that is, imbued with an inner domain of selfhood – replete with rational capacities, observational sensitivity, emotional and motivational wellsprings, and the capacity for conscious choice. The fully developed interiority, as we have come to understand, should form a coherent and integrated whole, and should be capable of independent deliberation (autonomy) and self-knowledge (authenticity). It is this interior self that serves as the basis for valuing persons over mere material, and without which it would be difficult to speak of love, trust, or intimacy. Without this self, the concept of democracy would wither; so too would institutions of public education designed to equip the self for full participation in the democratic form of life.

Yet, as we become increasingly aware of the modernist self as culturally and historically situated – not simply a self-evident truth – so has a deep uneasiness emerged. This pervasive consciousness – often indexed as postmodern – has been most fully articulated within the scholarly sphere. An enormous literature from all sectors of the academic world now casts doubt on the believability of the modernist self. We learn of the death of the author as agent of his/her works, the interpellated and decentered subject, and the end of logocentrism (rational agency). We find the very conception of self to be a byproduct of power/knowledge relations, inseparable from language-games, ideology, mass media, and the moment-to-moment construction (and dissolution) within ongoing relationships. Increasingly, within this literature, the self loses its sense of substance; increasingly we find no 'there' there.

My primary aims in this essay are threefold. First, I wish to trace the origins of this intellectual sensibility to a societal base. This is to propose that the postmodern 'loss of self' is not an invention of a restless and inter-textually dependent band of intellectuals. As they would be forced to agree, they are not the original sources of this sensibility. Rather, I propose that such argument gains its force primarily because it speaks into a social context that is already prepared. They essentially give rich articulation to understandings already embedded within the less re/markable stices of everyday life. In particular, I wish to trace the diminishing significance of interior selves to the emergence of a range of twentieth-century technologies. My particular concern is with the accumulating *technologies of sociation*, from the telephone, automobile, mass transportation systems, and radio in the early part of the century, to the jet plane, television, internet, satellite transmission, fax, and cellular phone in the latter. These relatively low-cost technologies dramatically expand and intensify the domain of social conjunction. Whether we speak in terms of the 'information age,' the 'globalization process,' or a 'new world order,' we find that daily life is marked by a steady expansion in the range of opinions, values, perspectives, attitudes, images, personalities, and information to which we are exposed and in which we are engaged.[1]

It is my view that the technologically based transformation of this century – and surely deepening within the next – significantly undermines both the intelligibility and the lived experience of the modernist self. My second aim, however, is to undermine postmodernism's otherwise univocal text of the loss of the subject. I wish to argue in this instance that what we confront here is not so much a loss as it is a transfiguration – essentially a transformation in related conceptions, experiences, activities, and institutions. Technology does not enter a uniform culture with coherent traditions. Rather, as the variegated conventions of Western culture interact with technologies in multiplicitous ways, so emerges a range of complex configurations – one might say, sub-cultures of the self. Thus the loss of self literature should be viewed with caution, for the outcomes of our contemporary engagement with technology yield not a single result, but a variegated range of self-related outcomes[2]. Three such transfigurations will receive attention: *fractionated being*, *techno/communal identity*, and *specular solipsism*.

Finally, to place these arguments within a context of action, I will focus particularly on the implications for moral and political action. We have traditionally viewed the single individual as the atom of the moral society. Whether we speak in terms of psyche, soul, agency, rational deliberation, or conscious choice, we generally hold that moral action is derived from particular conditions of individual mind. Thus, philosophers seek to establish essential criteria for moral decision-making, religious institutions are concerned with states of individual conscience, courts of law inquire into the individual's capacity to know right from wrong, and parents are concerned with the moral education of their young. The general presumption is that the virtuous mind propels meritorious conduct, and that with sufficient numbers of individual's living moral lives, we achieve the good society. However, in the following we shall ask: with the transfiguration of the individual self, are we also witnessing the loss of the moral atom? Or more broadly, what are the moral and political consequences of the emerging ethos of postmodernism? As we shall find, a fourth order of transformation may be the optimal outcome for future well-being.

Technology and the Fractionated Being

As Walter Ong's (1982) classic exploration of oral and print cultures suggests, our conception of individual minds is vitally dependent on the technological ethos. The shift from an oral to a print culture, Ong proposed, significantly altered the common forms of thought. For example, in oral societies people were more likely to depend on recall, concrete as opposed to abstract categories, and redundancy as opposed to precision. Yet, there is an important sense in which this fascinating thesis is insufficiently realized. While Ong wished to locate forms of mental life within a cultural context, he had no access into mental conditions themselves. That is, the analysis may be viewed as a treatise not on mental conditions but on cultural constructions of the mind. It is not thought in itself that changed but our way of defining what it is to think. To extend the implications of Ong's analysis, we may ask whether the conception of mind as a critical focus of study – something we must know about – was not solidified by the expansion of printed media. In an oral society, where the determination of the real and the good grows from face-to-face negotiation, there is little reason to launch inquiry into the speaker's private meaning. Through words, facial expressions, gestures, physical context, and the constant adjustments to audience expression, meanings are made transparent. However, when print allows words to spring from the face-to-face relationship – when the discourse is insinuated into myriad contexts separated in time and space from its origins – then the hermeneutic problem becomes focal. To wonder and speculate about 'the mind behind the words' is to create the reality of this mind. To grant this mental condition the status of originary source of action is to solidify its importance and to aid the growth of those institutions now identified with cultural modernism.

Given the potential dependency of conceptions of self on technological conditions, let us consider our contemporary ethos. In particular, what is to be said about the increasing insinuation of the technologies of sociation into our lives and its implications for our beliefs in substantive interiors? In my view the transformation of the technological ethos slowly undermines the intelligibility of the integral self as an originary source of moral action. The reasons are many and cumulative; I limit discussion here to several concatenating tendencies.

Polyvocality

By dramatically expanding the range of information to which we are exposed, the range of persons with whom we have significant interchange, and the range of opinion available within multiple media sites, we become privy to and engaged within multiple realities. Or more simply, the comfort of parochial univocality is disturbed. From the spheres of national politics and economics to local concerns with education, environment, or mental health, we are confronted with a plethora of conflicting information and opinion. And so it is with matters of moral consequence. Whether it is a matter of Supreme Court nominees, abortion policies, or affirmative action, for example, one is deluged with conflicting moral standpoints. To the extent that these standpoints are intelligible, they also enter the compendium of resources available for the individual's own deliberations. In a Bakhtinian vein, the individual approaches a state of radical polyvocality.

If one does acquire an increasingly diverse vocabulary of deliberation, how is a satisfactory decision to be reached? The inward examination of consciousness yields not coherence but cacophony; there is not a 'still small voice of conscience' but a chorus of competing contenders. It is one's moral duty to pay taxes, for example, but also to provide for one's dependants, to keep for oneself the rewards of one's labor, and to withhold monies from unjust governmental policies; it is one's moral duty to give aid to starving Africans, but also to help the poor of one's own country, to prevent population growth, and to avoid meddling in the politics of otherwise sovereign nations. Where in the mix of myriad moralities is the certitude of coherent conscience?

If immersion in a panoply of intelligibilities leaves one's moral resources in a state of complex fragmentation, then in what degree are these resources guiding or directing? Or, more cogently for the present analysis, if 'inward looking' becomes increasingly less useful for matters of moral action, does the concern with 'my state of mind' not lose its urgency? The more compelling option is for the individual to turn outward to social context – to detect the ambient opinion, to negotiate, compromise, and improvise. And in this move from the private interior to the social sphere, the presumption of a private self as a source of moral direction is subverted. If negotiating the complexities of multiplicity becomes normalized, so does the conception of mind as moral touchstone grow pale.

Plasticity

As the technologies of sociation increase our immersion in information and evaluation, so do they expand the scope and complexity of our activities. We engage in a greater range of relationships distributed over numerous and variegated sites, from the face-to-face encounters in the neighborhood and workplace, to professional and recreational relationships that often span continents. Further, because of the rapid movement of information and opinion, the half-life of various products and policies is shortened, and the opportunities for novel departures expanded. The composition of the workplace is thus in continuous flux. The working person shifts jobs more frequently, often with an accompanying move to another location. In the early 1990s, one of three American workers had been with their employer for less than a year, and almost two out of three for less than five years.

As a result of these developments, the individual is challenged with an increasingly variegated array of behavioral demands. With each new performance site, new patterns of action may be required; dispositions, appetites, personae – all may be acquired and abandoned and reappropriated as conditions invite or demand. With movements through time and space, oppositional accents may often be fashioned: firm here and soft there, commanding and then obedient, sophisticated and then crude, righteous and immoral, conventional and rebellious. For many people such chameleon-like shifts are now unremarkable; they constitute the normal hurly-burly of daily life. At times the challenges may be enjoyed, even sought. It was only decades ago when David Riesman's celebrated book *The Lonely Crowd* (1953) championed the virtues of the inner-directed 'man,' and condemned the other-directed individual for lack of character, a person without a gyroscopic center of being. In the new techno-based ethos there is little need for the inner-directed, one-style-for-all individual. Such a person is narrow, parochial, inflexible. In the fast pace of the technological society, concern with the inner life is a luxury, if not a waste of time. We now celebrate protean being (see, e.g., Lifton, 1993).

Repetition

Let us consider a subtler mode of self-erosion, owing in this instance to the increasing inundation of images, stories, and information. Consider here those confirmatory moments of individual authorship, moments in which the sense of authentic action becomes palpably transparent. Given the Western tradition of individualism, these are typically moments in which we apprehend our actions as unique, in which we are not merely duplicating models, obeying orders, or following conventions. Rather, in the innovative act we locate a guarantee of self as originary source, a creative agent, an author of one's own morality. Yet, in a world in which the technologies facilitate an enormous sophistication in 'how it goes,' such moments become increasingly rare. How is it, for example, that a young couple, who for twenty years have been inundated by romance narratives – on television and radio, in film, in magazines and books – can utter a sweet word of endearment without a haunting sense of cliché? Or in Umberto Eco's terms, how can a man who loves a cultivated woman say to her, ' "I love you madly," when he knows that she knows (and that she knows that he knows) that these words have already been written by Barbara Cartland?' (1983: 67). In what sense can one stand out from the crowd in a singular display of moral fortitude, and not hear the voices of John Wayne, Gary Cooper, or Harrison Ford just over one's shoulder?

Should one attempt to secure confirmation of agency from a public action – political remonstrance, religious expression, musical performance, and the like – the problems of authenticity grow even more acute. First, the existing technologies do not allow us to escape the past. Rather, images of the past are stored, resurrected, and re-created as never before. In this sense, the leap from oral to print memory was only the beginning of a dramatic technological infusion of cultural memory. Thus, it becomes increasingly difficult to avoid observations of how any notable action is historically prepared (predetermined). To perform publicly is to incite incessant commentaries about how one, for example, 'has roots in Billy Sunday revivalism,' or 'draws inspiration from Jimi Hendrix.' Should the public demonstration gain media interest, there is also a slow conversion from the authentic to the instrumental. That is, what may have once seemed spontaneous is now converted to a performance 'for the media' and its public. Indulgence in political passion, for example, becomes muted by the attentions one must give to wardrobe, voice projection, and facial expression. One cannot simply 'play the music,' but must be concerned with hair styling, posture, and girth. In a world in which the local is rapidly transported to the global, the half-life of moral authenticity rapidly diminishes.

Transience

To the extent that one is surrounded by a cast of others who respond to one in a similar way, a sense of unified self may result. One may come to understand, for example, that he is the first son of an esteemed high school teacher and of a devoted mother, a star of the baseball team, and a devout Catholic. This sense of perdurable character also furnishes a standard against which the morality of one's acts can be judged. One can know that 'this just isn't me,' that 'if I did that I would feel insufferable guilt.' However, with the accumulating effects of the technologies of sociation, one now becomes transient, a nomad, or a 'homeless mind' (Berger et al., 1973). The continuous reminders of one's identity – of who one is and always has been – no longer prevail. The internal standard grows pallid, and in the end, one must imagine that it counts for little in the generation of moral action.

There is a more subtle effect of such techno-induced transience. It is not only a coherent community that lends itself to the sense of personal depth. It is also the availability of others who provide the time and attention necessary for a sense of an unfolding interior to emerge. The process of psychoanalysis is illustrative. As the analyst listens with hovering interest to the words of the analysand, and these words prompt questions of self-reflection, there is created for the analysand the sense of palpable interiority, the reality of a realm beyond the superficially given, or, in effect, a sense of individual depth. The process requires time and attention. And so it is in daily life; one acquires the sense of depth primarily when there is ample time for exploration, time for moving beyond instrumental calculations to matters of 'deeper desire,' forgotten fantasies, to 'what really counts.' Yet, it is precisely this kind of 'time off the merry-go-round' that is increasingly difficult to locate. In the techno-dominated world, one must keep moving; the network is vast, commitments are many, expectations are endless, opportunities abound, and time is a scarce commodity.

Each of these tendencies – toward polyvocality, plasticity, repetition, and transience – functions so as to undermine the longstanding presumption of an integral self, personal consciousness as an originary source, and interior character as a cornerstone of daily action. If this argument is viable, there is a sense in which the person ceases to function as a font of moral action. There is no depending on depth of character, moral commitment, or inner resources of the self for sustaining a livable social order. However, it is important to realize here that we are speaking less of a vanishing interior than a transfiguration in conception and realization. It is not so much an emptying of conscience – a sense of moral consciousness – as a fragmentation. That is, while substance, durability, depth, and unity may be shattered, what remains are loosely connected fragments, senses of self embedded within separated, shifting, and often isolated circumstances. As ventured above, we might characterize the postmodern being as radically polyvocal, capable of speaking many moral tongues, each within a particular circumstance of relationship.

Many would lament such a condition. Our technological condition may be giving rise to a generation of morally incoherent, superficial, and spineless individuals, a society that has no courage or direction but simply muddles through. Such a society, the critic might add, would be little able to resist the return of fascism and the further possibilities of genocide. Or as most ethical theorists would decry, these are the moral relativists for whom anything goes. However, there is a more promising view that may be taken of fragmented being. Its elaboration must be postponed while we consider two additional forms of self-transfiguration.

Techno/Communal Identity

Many analysts would welcome a decline in attempts to lodge moral action in independent minds. I am not speaking here simply of the conceptual and political limits inherent in individualism. Rather, for many there is a far superior candidate available for achieving a viable society, namely the community. As MacIntyre (1984) has proposed, to be an individual self – that is, one who is identified within a narrative of past, present, and future –

requires a community. Moral conduct, then, derives from being 'accountable for the actions and experiences which compose a narratable life within a community' (1984: 202). In this sense, the moral society is achieved by sustaining the best of a community's traditions. In effect, 'the virtues find their point and purpose not only in sustaining those relationships necessary if the varieties of goods internal to practices are to be achieved . . . but also in sustaining those traditions that provide both practices and individual lives with their necessary historical context' (MacIntyre, 1984: 207). On the more political level, this view resonates with the shift from a rights-based to a duty-based orientation to societal life, as advocated by the communitarian movement.

Let us consider, however, the possibility of communally based identities as moral resources in the age of technology. Again the way is paved for such reflection by an earlier classic, in this case Benedict Anderson's *Imagined Communities* (1983). As Anderson proposes, the emergence of nation states was importantly facilitated by the development of print technology – which not only succeeded in unifying and codifying particular languages, but could be used to generate a sense of common interest and common future. In effect, we cannot separate issues of social organization from the technological context. In light of the contemporary context, then, what are the potentials of communally based identity?

If by community we mean a group of people relating face-to-face across time in a geographically circumscribed habitat, there would appear little hope for success in the moral project. As I attempted to outline in *The Saturated Self* (1991), twentieth-century technologies of sociation are everywhere eroding the traditional face-to-face community as a generative matrix for self and its associated commitments. Mass transportation systems have separated home from workplace, and neighborhoods from commercial and entertainment centers; families are frequently scattered across continents; and, largely owing to career demands, the average American now moves households over eleven times during his or her life. Even when neighbors or families are within physical proximity, face-to-face interaction has dramatically diminished. Technologically mediated exchange – through telephone, television, radio, CD players, computers, and the like – is steadily reducing dependency on those in the immediate surrounds. In these and many other ways, both the geographically circumscribed neighborhood and the traditional family unit are losing their capacity to generate and sustain an accountable identity.[3] Thus, while possessing a certain theoretical appeal, the emerging technological ethos poses substantial and ever-intensifying limits to lodging morality in geographically based communities.

Yet, while technological developments are reducing the significance of face-to-face communities in building identity, we are also witnessing a striking increase in the number and importance of *technologically mediated communities*. These are communities whose participants rely largely on communication technologies for sustaining their realities, values, and agendas. Television evangelism is an obvious case in point. Several million Americans are linked primarily through mediated communication to a set of beliefs that affect decisions from local school systems across the country to the posture of national political parties (Hoover, 1988). Less obvious is the organization of over 20,000 non-governmental organizations (NGOs) operating internationally to combat starvation, overpopulation, AIDs, environmental erosion, and other threats to human well-being, and over a million such private organizations advancing human welfare within the United States. Such organizations are vitally dependent on existing communication technology for continuing sustenance.

Less public in their moral agenda are also the countless numbers of computer-mediated or virtual communities emerging over the past decade. The sense of community often created within such groups is illustrated in Howard Rheingold's *The Virtual Community*:

> Finding the WELL [a computer-mediated community] was like discovering a cozy little world . . . hidden within the walls of my house; an entire cast of characters welcomed me to the troupe with great merriment as soon as I found the secret door. . . . A full-scale subculture was growing on the other side of my telephone jack, and they invited me to help create something new. The virtual village of a few hundred people I stumbled upon in 1985 grew to eight thousand by 1993. (1994: 7)

The emergence of these communities is now facilitated by the World Wide Web, on which virtually any organization can mount a colorful invitation to participate. At present there are, for example, highly active web sites inviting participation in virtually all the major religious sects and political movements, and many of the minor ones as well – including Pantheism, Druidism, Wiccanism, and Discordianism in the case of religion, and the Zapatistas, KKK, and militia movements in the political sphere. The potential power of these forms of mediated engagement in people's lives is perhaps most dramatically evidenced in the ability of the techno-generated cult, Heaven's Gate, to precipitate mass suicide.

In terms of the self, we find here a fascinating transfiguration, one that echoes pre-modern and pre-individualistic times of tribalism, familialism, and feudalism. It is a transfiguration that may be fed as well by the above discussed loss in the sense of foundational self. In any case the movement here is away from the independent (or individuated) self of high modernism, and toward the identification of self with the group through which one is constituted: 'I am I by virtue of the We.' There is little here in the way of the individualist tension between self and group, no yearning to be free, or seeking of independent judgment. Without the group, one's identity wears thin. In the present era we are likely to speak of many such movements in terms of identity politics. Or to put it otherwise, identity politics represents the most visible manifestation of widespread movement toward techno/communal identity.

In terms of moral implications, one might applaud the emergence of this form of identity. For the religious and political enclaves, among many others, do furnish moral standpoints. Because they are lodged within orders of articulation, each contributes to the resources available in the society for moral deliberation. In effect, it may be argued, the technologies enable us to enter a new period of radical democracy, where all groups may put their claims forward for debate. Yet there is also a sense in which the very advantages of techno/communal identity simultaneously pose a societal danger. Rapidly, inexpensively, and with little regard to geographic distance, self-organizing enclaves are created and sustained. At the same time, however, the ease and efficacy of organization is accompanied by strong centripetal or inner-directed tendencies. With the flick of a switch the individual enters the totalizing reality of the group. In many cases, the techno-mediated relationships are complemented by printed media (newsletters, newspapers, magazines) and face-to-face meetings (religious services, conferences, demonstrations). Social and political agendas invite a life-style of full engagement. David Healy comments on the tendencies toward cyber-segmentation:

> At my university . . . the IRC [Internet Relay Chat] addicts are just as segregated as the occupants of my son's high school lunchroom. In our computer lab the Vietnamese students hang on out on Vietnamese channels, just as at Ben's school they all sit at their own tables at lunch. . . . On the net . . . talk tends not to get overheard; the boundaries separating virtual conversants are less substantial, but their effect is more dramatic. Two virtual places may be separated by only a keystroke, but their inhabitants will never meet. (1997: 62)

Accompanying such segmentation is a tendency for moral/political positions to become polarized and rigidified. The in-group reality becomes more convincing, the out-group is seen as more malevolent. When the moral/political agendas become manifest in public action, jarring conflict is almost inevitable. And it is thus that our technologies have hastened what James Davison Hunter (1991) has called 'the culture wars' – with myriad groups set against each other (as in pro-life vs pro-choice), against the dominant order, or both. We confront the bleak future of techno/communal identity when we find that a commitment to justice, dignity, freedom, and moral integrity can lead to the bombing of the Federal Building in Oklahoma City.

Mediated Being: The Emergence of Specular Solipsism

We find that while the technologies of sociation tend toward the dissolution of palpable selves, so do they lend themselves to the appropriation of self by techno-communities. While the flames of moral passion are thus inflamed, the societal results prove daunting. Yet there is a third transformation in selves emerging from the technological ethos, and while I must necessarily be speculative, it is a transformation that in certain respects is the most formidable of the three. It is Guy Debord's *The Society of the Spectacle* (1987) that sets the stage here. As Debord proposed, increasingly we live in a world of artificially created realities – media-generated spectacles – as opposed to relations in the raw. 'The concrete life of everyone has been degraded into a speculative universe' (1987: 12). For Debord, the condition of the spectacle largely results from capitalist economic domination, and is ultimately soporific in its effects. This line of argument also furnished a generative context for Baudrillard's (1983) subsequent writings on the way in which the use-value of signs (within concrete transactions) has been undermined by the information society, with signification now circulating, expanding, and accumulating autonomously. From this 'vast precession of simulacra,' proposes Baudrillard, there is no returning to 'the real.'

While for dramatic purposes Debord and Baudrillard perhaps overstate the case, they do draw our attention to a steadily increasing dependency – for information, entertainment, sexual stimulation, etc. – on artificial or mediated representations (on television, in film, newspapers, audio and video recordings, books, magazines, on computer screens, and so on). In the average household the television alone is in operation for over seven hours a day. At the same time, broad differences exist within the population in the extent of immersion in mediated worlds. For example, there are significant age and class differences in hours of television viewing. It follows, then, that certain sectors of the population may be singled out for the extremity of their engagement in technologically refracted realities. While there may be many routes toward mediated being, much demographic and sociological literature suggests that there will be a tendency for such persons to be unmarried, to live alone, to be unemployed or to have uninspiring jobs, to have few friends, and to be male. Moreover, this is a steadily growing population: over a fifth of the US population now lives alone. Or as one commentator has put it, 'this is a population in a permanent state of intermittent attachment. Inevitably, the silent apartment lies in wait' (Gornick, 1996; also see Sweet and Bumpass, 1987).

How are we to characterize the self that emerges from a life of mediated being? Here it is useful to return to the arguments for the communal lodgement of self and morality. There is now an extensive literature treating the ways in which selves are constructed through relationships. It is a literature with roots in the early theories of George Herbert Mead and Charles Horton Cooley, but which has multiplied many-fold under the current impetus of post-structuralist, discursive, or postmodern arguments. Embedded within this latter literature we find extensive accounts of the ways in which people are interpellated within structures of ideology (Althusser), defined within power/knowledge relationships (Foucault), positioned within conversations (Harré), called by others into accountability as persons (Shotter), and fashioned within the subtle stices of social interchange (Garfinkel). In effect, we find here a rich elaboration of the way in which individual selves emerge within the ongoing processes of relationship. Or to put it another way, persons as selves do not come together to create relationships; rather, processes of relationship are essential to creating the sense of a palpable self.

Informed by this view, the condition of mediated being essentially lacks the germinating processes necessary to becoming a self, a recognizable agent with distinctive features. There is little in the kind of significant interchange through which one is treated as this and not that, given value for particular features, identified as an integral identity, or held accountable for being a particular person. Rather, we might characterize the state as one of *specular solipsism*, a condition of relatively free-floating experience in which there is no important distinction to be made between an 'in here' and an 'out there,' in which all that might otherwise be characterized as the mediated world ('out there') serves as a mirror to experience. There is no self to be recognized in this mirror; one does not learn who one 'truly' is through interrogation of the image. Rather, the images function to define the parameters of the world. Nor is this the world that others are more accustomed to living in in an unmediated way; there are few 'reality' checks (in the form of reactions by significant others) against which the representations can be compared. For the specular solipsist there is an undifferentiated world-as-media. Maia Szalavitz's commentary on her virtual life is suggestive here:

> At times, I turn on the television and just leave it to chatter in the background, something that I'd never done previously. The voices of the programs soothe me. . . . I find myself sucked in by soap operas, or compulsively needing to keep up with the latest news and the weather. Dateline, Frontline, Nightline, CNN, New York 1, every possible angle of every story over and over and over, even when they are of no possible use to me. (1996: 50)

Specular solipsism is to be distinguished from the dissolution of self outlined in the earlier discussion. Such dissolution was in terms of singularity – a sense of an integral, isolable, 'oneness.' However, this transformation is accompanied by malleable movement across relationships, within which situated authenticity can be realized. The dissolving of a coherent and substantive self is indeed hastened by broadening of active, self-defining relationships. For the specular solipsist, there is not so much a multiplicity of conditional selves, but movement without articulation, without the punctuations, corrections, reminders, and reminiscences furnished by concrete interchange across time.

What is to be said of the moral consequences of mediated being? In a certain sense we find here the least promising trajectory. Where the loss of self lent itself to a situationist morality, and immersion in techno/communities was accompanied by strong but narrow commitments, for the specular solipsist there is little by way of an identifiable self or community in terms of which moral issues are significant. There is no identity to form the basis for moral accountability, no lodgement within a tradition to which one is held responsible. In this sense we might anticipate a high degree of moral lability – ranging from passive disengagement, to quixotic commitments, and ultimately to acts of morally reprehensibility (in the terms of the broader society). Szalavitz's comments on her on-line relations are again relevant:

> I find myself attacking everyone in sight. I am irritable, and easily angered. I find everyone on my mailing list insensitive, believing that they've forgotten that there are people actually reading their invective. I don't realize that I'm projecting until

> after I've been embarrassed by someone who politely points out that I've flamed her for agreeing with me. (1996: 50)

Also relevant to the case is the dramatic increase in the incidence of celebrity stalking. The very category of 'celebrity' is a byproduct of technology, as are the imaginary relationships they invite in the population more generally. What many find striking about these relationships is the incapacity of many of the affected to distinguish their fantasy from the accepted reality of the culture. Particularly when these individuals live within a technologically mediated world, they come to believe they occupy a special place in the life of the celebrity. They plan visits, marriages, and – out of jealous ire – assassinations.[4] It is now virtually essential that anyone reaching celebrity status employ a specialist at screening fan mail for signals of impending danger.

Fourth-Order Transfiguration: Relational Being

Although consistent with much social commentary on the erosion of moral value in contemporary society, the picture painted in the present essay is scarcely sanguine. I have argued that the intense infusion of technology into social life functions to dissolve the traditional reliance on integral selves as moral atoms, and simultaneously invites two dead-end trajectories: techno/communal identity and specular solipsism. The former conduces to a conflict of all against all and the latter to an aimless amoralism. Are these bleak conclusions, then, without respite? I don't think so. There is an opening within these lines of argument to a fourth order of transfiguration, a trajectory of substantial hope and possibly profound potential. To appreciate this possibility, let's return to the issue of moral relativism emerging in the earlier discussion of polyvocal identity. As I proposed, in the first order of transformation the self was not so much obliterated as splintered. The end result was a posture of situated morality. This conclusion then opened itself to the charge of jellyfish relativism. It is in revisiting this charge that we locate the possibility for a new and more promising formation of self.

The argument against moral relativism springs from its antithesis, namely a commitment to (or quest for) some form of foundational morality (e.g. absolutism). Yet how does this commitment play out in the daily life of the society? At least one manifestation is given in the forms of techno/communalism discussed above. Although there is certainly righteousness in abundance in these cases, the implications seemed disastrous. Writ large, they suggested that there is no form of intelligible action that is not morally credited from at least some standpoint. One person's 'rape' is another's 'right'; 'robbery' a 'revenge,' 'murder' a 'moral imperative,' and so on. And in the case of moral conflict – a battle of absolutes – we are truly speaking of incommensurable paradigms.[5] If this argument is viable, then we may revisit situated morality with a more appreciative eye. For in a positive sense there is something more societally integrative (or less annihilative) in such a posture. Let us press further the possibilities. Is there a sense in which situated morality could imply the emergence of a new conception of self, one not grounded in division, inferiority, and self as origin? I believe so. Specifically, if by 'situated' we mean action within a particular configuration of relationship – for example, when persons from differing matrices of tradition are conjoined – then situated morality essentially bespeaks of a relational self, a self that gains identity or self-hood within the process of relationship. This is not a variation on communally determined identity. Rather, it is out of relational process that concepts of both self and community emerge. The familiar binaries of self/other and individual/society are dissolved.

In certain respects the emerging technologies again create the space for a relational imaginary. Of particular relevance is the development of chat rooms, bulletin boards, list-serves, and other internet facilities that enable relationships to take place without specific lodgement in individual bodies (see especially Stone, 1995; Turkle, 1995). That is, identities can be put forward that may or may not be linked in any specific way to the concrete existence of the participants, and these cyber-identities may carry on active and engaging relationships. Most significant for our purposes, we have here relationships that proceed not on the basis of 'real selves' (originary minds within a body), but on the basis of self-positionings or discursive formations. (One 'real self' may indeed generate multiple self-positions, and in some cases even set these into animated public interchange.) Further, it is only the coordinated functioning of these discursive formations that enables community to be achieved. In effect, community has no geographic locus outside the web of discourse by which it is constituted. We approach here a process of pure relatedness, without self or community in the traditional sense.

The image of relationship without individual selves or community has other sources in the techno-sphere. For several decades the computer has served as one of the chief metaphors for human functioning. The cognitive revolution in psychology, along with the artificial intelligence movement and cognitive science, have derived much of their intelligibility from various equations of person and computer. However, with the dramatic expansion of the internet and World Wide Web, the computer gradually loses its rhetorical fascination. The internet is a domain that brings instantaneous relationship to an exponentially increasing population throughout the globe. It is a domain so vast and so powerful that it can scarcely be controlled by any nation state. It is legislated by no institution; it functions virtually outside the law. In this context the computer is merely a gateway into a domain without obvious end. The metaphor of the computer, limited and parochial, is gradually placed by the imaginary of the *network* – a world that stretches toward infinity.

In the same way that the technological ethos has stimulated scholarship on the loss of self, so does it now function as an impetus to scholarly inquiry into relationship. The waves of innovation are numerous, including many feminist writings,[6] the cultural psychology movement (see esp. Bruner,

1990), and the broad-scale revitalization of Vygotsky and Bakhtin. Most of this work, however, retains a strong footing within the modernist tradition of individual subjectivities. More radical departures grow from the soil of social constructionist inquiry, and its emphasis on the discursive creation of selves. From this perspective, the presumption of meaning as performatively and publicly generated among persons (as opposed to intersubjectively) simultaneously contributes to a conception of relational being and an appreciation of the primacy of relationship over persons and communities.[7]

The moral implications of these various conceptualizations of relational being are substantial. However, there is a pervasive sense among theorists in this realm that theoretical work is insufficient. If scholarly theory does not so much dictate actions within the culture as reflect and formalize its sensibilities, then moral transformation will not derive from theory alone. Attention thus turns to specific domains of practice. There is the further question of defining 'moral' action in a world of pluralist realities and relationships. Here the answers lean not toward predetermined utopias but to processes by which futures may less antagonistically emerge. As Caputo proposes, 'the violence is to stop the slippage, to erase the ambiguity . . . to put events out of play and into order, to hierarchize them, to erect principal authorities who would give authorized interpretations and definitive solutions and judgments' (1993: 222). Essentially, then, interest shifts to forms of practice that function at the boundaries of human connection, that can soften lines of conflict, blur meanings that are otherwise divisive, and locate common lines of agreement.[8] Such practices, it is reasoned, function to sustain or increase the possibilities for a mutually generative and ever-expanding domain of relationship. The alternative is mutual annihilation, which is the end of relationship altogether.

Notes

1. For an extended treatment of this process, see Gergen (1991).
2. For further analysis of the 'loss of self' in the information age, see Gergen (1996) and Turkle (1995).
3. For further elaboration of technology and the erosion of the traditional family, see Meyorowitz (1985).
4. In my own work with a security management agency, research on sixty stalkers who had attempted to, or succeeded in, inflicting injury (or death) on a celebrity revealed that in virtually every case the stalker lived alone and was heavily engaged in 'mediated' relationships.
5. For more on the problem of moral principles, see Caputo (1993).
6. Chief among these are the writings of the Stone Center at Wellesley College.
7. For further elaboration, see Gergen (1994).
8. For a summary of such practices, see Gergen (1999).

References

Anderson, B. (1983) *Imagined Communities*. London: Verso.
Baudrillard, J. (1983) *Simulations*. New York: Semiotext(e).

Berger, P., Berger, B., and Kellner, H. (1973) *The Homeless Mind*. New York: Vintage.
Bruner, J. (1990) *Actual Minds, Possible Worlds*. London and Cambridge, MA: Harvard University Press.
Caputo, J.D. (1993) *Against Ethics*. Bloomington: University of Indiana Press.
Debord, G. (1987) *Society of the Spectacle*. New York: Rebel Press.
Eco, U. (1983) *Postscript to the Name of the Rose*. San Diego, CA: Harcourt Brace Jovanovich.
Gergen, K.J. (1991) *The Saturated Self: Dilemmas of Identity in Contemporary Life*. New York: Basic Books.
Gergen, K.J. (1994) *Realities and Relationships: Soundings in Social Construction*. London and Cambridge, MA: Harvard University Press.
Gergen, K.J. (1996) 'Technology and the Self: From the Essential to the Sublime,' in D. Grodin and T. Lindlof (eds), *Constructing the Self in a Mediated World*. London and Thousand Oaks, CA: Sage. pp. 127–40.
Gergen, K.J. (1999) *An Invitation to Social Construction*. London and Thousand Oaks, CA: Sage.
Gornick, V. (1996) *Approaching Eye Level*. Boston: Beacon.
Healy, D. (1997) 'Cyberspace and Place,' in D. Porter (ed.), *Internet Culture*. New York: Routledge. pp. 55–68.
Hoover, S.M. (1988) *Mass Media Religion*. London and Thousand Oaks, CA: Sage.
Hunter, J.D. (1991) *Culture Wars: The Struggle to Define America*. New York: Basic Books.
Lifton, R.J. (1993) *The Protean Self*. New York: Basic Books.
MacIntyre, A. (1984) *After Virtue*. 2nd edn. Notre Dame, IN: University of Notre Dame Press.
Meyorowitz, J. (1985) *No Sense of Place: The Impact of Electronic Media on Social Behavior*. New York: Oxford University Press.
Ong, W.J. (1982) *Orality and Literacy*. London: Methuen.
Rheingold, H. (1994) *The Virtual Community*. London: Minerva.
Riesman, D. (1953) *The Lonely Crowd*. New Haven: Yale University Press.
Stone, A.R. (1995) *The War of Desire and Technology at the Close of the Mechanical Age*. Cambridge, MA: MIT Press.
Szalavitz, M. (1996) 'A Virtual Life,' *The New York Times Magazine*, July 28. p. 50.
Sweet, J.A. and Bumpass, L.L. (1987) *American Families and Households*. New York: Russell Sage Foundation.
Taylor, C. (1989) *Sources of the Self*. London and Cambridge, MA: Harvard University Press.
Turkle, S. (1995) *Life on the Screen: Identity in the Age of the Internet*. New York: Simon & Schuster.

6

Modernists at Heart? Postmodern Artistic 'Breakdowns' and the Question of Identity

Mark Freeman

'Illness' and 'Health'

There is perhaps no better introduction to (certain notable) 'dilemmas of identity in contemporary life' than Kenneth Gergen's well-known book *The Saturated Self*. As Gergen argues in the opening chapter of the book ('The Self Under Siege'), 'the process of social saturation is producing a profound change in our ways of understanding the self. . . . As we enter the postmodern era, all previous beliefs about the self are placed in jeopardy, and with them the patterns of action they sustain,' such that 'the very concept of personal essences is thrown into doubt. Selves as possessors of real and identifiable characteristics – such as rationality, emotion, inspiration, and will – are dismantled' (1991: 6–7). As Gergen explains, 'In the postmodern world we become increasingly aware' – or increasingly come to believe – 'that the objects about which we speak are not so much "in the world" as they are products of perspective . . . the outcome of our ways of conceptualizing them.' As a result, 'The center fails to hold' (1991: 7). Indeed, the supposition begins to emerge that there *is* no center, no foundational principle or set of principles that can be adduced to contain the infinite play of meaning.

There are, clearly, certain potential liabilities to such a state of affairs. Gergen notes, for instance, that individuals may possess 'a sense of coherent identity or self-sameness, only to find themselves suddenly propelled by alternative impulses. They seem securely to be one sort of person, but yet another comes bursting to the surface. . . . Such experiences with variation and self-contradiction may be viewed as preliminary effects of social saturation.' Moreover, they may entail what Gergen calls a 'populating' of the self, 'the acquisition of multiple and disparate potentials for being' – which, at an extreme, may assume the form of a 'virtual cacophony,' such that 'committed identity becomes an increasingly arduous achievement' (1991: 68–9). The task may be challenging indeed, particularly for those 'romantics' who prize coherence and integrity: 'How difficult for the romantic to keep firm grasp on the helm of an idealistic understanding when a chorus of internal voices sing the praises of realism, skepticism, hedonism, and nihilism' (1991: 73). Roland Barthes, a somewhat 'qualified' romantic, puts the matter well: 'How do you explain, how do you tolerate such contradictions?' he asks himself.

> Philosophically, it seems that you are a materialist (if the word doesn't sound too old-fashioned); ethically, you divide yourself; as for the body, you are a hedonist; as for violence, you would rather be something of a Buddhist! You want to have nothing to do with faith, yet you have a certain nostalgia for ritual, etc. You are a patchwork of reactions: is there anything *primary* in you? (1989: 143)

For Barthes, it would appear, the populated self exists irrespective of processes such as social saturation. Following Gergen, however, it may be the case that 'as social saturation adds incrementally to the population of the self, each impulse toward well-formed identity is cast into increasing doubt; each is found absurd, shallow, limited, or flawed by the onlooking audience of the interior' (1991: 73). From this perspective, social saturation thus potentiates and exacerbates a condition of identity that may already be present, transforming what might once have been mere inner dissension into full centrifugal dispersion.

Alongside the populating of the self, Gergen goes on to note, there emerges 'a new constellation of feelings or sensibilities, a new pattern of self-consciousness,' which he terms '*multiphrenia*, generally referring to the splitting of the individual into a multiplicity of self-investments' (1991: 73–4). Now, as Gergen is quick to add, 'It would be a mistake to view this multiphrenic condition as a form of illness, for it is often suffused with a sense of expansiveness and adventure' (1991: 73). As with the populating of the self, however, there is no denying that multiphrenia may present its own share of potential difficulties. It is a condition 'in which one swims in ever-shifting, concatenating, and contentious currents of being,' in which 'one bears the burden of an increasing array of oughts, of self-doubts and irrationalities' (1991: 80). It is therefore a precarious condition at the very least. But of course precarious conditions, depending on where they lead, can also be very positive. After the distress of dispersion wears off and the 'pastiche personality' takes over, 'the individual experiences a form of liberation from essence, and learns to derive joy from the many forms of self-expression now permitted.' As Gergen puts it:

> The pastiche personality is a social chameleon, constantly borrowing bits and pieces of identity from whatever sources are available and constructing them as useful or desirable in a given situation. If one's identity is properly managed, the rewards can be substantial – the devotion of one's intimates, happy children, professional success, the achievement of community goals, personal popularity, and so on. All are possible if one avoids looking back to locate a true and enduring self, and simply acts to full potential in the moment at hand. Simultaneously, the somber hues of multiphrenia – the sense of superficiality, the guilt at not measuring up to multiple criteria – give way to an optimistic sense of enormous possibility. The world of friendship and social efficacy is constantly expanding

> and the geographical world is simultaneously contracting. Life becomes a candy store for one's developing appetites. (1991: 150)

Quick! Let me in!

If all goes well, one finally arrives at what Gergen calls the 'relational self': 'as the distinction between the real and the contrived, style and substance, is eroded, the concept of the individual self ceases to be intelligible. At this point one is prepared for the new reality of relationship' (1991: 170; see also Gergen, 1994; Sampson, 1993). The near-illness of multiphrenia is replaced by a joyous romp through the candy store of the pastiche personality and, ultimately, the fulfilling and, by all indications, healthy world of relationship. Or so one hopes. Indeed, make no mistake about it: Gergen's entire framework in the book rests on hope as well as a kind of *faith* – that we're heading someplace good, that even amidst the confusion of contemporary life there are the seeds of better days.

I should qualify this interpretation by noting that, by and large, Gergen's aim in this book is neither to condemn nor to celebrate the emergence of postmodern discourse and its associated views of personal identity but simply to document it: we are in the midst of a cultural upheaval that is leading to entirely new and different ways of thinking about our selves and our world, and it behooves us to explicate its features. It does seem fair to say that he is inclined more toward celebration than condemnation, but he remains measured in his appraisal. 'What are we to conclude about our emerging condition?' he asks in the final chapter. 'I have pointed to numerous ways in which our traditions of understanding and action are being eroded'; there is no doubt, therefore, that he is fully aware of the possible liabilities of the worldview being explored. 'At the same time,' he goes on to say, 'I have been indulgent in my elaboration and reticent in my criticism of postmodern influences.' In other words, rather than succumbing to conservative or traditionalist lamentations about what has been lost, he has sought to raise the possibility that there is, again, a hopeful or even 'redemptive' moment to the upheaval at hand. The question, of course, is: 'Can we now press beyond this ambivalence, establish an evaluative posture, and clarify issues of significance? Of particular concern is the question of the future under postmodernism. If romanticist and modernist traditions are slipping away, is there a positive case to be made for the postmodern replacement?' (1991: 226). Will we move in the direction of illness or of health?

The Path to the Postmodern

What I wish to suggest in much of the remainder of the present essay is that, within the domain of contemporary art, there are important clues about how we might best answer the sorts of questions posed by Gergen. Or, to put the matter somewhat differently, what I wish to suggest is that, in a distinct sense, 'the future under postmodernism' has already arrived in the form of art's recent history. In order to explore this suggestion, a brief excursion into this history may be in order. As far back as 1913, when the famous French Dadaist Marcel Duchamp stunned the art world by displaying a number of commonplace objects – a bicycle wheel, a snow shovel, a gleaming white urinal – in the context of the museum, thereby transforming them into 'works of art,' there began to emerge the contours of many of the ideas Gergen and others have sought to address. In order for an object to be deemed art, Duchamp seemed to be saying, it needs to be seen in a particular way, placed in a particular context: an object needs to be seen *as* art for it to *be* art. As a variety of philosophers of art have argued since that time, there simply is no art without an interpretation on the part of some audience, virtual or actual, constituting it as such (e.g. Danto, 1981; Dickie, 1974; Goodman, 1976). This does not mean that the work of art is a mere nothing, a blank screen onto which the 'interpreter' is to project his or her own designs and desires. It means that in order to distinguish what is art from what is not art, one cannot rely on the (supposedly) self-evident properties of objects themselves, for there simply *are* none – at least not outside of some interpretive community able to see/construct things in a common way (see Fish, 1980).

The same may be said of artistic value. 'To hold that one kind of art must inevitably be superior to another kind,' Clement Greenberg has written, 'means to judge before experiencing; and the whole history of art is there to demonstrate the futility of rules of preference laid down beforehand: the impossibility, that is, of anticipating the outcome of aesthetic experience' (1961: 134). However good or bad we may feel, believe, or even *know* certain works of art to be at some specific moment in time, there remains the need to acknowledge that all of this certainty may in fact be swept away in the future, as different modes of life and different standards of appreciation come along and supplant current ones. Again, none of this is meant to imply that the value of a work of art is strictly arbitrary, a free-for-all, a matter of mob rule or the like – Greenberg, one of the foremost formalist art critics of our time, would certainly reject a wholesale relativism of this sort – but only that the ascription of value must be made contingent upon experience. In short, then, from the point of view offered by Duchamp and, later, by a good many philosophers, critics, and artists alike, there is neither 'art' nor artistic value outside of interpretation and experience. Furthermore, it follows that there is neither interpretation nor experience, however 'raw' experience may seem, outside of more or less specific norms or constructions. This is why what counts as art in one culture or one generation often becomes discounted in another, why what is considered good becomes considered bad, and so on.

As for how these ideas came to be played out in the recent history of art, the story is approximately as follows. What we find throughout much of this history is precisely the attempt to cast into question not only the presumption of a unitary art object possessing 'essential,' self-evident properties but also that of a unitary creative process. If there was any rule at all to be followed by many artists working during this period, it was to subvert, undermine, and 'deconstruct' all rules. Or, in a rather less extreme vein, the goal was to let artists and their works determine their *own* rules rather than having them follow those laid down ahead of time. In the late 1940s and throughout the 1950s, the art world saw, for instance, the emergence of the Abstract Expressionists, painters such as Jackson Pollock and Willem De Kooning, who, the story often went, plunged into the depths of their souls and, as some came to believe, seemed able to reveal a reality somehow 'truer' than the one ordinary perception allowed. Several of them were thus hailed by important critics as being the bearers of an entirely new way of thinking about art and creativity: rather than seeking to depict the outer world, an aim which remained at the forefront of artists' efforts even in such progressive movements as Cubism and Surrealism, the work of art came to be a world of its own, perhaps referring to little else than its own singular self. And even though there were many who rejected the view of the purely self-referential work, including a number of the Abstract Expressionists themselves, most agreed that something new and different was being inaugurated. Most centrally, the Abstract Expressionists seemed to embody a completely new brand of creative process and a new sense of what it might mean to be creative. Compared to the Impressionsts, say, or, again, even to the Cubists or the Surrealists, theirs was an art of spontaneity and freedom; with the abandonment of the attempt to depict the outer world, there was much more room to move. More to the point still, it might be said (somewhat crudely) that, whereas in times past the conception of the work customarily preceded its execution, for much of this new art the order had effectively been reversed: the artist, through the creative process itself, this frequently profound encounter with an indeterminate yet ever-congealing form coming into being, came to realize an idea or feeling or dimension of Being that had never been witnessed until this very act. In De Kooning's 'laboratory,' as Harold Rosenberg called it, for instance, 'the animated paint takes its form from the artist's personality, while the artist discovers the changing form of his personality in the physical potentialities of his medium' (1972: 61). For some of these artists, painting had become a kind of personal archeology, a process of simultaneously retrieving and constructing, via the directives of their work, lost, split-off, and unrealized dimensions of their selves: as they created paintings, paintings created them. Not surprisingly, there was often talk of the unconscious among some of the Abstract Expressionists, the artist being seen as a kind of medium through which those human depths unable to speak in ordinary language might have their say. Like free associations, bubbling up from the secret strata of the unconscious, the work of many of these artists came to be interpreted as highly revealing signs of their (frequently tormented) inner lives.

Given the thrust of Abstract Expressionism, it is all the more noteworthy that when we continue on into the 1960s and see the ascendancy of such movements as Pop Art and Conceptual Art, things change drastically yet again. In the wake of such revolutionary artists as Robert Rauschenberg and Jasper Johns, and taken up by the likes of Andy Warhol, Roy Lichtenstein, and others, there is all but an about-face. Gone, for many, is the passion (except, perhaps, as simulated), the intense personal encounter with the work that had been the hallmark of many of those in the previous generation. Gone are the attempts to reveal one's inner depths, to express that (supposedly) truer interior reality. In fact, a good portion of the art of the 1960s was seen as an art of 'impersonality and disengagement, an art of anonymity, where the artist stood aloof from his work, refusing commitment and presenting it as an object among other objects, more like a factory product than a personal document' (Osborne, 1979: 149). As Kostelanetz has added, 'Scarcely a work will reveal much that is personal about its individual creator, though a body of achievement might offer a few clues' (1980: 50). There was less reference to feeling and to the artist's psychological history than there was to earlier works of art and aesthetic premises. As Jameson puts the matter,

> Modernism was predicated on the achievement of some unique personal style that could be parlayed out to the subject of genius, the charismatic subject, or the supersubject, if you like. If that subject has disappeared, the styles linked to it are no longer possible. A certain form of depersonalization thus seems implicit in all of this. (1988: 21)

Alongside this dimension of depersonalization, much of the work done at this time was an art of surfaces, avowed as such by its creators, with 'depth' being seen by some not only as illusory, the product of an outdatedly romantic brand of humanism (we might think of the rise of structuralism and post-structuralism in this context), but a bit defensive: the positing of depth, personal and artistic alike, was perhaps best seen as a way of warding off the distinct possibility that there was not in reality much depth to be had. As far as many of these artists were concerned, the heroic individuality of the sort exemplified by the Abstract Expressionists, with their Hemingwayesque craving for life (and, for some, death), simply did not fit a culture inundated with boredom and with banal images from the media: the 'truth,' such as it is, lies on the surface of things, nowhere else. Jameson goes so far in this context as to write about the virtual disappearance of depth in much of postmodern art. 'I mean not only visual depth,' he explains, 'which was already happening in painting – but also interpretive depth, the idea that the object is fascinating because of the density of its secrets, which are then to be uncovered by interpretation. All this vanishes' (1988: 4). What happens, in turn, Jameson goes on to suggest, is that there emerges

> a transformation of the depth of psychological *affect*, in that a particular kind of phenomenological or emotional reaction to the world disappears. Symptomatic here is the changeover from anxiety – the dominant feeling or affect in modernism – to a different system in which schizophrenic or drug language gives the key notion. (1988: 4; see also Jameson, 1983; Sass, 1992)

Jameson is referring here

> to what the French have started to call *intensities* of highs and lows. These have nothing to do with 'feelings' that offer clues to meaning in the way anxiety did. Anxiety is a hermeneutic emotion, expressing an underlying nightmare state of the world; whereas highs and lows really don't imply anything about the world, because you can feel them on whatever occasion. (1988: 4–5)

For present purposes, let us simply note for the time being that accompanying the emergence of (certain variants of) postmodern art is an entirely new way of viewing not only identity but the very texture of lived experience and emotional life.

I need not take this excursion into art history much further. The point here is simply that over the course of a relatively brief span of time, the idea of art – and with it, the idea of the creative process as well as the creative person – underwent a massive change: alongside the 'desacralization' of the art object is the 'desanctification' of the artist him- or herself (Gottlieb, 1976), the much-touted creative process deconstructed in turn. Of course, it could be argued that an artist like Andy Warhol, with his somewhat tedious paintings of identical soup cans, for instance, or, later, certain postmodern feminist artists, weren't engaged in the creative process at all: there might be little in the way of discovery, whether of inner self or outer world, little in the way of personal expression, little in the way of deep meaning, and little in the way of a good many other qualities customarily associated with the idea of Art and what it means to create it. But it was precisely these customary associations that were being cast into question.

As Arthur Danto was to write back in 1989, reflecting on the recent past and gazing into the near future, 'No one, I think, feels in the art world today that our nineties are going to be gay or that the century before us will have the same thrilling artistic history many of us have lived through. No one really expects the twenty-first century to shoot out of the neck of the twentieth like a champagne cork!' (1997: 298). But perhaps the time had finally come, he goes on to suggest, when those sorts of hopes and dreams were beside the point. Among the many ideas gaining currency in the art world was the notion that 'the very idea of a masterpiece' – a sacred art object with a transcendent presence or essence – 'goes with a form of privilege and elitism that has the political consequence of excluding women and minority artists by imposing upon them an alien imperative – namely, to be a "great artist" – when this concept but exalts forms that define white male domination. Rather, in the name of a certain kind of liberation, one must,' from this perspective (not entirely Danto's own, it should be emphasized), 'shun the propensity to define art in terms of what one group of feminist aesthetic activists disparages as "genius-type objects." And "good aesthetics" may be part of the apparatus of privilege disguised as a standard of taste' (1997: 298). Much of postmodern art, Danto continues, might appropriately be called 'disturbatory' art. 'This is art that does not just have disturbing contents, for a lot of traditional male (if you insist) art and even some of its masterpieces are filled with disturbing content. . . . Disturbatory art is intended, rather, to modify, through experiencing it, the mentality of those who do experience it' (1997: 299), thereby jarring their preconceived and often reified ideas of the very categories at hand:

> The injunction is to sneer at genius, mock the masterpiece, giggle at aesthetic values – and to try to begin a new history, nonexploitative, in which art is put to some end more immediately human and important than to hang in the museum,

> ornament the brilliant collection, draw gasps in the dramatic auction space and be interred in the graphic tomb of the expensive art book and the real tomb of the Japanese bank vault. The charge is to end one form of history and to begin another one. (1997: 303)

As Crimp adds, postmodern art rids itself of the 'aura' of the art object, defined and constituted in terms of putatively essential qualities: 'The fiction of the creating subject gives way to the frank confiscation, quotation, excerptation, accumulation and repetition of already existing images. Notions of originality, authenticity and presence, essential to the ordered discourse of the museum, are undermined' (1983: 53).

What we find in the emergence of much of postmodern art, in short, is the replacement of that sort of 'ordered discourse' referred to by Crimp with an entirely different kind of discourse. As suggested earlier, this discourse is framed in fundamentally negative (which is not say pejorative) terms – depersonalization, desacralization, desanctification. That is, it is framed in terms of what art and artist are *not*. In addition, however, the discourse of postmodern art and postmodern thought more often has a decidedly positive spin, tied to such ideas as plurality, freedom, and play (see Freeman, 1990, 1994). The 'charge' to which Danto refers, above, is not only 'to end one form of history,' to negate, deconstruct, and dismantle, but 'to begin another one.' Acknowledging that there are many possible ways to do so, Lyotard's consideration of how we might distinguish modern from postmodern aesthetics may be helpful at this point:

> Here, then, lies the difference: modern aesthetics is an aesthetic of the sublime, though a nostalgic one. It allows the unpresentable to be put forward only as the missing contents; but the form, because of its recognizable consistency, continues to offer to the reader or viewer matter for solace and pleasure. Yet these sentiments do not constitute the real sublime sentiment, which is an intrinsic combination of pleasure and pain: the pleasure that reason should exceed all presentation, the pain that imagination or sensibility should not be equal to the concept. (1984: 81)

Abstract Expressionism, from this point of view, would fall squarely within the discourse of modern aesthetics; for even amidst the desire to move into the interior of the soul, into the heart's dark stirrings, there is often a sense of loss and impossibility, a sense that one is destined to fall short of being able to say everything that needs to be said. Modern discourse, therefore, whatever its apparent break from the past, remains tied to some form or other of the idea of 'totality' (see also Derrida, 1978, on the idea of 'totalization'), the idea that the world, including the world of the self, is *in principle* capable of being made known, unearthed, revealed. The problem is in the practice: luminously present and 'available' though the world may be, there is simply no way to quite get to it. So it was, perhaps, that so many of the Abstract Expressionists, among others, succumbed to profound feelings of despair and loss.

Postmodern discourse, on the other hand, seeks to move beyond this nostalgic and often self-destructive take on the world. The postmodern, Lyotard writes,

> would be that which, in the modern, puts forward the unpresentable in presentation itself; that which denies itself the solace of good forms, the consensus of a taste which would make it possible to share collectively the nostalgia for the unattainable; that which searches for new presentations not in order to enjoy them but in order to impart a stronger sense of the unpresentable. A postmodern artist or writer is in the position of a philosopher: the text he writes, the work he produces are not in principle governed by preestablished rules, and they cannot be judged according to a determining judgment, by applying familiar categories to the text or to the work. Those rules and categories are what the work of art itself is looking for. The artist and the writer, then, are working without rules in order to formulate the rules of what *will have been done*. Hence the fact that work and text have the character of an *event*; hence also, they always come too late for their author, or, what amounts to the same thing, their being put into work, their realization (*mise en oeuvre*) always begins too soon. *Post modern* would have to be understood according to the paradox of the future *(post)* anterior (*modo*). (1984: 81)

The bottom line for Lyotard is simply this:

> We have paid a high enough price for the nostalgia of the whole and the one, for the reconciliation of the concept and the sensible, of the transparent and the communicable experience. Under the general demand for slackening and for appeasement, we can hear the mutterings of the desire for a return of terror, for the realization of the fantasy to seize reality. The answer is: Let us wage a war on totality; let us be witnesses to the unpresentable; let us activate the differences and save the honor of the name. (1984: 81–2)

I have no wish whatsoever to be among the 'mutterers' in what follows. Nor do I wish to offer some sort of blanket indictment of postmodern art and postmodern thought. Having just recently visited the Robert Rauschenberg exhibit at the Guggenheim in New York only to be swept away by its incredible heterogeneity and otherness, it would simply be impertinent to launch into a diatribe against the movement as a whole. What I wish to do instead is pursue a relatively straightforward question. Following Lyotard and countless others, it seems fair to say that the *discourse* of postmodern aesthetics – and one might generalize here to include the discourse of postmodern renditions of identity as presented by theorists such as Gergen – is most promising; it would appear to herald a new dawn, as it were, taking us into 'new forms of serious games' (Gergen, 1991: 289) that those who are up to the challenge would surely want to play. The question is: How might we begin to understand the relationship between *discourse* and *experience*? Does the discourse 'deliver' in regard to the forms of experience it yields?

Postmodern Artistic 'Breakdowns'

I will not pretend to offer a simple answer to the questions just posed. What I will do instead, with the help of several case histories gathered in a study of aspiring painters and sculptors schooled in Chicago in the mid-1960s, is suggest that for a number of artists who have been part of the contemporary art scene, it has proved to be much easier to *think* postmodernism than it has been to *live* it. On the basis of what has been said thus far, it should be clear enough that at the level of discrete propositions, there is much in post-modern thinking, broadly conceived, that commands attention and belief. It is fairly clear, for instance, that works of art along with the artists who make them, far from being able wholly to escape the confines of the earthly world (as in Romanticism, say), are in fact bathed in 'constructions' of a wide variety of sorts. It is therefore difficult to imagine, *à la* modernist aesthetics, how one could ever encounter Reality or Being face to face – devoid of constructions, devoid of discourses; it would mean stepping out of language, out of culture.

Relatedly, it is on some level difficult to imagine that works of art could ever be about anything *but* these constructions and discourses and, of course, other works of art. In the end, how could they be? 'Indeed,' Gergen has suggested, 'with this shift from objects to objectifications, from reality to constructions of reality, we cross the threshold into a virtual vertigo of self-reflexive doubt. For the focus on how things get constructed is, after all, born of doubt – doubt of all authority and all claims to truth' (1991: 134). The main point here is simply that, at least for those whose business it is to ponder such things, it is extraordinarily difficult to avoid raising these sorts of doubtful suspicions at this particular moment in history: insofar as these suspicions are grounded in a pervasive and thoroughgoing skepticism and insofar as skepticism itself may itself be considered the premier 'religion' of postmodernity, it stands to reason that lots of artists have found themselves drawn in by its creeds.

It should also be emphasized that, in addition to making a great deal of sense to many artists, the postmodern moment has surely been liberating in some ways, and in that sense has in fact fulfilled a portion of its promise. There has been less of a burden, perhaps, for artists to hole themselves up in a garret in the hope of somehow breaking through to the 'really real' and less of a need to drink themselves into oblivion, Abstract Expressionist-style, on account of the felt impossibility of ever being able to say everything that needs to be said. With the 'really real' out the door, along with the angst that can emerge with the project of seeking to capture it in some total fashion, there would seem to be much more room to move. The much-discussed pluralism of the contemporary art world has also undoubtedly been liberating (see, e.g., Adams, 1978; Kostelanetz, 1980; Robins, 1984; Smagula, 1983). The greater the measure of doubt cast upon proclamations of what constitutes legitimate – not to mention good – art, the greater, it would seem, the measure of freedom for artists to go their own ways and to test the boundaries of art itself. But as the artists I shall be discussing here testify, in virtue of their each having suffered some form or other of postmodern 'breakdown' in the course of their pursuits, there had been some quite definite problems – or syndromes, as I'll call them here – along the way (see Foster, 1985; Freeman, 1993; Gablik, 1984).

Several qualifications are in order. The first is that some of the artists who were studied for the present project suffered no breakdowns whatsoever. However, there were very few who felt that their lives in the contemporary art world had become a candy store, and I would even go so far as to say that breakdowns, of some sort, were more the rule than the exception. As Danto (1997) has argued, borrowing the language of the critic Elizabeth Frank, significant portions of the 1970s and 1980s especially were simply 'bad aesthetic times' and thus difficult ones within which to thrive. Nevertheless, I emphatically do not wish to claim that artistic breakdowns were in any way necessary or inevitable. They were only *possible*, quite possible, in fact. It is this very possibility that I shall be exploring. The second and related qualification is that the syndromes I am about to discuss in no way exhaust the vast array of phenomena that might be considered in this context; they are simply notable examples of such phenomena that may serve to point us in the direction of some important issues. The third qualification concerns the concept of 'breakdown.' In one sense, it would surely be stretching things a bit to claim that breakdowns of the sort we are about to consider are at all comparable to those that land people in psychiatric institutions and the like. Along these lines, one might therefore be tempted to say that, in speaking of artistic breakdowns, I am only doing so metaphorically – as if they were like 'real' ones. But of course these 'real' ones to which they may be compared are on some level metaphorical constructions in their own right; they involve the constitution of a set of behavioral phenomena as phenomena of a quite specific sort, 'pathological' in their essence. The comparison between the two 'breakdowns' at hand are, therefore, to be understood as being not between a 'metaphorical' one and a 'real' one, but rather between two distinct modes of metaphorization, the one referring to artistic 'illness' and other to mental 'illness.'

Thus, even though I shall refrain from claiming that the two are strictly comparable, in the sense of there being a relationship of identity between them, I am quite comfortable claiming that there is a substantive *affinity* between them. As Sass argues in his important book *Madness and Modernism*, 'Many modernist artists, and particularly postmodernists, might be viewed as expressing – and many schizoid and schizophrenic individuals as living out – something akin to the philosophical aberrations or distortions that emerge when one loses contact with the prereflective world that is the normal dwelling place of human existence' (1992: 347). With this in mind, it could very well be that artistic breakdowns and those more widely discussed breakdowns we usually associate with the process of going mad have a good deal in common.

Self-Enclosure

The first form of artistic breakdown to be considered may be referred to as 'self-enclosure,' and it had mainly to do with the relative absence of a shared symbolic vocabulary with which artists might create. Along with several others in the group, the man I am to discuss, while in art school, had been a member of a tightly knit group of Chicago artists, with their own unique brand of work. They were successful as well, gaining acclaim not only in their hometown but elsewhere. In fact, this group had gained more recognition for their work early in their careers than many other artists had ever gained. Nevertheless, there were problems as well. There was the problem, for instance, of 'being so solidified an image' in the eyes of others. As the man explains, the art became 'too openly, readily identifiable in terms of a type of work.' In a sense, he said, he felt that he had been 'typecast' back then and that, consequently, there had been too great a loss of his own identity, as an artist and as a person. He also came to feel that 'as you progress in terms of working in the world of art or working in the world of *careers* in art, there is a certain sense of professionalism, even a kind of boredom. . . . You can get wrapped up in the methodologies,' he explained. 'I was constantly getting wrapped up in an internalized process which really is a kind of interiorized game that has no external rules,' the result being that he felt that he'd cut himself off from the world, that he'd become secluded in what amounted to a self-defining, autistic mode of activity that ultimately had no rationale other than that which had been fashioned out of the esoteric demands of the art world. 'It's like consumer goods in a way,' he went on to say;

> it's a marketable kind of commodity, with its own rules and its own little genres of doing things. . . . You're kind of like a little self-employed businessman or something; you worry about all the things in the world and all the things that surround you; you become almost a hermit unto yourself, tremendously self-absorbed – the fact that you just sit there in front of a canvas, trying to figure out what will work.

Part of the problem, he went on to explain, was that he had expected so much from art; like a lot of others, he had thought of painting 'as almost this sacred bond to the medium,' as a sphere of activity that moved beyond 'all the norm and logic rules,' as he put it, that exploded the boundaries of socially constructed and socially ratified taste. But it really wasn't like this at all. Ironically enough, it was precisely the alleged *impossibility* of exploding these boundaries that had come to occupy center-stage in a significant sector of the art world. On some level, he understood this; if there was anything that postmodern art had taught him, it was that art objects always existed within a highly circumscribed region of artistic discourses and conventions. The problem, however, was that many of the discourses and conventions these people often found themselves following, rather than being experienced as integral parts of a valid tradition, were instead experienced as self-validating and essentially arbitrary, bearing little identifiable relationship to anything outside themselves. In the end, he simply couldn't endure the 'isolating impact' his work had upon him.

As for the art world, he couldn't find much worth in it, either. It was a terribly insecure world, he said, 'peopled by people who have actually built up these mechanisms to defend themselves and their friends.' He couldn't respect most of them, he admitted, and he felt that the entire market situation was 'all out of kilter,' that it had become 'inflated' and 'magnified' in recent years, to the extent that it had come to appear bigger than life. Appearances aside, however, it was actually 'a very small kind of world,' in which one could reach a point of being 'too ornamental to function.' The New York art scene, he said, was like Malibu, where people would drive by the homes of the stars. All of this had added to his profound sense of self-enclosure and, finally, his decision to stop painting altogether. At various times, he said, he had 'felt a certain repugnance about it actually' and believed that he 'really wouldn't ever consider painting again.' The ultimate reasons were difficult to discern: 'I don't know whether it was a decision on my part to do other things or whether it was a decision to stop painting or whether it was a decision to stop isolating myself.' It didn't much matter; the entire rationale behind the activity of painting had broken down.

As for whether he would ever return, he had actually been thinking a lot about that recently, he told me. And interestingly enough, the kinds of paintings he had been thinking about were not unlike those he did many years ago, when he was a first-year student at art school: he described them as trying to picture a

> shimmering fantasy miracle state . . . trying to picture something that had this state in it; that in the actual physical objects, what was there was just a kind of almost simple and objective, kind of dumb in some ways, but that somehow the magic of it – or the relationship of it, the placing of all these things in it – had a kind of transcendence.

They were paintings, he felt, that would be able to step out of all of those 'norm and logic rules' referred to earlier, that would move beyond the paralysis of hyper-reflexivity, that would express, through their simplicity and dumbness, the wonder of there being anything at all: they were paintings that sought precisely to explode his own sense of self-enclosure. It is of course no easy task to discern how such 'modernist' desires emerge. It could simply be that old habits die hard, and that the face-to-face encounter with the arbitrariness of the sign – not to mention the arbitrariness of the *world* – sometimes sends people reeling backward, to the old ways, when reality seemed firm, secure, and good. There are of course other interpretive possibilities as well, which we will turn to shortly.

Dissimulation

The second artist we will consider is renowned within the New York art world (see Freeman, 1994, for an extended treatment). His work has been described by one critic as looking like 'flimsy approximations of oil paintings. . . . Their surface,' he writes, 'mimics and mocks a "rich surface",' the work overall being fundamentally about 'kinds of fakeness, of simulation.' In his work, this critic continues, 'one sees American art of the past twenty-five years as an ongoing tale about irony and fakery, about feeding off popular art, about the worship of formalism and craft.' For another critic, this man's painting encompassed 'an expansive contradiction, straddling that deep dichotomy between the woolly, uncivilized imagination that we associate with his hometown of Chicago and the theorizing, formalist sensibility associated with New York.' Not only has he 'never resolved that contradiction into an art of seamlessly unified wholeness,' but he has 'thrived' on it, 'gathering out of it an exuberantly impure art that indiscriminately gathers together the form and the theory of modernism with that which the modern traditionally abhors.' His latest work, this critic adds, 'offers a combination of arrestingly perverse technique and highly abstracted, vacantly illustrative and vaguely comic imagery.' It was nothing short of an 'intricate parody of modernist reflexivity,' the work's 'real center of gravity' being 'the absurd process of painting.' On the face of it, therefore, this man was the postmodern painter *par excellence*, engaged in a kind of playful romp through and beyond the dark sobriety of modernism, with its seemingly incessant yearning for coherence, wholeness, and depth. Many 'unlikely elements' went into his work, this artist acknowledged, the images employed being essentially arbitrary. There was no great mystery about his 'creative process' either, he told me. 'This is not Versace. . . . This is Robert Hall' (a popular New York clothier): 'It's on the racks . . . small, medium, and large. These are made to order.'

He wasn't entirely comfortable with his situation, however, success and all. 'I once had a notion,' he said, 'I wanted to do a painting of myself where I'd put the paint on the bathroom scale for structure, and then I'd paint on it until it weighed as much as I did; and then [I would] be stuck with this damn thing until the day I died.' The only dilemma, then, would be 'either painting it heavier or reducing it somehow.' There would be 'a lifelong commitment to a single problem, where it's you but not you, where all of those things are in balance.' This project would allow for some measure of continuity, and it would serve as a secure starting point for making artistic decisions. What's more, he would be able to reveal who he was, but without really disclosing anything personal at all. But the whole thing was far too simple a solution to the problems he faced as an artist.

There was another painting he spoke of, a real one that he had completed back in the late 1960s. It was a painting that had within it a multiplicity of different styles, 'like a Sears catalogue,' as he put it, from which he could draw ideas for his work, perhaps forever. But this too was 'an existential problem that failed.' This was because 'the notion of painting every day a different style is ultimately as confining as trying to develop one style: because the limitation is you. So the only way you could beat the problem is you become a stylistic entrepreneur. And the only way to create that is to hire people to paint for you, thus becoming, in a sense, a patron of your own art.' This idea interested him, he admitted. But he also acknowledged that ideas like these, when pushed too hard, could lead toward too 'nihilistic' an attitude. His dilemma was a painful and difficult one; there was a tendency on his part to go back and forth between contradictory beliefs. Philosophically speaking, it was easy enough to conclude that the world was meaningless; and sometimes, this sort of conclusion suited him just fine. More often than not, though, it seemed to bother him; there was something about it that was not only uncomfortable but, in a way, dishonest. Like a number of others, in any case, he often found himself suspended in a kind of in-between artistic space, 'balancing the tightrope between non-objective art, conceptual art, and figuration.' They were 'like the Walendas, all on this thing.' It was dizzying and dangerous.

'I sometimes think,' he said, 'that with the death of modernism, in a sense what I'm doing is *performing* the notion of painting, that all of this is a highly realistic theater that comes with real painting and real pleasure. . . . But possibly that's what some of us are doing: talking about the end and not the beginning of an art form.' There were lots of artists, he went on to say, who 'never learn anything from the paint because they're so involved with a didactic idea about history or philosophy.' The problem, however, was that without this felt sense of what paint could do, without attention to what he called the 'skin' of the work, the 'magic' that paintings could sometimes embody couldn't be 'released.' He spoke about Magritte and Rousseau in this context. Some of their paintings were 'very intense abstract realities' that were able to present themselves 'in an existential sense of, like, a *thing*.' He felt that he, unlike many others, recognized 'the importance of trying to control the paint and understand what it does.' But there wasn't much consolation in this. Maybe, in fact, he mused, 'It's that artists can only make these . . . fake careers, that painting is so bankrupt that your whole career becomes an intellectual construction. It's such an unmeaningful art in this century,' he felt, that maybe the only thing people like himself were really doing was 'constructing a life that has documentation.' There was so much uncertainty about the validity of contemporary art, he went on to explain, that one couldn't help but raise suspicions of this sort. Again, philosophically speaking, there was no reason to lament this situation: a good deal of contemporary art was precisely *about* this uncertainty; it sought to cast into question its own validity and it avowed its own movement toward theater, toward simulation. But at the very same time that he could affirm these ideas philosophically, he couldn't shake the idea that there was something more to the world – and to art – than what they suggested. He recalled at one point in the interview with him a painting he had done some years ago. It was a giant painting of dinosaurs, elegant and colorful, living in the scene of a time 'before man existed: almost a perfect world,' as he described it. The painting 'rejoiced in its big, dumb shapes' – the language of 'visual stupidity,' he called it, but 'elegant . . . and beautiful.' The problem was that it was too late in the game to have this sort of connection to his art; he'd simply come too far. His voice seemed to be cracking as he spoke.

In a distinct sense, this man was in the middle of a breakdown of sorts at the time we spoke; it was tough for him to comprehend how he'd come to be doing the sort of work he had. In lighter moments, he believed that it had a rationale, a reason for being, and critics helped to confirm this. But other times he couldn't help but feel that there was something about his work – and much of his friends' work – that was, to use his own word, 'bankrupt': an art of simulation that bore within it a painful element of *dis*simulation. It had become poisoned and compromised through its complicity with an anti-aesthetic ideology that, ultimately, he felt was false and entirely too cynical. Unfortunately, it seemed that there was no turning back.

Derealization

At one point in his career the artist we will consider next had also come to find himself preoccupied with a number of perplexing philosophical ideas, concerning whether we saw the world for what it was or merely projected onto it; concerning the artificiality of existence; concerning, as he put it, the 'unreality of reality' and in turn the 'reality of unreality.' The world had actually opened up for him at this point in an interesting and compelling way: the conventions that were inherent in painting, he had realized, were part and parcel of the conventions inherent in the world. For some time, everything for him had been bathed in a kind of luminous duplicity. As for his own work, it had appeared to him that a terrific burden was in the process of being lifted. The task of linking up what was on the canvas to what was in the world had been obviated; the 'text' of his painting was merely a link in an infinite chain of other texts, none of which were to be given any privileged place in regard to the 'real.' He could therefore rest content within the confines of the canvas; he would paint fictions, which needn't aspire to the status of being windows on the world; they were their own realities, neither more nor less than any others.

Liberating though this entire set of realizations had been for this man, he eventually came not only to question them but to *hate* them; he wanted to 'just get the message across,' like he used to. In certain important respects, his problem was not unlike the previous man's. Although he wasn't a realist philosophically, he still was experientially. Despite having spent a good many years pursuing it, he found that he just wasn't into 'art about art,' like so many others were. There were too many 'removals,' he had come to feel; the sources had to come from somewhere else. In part, his problem was one of self-enclosure: by virtue of his having succumbed for some years to creating art about art, such that he became locked within the confines of his own constructions, he'd come to feel that everything had become too insular and self-perpetuating. There was too much art, he said, that was just a 'high-priced form of autograph collecting,' devoid of emotion and spirit. In addition, there was the problem of dissimulation; there was somehow something false about the work he had been doing, something that didn't quite square with how he felt about the world, at least occasionally. The main problem, though, went beyond both of these syndromes. Most significant was this man's inability, despite his having cast into question the very existence of reality, to rid himself of the belief that it was somehow possible – and maybe even necessary – to deal with it in some way in his art. What had happened, he eventually came to believe, was that in concentrating his attention so thoroughly on the ostensibly fictive dimension of his art, in severing its possible ties to the real, it had become *derealized*, as had he; there was a sense in which he himself, as an expressive, feeling human subject, dwelling in what for the most part seemed to be a quite real world, had been effaced. And while there was still something interesting and compelling about the idea of the unreality of reality and so forth, he couldn't quite bring himself to live in the land of unreality itself. He *didn't* live there; and it became strange and alienating to carry out his work as if he did.

So it was that he eventually decided to shelve this way of working. He would do something simple and strong, something that would 'knock 'em dead,' so 'they'd run into the streets, bleed from their ears. . . . Close the lines in case there's a riot!' someone would have to shout. He would continue to make use of strange, artificial images, he went on to say, so it wasn't as if he would completely leave behind some of the concerns he had sought to address earlier. But his work would become a kind of 'parade,' in which these images would serve to mirror the multiplicity of existence itself. The entire change had to do with 'a longing for absolute reality or something.' It also had to do with his desire to speak to people, to *give* them something: 'If somebody's interested in patterns, I've got patterns. If somebody's interested in color, I've got color. Whatever.'

But what exactly was he to do with his earlier philosophical convictions about the constructedness of reality? If everything that could be experienced, in art and elsewhere, was bathed in constructions, as it seemed to be, wasn't his own 'longing for absolute reality' merely nostalgic, a sign of his weakness in the face of the truth? Perhaps; there was no way of knowing for sure. And finally, it didn't much matter: he had decided that he was willing to suffer the philosophical culpability involved. The way he had been working had made him sad, he said at one point; it made him feel that something – something eminently real – had been lost. He certainly wasn't in a position of identifying what this lost something was, of course, for it would entail positing just that sort of 'presence' that he'd earlier learned to reject. Hence the 'or something' part of his longing for the absolute. Most importantly, though, his newer work lifted him out of his sadness. Some of his recent paintings were like 'fever dreams.' There would be skating, for instance, on smooth, glittering ice through debris and junk. The sublime and the banal would work together; there would be something like beauty even amidst the cheapness and artificiality of things. This, he felt, was what the world really was.

Mutism

The final syndrome I shall discuss might be appropriately called 'reduction to the point of no return.' It might also be called 'privatization.' But for simplicity's sake I will simply refer to it as 'mutism.' Not unlike the others from whom we have heard, the woman I shall consider had become immersed in a world of ideas that had become terrifically compelling to her. As formative as her schooling in Chicago had been and as successful as she had become, she had found herself questioning her work. At one point, in fact, she said, 'I began working against everything I learned in school.'

Having rejected the somewhat boisterous imagistic art she'd done earlier, she became more and more interested in how paintings were constructed, how colors on a canvas, along with the canvas itself, came to *mean*, came to possess a specific discursive power. As a result, her work got more and more formal and 'reductive.' She described this entire process as one of 'elimination,' by which she meant that she would continue to remove from her work everything that was unnecessary until finally she would be able to determine exactly what it was that paintings required in order to exist, to be constituted as art. What wound up happening, however, was that her work became so reductive, so thoroughly purged of what could arguably be deemed inessentials, that it reached a point of no return. The conclusion was straightforward enough: *nothing* was essential, she realized; there *was* no foundation or ground for a painting's existence; not unlike what Gergen had to say earlier regarding the loss of the self's 'center,' there was no principle or set of principles that could be brought to bear on the issues at hand that would lead her toward art's alleged intrinsic and necessary qualities. Indeed, strictly speaking – and she took this very seriously – there was no reason to do *anything*, not for her and not for anyone else. If she kept moving in this eliminative direction, therefore, there would soon be nothing left at all. She had deconstructed her art and, in the process, her own existence as an artist. Hers was a full-blown artistic breakdown. In its wake, there was silence. She had been rendered mute.

But there was also confusion. Years ago, she had been passionate about painting; it had been her whole world. Was all that passion simply illusory, the product of cultural myths regarding the enraptured engagement of the artist, aswirl in paint, day and night, as if nothing else mattered? Or was it real? Clearly, there was no possible way of knowing. How could one distinguish between what was illusory and what was real anyway? What it came down to, finally, was that she had to make a decision – about whether there really was enough in painting, in the *experience* of painting, that could sustain her. She had to make a wager, one might say, about whether she truly loved it, about whether there was any justifiable reason to go on. For all of the profound existential puzzlement these sorts of questions entailed, the answers, she found, turned out to be rather simple. She was an artist, and would need to figure out some way of reconnecting herself to the potential fullness of art for her future to be viable. 'It became a process,' she explained, 'of accepting the tradition of painting and introducing additive thinking.' The first of these works, she told me, 'looked almost as reductive as the work which preceded it.' At a manifest level, in other words, it was difficult to discern the revolution she had undergone. But 'there was a different construct underlying it,' a different orientation to what it was. Much of her earlier work had been about perceptual 'issues'; they were paintings that 'the eye scanned in a certain way.' But there had been something 'manipulative' about them, she had come to feel. More generally, she had come to find herself less and less interested in playing out 'issues' of any sort in her work. At one time, they were interesting and important. But now, she said, 'I just don't care about those issues any more.' Her work would become 'operatic'; it would be 'inclusive of everything I know that seems appropriate for that painting.' Rather than being subservient to some art world issue, it would be 'more or less its own entity.' What she cared about, finally, was painting: not ideas about the thing, as a Wallace Stevens poem puts it, but the thing itself, its existence, its presence. It was true: there was no reason to do anything at all. But nor was there any reason to do nothing, to be mute. She wanted to speak. 'I want to do a really good painting,' she said.

One of the things this woman had learned through her own breakdown and subsequent 'recovery' was that she was 'still a romantic' and that she wanted her work to be expressive in some fashion. Even during that 'tight, tough analytical period' when she had sought to reduce her paintings to their barest essentials, the desire to express had been there. In her 'hearts of hearts,' she confessed at one point, she was most comfortable with work by artists like the Abstract Expressionists, modernist angst and all; at least they were expressively engaged with what they were doing. She was not especially interested in 'that form of male heroic' which frequently accompanied their work, she was quick to add; there was no denying that they could be self-indulgent as well as self-destructive. But there was a great deal to be said, she believed, about their passion and commitment, their refusal to efface their own subjectivity in the name of an idea.

This woman was well aware that some of the issues that had once preoccupied her would surface every now and then and render her suspicious and skeptical once more. 'Doubt,' she said, 'is simply a part of it on one level'; it was an intrinsic facet of the twentieth-century condition. Not only were there no set rules that could ever justify a painting's existence, there was no way of ever knowing, definitively, whether a given work was any good or not; the criteria were just too ambiguous and ephemeral. The task, therefore, as she saw it, was 'to always measure your feeling against what you really do in the world,' however difficult this may be. Given the particular climate in which we live, she acknowledged, 'It's very easy to give more credibility to doubt than one ought to.' Indeed, the only thing that really saved her from becoming consumed by doubt was the 'connection that periodically gets made between the material, the person doing it, and the thing being done – where it all fuses.' What was required, in short, was a kind of faith, one that could allow her to carry on with some measure of conviction that what she was doing was worthwhile.

The Question of Identity

It may be worth noting that each of the four artists discussed not only suffered a 'breakdown' of one sort or another; they either recollected better days, when their art felt more connected and real (the first two artists), or actually 'recovered' by going on to do work that was closer to their 'hearts.'

To put the matter somewhat differently, for each of these artists there was a marked tension between a postmodernist orientation to their art, which they generally seemed ready to accept philosophically, and a modernist orientation to their art, which generally seemed more consonant with their experiential worlds. Admittedly, these artists' brief stories were selected for inclusion here because of this tension, and there are no doubt plenty of artists whose own tension is either much less severe or, perhaps, non-existent. That said, the task remains of making sense of these artists' stories. What has been learned from these artists?

One possible answer, of course, is nothing whatsoever. These artists, one might argue, are in varying degrees simply anxious and fearful, weak and defensive; they're retreating from the challenges of postmodernity because they can't stand the heat. There is surely some compelling evidence for this interpretation; for even though each and every one of them seemed to 'know' that postmodern thought was the way to go, they couldn't quite follow the directives of their own knowledge. They retreated, this argument might continue, to 'feeling,' 'belief,' even 'faith,' and all the while they must have known that these were merely 'rear-guard' actions, designed to fend off their shame. A world comprised only of constructions may be difficult to endure for some people. Perhaps these artists are among them.

Another possibility is that these artists were simply nostalgic. As suggested earlier, old habits die hard; perhaps these artists had been so thoroughly habituated to modernist modes of creating and of *being* that they were unprepared to undergo changes as radical as the ones being proposed. Lukacher, borrowing from Derrida, refers to the idea of 'half-mourning' in this context. This 'describes the fate of thinking where one is in part outside metaphysics, but still under its spell, where one has forgotten metaphysics but still remembers that something has been forgotten' (1986: 90). These artists, albeit in different ways, implied that their thinking had moved wholly outside metaphysics, outside 'presence.' But maybe they were wrong about this. Maybe they were 'still under its spell,' still working their way out of a set of convictions that might never fully die.

Relatedly, one might also offer a constructionist interpretation of these artists' problems and dilemmas, focusing on their being caught in-between postmodernist and modernist ways. Insofar as their identities, and their ideas about their identities, were formed in a predominantly modernist mode, highlighting their own depth, uniqueness, mysteriousness, and so on, it could be that postmodernist thought had placed them in a contradictory discursive situation. First they were told one thing about artists and identities, then they were told quite another. As a result, perhaps there came to be a kind of inner crossfire, tied not so much to nostalgia for 'lost objects' and the like as to competing discourses, vying for recognition.

There are numerous other interpretations one might offer here as well. We need not choose between them; perhaps each is in some way applicable. One thing seems relatively clear, and that is that these four artists were, by all indications, modernists at heart, committed to just that sort of 'sublime sentiment' of which Lyotard and others have spoken. With this in mind, let me suggest that there are at least three ideas that seem worth exploring in this context. As the last artist we considered implied, it may be important to doubt doubt itself, to expose its very mode of operation by relegating it to the same constructed status as everything else in the world. It was relatively easy, she and the others told us, to be drawn in by doubt. The entire world *could* be a construction. But maybe it wasn't. Maybe, in fact, this notion of everything being constructed was *itself* a construction – a sign of the times, as it were. So there existed the need to entertain other possibilities. The second idea follows from the first. Given the ease with which people can become doubtful and skeptical, and given the fact that there are a lot of things people might commit themselves to that are utterly *devoid* of any discernible foundation or justification, there also exists the need to rely sometimes on a kind of faith in carrying out one's commitments. There may be nothing 'essential' in a work of art, no 'reason' for it to exist. And the criteria that might be employed to discern its worth may be thoroughly contestable. But all that this meant, as the last person we heard from insisted, was that there was really only one way to carry on as an artist, now, with any sense of conviction: to do the sort of work that, in her 'heart of hearts,' as she put it, was real and that engaged not only her mind, but her being. For artists, doing anything less would come back to haunt them, transforming them into yet another crop of alienated workers. As for the third idea, what these artists each seemed to suggest in their own ways was that, in the end, one had to trust *experience*; one had to be honest about it and take it, occasionally, for what it seemed to be. There were aspects of the world that moved these artists, making them want to create things. There were ways that colors came together on a canvas that they felt were somehow right, that achieved what they had been working toward, that somehow managed to exist in a way that seemed meaningful and significant. They also had an interest in reaching people, maybe even people outside the borders of the art world. More than anything, therefore, the 'cure' for these artists' respective breakdowns would have to do with their recollecting those dimensions of their own experience that had become occluded by certain constructions of what art was all about and, ultimately, by doubt; only then would they be able to carry on with a surer sense that what they were doing was worthwhile.

Gergen, you may recall, held out the hope that the saturated self, after some initial discomfort with having become 'populated,' 'multiphrenic,' and so on, would in the end become transformed into the relational self, divested of ego and hyper-autonomy; the 'individual' would become absorbed into the web of relationship and a better, more interconnected world would follow. Gergen is certainly to be praised for working toward a better world, which is to say, for working toward the *good*; given the ethical commitments entailed in such work, it has become something of a rarity. The problem, however, is that the idyllic future he projects may never arrive – not, at least, if we rely on postmodern thought to carry us to this promised land. Indeed, if the artists from whom we have heard are to be believed at all – which, I think, they should – their accounts may in fact lead us *away* from the relational self and its associated virtues. By stripping the world of its presence and replacing it only with our constructions, it may be that we become that much more 'undernourished,' starved for that sort of stimulation only the Other in its otherness – people, nature, art, God, or what have you – can provide.

The arbitrariness of artistic rules, their mere conventionality, could lead to self-enclosure. The project of artistic simulation could lead to a sense of dissimulation, a sense that one was betraying not only oneself but the world. There could emerge derealization, which could be concomitant with a profound distance from others, along with a desire to reach them. And reducing art to its least common denominator, which may be *nothing*, could render one effectively mute, unable to communicate, to speak. I have no evidence whatsoever that these are *necessary* outcomes of postmodern artistic practice. Nor do I know if they are probable ones. But they are certainly possible ones. Perhaps we should be aware of this possibility, if only to temper our potential enthusiasm for the deliverances of the future.

'Cultural production,' Jameson writes, 'has been driven back inside the mind, within the monadic subject: it can no longer look directly out of its eyes at the real world for the referent but must, as in Plato's cave, trace its mental images of the world on its confining walls. If there is any realism left here,' he continues, 'it is a "realism" which springs from the shock of grasping that confinement and of realizing that, for whatever peculiar reasons, we seem condemned to seek the historical past through our own pop images and stereotypes about that past, which itself remains forever out of reach' (1983: 118). Jameson goes on to discuss the relationship of postmodernism to schizophrenia by suggesting that when signifiers lose contact with what colloquially goes by the name of the 'real,' they can lead to fragmentation, temporal and experiential: 'schizophrenic experience is an experience of isolated, disconnected, discontinuous material signifiers which fail to link up into a coherent sequence. The schizophrenic thus does not know personal identity in our sense, since the feeling of identity depends on our sense of the persistence of the "I" and the "me" over time' (1983: 119). The result on initial inspection may appear to be exciting – 'an increase in our perceptions, a libidinal or hallucinogenic intensification of our normally humdrum and familiar surroundings.' In actuality, however, it is more often 'felt as loss, as "unreality" ' (1983: 120). Loss of reference, predicated on the materialization of the signifier, culminates in loss of world; and what had once been relationship folds in upon itself, shrinking to the status of a solitary onlooker, unsure what else there is but images, phantasms.

According to Sass, in both madness and certain variants of modernism and postmodernism, 'we find, tightly intertwined, a solipsism that would elevate the mind and derealize the world and a self-objectification that would rob the subject of its transcendental role as a center of power and knowledge. This parallelism of paradoxes is no mere coincidence,' he argues; 'what we are discovering in both domains are the characteristic paradoxes of the reflexive –

contradictions generated by the alienation and hyper-self-consciousness that are central both to schizophrenia and to the modern episteme' (1992: 338). Sass even goes so far as to argue that if one were actually to take what he refers to as 'hypermodernist' philosophy (which, for him, includes post-modernist) literally, 'imagining an actual living out of its claims,' the resultant mode of existence 'might well resemble the schizophrenic condition' (1992: 348).

A short while back, I explored the issue of whether the artists who had been discussed were modernists at heart. Let me work toward closing with a question that is fairly audacious in its scope: Are *we* modernists at heart, destined to remain so for the foreseeable future? That is, could it be that we too, human beings who have come to possess qualities that often feel decidedly like depth and dimensionality, somehow require a kind of 'nourishment,' as I put it earlier, that is simply unavailable in postmodernist renditions of identity? Initially, this question may appear to involve a retreat to individualism, and a perniciously monadic one at that; it may appear to signal essentialism once more, the self being restored to its former status as master, free and omnipotent, willful and powerful. 'On the whole,' McGowan has written,

> modernists . . . work to ensure the primacy of the will, since they believe that only the integrity of the willful, autonomous self can afford them an escape from the general cultural condition they abhor. Alone in the wasteland, threatened by the madness of being overwhelmed by society's decay and his own isolation, the poet can still assert that 'these fragments I have shored against my ruin.' This heroic maintenance of the self and its ability to create the artwork that represents and encapsulates its will stands as the quintessential modernist gesture when all hope of having any impact on the culture at large has been lost. (1991: 11)

Modernism, for McGowan, necessarily brings in tow the 'willful, autonomous self.' But there is a quite different picture that may be drawn as well. Many of the artists whom we studied noted that it was important for them to maintain continuity in their work. Partly for marketing reasons, they needed to maintain a singular 'brand image,' a unique signature, that would testify to their having an identity worth knowing. Some, however, complained that this identity was artificial, that it was a mock-identity, having less to do with their desires as artists than with the demands of consumers, hungry for more of the same. Their artistic identities thus became interiorized, the continuities between one moment of their histories and the next largely being a function of their need to keep up appearances. On the surface of things, there was coherence, connection. But it was a simulation of a meaningful history. To have actually lived such a history would require something entirely different than interiorization; it would require devotion to something outside themselves, something worthy enough of their attention to carry them forward. These artists, modernists at heart, seemed much less interested in restoring the Self than in restoring the Other. This was the condition for their having an identity that was something other than a simulation; it was what could bind together the moments of their histories into something 'real.'

Postmodern thinking had led to their folding in upon themselves; their aim was to move out again, into the world. It could therefore be that some of what we imagine will lead us to 'health' might actually lead to 'illness.' And, of course, vice versa: that which seems most ill may hold it within the promise of health. The future remains uncertain. What is not uncertain is that we should approach it very carefully.

Author's Note

I wish to thank the Spencer and MacArthur Foundations, who supported the research from which the life history information considered herein was drawn, as well as Mihály Csiksentmihályi, Jacob W. Getzels, and Stephen P. Kahn, who provided direction in carrying out the project itself.

References

Adams, H. (1978) *Art of the Sixties*. Oxford: Phaidon Press.

Barthes, R. (1989) *Roland Barthes*. New York: Noonday Press.

Crimp, D. (1983) 'On the Museum's Ruins,' in H. Foster (ed.), *The Anti-Aesthetic: Essays in Postmodern Culture*. Port Townsend, WA: Bay Press. pp. 43–56.

Danto, A.C. (1981) *The Transfiguration of the Commonplace*. London and Cambridge, MA: Harvard University Press.

Danto, A.C. (1997) *Encounters and Reflections: Art in the Historical Present*. Berkeley: University of California Press.

Derrida, J. (1978) *Writing and Difference*. Chicago: University of Chicago Press.

Dickie, G. (1974) *Art and the Aesthetic: An Institutional Analysis*. Ithaca, NY: Cornell University Press.

Fish, S. (1980) *Is There a Text in this Class?* London and Cambridge, MA: Harvard University Press.

Foster, H. (1985) *Recodings: Art, Spectacle, Cultural Politics*. Seattle: Bay Press.

Freeman, M. (1990) 'Artistic Creativity and the Meaning of Freedom,' *Journal of Humanistic Psychology*, 30 (2): 109–25.

Freeman, M. (1993) *Finding the Muse: A Sociopsychological Inquiry into the Conditions of Artistic Creativity*. Cambridge: Cambridge University Press.

Freeman, M. (1994) 'What Aesthetic Development is Not: An Inquiry Into the Pathologies Postmodern Creation,' in M. Franklin and B. Kaplan (eds), *Development and the Arts: Critical Perspectives*. Hillsdale, NJ: Lawrence Erlbaum Associates. pp. 145–64.

Gablik, S. (1984) *Has Modernism Failed?* New York: Thames & Hudson.

Gergen, K.J. (1991) *The Saturated Self: Dilemmas of Identity in Contemporary Life*. New York: Basic Books.

Gergen, K.J. (1994) *Realities and Relationships: Soundings in Social Construction*. London and Cambridge, MA: Harvard University Press.

Goodman, N. (1976) *Languages of Art*. Indianapolis: Hackett Publishing Company.

Gottlieb, C. (1976) *Beyond Modern Art*. New York: E.P. Dutton.

Greenberg, C. (1961) *Art and Culture*. Boston: Beacon Press.

Jameson, F. (1983) 'Postmodernism and Consumer Society,' in H. Foster (ed.), *The Anti-Aesthetic: Essays in Postmodern Culture*. Port Townsend, WA: Bay Press. pp. 111–25.

Jameson, F. (1988) 'Regarding Postmodernism – A Conversation with Fredric Jameson' (with Anders Stephanson), in A. Ross (ed.), *Universal Abandon? The Politics of Postmodernism*. Minneapolis: University of Minnesota Press. pp. 3–30.

Kostelanetz, R. (1980) *Metamorphosis in the Arts: A Critical Anthology of the 1960s*. New York: Assembling Press.

Lukacher, N. (1986) *Primal Scenes: Literature, Philosophy, Psychoanalysis.* Ithaca, NY: Cornell University Press.

Lyotard, J.-F. (1984) *The Postmodern Condition: A Report on Knowledge.* Minneapolis: University of Minnesota Press.

McGowan, J. (1991) *Postmodernism and Its Critics.* Ithaca, NY: Cornell University Press.

Osborne, H. (1979) *Abstraction and Artifice in Twentieth-Century Art.* Oxford: Clarendon Press.

Robins, C. (1984) *The Pluralist Era: American Art, 1968–1981.* New York: Harper & Row.

Rosenberg, H. (1972) *The De-definition of Art.* New York: Macmillan.

Sampson, E.E. (1993) *Celebrating the Other: A Dialogic Account of Human Nature.* Boulder, CO: Westview Press.

Sass, L.A. (1992) *Madness and Modernism: Insanity in the Light of Modern Art, Literature, and Thought.* New York: Basic Books.

Smagula, H. (1983) *Currents: Contemporary Directions in the Visual Arts.* Englewood Cliffs, NJ: Prentice Hall.

7

A Dangerous Symbolic Mobility: Narratives of Borderline Personality Disorder

Janet Wirth-Cauchon

> Societies do not succeed in offering everyone the same way of fitting into the symbolic order; those who are, if one may say so, between symbolic systems, in the interstices, offsides, are the ones who are afflicted with a dangerous symbolic mobility. Dangerous for them, because those are the people afflicted with what we call madness, anomaly, perversion. . . . And more than any others, women bizarrely embody this group of anomalies showing the cracks in an overall system.
>
> (Clément, 1986: 7)

> My self-image was not unstable. I saw myself, quite correctly, as unfit for the educational and social systems. But my parents and teachers did not share my self-image. Their image of me was unstable, since it was out of kilter with reality and based on their needs and wishes.
>
> (Kaysen, 1993: 155)

> Borders are set up to define the places that are safe and unsafe, to distinguish us from them. A border is a dividing line, a narrow strip along a steep edge. A borderland is a vague and undetermined place created by the emotional residue of an unnatural boundary.
>
> (Anzaldua, 1987: 3)

> The 'border' has existed in the myths of many cultures. It is the area in the psyche where the ego's orientation begins to fail and where powerful forces, over which one may have little control, constellate.
>
> (Schwartz-Salant, 1989: 9)

In this essay I present a feminist sociological reading of psychiatric and psychoanalytic case narratives of women diagnosed with *borderline personality disorder*. Borderline personality disorder is a condition diagnosed predominantly in women, characterized by symptoms such as instability of self-identity, unstable interpersonal relationships, and labile mood. The term 'borderline' was first used in 1938 by analyst Adolph Stern to describe patients who appeared more severely disturbed than the neurotics who Freud felt were suitable for psychoanalysis, yet who did not show signs of outright psychosis (Stern, 1938). In current psychiatric nomenclature, it is one of the personality disorders and is recognized as a severe form of the self disorders emerging with increasing frequency in clinical settings (American Psychiatric Association, 1994: 654). Those described as borderline personalities are predominantly women (Castaneda and Franco, 1985; Gibson, 1991; Gunderson and Zanarini, 1987; Swartz et al., 1990).

The intent here is to perform a sociological deconstruction of the psychiatric category of 'borderline' in order to analyze its gendered underpinnings, how the psychiatric construction of the female borderline patient is highly gendered, and draws upon and reproduces cultural assumptions about women's selfhood and subjectivity. I argue that this medicalized construction of women as borderline has the effect of pathologizing some of the fundamental conflicts women face in contemporary society, and within which they construct a sense of self. Specifically, the social construction of the borderline in women is accomplished through the medicalization of women's unease or resistance to their social and cultural status. Thus, the dual aims of this essay are, first, to illustrate this medicalized construction of the female borderline patient within psychiatric case narratives, and, second, to offer an alternative perspective through which to understand the borderline disorder as some women's response to their contradictory, marginal status.

My approach is informed by Foucault's conception of the operation of modernized power within institutionalized discourses such as psychiatry and penology (Foucault, 1965, 1977, 1980). Foucault focuses on the domination of the individual through psychiatric discourse, by making the human experience of madness the object of scrutiny and analysis. In effect, such experiences are reframed within psychiatric discourse as objects of management, manipulation, and control. Drawing on Foucault's project of locating the emergence of the subject within sites of knowledge and power, I explore the psychotherapeutic encounter as a site of knowledge and power, within which is constructed a specific psychiatric subject – the borderline woman.

My analysis is also informed by recent feminist analyses of women's disorders which read women's symptoms as embodiments of gender conflicts (Bordo, 1993; Flax, 1987; Showalter, 1985). Susan Bordo, for example, argues that women's symptoms have symbolic social and political meaning in the context of prevailing gender codes and women's attempts to conform to them. She argues that the symptoms of anorexia nervosa can be read as exaggerated forms of a regime of femininity that demands women exert strict control and discipline over their bodies. Madness in women, then, is culturally significant as the visible (or even audible) signs of wider paradoxes and conflicts in the construction of gender.

In analyzing the borderline experience, I focus on published case accounts of patients diagnosed as borderline in the psychiatric literature, including the psychoanalytic literature. This literature is primarily North American, with case articles drawn from professional clinical and psychoanalytic journals, most of them published between 1970 and 1988. As a story told by the interpreter, the psychoanalytic case study is, as critics of Freud's narratives of cases of hysteria point out, 'a vivid record of the construction of [cultural assumptions] as they emerge from the desire of the interpreter' (Kahane, 1985: 24–5). Stories of the treatment of personality disorders are sites where the negotiation of the meaning of selfhood, gender, and psychic disturbance is played out. As feminist critics of psychoanalysis have shown, psychoanalytic narratives have long been the sites where gender subjectivity is contested and produced – particularly that of women. The case histories of hysterical women patients – Breuer and Freud's Anna O, Freud's Dora – are perhaps the paradigmatic instance of the cultural representation of female subjectivity through narrative (Cixous and Clément, 1986; Gallop, 1982; Irigaray, 1985).

The post-Freudian psychoanalytic and psychotherapeutic narratives of borderline personality disorders constitute a set of texts largely unexamined from a feminist critical perspective. I read the clinical texts of borderline cases as cultural artifacts that are produced in particular social relations of power. My aim, as Kathy Ferguson writes, is to 'deconstruct meaning claims in order to look for the modes of power they carry and to force open a space for the emergence of counter-meanings' (1991: 323).

Borderline: Women, Marginality, and Unstable Selfhood

> There is a strange, uncomfortable, somewhat inhuman feeling to her. It feels somewhat like having a dream with an archaic figure who speaks in a stilted language from a distant century, yet carries a strong affect. She speaks to me in plain English, has affects I clearly recognize, is suffering, yet also seems inhuman, of a different species. Her words each carry a fullness that feels like they each link to greater whole, yet they are expressed in a strangely shallow manner. Alternatively, she has great depth and insight. But each moment is strained, too full and also too empty. She seems an outcast, living on the fringes of the world, cast into a dark shadow of inhuman, archetypal processes and speaking through them as if she were partaking of a human dialogue. She seems a princess, a witch, a clown, a trickster. We are in a fairy tale world of abstract characters which quickly turn back to flesh and blood reality. I am left feeling guilty for ever thinking of her as anything other than genuine.
>
> (Schwarz-Salant, 1989: 9).

> Our clinical experience tells us that the border of insanity is not a line; it is rather a vast territory with no sharp division: a no-man's-land between sanity and insanity.
>
> (Green, 1977: 19)

Who is the Borderline?

How do women come to be placed in this 'no-man's land' – this borderland of madness? As Elaine Showalter points out, in her study of women and madness, *The Female Malady*, feminist social theorists have called attention to women's marginality within the Western cultural order. Women are 'typically situated on the side of irrationality, silence, nature, and body, while men are situated on the side of reason, discourse, culture, and mind' (Showalter,

1985: 3–4). Closely associated in Western perception with nature and body, and structurally positioned as both the object of scrutiny, and as a subject in her own right, 'Woman' occupies a position at the borders, representing 'something intermediate between culture and nature . . . on the continuous periphery of culture's clearing' (Ortner, 1974: 85).

> [W]omen's social or cultural marginality seems to place them on the borderline of the symbolic order, both the 'frontier between men and chaos' and dangerously part of chaos itself, inhabitants of a mysterious and frightening wild zone outside of patriarchal culture. (Showalter 1990: 4)

Gloria Anzaldua (1987) writes of the psychic conflicts of what D. Emily Hicks (1991) has termed the 'border subject.' Anzaldua describes the subjective experience of living in cultural borderlands, created around an 'unnatural boundary' (national/cultural borders that split off and marginalize 'others'). She helps us see the connection between colonial/racial borders and the Western cultural split between a masculine reason/*logos*/culture and devalued feminine/pagan nature. The key feature of the borderland is the clash or confusion of meanings that occurs when a dominant culture attempts to enforce certain meanings or identities and renders others unthinkable or illegitimate, unreal or even pathological. Yet these unnatural borders can never be fully enforced; fragments of the suppressed identities remain, in symptomatic traces or hauntings, preserved in muted form in the psyches or bodies of border subjects.[1]

Robert Romanyshyn writes of such cultural symptoms,

> To be sure, a symptom as a way of ignoring or forgetting something is also a way of preserving or remembering it. . . . In every symptom there is, so to speak, the whisper of a direction, the hint of a path about how one can find one's way back to health or balance or, perhaps most descriptively, home. Symptoms are a memory of this path, this way home, this way back to what has been forgotten, lost, ignored, or otherwise left behind. (1989: 13).

What Are Borderline Symptoms Memorializing?

In psychiatric discourse, women deemed borderline are not only placed 'on the borders,' at the edges of sanity. They are also placed at the very margins of *selfhood.* This interpretation arises from the contemporary psychoanalytic assumption that the 'normal' self is a unified, coherent, singular entity. As Roy Schafer has written, in contemporary psychoanalysis, 'The self has become the most popular figure in modern, innovative psychoanalytic accounts of human development and action . . . it is the unity, the essence, the existential core, the gestalt, and the mastermind of one's life' (1989: 154). Borderline patients are described as lacking this unified mastermind.

In psychiatric discourse, clinicians rely on the theme of a lack of stable selfhood in their descriptions of borderline patients. Their selves are described as 'dead' (Schwarz-Salant, 1989) or 'empty' (Singer, 1977), as 'unstable' or 'split' among 'part-selves,' (De Chenne, 1991), as containing a 'defect in the organizing structure of the self' (Ross, 1976); alternatively, such patients are said to manifest a 'blurring of ego boundaries' (i.e. confusion between one's own thoughts and feelings and those of others) (Boyer, 1977: 403).

As the above examples show, the interpretation of the borderline case is dominated by a concern with the presence and coherence of the conscious, stable 'self.' A language of selfhood dominates contemporary clinical description and interpretation of the borderline patient. As such, the borderline is defined negatively in comparison to the healthy norm: the possession of a firm, full, unified, and well-bounded self. My approach is to analyze case narratives to explore how women are defined as 'marginal' or unstable when judged according to cultural norms of selfhood. From this perspective, the diagnosis of women as borderline suggests the reproduction, in psychiatric discourse, of the symbolic and linguistic equation of women with marginality and instability.

From Borderland to Borderline: Tracing the History of the Borderline in Psychiatry

> Darwinian, determinist, or evolutionist psychiatry dominated the English scene from about 1870 to the First World War, and brought with it changes in the . . . definition of madness itself. . . . The most characteristic and revealing metaphor of Darwinian psychiatry was that of the 'borderland,' the shadowy territory between sanity and madness which sheltered 'latent brain disease' and the 'seeds of nervous disorders.'
>
> (Showalter, 1985: 105)

Before addressing the case narratives, some brief historical background is presented here to sketch the emergence of the borderline category in psychiatric discourse, and the growing emphasis placed on deficits in character, personality, or 'self' as the source of psychic disturbance.

The borderline category first appeared in the official nomenclature of psychiatry in 1980, in the third edition of the *Diagnostic and Statistical Manual of Mental Disorders* (*DSM-III*) (American Psychiatric Association, 1980). However, the borderline category had been in use in psychiatry prior to this, beginning in 1938 when psychoanalyst Adolph Stern began treating patients who, he wrote, 'occupied the border line between neurosis and psychosis' (1986: 467). These patients appeared to be more profoundly disturbed than those suffering from neurotic symptoms. Yet they could not be classified as psychotic. Stern felt that such patients showed signs of regressing to an early narcissistic state in which they had withdrawn libidinal energy from the outside world and turned it upon themselves. Hence, such patients showed evidence of pre-Oedipal conflicts having to do with the earliest acquisition of a self, rather than the Oedipal neurotic symptoms of other patients. This marked the emergence of a new category of patients that later psychiatrists said were suffering from 'self disorders.' This was a shift 'from people concerned with troubling unconscious desires, as in the classical images [of Freudian analysis], . . . to people desperately seeking for a secure core of self' (Frosh, 1991: 45).

This was not the first time that psychiatry had identified a 'borderline' region between sanity and madness. In the late nineteenth century, physicians began to recognize certain patients who retained their powers of reason, yet nonetheless appeared highly disturbed or showed emotional anguish. They suffered from what Phillipe Pinel termed *manie sans délire*, also termed 'moral insanity' by James Cowles Prichard in England, which he defined in 1835 as 'madness consisting in a morbid perversion of the natural feelings, affections, inclinations, temper, habits, moral disposition, and natural impulses, without any remarkable disorder or defect of the intellect or knowing and reasoning faculties, and particularly without any insane illusion or hallucination' (quoted in Mack, 1975: 2).

This ambiguous madness was captured in the metaphor of the *borderland*, where dwelt, as physician Henry Maudsley wrote in 1874, 'many persons who, without being insane, exhibit peculiarities of thought, feeling, and character which render them unlike ordinary beings and make them objects of remark among their fellows' (in Showalter, 1985: 105). Such peculiarities, it was thought, could be expressed by a lack of control of one's 'lower nature,' and Maudsley, like other physicians, placed emphasis on the urban classes and their lack of control as signs of hereditary regression and potential lunacy. Early psychiatrists, such as George Beard in 1884, depicted the inhabitants of the borderland as able to mask their potential madness: these 'incipient lunatics' may 'pass about the world with a clean bill of health,' yet a trained psychiatrist would be able to spot the signs of hereditary taint which betrayed their evolutionary and moral degeneracy (Beard, in Showalter, 1985: 105).

The borderland, Elaine Showalter points out, was a concept that reflected the Darwinian psychiatry of the nineteenth century, with its hereditary evolutionary theories that legitimated inequalities of race, class, and gender. Persons located in the borderland had transgressed the moral social codes of middle-class Victorian society. The borderland, she writes, 'reflected the anxieties of late Victorian psychiatrists, who felt that they were in a temporal and sexual limbo where the traditional boundaries of gender, labor, and behavior were being challenged by New Women and decadent men' (Showalter, 1985: 105–6).

In later developments of the borderline concept in psychiatry, it acquired some of the features of its contemporary meaning. Rather than depicting it as an ambiguous realm between existing categories (i.e. as a 'severe neurosis' or a 'weak schizophrenia'), psychiatrists began to systematically map the specific features of the borderline personality type. This is most evident in the work of analyst Otto Kernberg, who used the term 'Borderline Personality Organization' to refer to patients showing inconsistency in behavior and a lack of clear sense of identity. These characteristics predominate in the contemporary definition of the borderline. The current official definition of borderline disorder appears in the fourth edition of the *Diagnostic and Statistical Manual of Medical Disorders*: 'A pervasive pattern of instability of interpersonal relationships, self-images, and affects, and marked impulsivity beginning by early adulthood and present in a variety of contexts' (American Psychiatric Association, 1994: 654).

> There are sudden and dramatic shifts in self-image, characterized by shifting goals, values, and vocational aspirations. . . . These individuals may suddenly change from the role of a needy supplicant for help to a righteous avenger of past mistreatment. Although they usually have a self-image that is based on being bad or evil, individuals with this disorder may at times have feelings that they do not exist at all. (1994: 651)

After its first entry into *DSM-III* in 1980, it had become 'by far the most common personality disorder,' according to researchers John Gunderson and Mary Zanarini (1987: 8), accounting for 15 to 25 percent of hospital and outpatient cases. A recent overview of borderline personality disorder profiled the typical borderline patient as 'an 18–30 year old white female inpatient' (Gibson, 1991: 66).

Since the borderline diagnosis was codified in *DSM-III* in 1980, it has not been without controversy. Critics have pointed out that with such a diverse array of symptoms, its meaning is inconsistent and obfuscated (Aronson, 1985: 209). Further, research has shown that the term 'borderline' is used as a derogatory label for difficult patients (Lewis and Appleby, 1988; Reiser and Levenson, 1984). Reiser and Levenson conclude: 'We believe that the extent of this abuse is serious enough to put the term in danger of becoming clinically meaningless' (1984: 1529).

The lack of agreement on the meaning of the borderline diagnosis raises questions about how the diagnosis is used, and for whom. Given the predominance of women among those diagnosed as borderline, the question of gender is central to the manner in which the borderline category is deployed in clinical settings. In this analysis I focus on case narratives to explore how women receiving this diagnosis are described and interpreted.

Fluid Metaphors of the Feminine: Fragmented Borderline Selves

In a clinical article published in 1929, 'Womanliness as Masquerade,' Joan Rivière described the behavior of some of her women patients as a 'masquerade' of femininity, the putting on of an exaggerated mask of feminine traits, in order to disguise or cover a fantasized forbidden 'masculine' self. Rivière suggests that her patients are divided into a strategically performed artificial femininity and some forbidden aspect of self that, when exposed or performed, is threatening to others, and makes these women the target of retribution. Rivière traces this fantasy to a desire to take the position of men, and, more specifically, to a rivalry with the father in an Oedipal drama (Rivière, 1929).

In the examples of borderline cases that follow, psychoanalyst Melvin Singer notices a sense of artificiality in his borderline patients' behavior, but, in contrast to Rivière, finds nothing under the mask. The patients appear to be divided into a false persona or outer surface self and an underlying emptiness. In my reading of the cases, I explore how these themes of emptiness, numbness, and artificiality are represented and interpreted in the language of psychiatry. Specifically, I examine how Singer linguistically constructs the borderline patient's emptiness of self in the narrative, projecting onto the borderline patient a literal intangibility and fluidity of self that is culturally associated with femininity.

Singer, in an article published in the *International Review of Psycho-Analysis* in 1977, describes a pervasive symptom that he finds in his borderline patients: 'a chronic state of emptiness or being nothing, gone and missing,' which can lead ultimately, he writes, 'to the conviction of personal extinction' (1977: 460). Singer's discussion focuses on several female patients and one male patient who was experiencing gender and sexual conflicts. For such patients, this feeling of emptiness is frequently experienced as a physical feeling of hollowness or hunger; Singer notes that commonly heard symptoms include 'hollowness, deadness, nothingness, an inner void, or "something's missing" ' (1977: 472).

> Sudden or acute states of anguish and despair over this feeling of an inner world emptiness, especially when associated with an outer world emptiness (aloneness) are at times so exquisitely painful that suicide seems the only escape. Borderline patients dread the appearance of this emptiness and view it paradoxically as equivalent to a death experience – only a phenomenological, not physical death. (1977: 472)

Singer describes this experience as patients' loss of an 'I,' particularly in relation to powerful others:

> Some borderline patients will describe a loss of their 'I' experience regardless of what it is, if the other person is too dominating – they fear getting swallowed up by the other's power. One patient, graphically and concretely, describes this loss of self in a dream, in which her face, although partially formed, was still without an 'eye.' (1977: 475)

Singer describes his patients as cut off from object relations with others, relying on fragmentary feeling-states or sensations to 'anchor' their identities. According to Singer, his patients used these feeling-states to create 'false selves' to ward off the horror of feelings of inner emptiness or deadness. For some patients, any physical feeling, whether pleasant or unpleasant, can become a kind of anchor point to the external world, providing a partial sliver of existence in place of a sense of internal void.

> One borderline patient felt real, human, or some semblance of herself only when she experienced a queasy anxiety in the pit of her stomach which relieved her emptiness. This was her psychological center of gravity and she would look for that feeling to position herself in the world, to know who she was. Without anxiety, even if it was very discomforting, she felt as if she had disappeared or was nothing. Another patient generally felt so unreal because of her emptiness and lack of a substantial self-image or 'identity' that any feeling she could experience in herself was her only sign that she was a living human being. She held on to any feeling that reached awareness, for as she conceptualized it, if it dis-

> appeared, so did her humanness. Thus, she lived every feeling to its completion, be it hunger, anger or sex. (1977: 473)

Aside from such physical anchor points to ward off the threat of extinction of self, Singer notes another, perhaps more disturbing strategy of being in the face of nothingness, where the patient constructs a non-human, or even inanimate, 'false self.' Some patients created fantasied, non-human selves, thereby turning themselves into objects: 'In this way, they had defensively already died, so they could not be abandoned and thus suffer the excruciating agony of annihilation of the self.' To preserve their fragmentary and fleeting selves, Singer's women patients constructed a state of 'living death' to survive in a kind of subdued state, neither fully alive nor dead, at the border. They felt like objects, or parts of the landscape: like a 'blade of grass' or 'like the scenery':

> One woman, in the secrecy of her inner thoughts, felt she must be like a tree, since she did not feel human. She knew that her parents were human, but since they did not attend to her, she felt she was more like the scenery, which is also unattended. Thus, she might as well be a tree, which at least has roots deep in the ground. (1977: 474)

> Another patient, similarly, felt she was like a blade of grass stretching and bending with the breeze, deeply rooted and attached to the soil. A third patient felt at times like stone, or at other times like wood (which was a further regression from a hairy ape – a past, unacceptable, split-off sexual self) in order to deal successfully with a period of my absence. In that way she avoided the pain of her dying by my loss, i.e. she was now a 'living dead.' (1977: 478)

In further descriptions of the fragmentation of self, Singer's language is revealing of the metaphoric connotations he has layered onto the borderline's sense of inner emptiness. Singer describes these defensive false part-selves as patients' attempts to combat the 'dissolution' or fluidity of the empty self. Masochism, for example, is described as a way for patients to avoid dissolving:

> Another common method used by borderline patients to preserve this self-experience and to feel alive is to suffer masochistically, be excited, or in danger. Thus, by bombarding the outer boundaries of the body or psychic self with painful stimuli, cathexis is kept at the periphery and a sense of intactness, definition, delineation and aliveness is temporarily achieved. Hardness, physical pain and psychic combativeness gives some borderline patients the feeling of definition and limits, not unbounded extensiveness and dissolution. (1977: 474)

Such descriptive terms as 'hardness' and 'intactness' express Singer's notion of the flip-side of the empty, fluid, dissolved self – one characterized by solidity, firmness, and constancy over time. But such 'hard' defenses don't always hold the fluid self inside its borders:

> I have treated two patients who described feeling like a block of ice. The difficulty with this defensive posture is that one can readily be melted with the heat of emotions and become nothing but a puddle of water. (1977: 474)

Singer also describes a type of borderline patient who keeps up a continual flow of talk, which he interprets as a wish to merge with the analyst by maintaining constant contact with him, and to avoid a sense of separateness. Such a flow of talk, which Singer likens to the need for 'small talk,' is accompanied by 'inexorable panic when the person feels any degree of "me" feelings separate from "us." ' Again, a liquid metaphor is invoked here as Singer cites Katan's classic drive interpretation of incessant talk as 'equivalent to feeding and a continual flow of milk and urine' (1977: 474).

In addition to metaphors of liquidity, Singer describes the intangibility of the empty self as mist or smoke:

> Other patients used the reverse defense to avoid dissolution: rather than hard firmness, they present a misty, airy smoke-screen effect which dynamically expresses their lack of structural integrity while simultaneously keeping the other away, unpenetrating and safely uninvolved. (1977: 474)

In another example, Singer depicts the dissolution of self in highly gendered terms, counterposing a feminine 'dissolution' with masculine intactness:

> One woman, mentioned above, feared closeness, especially close physical contact, with another woman not primarily because of homosexual danger, although that certainly was present, but on this same level, out of her fear of dissolution into the other woman. She chose hard, muscular men whose firmness made her feel insoluble: into whom she could press but not sink and fall, dispersed into an eternally bottomless abyss. Her desire, it seemed, was to press into the other's body – through the outer integument, and insinuate herself between the muscles, tendons and fasciae. Here the merger, closeness and warmth of the other's body, especially the outer rind, was primary. (1977: 477)

The use of metaphors of liquidity to refer to women reproduces the cultural association of femininity with nature. Klaus Theweleit, in his analysis of the writings of Freikorps soldiers in pre-fascist Germany, found that 'floods' and flows were central metaphors to represent the threat of the emergent socialist revolution, the 'Red Tide' that threatened Germany from within its borders, and that this flood was equated with the threat of women. Women became a 'code word for the whole complex of nature' in the writings of the Freikorps soldiers (Theweleit, 1987: 215). The image of 'woman-in-the-water' is one running through Western literature, 'over and over again: the women-in-the-water; woman as water, as a stormy, cavorting, cooling ocean, a raging stream, a waterfall; as a limitless body of water that ships pass through, with tributaries, pools, surfs, and deltas; woman as the enticing (or perilous) deep.' This imagery is a 'depersonalization of women . . . the dissolving of their boundaries' (1987: 283).

> What is really at work here, it seems to me, is a specific (and historically relatively recent) form of the oppression of women – one that has been notably underrated. It is oppression through exaltation, through a lifting of boundaries, an 'irrealization' and reduction to principle – the principle of flowing, of distance, of vague, endless enticement. Here again, women have no names. (Theweleit, 1987: 284)

Theweleit explores the relationship of these metaphors to the anxiety of the Freikorps 'soldier males' over the dissolution of their own boundaries, particularly those of male identity, of the body, and of the 'pure' race of

Germany: 'Our soldiers, conversely, want to avoid swimming at all costs, no matter what the stream. They want to stand with both feet and every root firmly anchored in the soil. They want whatever floods may come to rebound against them; they want to stop, and dam up, those floods' (Theweleit, 1987: 230).

Singer reads a diverse array of women's symptoms as signs of the literal intangibility and solubility of the borderline's empty self. For him, these experiences are signs of an underlying structural flaw in the patient's self. He interprets the borderline symptoms as defenses against facing the horror of this emptiness and dissolution. Thus, for Singer, the borderline patients' selves are indeed dissolved, fluid, insubstantial – and this lack of a stable self causes mental anguish.

But would it be possible to understand these symptoms as signs not of an underlying dissolution of self, but of subjective responses to the patient's situation and her social status? Can these symptoms be interpreted as intelligible responses to gender relations? What is missing from the account that would enable us to answer that question?

Borderline Double: The Return of the Repressed

Like Singer's narrative, the following case illustrates the linguistic construction of the borderline's unstable, fragmented self. The case of 'Marge,' described by Irving Yalom (1989) in a piece entitled 'Therapeutic Monogamy,' is a vivid portrayal of the borderline's fragmentation between a surface self and an underlying lost self. But here, the lost self returns in the form of a second personality. Marge, a depressed borderline patient, undergoes a transformation during a therapy session when a second self emerges, an empowered 'double' that attacks the first self.

In introducing the reader to Marge, Yalom acknowledge his immediate dread of her when first meeting her as he recognizes that she may very well be a borderline:

> It didn't take much experience to recognize the signs of deep distress. Her sagging head and shoulders said 'depression'; her gigantic eye pupils and restless hands and feet said 'anxiety.' Everything else about her – multiple suicide attempts, eating disorder, early sexual abuse by her father, episodic psychotic thinking, twenty-three years of therapy – shouted 'borderline,' the word that strikes terror in the heart of the middle-aged comfort-seeking psychiatrist. (1989: 213)

At the next therapy session, Marge speaks 'like a simulacrum – with uncanny stillness, with nothing moving but her lips, not her breath, or her hands, or her eyes, or even her cheeks':

> I am forty-five years old. I have been mentally ill all my life. I have seen psychiatrists since I was twelve years old and cannot function without them. I shall have to take medicine the rest of my life. The most I can hope for is to stay out of a mental hospital. I have never been loved. I will never have children. . . . My father, who molested me when I was a child, is dead. My mother is a crazy, embittered lady, and I grow more like her every day. (1989: 216)

Yalom writes that the 'simulacrum' speaking was not exactly the woman, Marge, but a tormented part of her: 'It was her depression speaking.' In an effort to give back Marge's 'self' to her, Yalom reads back to her one of her own letters that she had sent to him, in effect giving her back her own self-narrative that she had lost. Marge appears visibly improved. This seemingly 'healthy self,' however, dissolves three weeks later, when Marge undergoes a transformation:

> In the middle of her dirge, she suddenly closed her eyes – not in itself unusual since she often went into an autohypnotic state during the session. . . . I said, 'Marge,' and was about to utter the rest of the sentence, 'Will you please come back?' when I heard a strange and powerful voice come out of her mouth: 'You don't know me.' . . . The voice was so different, so forceful, so authoritative, I looked around the office for an instant to see who else might have entered. 'Who are you?' I asked. 'Me! Me!' (1989: 222)

The emergence of Marge's monstrous double creates a nausea in Yalom, as he evokes the experience of witnessing the 'forbidden':

> For a brief time I felt a wave of eerie nausea, as though I were peering through a rent in the fabric of reality, at something forbidden, at the raw ingredients, the clefts and seams, the embryonic cells and blastulas that are, in the natural order of things, not meant to be seen in the finished human creature. (1989: 222)

Yet in spite of his nausea, Yalom is also riveted by the performance of Marge. The narrative evokes vividly Yalom's response to Marge's double, and this narrative evocation constructs 'Me,' the second self, as a seductive, powerful, yet threatening woman, whom Yalom calls a 'Lorelei.' In this narrative, therefore, Yalom constructs the borderline's fragmented self in highly gendered terms, reproducing the cultural split between passive femininity and forbidden sexual autonomy. Yalom is attracted to 'Me,' and in the narrative draws out his own associations to this powerful double. The image of the beautiful woman as both seductive and deadly is openly embraced in his narrative:

> This new Marge was vivacious and outrageously, but enjoyably, flirtatious. She was savvy, willful, very sexy. What a relief to have a break from Marge's droning voice and relentless whining. But I was beginning to feel uneasy; I enjoyed this lady too much. I thought of the Lorelei legend, and though I knew it would be dangerous to tarry, still I visited awhile. . . . Perhaps I was staying longer with her than I should. It was wrong to talk to her about Marge. It was not fair to Marge. Yet this woman's appeal was strong, almost irresistible. (1989: 222)

Yalom is captivated by Marge's double, which creates a dilemma for him: Marge was split, with two selves; which of her 'selves' was he treating? Which self was 'real'?

> I felt bewildered by what had happened. My one basic rule – 'Treat Marge as an equal' was no longer sufficient. Which Marge? The whimpering Marge in front of me or the sexy, insouciant Marge? (1989: 224)

Yalom struggles with the question of not only which self is real, but with which self does he have a relationship; he is concerned about 'being faithful to his patient,' about 'fidelity': 'Above all I must not permit myself to be seduced by that other Marge.'

Yalom interprets Marge's double as a false creation of her father, caused by his sexual abuse. Yalom is therefore wary of falling into the role of Father in relation to this seductive yet artificial feminine self:

> My implicit contract with Marge (as with all my patients) is that when I am with her, I am wholly, wholeheartedly, and exclusively with her. Marge illuminated another dimension of that contract: that I must be with her most central self. Rather than relating to this integral self, her father, who abused her, had contributed to the development of a false, sexual self. I must not make that error. (1989: 225)

Thus, Yalom advocates 'Marge' as the real, central self, the integral self, and 'Me' – the seductive powerful other – as false, a creation of an incestuous relation to her father, a literal creation of patriarchal fantasy. Yet Yalom is nonetheless seemingly under this powerful double's spell; staying faithful to Marge was difficult:

> It was not easy. To be truthful, I wanted to see 'Me' again. Though I had known her for less than an hour I had been charmed by her. The drab backdrop of the dozens of hours I had spent with Marge made this engaging phantom stand out with a dazzling clarity. (1989: 225)

Yalom is not successful in preventing himself from re-creating the role of Marge's father in the creation of 'Me,' as he expands on his own romantic associations to this attractive 'engaging phantom':

> I didn't know her name and she didn't have much freedom, but we each knew how to find the other. In the next hour she tried several times to come to me again. I could see Marge flicker her eyelids and then close them. Only another minute or two, and we would have been together again. I felt foolish and eager. Balmy bygone memories flooded my mind. I recalled waiting at a palm-edged Caribbean airport for a plane to land and for my lover to join me. (1989: 225)

'Me' embodies not only the false Lorelei image, but the rage of that persona aimed against the other, passive self, Marge. 'Me' says to Yalom, 'You could have her in therapy for thirty years, but I'd still win. I can tear down a year's work in a day. If necessary, I could have her step off a curb into a moving truck. . . . Marge is a creep. You know she's a creep. How can you stand to be with her?' (1989: 223) 'Me' proceeds to parody Marge, providing, in Yalom's words, 'an astounding theatrical performance,' imitating Marge, her timidity, her fear, and despair:

> It was a virtuoso performance. But also an unspeakably cruel performance by 'Me.' . . . Her eyes blazed as she continued to defile Marge, who, she said, was incurable, hopeless, and pathetic. (1989: 223)

'Me' is not only alluring but also an 'equal,' in collusion with Yalom.

> This woman, this 'Me,' she understood me. . . . She knew I wanted a real woman. . . . 'Me's' theatrical performance, in which she regurgitated all those snippets of Marge's behavior, convinced me that both she and I (and only she and I) understood what I had gone through with Marge. She was the brilliant, beautiful director who had created this film. . . . If she could play all those roles, she must

> be the concealed, guiding intelligence behind them all. We shared something that was beyond language. (1989: 225)

As this example shows, 'Me' is a narrative construction, created by Yalom's graphic and vivid rendering of the eruption of the 'beautiful and intriguing, but also lethal,' Me. Yalom projects his own romantic associations onto this 'engaging phantom.' With his attraction to Me, Yalom projects the image of the powerful and dangerous seductress onto Marge's performance. As depicted in the text, he 'sees' 'Lorelei' when Marge's 'other' personality emerges. It is not possible to discern how Marge's double 'really' appeared. We cannot move beyond the level of Yalom's text to get the 'real' events. Yet Yalom's counter-transferential captivation and fascination with 'Me' finds its way into the text. Thus, the split Yalom describes for us is partly his own creation.

The title of the piece, 'Therapeutic Monogamy,' encapsulates the metaphor of therapy as marriage and fidelity to Marge, and the emergence of 'Me' as a seductive figure, an 'Other woman,' that conjures up Yalom's romantic fantasies. Clearly, these figures are intentionally exaggerated by Yalom for effect. Yet this metaphor of fidelity and temptation appears to magnify the dual images of women that constructed the Marge/Me split; the shrinking pathetic Marge versus the beautiful and lethal seductress, Me. Yalom tells the story of continuing faithful to Marge, and keeping 'Me' at bay, in spite of his temptation, and in spite of Me's 'gathering strength and desperately trying to return to me.'

Yalom's therapeutic ritual is aimed at bringing together these mutually exclusive opposites, to 'establish a confederacy or fusion of the two Marges.'

> I would sacrifice her rival to her, pluck her feathers, pull her asunder, and, bit by bit, feed her to Marge. The feeding technique was to repeat one standard question: 'Marge, what would "she" say if she were here?' (1989: 226)

The expectation is that a reconciliation of these conflicting personalities can be expected to occur within the bounds of Marge's 'integral self' – her 'most central self.' Yalom 'feeds' Me – the empowered, yet forbidden self – to Marge, in hopes that Marge will 'ingest' or 'appropriate' the best aspects of Me, while neutralizing her destructive power. Yet, from a feminist perspective, Marge's split self can be understood as the embodiment or personification, in exaggerated form, of the dual image of women in Western perception; a duality that makes the passive, subordinate 'shrinking' Marge irreconcilable with the powerful 'Me.' The double, 'Me,' appears to carry all of Marge's power, self-assertion and sexuality. These aspects of Marge are split off and embodied in another persona. They are forbidden from being part of Marge's personality, not solely as the result of Marge's mental pathology, but as a prohibition in the culture against women's power. Thus, the split between Marge and 'Me' is a creation of her culture, a contradiction in the construction of gender, literalized in Marge's relationship to her father.

Yalom wants the integration of this feminine duality – a cultural projection of the passive–powerful images of women, the double bind within which Marge constructs her self – to occur at the individual, rather than the cultural, level. This expectation speaks less to the limits of Yalom's own intentions than it does to the limits of the goal of a therapeutic reconciliation of the cultural contradiction of current gender relations.

Forbidden Selves: Repressing Gender

In order to provide a contrast to Singer's and Yalom's decontextualized depiction of the borderline patients' unstable self, I will discuss a case narrative of a borderline patient written by a feminist therapist, Jane Flax. Flax (1987), in her discussion of her patient 'Laurie,' presents a more socially informed interpretation of the borderline patient's fragmented sense of self.

Flax analyzes Laurie's unstable sense of self in relation to gender and women's contemporary cultural position, arguing that the borderline patient's 'core self' is split between an outward false self that conforms to the feminine role, and a repressed, split-off, autonomous self that is forbidden expression in contemporary Western culture. Thus, the source of the borderline patient's fragmented self is ultimately a cultural source – the construction of femininity in Western culture. The patient's borderline symptoms are expressions of the confusions, ambiguities, and contradictions faced by women as each of these parts of the self struggle for expression. According to Flax, her patient 'Laurie' was split into a 'mostly false' (but predominant) 'social self – the conforming, nurturing feminine self 'that women are usually praised for,' and two repressed selves, forbidden for women in Western culture: 'an autonomous (and highly underdeveloped) self, and a "sexual" self (also underdeveloped, but not as forbidden or constricted as the autonomous self)' (1987: 98). Such splitting off of forbidden selves created Laurie's borderline fragmentation: 'in order to survive she split off parts of her self, protecting some with rigid defenses and repressing others.' This denial and repression created turmoil in Laurie's relationships with people and her 'internal worlds,' which were marked by 'rigidity, rage, terror, loneliness, self-hate, and a (disavowed but desperate) need for love.' Flax notes that these conflicts were evident in Laurie's relationship to her in the therapy:

> Laurie fears that I will not give her what she needs in order to grow and develop as a separate person (or that I will actively inhibit her from doing so). Alternatively, she fears that I will hate her for becoming her 'real self,' as Laurie believes every member of her family did, each for their own distinct reasons. (1987: 97)

Flax's reading of the causes of the borderline patient's psychic fragmentation and turbulence is very different from Singer's in that her analysis is oriented toward the cultural context within which women construct selves.

> While the contents of Laurie's repressed [selves] can be understood by mapping out and locating them within her family dynamics, I think that her repressed material is widely shared by other women in Western culture. This commonality makes her case relevant to the more general questions of gender, repression, and subjectivity. (1987: 96)

Laurie, according to Flax, was enmeshed in a family and cultural milieu that demanded her conformity with their demands; hence her false, nurturing and caretaking 'social self' predominated at the cost of 'the mutilation or denial of the other selves.' As Flax argues: 'The social self is the part of the self that women are usually praised for – it strives to satisfy the needs of others; it is capable of empathy; it desperately wants and needs interpersonal interaction' (1987: 98). Flax argues that Laurie played this role as 'echoes' of her family's own selves:

> Here it is not the self which is to blame but the context in and conditions under which it comes to be and must exist (and how these conditions are taken into and become part of this self). In Laurie's case, her family wanted this part of her to exist only to service other people's needs, not her own. She could only be in relationships with her mother, father, or brother on their terms and as a means to their ends – symbiotic fusion for the mother, narcissistic echo for the father, scapegoat and actor-out of forbidden feelings for the brother. (1987: 99)

Flax traces the repression of the 'sexual self' directly to cultural perception of women's bodies, particularly in relation to hunger and sexuality, transmitted to Laurie by her parents: Laurie's mother, Flax writes, 'regarded the body as an enemy that needed to be regulated and controlled. . . . The dangers of the body were condensed, focused, and expressed through the mother's intense, persistent preoccupation with food and weight' (1987: 100). Her mother's control of Laurie's appearance and food consumption contributed to Laurie's anorexia and bulimia. Laurie's father gave her similar messages about women's bodies as passive objects to be regulated. Her father's messages about sexuality portrayed women as passive objects or victims:

> The father's messages to Laurie about sexuality were frightening. He warned her that men have a powerful sexual drive, that they are really only interested in their own pleasure, and that they seek to use women solely for their own sexual ends. Once men have attained satisfaction, they will feel contempt for the woman and abandon her. Any woman would be a 'fool' to give in to a man's sexual pleadings. (1987: 100)

Thus, Laurie's 'domestic metaphysics' center on the assumption that 'minds and bodies are two completely distinct entities' (1987: 103). Flax's interpretation makes a direct connection between Laurie's split borderline identity and the gendered, cultural split between the abstract mind and the uncontrolled body. Laurie appears caught in the double bind created by this duality: she cancels out her own desires in her regulation of her body's appearance, thereby meeting her family's and society's expectations to transform herself into a passive feminine (sexual) image or object, yet is warned of the dangers of this very acquisition of a feminine body. In order to enter her father's world, she must *disembody* herself. Thus, Laurie cancels out her autonomous selfhood because she wants to be accepted into the world and to meet her family's (and society's) expectations.

More forbidden than the 'sexual self' is Laurie's repressed 'autonomous self.' 'Laurie believes this to be the most "mutilated" and underdeveloped of her three selves. She likens it to the binding of feet – the toes curled under and deformed – to render woman helpless and pleasing to men.' In Flax's words, the autonomous self 'would enjoy mastery, aggression, competition, and define its desires independently of, even against, the wishes of others' (1987: 105). And yet, Flax is concerned lest this self begin to resemble the sort of rigid, bounded self that feminist theory has identified as 'masculinist': 'By autonomous, however, Laurie (and I) do not mean a self that denies its embeddedness in many kinds of social relations. For a notion of autonomy that is opposed to the "social" or to "connection to others" is itself a barrier to the development and enjoyment of such a self' (1987: 104). The 'autonomous self' denied women is neither the fully relational nurturing self, congruent with cultural definitions of femininity, nor the ' "unitary," mentalist, deeroticized, masterful, and oppositional' self that is congruent with cultural definitions of masculinity (1987: 93). The autonomous self that Laurie's family and her culture won't allow her access to is defined by Flax as transcending such gendered splits between dependence or engulfment, on the one hand, and isolation and separation, on the other.

Clearly, Flax's feminist orientation enables her to 'see,' and to help Laurie discover this very feminist self. It is a utopian self, since, as Flax states, it does not and cannot yet exist in contemporary culture, due to the powerful forces of repression at work which mitigate against such selfhood for women. But collective feminist action may enable its emergence.

> By retrieving repressed aspects of the self together – our anger, our connections with, attractions to, and fear of other women, our self-hate – we also begin to find in this 'new' memory a powerful impulse toward political actions. Experiences in therapy and consciousness raising confirm that memory in its fullness requires access to the various aspects of the self. (1987: 106)

Thus, Flax locates Laurie's fragmentation within the wider cultural splits and fragmentations that impact on women's construction of identity. As a feminist, Flax is oriented not only to early childhood experiences and relationships, but to cultural prohibitions and repressions and their psychic and bodily costs for women. Borderline subjectivity, then, is potentially all Western women's subjectivity, crystallizing in particularly intense form in borderline patients such as Laurie through an especially extreme degree of repression by her family.

Gender and the Borderline Self: A Cultural Analysis

As the discussion of the cases shows, the symptoms of women diagnosed borderline may be read as meaningful or intelligible responses to the double bind of feminine subjecthood. The borderline patients discussed here experienced an uncertainty or crisis in subjecthood, manifest in a split or fracturing of self, a split between irreconcilable aspects of being. This is most explicitly expressed in the case of Marge. We saw how Marge's crisis of identity was expressed as a split between a passive, dependent, powerless persona, and an empowered, yet forbidden, double. Laurie, too, as Flax shows, appeared to be responding to the contradictory demands of a socially sanctioned feminine selfhood and a forbidden autonomy and empowerment.

In the context of the double bind of women's subjectivity, the borderline patient's split self has its sources not in a flawed psyche, but in the overall context of the Western cultural split between a devalued realm of the feminine and the body, and the realm of the autonomous subject – the realm of reason and the mind. Women, on the borderline between these two realms, must negotiate both. We can characterize this fragmentation and oscillation not as pathological instability, but as a fluctuation between subject positions. Borderline patients appear to be aware of the contradictions they experience: Marge and Laurie appeared to recognize the existence of these 'split-off' aspects of themselves. One senses Marge's conscious performance of the forbidden 'Me.'

This double bind of feminine subjecthood was transmitted to Marge and Laurie through the family: in Laurie's case, through cultural messages from her parents about women and the management of their bodies; and in Marge's case, her father's sexual abuse. Yet this double bind goes beyond the family; it is located in the Western cultural images of femininity. Thus, these images cannot be integrated into a coherent, unified gender identity.

The patients discussed by Singer, however, seem to show an irrevocable split between these dual images. Their sense of artificiality suggests that, like Laurie and Marge, they present an outer mask of conformity, a false, surface, socially adaptable persona. Yet their emptiness and numbness also suggests that there is nothing suppressed, nothing underneath the mask. In place of a split-off, forbidden self, there is only numbness. What does this numbness signify? If symptoms are traces, carriers of repressed cultural meanings, as Romanyshyn states, or literalizations of contradictions in the construction of gender (Bordo, 1993), what is numbness signifying about contemporary culture?

The construction of gender, as De Lauretis notes, occurs in relation to ideology – the 'always provisional encounter of subject and codes' (1984: 14). Considered in the context of the cultural conditions for women's selfhood, the borderline patient's symptomatic fragmentation between a false surface self and an underlying emptiness is perhaps not as far removed from 'normality' as the psychiatric account would suggest. The symptoms of the borderline patients suggest that they have become nothing but surface, feeling such a profound sensation of emptiness that they begin to experience themselves as rigid surface only, as objects that cover a void. Unlike Rivière's patients, who don a mask of femininity to cover a suppressed or forbidden 'masculine' self, the borderline patient appears to have lost touch with any form of being outside of the boundaries of the mask, and thus manifests an empty conformity. Borderline patients thus literalize the effects of the production of femininity within consumer culture, a culture that, as Christopher Lasch writes, creates social conditions which 'encourage an unprecedented attention to superficial impressions and images, to the point where the self becomes almost indistinguishable from its surface' (1984: 30).

The feelings of numbness and artifice might suggest that the border between this reified image of femininity and anything outside its boundaries is eroding or blurring, leaving open the question of whether there remain any possible actions or lines of behavior outside that pre-given image. In a society dominated by electronic media, the borders between what is simulated under circulating images of 'woman' and potential alternatives to that dominant image may be disappearing. The question of what 'woman' is, or of what 'femininity' might be, has been plagued by the uncertainty of naming any characteristics not already pre-constructed in advance by the dominant culture. Can a border be located between the mask and what lies beneath; between the mass-media image and the 'real'? Did such a boundary ever exist? Or is it increasingly in danger of being erased under the ultra-modern invasion or 'infestation' of the body by an abstract, disembodied power, a power 'positive, charismatic and seductive' (Kroker, 1986: 75)?

This blurring or erosion of the boundary between this reified image and women's lived experiences is taken up by Susan Griffin in her book *Pornography and Silence* (1981). In the chapter 'Silence,' her analysis is focused on the vanishing border between the mask and the 'real.' Arguing that Western industrialized culture is involved in a massive 'participation mystique,' in which we confuse the image for the 'real,' Griffin describes the power of the 'pornographic ideal' of women as a false, disembodied, doll-like image. This false image is taken as real, however, and no other possibilities for feminine selfhood are imaginable. Yet Griffin argues that there exists a trace, in women's subjectivity, of an alternative, lost self, a haunting feeling, an unconscious sense of some other way of being.

Griffin writes that this haunting feeling can be read as a hopeful sign of the traces of an 'authentic' self whose loss is memorialized in symptoms: 'When one has lost one's self, one does not say, I am one way but I behave another. Rather, one has forgotten that the lost self ever existed. Only a feeling of falsity remains. One may feel empty inside. Or one may have a continual feeling of loneliness.' Griffin quotes Marilyn Monroe, the quintessential icon of ideal femininity in the 1950s, as saying, 'I used to get the feeling, and sometimes I still get it, that sometimes I was fooling somebody, I don't know who or what – maybe myself' (1981: 205).

Thus, these 'symptoms' of numbness and emptiness carry the haunting memory or trace of a lost feeling part of the self. 'We must recognize that in our own experience of emptiness, that even though one feels "empty," one must have a self in order to feel this emptiness; a loss cannot be felt unless what is missed is really a lost part of the self' (1981: 206).

> But always there is something unreal, uncannily unreal, about her. Knowing she has fulfilled her role perfectly, the mind casts back, the heart longs, for something more. But always finds only a flat, perfect image reflected back, a deathlike and still mask of being. Inside, then, this supposedly perfectly mothered woman feels the same pâpier-mâché self. Polite. Correct. Normal. Empty. (1981: 209)

These symptoms, as visible signs of the material effects of contemporary gender constructions, may operate as points of resistance, in revealing a fracture between the dominant image and its material effects in the psyches and bodies of women diagnosed borderline. They may, like women's symptomatic practices of starvation under the contemporary Western cultural 'tyranny of slenderness,' thus 'expose and indict' the cultural dictums of the construction of gender, 'precisely by pursuing them to the point where their destructive potential is revealed for all to see' (Bordo, 1993: 176).

Conclusion

In the cases discussed here, the psychiatric interpretation of the borderline patient, based on a definition of a healthy self as a gender-neutral, coherent, unified, and bounded entity, yields ahistorical and decontextualized readings of the borderline patient's symptoms as an inner pathology. The selves of these women are depicted as lacking coherence and integration – without firm borders – and are furthermore linguistically created within those very narratives. Singer reconstructed his borderline patient's 'tenuous self-experience' in vivid ways, relying on the metaphor of emptiness and liquidity to depict the borderline's self as dissolving, fluid, and intangible. Yalom's expressive portrayal of the borderline patient's attractive and seductive double is a clear example of the representation of the borderline patient that draws on explicit images of women.

I have argued that borderline symptoms can be read not as pathology, but as meaningful or intelligible responses to the contradictions of gender. The women diagnosed borderline appear to be caught in the transition between the position of passive, dependent, object of other's wills and desires (Laurie's family; Marge's abusive father), and the forbidden, yet increasingly accessible, position of active, desiring subject. This transition is fraught with contradictions. For these women, shedding the dependent passive self is more than a matter of individual adjustment; since it is a position structured into the logic of gender within which they construct their identities, they cannot step outside of these gender relations to reconstruct their identities. In addition, to enter the realm of the subject, the realm formerly excluded them, women must disavow their feminine embodied qualities, which are viewed as threatening or dangerous ('lethal,' in Yalom's words, to Marge's 'central' self). Thus, women who come to be diagnosed borderline can be said to be expressing in exaggerated form the effects of the very conditions for women's construction of self; these symptoms are thus readable as the embodiments or literal inscriptions of the contemporary construction of gender.

Note

1. Here I speak of the binary logic between the dominant white rational culture and its projected others that Anzaldua writes of. It is important to acknowledge, however, that Anzaldua's 'border subject' is historically situated in relation to national and racial borders as well, specific to the contested US–Mexican border and the cultural clash created by the dominance of US hegemony on the Mexican and indigenous cultures. I speak of gender borders in a somewhat more abstract sense, relying on Anzaldua's insights regarding the workings of cultural borders and their effects. In regarding women, or, more specifically, women who come to be diagnosed 'borderline,' as 'border subjects,' I do so in the spirit that Anzaldua's work evokes: that all cultural identities are partial, hybrids constructed from fragments; a recognition that calls into the question the notion of a pure or unified identity.

References

American Psychiatric Association (1980) *Diagnostic and Statistical Manual of Mental Disorders*. 3rd edn. Washington, DC: American Psychiatric Association.

American Psychiatric Association (1994) *Diagnostic and Statistical Manual of Mental Disorders*. 4th edn. Washington, DC: American Psychiatric Association.

Anzaldua, G. (1987) *Borderlands/La Frontera: The New Mestiza*. San Francisco: Spinsters/Aunt Lute.

Aronson, T. (1985) 'Historical Perspectives on the Borderline Concept: A Review and Critique,' *Psychiatry*, 48: 209–22.

Bordo, S. (1993) *Unbearable Weight: Feminism, Western Culture, and the Body*. Berkeley: University of California Press.

Boyer, L. (1977) 'Working with a Borderline Patient,' *Psychoanalytic Quarterly*, 46: 386–424.

Castaneda, R. and Franco, H. (1985) 'Sex and Ethnic Distribution of Borderline Personality Disorder in an Inpatient Sample,' *American Journal of Psychiatry*, 142 (2): 1202–3.

Cixous, H. and Clément, C. (1986) *The Newly Born Woman*. Minneapolis, MA: University of Minnesota Press.

Clément, C. (1986) 'The Guilty One,' in H. Cixous and C. Clément, *The Newly Born Woman*. Minneapolis: University of Minnesota Press. pp. 3–59.

Clément, C. (1987) *The Weary Sons of Freud*. New York: Verso.

De Chenne, T. (1991) 'Diagnosis as Therapy for the Borderline Personality,' *Psychotherapy*, 28 (2): 284–91.

De Lauretis, T. (1984) *Alice Doesn't: Feminism, Semiotic, Cinema*. Bloomington: Indiana University Press.

Ferguson, K. (1991) 'Interpretation and Genealogy in Feminism,' *Signs*, 16: 322–39.

Flax, J. (1987) 'Remembering the Selves: Is the Repressed Gendered?,' *Michigan Quarterly Review*, 26: 92–110.

Foucault, M. (1965) *Madness and Civilization: A History of Insanity in the Age of Reason*. New York: Vintage.

Foucault, M. (1977) *Discipline and Punish: The Birth of the Prison*. New York: Pantheon.

Foucault, M. (1980) *The History of Sexuality, Vol. I*. New York: Vintage.

Frosh, S. (1991) *Identity Crisis: Modernity, Psychoanalysis and the Self*. London and New York: Routledge.

Gallop, J. (1982) *The Daughter's Seduction: Feminism and Psychoanalysis*. Ithaca, NY: Cornell University Press.

Gibson, D. (1991) 'Borderline Personality Disorder: Issues of Etiology and Gender,' *Occupational Therapy in Mental Health*, 10 (4): 63–77.

Green, A. (1977) 'The Borderline Concept: A Conceptual Framework for the Understanding of Borderline Patients,' in P. Hartcollis (ed.), *Borderline Disorders: The Concept, the Syndrome, the Patient*. New York: International Universities Press. pp. 15–44.

Griffin, S. (1981) *Pornography and Silence: Culture's Revenge Against Nature*. New York: Harper & Row.
Gunderson, J.G. and Zanarini, M.C. (1987) 'Current Overview of the Borderline Diagnosis,' *Journal of Clinical Psychiatry*, 48: 5–11.
Hicks, D.E. (1991) *Border Writing: The Multidimensional Text*. Minneapolis: University of Minnesota Press.
Irigaray, L. (1985) *The Speculum of the Other Woman*. Ithaca, NY: Cornell University Press.
Kahane, C. (1985) 'Introduction: Part Two,' in *In Dora's Case: Freud-Hysteria-Feminism*. New York: Columbia University Press.
Kaysen, S. (1993) *Girl, Interrupted*. New York: Turtle Bay Books.
Kroker, A. (1986) 'The Disembodied Eye,' in A. Kroker, and D. Cook (eds), *The Postmodern Scene: Excremental Culture and Hyper Aesthetics*. New York: St Martin's Press.
Lasch, C. (1984) *The Minimal Self: Psychic Survival in Troubled Times*. New York: Norton.
Lewis, G. and Appleby, L. (1988) 'Personality Disorder: The Patient Psychiatrists Dislike,' *British Journal of Psychiatry*, 153: 44–9.
Mack, J.E. (1975) 'Borderline States: An Historical Perspective,' in J.E. Mack (ed.), *Borderline States in Psychiatry: An Historical Perspective*. New York: Grune & Stratton. pp. 1–27.
Ortner, S. (1974) 'Is Female to Male as Nature is to Culture?,' in M.Z. Rosaldo and L. Lamphere (ed.), *Woman, Culture, and Society*. Stanford, CA: Stanford University Press. pp. 67–87.
Reiser, D.E. and Levenson, H. (1984) 'Abuses of the Borderline Diagnosis: A Clinical Problem with Teaching Opportunities,' *American Journal of Psychiatry*, 141 (12): 1528–32.
Rivière, J. (1929) 'Womanliness as Masquerade,' *The International Journal of Psychoanalysis*, 10: 303–13.
Romanyshyn, R. (1989) *Technology as Dream and Symptom*. London and New York: Routledge.
Ross, M. (1976) 'The Borderline Diathesis,' *International Review of Psycho-Analysis*, 3: 305–21.
Schafer, R. (1989) 'Narratives of the Self,' in A. Cooper, O. Kernberg, and E. Person (eds), *Psychoanalysis: Toward the Second Century*. New Haven, CT: Yale University Press. pp. 153–67.
Schwartz-Salant, N. (1989) *Borderline Personality: Vision and Healing*. Wilmette, IL: Chiron Publications.
Showalter, E. (1985) *The Female Malady: Women, Madness, and English Culture, 1830–1980*. New York: Penguin.
Showalter, E. (1990) *Sexual Anarchy: Gender and Culture at the Fin de Siècle*. New York: Viking.
Singer, M. (1977) 'The Experience of Emptiness in Narcissistic and Borderline States I: The Struggle for a Sense of Self and the Potential for Suicide,' *International Review of Psycho-Analysis*, 4: 471–9.
Stern, A. (1938) 'Notes on the Border Line Group of Neuroses,' *Psychoanalytic Quarterly*, 7: 467–89.
Swartz, M., Blazer, D., George, L., and Winfield, I. (1990) 'Estimating the Prevalence of Borderline Personality Disorder,' *Journal of Personality Disorders*, 4 (3): 257–72.
Theweleit, K. (1987) *Male Fantasies: Volume I: Women, Floods, Bodies, History*. Minneapolis: University of Minnesota Press.
Yalom, I. (1989) 'Therapeutic Monogamy,' from *Love's Executioner and Other Tales of Psychotherapy*. New York: Basic Books. pp. 213–29.

8

Is It Me or Is It Prozac? Antidepressants and the Construction of Self

John P. Hewitt, Michael R. Fraser, and LeslieBeth Berger

Since the 1950s, psychiatry has increasingly turned toward drug therapy in the treatment of depression.[1] In the late 1980s, the use of antidepressant drugs accelerated greatly, drug therapy for depression became widely publicized, and the social construction of depression as a biological illness began to solidify. One of the drugs most responsible for this transformation of public attitude and medical practice is *fluoxetine hydrochloride*, marketed by Eli Lilly since 1987 under the trade name *Prozac*. In this essay we examine the implications of this and other antidepressants for self-theory. We probe the possible impact of Prozac on self-esteem and explore the social mechanisms through which it may exert its influence; reconceptualize self-esteem as an emotion grounded in mood and dependent upon discourse; consider self-esteem and depression as alternative and linked vocabularies for experiencing the self; discuss the linkage of contemporary culture, self-esteem, and depression; and theorize about how psychoactive drugs may affect the social construction of the self.

Although not demonstrably more effective than other drugs in treating major depression, Prozac has acquired almost legendary status since its introduction. It is one of a class of antidepressants termed SSRIs – selective serotonin reuptake inhibitors – so called because they act to inhibit the reuptake of the neurotransmitter serotonin from the synapse into the presynaptic neuron after its reception by the postsynaptic neuron. These drugs effectively prolong the action of serotonin, and in so doing significantly affect both mood and behavior. In a significant proportion of cases, they gradually counteract depression and permit people to live free of its weight.

Prozac is now one of the most widely prescribed drugs in the United States (*Consumer Reports*, 1993; Eli Lilly and Company, 1993a, 1993b). The drug's popularity is remarkable in view of the fact that its early history included widely publicized charges that it was responsible for several suicides. Thanks in part to widespread media publicity, most recently in the wake of Peter Kramer's (1993a) best-seller *Listening to Prozac*, proselytizing by psychiatrists and psychotherapists, favorable word-of-mouth advertising, and a reputation for fewer and milder side-effects than other antidepressants,

Prozac has become a drug patients actively seek from their physicians. Indeed, it has become generally perceived as a miraculous drug that not only relieves the painful symptoms of depression but also dramatically transforms some patients who before taking the drug led disorganized, unproductive, and desperately unhappy lives.[2]

In this essay we take up several important theoretical questions raised by the apparent success of the pharmacological treatment of depression: How is our sociological and social psychological understanding of the self modified, if at all, by the development of a drug that seemingly brightens mood, alters social perception, and enhances self-esteem? How can we assimilate findings about antidepressants into social psychological theory? Can we comprehend the action of the antidepressants in social psychological terms? How are such developments in psychopharmacology and the social construction of depression linked to postmodernity?

Our approach to these questions utilizes social psychological theories of self and emotion, existing scientific and popular literature that describes the effects of Prozac, and illustrations drawn from the clinical experience of one of the authors. There is a paucity of sound research on the effects of Prozac upon the self, but there is an abundance of clinical testimony and popular reports that suggest its impact is considerable. Even allowing for the likelihood that the developing Prozac culture has created a powerful and partially self-fulfilling set of expectations about the nature of the drug's effects on potential users, we are convinced that the drug has significant direct effects of the sort we describe.[3] Hence, there seems ample warrant for theoretical analysis of its implications even in the absence of the compelling evidence we would ideally wish to have.[4]

What Does Prozac Do?

An account of how Prozac affects the neurotransmission process is beyond the scope of this essay, and in many respects quite beside the point. There is not widespread agreement as to how any of the antidepressants achieve their results, beyond the fact that they in various ways prolong the presence of neurotransmitters in the synapse. Nor is it clear that depression is a single clinical entity, since drugs that are effective in some patients do not produce results in others. Thus, some who are diagnosed with depression will respond to Prozac, whereas others will respond only to one of a number of other available antidepressants. Some people must try several drugs before finding one that works.

There is substantial agreement, however, that in many individuals Prozac gradually relieves the suffering associated with clinical depression. Over a period of weeks from the beginning of treatment, patients gradually find their moods lifted or 'brightened.' They regain a sense of well-being, become mentally more focused, rekindle their interest in life, find their energy levels restored, and become more positive in their outlook. In short, their depressive symptoms gradually diminish. Moreover, it does not seem likely that Prozac merely 'masks' a depression, so that the underlying condition is simply covered by 'artificial' drug-induced feelings. Those who take Prozac feel no rush or high associated with ingesting the drug, and persons anxious for their depressions to be brought under control often feel impatient for the drug to take effect. Indeed, others may notice objective changes in behavior before the individual reports any change in mood or self-feeling. Once Prozac takes full hold, people feel not drugged, but 'normal.' As one woman, an amateur golfer, reported, she now 'felt on a par with the rest of the world.'[5]

The key effect of Prozac is a gradual improvement or 'brightening' of mood, accompanied by both cognitive and somatic changes. A clinically depressed person may be sad, irritable, and lacking capacity to experience pleasure. There may be no external reason for such feelings, and the person is essentially powerless to do much to alleviate them short of either some kind of therapeutic intervention or waiting for them to disappear of their own accord. The depressed person may find it difficult to think clearly or to concentrate, and may well have sleep disturbances (particularly early-waking insomnia) and feel unable to muster sufficient interest or energy to do even those things that were previously important or interesting. Prozac and the other antidepressants gradually lift mood, improve energy levels, and restore cognitive functioning. An accounting executive, for example, said that prior to Prozac she had gone through life 'as though Vaseline had been rubbed permanently' over her eyeglasses. Now, she said, she could 'think and see clearly and instantly.'

Four other effects of Prozac seem notable and especially consequential for the way we conceptualize the self. First, Peter Kramer (1993a: 67–97) reports that in some patients (though what proportion is not clear) Prozac seems to ameliorate the negative sensitivity to others that is sometimes associated with depression. The depressed often display 'morbid sensitivity' to the social world around them, treating as slights what others would not notice or easily ignore. They are keenly attuned to the social world, but they interpret much that is random or unintended in the behavior of others as meaningful or significant gestures. They anticipate the worst in others' reactions to them, and in particular seem affected by what they readily perceive as rejection, to which they react with a deepening of depression. Prozac seems to diminish not only the morbid sensitivity of the depressed but also the rejection sensitivity of those who are not clinically depressed or who only marginally meet the criteria of clinical depression. It appears in some way to make people less dependent on the approval of others or on acceptance by them, and less likely to define the actions of others as rejecting.[6]

Second, for some patients (again the exact proportion is unknown), Prozac seems to have direct effects on the low self-esteem that is a common symptom of depression. Depressed people often blame themselves for the bad things that happen, believe that they are evil, or feel a generalized sense of worthlessness. Prozac seems to raise self-esteem. Even for those who fall short of strict clinical criteria for depression, the drug seems to enhance self-esteem in a way that those taking the drug consider miraculous. Kramer (1993a: 217–20) reports the case of a patient who had received extensive psychotherapy, but who had not really achieved the kind of results either he or the therapist desired or anticipated. It was evident that in spite of extensive therapy – and considerable professional success and an impressive demeanor – the patient suffered from low self-esteem. On a course of Prozac, he improved dramatically, and reported that he not only felt better about himself but also could now make sense of the many years of therapy he had experienced and absorb its lessons.

Third, those for whom Prozac successfully treats depression tend to report either a restoration, or in some cases the discovery, of an avid interest in life, a sense of 'what all the excitement is about.' Those who are chronically or deeply depressed find it difficult to understand how others can possibly take an interest in life or find the energy to deal with its ups and downs. To be depressed is not only to feel that life is hopeless or pointless, but also to be baffled by the hope and purpose that others apparently find. Those who respond to Prozac feel either restored to 'normality,' by which they mean the capacity for interest and enjoyment, or that they have for the first time in their lives discovered what it is to be 'normal' in this sense. One client, a college junior, returned to Rome, where he had previously spent a junior year abroad. He walked the Forum, sat at a café at the Trevi Fountain, and couldn't believe that a year ago he 'had thought Rome was just one more overcrowded, dirty city with a few sights.' Now, on Prozac, he said he experienced for the first time 'all the excitement about travel.'

Fourth, successful Prozac users who later taper off or stop taking the drug after a typical use period of six months sometimes report that they no longer 'feel themselves.' Even when depression does not return, or does not do so immediately, for some users the cessation of the drug leads them to report that they are 'not themselves.' They feel that the desirable sense of a normal self they had achieved while taking the drug is beginning to slip away. Prozac, they feel, had restored or created a self that seems threatened when drug therapy is discontinued. One woman who discontinued use said she 'felt as though she were in mourning for a self she never even knew she had.'

What do these effects of Prozac imply for self theory? If a pill can elevate mood and shape a person's outlook on the world and capacity to function in it, what are the implications for our view of a creature who is capable of symbolically designating the world, acting toward the self as an object, and managing emotions? Is it the pill or the person presenting a self? If Prozac reduces rejection sensitivity, what does this say about our analyses of role-taking, in which it is the imagined response of the other that holds significance both for conduct and self-feeling? If a pill can enhance self-esteem without any change in one's life circumstances or position in the social world, what does this do to our view that the responses of others matter to one's view of self? And if a pill can create a self that feels 'normal' and removing it makes one feel 'not oneself,' is the self as much a social object as we had once thought? What and where is the self if a pill can make it whole and well again?

A Pill for Self-Esteem

Although clinical trials of Prozac were designed to test its effectiveness as a treatment for major depression, the current popularity of the drug owes a great deal to reports of its impact on lesser forms of depression and on personal problems as diverse as rejection sensitivity and low self-esteem. For significant numbers of users, a therapeutic dose of Prozac has the effect of raising self-esteem. There are no reliable reports of how many Prozac users are affected in this way, nor can we measure by what degree the drug elevates self-esteem in those for whom it has this effect. But it seems clear from both popular and clinical reports that Prozac not only makes people feel better but also makes them feel better about themselves. The question is, how? Formulating an answer to this question will help us understand the relevance of Prozac to the self.

One approach to assimilating the effects of Prozac into self theory is by examining the standard social psychological account of self-esteem. In this account, self-esteem arises incrementally through role-taking as the person lives in the social world and takes the attitudes of others toward self. If those attitudes are positive, self-esteem is enhanced; if they are negative, it is reduced. Self-esteem is thus formed, enhanced, sustained, or undermined as the person interacts with others and reflexively interprets not only their words and deeds but also his or her own possessions, attributes, and activities. More precisely, self-esteem arises in five basic ways, all dependent on role-taking (see Gecas and Schwalbe, 1983; Hewitt, 1994: 122–5; Rosenberg, 1981: 602–6).

First, the person's image of self rests upon others' direct appraisals, which shape feelings about the self through the ordinary processes of role-taking but leave little to the imagination. Direct appraisals do need some interpretation – the person must put himself or herself in the place of the other and imagine the meaning of the other's response – but they leave little room for it. Evaluations are so unequivocal that the recipient has little choice but to interpret them in ways that more or less coincide with the intentions of the evaluator.

Prozac may enhance self-esteem by promoting behavioral changes that others notice and reward through more positive direct evaluations of the user. Friends, spouses, and associates of Prozac users are apt to say that it makes them 'nicer,' easier to get along with, less abrasive, and more positive (Kramer, 1993a). Parents of an adult child living at home reported that their son, now on Prozac, suddenly began asking whether he should change the television channel, rather than just seizing the clicker. Once he even brought home milk and bread when he realized the family supply was low. When the mother mentioned how considerate the son was now being, he smiled and said, 'Well, you guys are making it easier now to be nice.' As a family physician who regularly prescribes the drug for depression puts it, 'Prozac brings out the best in people.' Any drug that relieved the behavioral manifestations of depression might have such an impact on the person's social surroundings, since depression makes people pessimistic, irritable, 'moody,' and in other ways unreceptive to social intercourse. If Prozac 'brightens' the person's mood, making him or her more socially agreeable, it may then promote behavior that others regard more positively and to which they will respond more positively.

Second, self-esteem is sustained or undermined by a process of reflected appraisals in which one imagines how others feel about one, briefly shares those feelings, and thereby adopts their imagined attitudes toward the self. Even when others are providing no direct appraisals, we find ways to imagine what they think of us. We worry about the significance of smiles or frowns, speculate about how our work will be received, and in similar ways imagine the opinions of important others. It goes without saying that reflected appraisals allow greater interpretive latitude than do direct evaluations. There is a loose fit between the other's word or deed and the significance attributed to it.

If we are to grasp the role of Prozac, we must think about its possible impact on this interpretive process. Prozac seems to exert a calming effect, not by tranquilizing the person or muting perception, but rather by diminishing anxious or panicked responses to ordinary stimuli. Whereas the depressed person is apt to be irritable and to overreact to social slights or negative comments from others, the individual taking Prozac seems capable of responding in a more measured way. The medication seems to alter role-taking, not by making it more accurate but by making it more benign. The role-taker on Prozac seems more willing or able to attribute positive motivations or attitudes to the other, and hence to imagine the self in a more positive light.

Third, self-esteem is constructed by comparing one's own characteristics and accomplishments with those of others, with additions to or subtractions from the fund of self-esteem, dependent on how we are able to interpret ourselves in comparison with them. We gain in self-esteem when we can imagine that some relevant community of reference looks favorably on us in comparison with others. Prozac may increase self-esteem derived from social comparisons in much the same way as reflected appraisals, by allowing the person more latitude to imagine the community's positive appraisal. Freed from the perceptual influence of depression, for example, the person can more readily attribute a positive attitude to the generalized other and see himself or herself as a valued member of the community rather than as a despised or blameworthy person. It is even possible that Prozac mutes the tendency to rely on social comparison. The reduced sensitivity to social rejection that Prozac reportedly achieves may be a facet of a more pervasive reduction in sensitivity to all appraisals. If so, a lessened sensitivity to social evaluations reduces the salience not only of social comparison but of direct evaluations and reflected appraisals as well.

Fourth, people experience themselves in a positive or a negative light by observing their own performances and holding them up to the social scrutiny of the generalized other. The action of Prozac here probably resembles that in the preceding discussion of reflected appraisals and social comparison. That is, Prozac may allow the person to attribute a more positive or tolerant view to the generalized other. It suppresses anxious or panicked imaginations of the other's attitudes. And it may also simply make the person less sensitive to evaluations of all kinds, whatever their direction.

Fifth, self-esteem arises from the person's sense of efficacious action on his or her surroundings. Although this form of self-esteem seems to rest more on the person's sense of autonomy and agency and less on the judgments of others, it is worth noting that it, like all constructions of the self, depends to some extent on a process of imagining the self as it may appear to others. The person feels efficacious, in other words, not directly as a result of experiences with self, but indirectly because he or she can imagine an audience that views those performances as efficacious. Here again, then, the argument is much the same: Prozac allows for a more positive and more benign imagination of others' attitudes.

The preceding discussion treats self-esteem as a product of social experience, and explains the effects of Prozac as a result of its impact upon behavior, role-taking, and sensitivity to evaluation. Hypothetically, Prozac earns the person more favorable evaluations by adjusting behavior in a more socially desirable direction. It enhances the person's capacity for positive role-taking by making it more likely that the real or imagined responses of both particular and generalized others will be seen as positive. And it reduces sensitivity to evaluations of all kinds, in effect making the person less dependent on others for the maintenance of self-esteem.

Although this approach to the effects of Prozac seems entirely plausible in the light of social psychological self theory, there are indications in clinical reports on Prozac that it has a more direct impact on self-esteem than this approach is capable of explaining. Some users portray Prozac as a pill that directly enhances self-esteem without regard to the attitudes of others. They report not a gradual and indirect improvement in self-esteem, but a direct and unmediated effect. Although there is the usual time lag between beginning a course of Prozac therapy and subjectively noticeable effects, one of the reported first effects is the enhancement of self-esteem. With no discernible change in social milieu, and with no lengthy period of time during which altered behavior might influence the responses of others, the person feels better about himself or herself. Self-esteem simply rises as if it was independent of the real or imagined appraisals of others. Thus, for example, a retired physician said he awakened one morning feeling as though he had 'just performed the most complex surgery – and could do two more.' And a middle-aged woman who was facing divorce reported that she 'suddenly had a hardier, more confident self that could face the world' no matter how much it had changed since her dating days. For such people, Prozac appears to act as a self-esteem pill, shaping attitudes toward the self as directly as insulin affects the metabolism of sugar.

If we give credence to the idea that Prozac *directly* raises self-esteem, then we have a theoretical problem of greater magnitude. For on the surface, at least, the possibility of a self-esteem pill seems to undermine the very foundations of self theory. If *fluoxetine* can accomplish what we had thought required social interaction, where does this leave our theory of a self grounded in social interaction? The problem can be solved if we think more carefully about the meaning of 'self-esteem' as a social psychological construct.

Self-Esteem as Mood and Discourse

Self-esteem is commonly defined as the evaluative dimension of the self. Where identity locates the self as an object in relation to others, self-esteem refers primarily to self-evaluations. One either likes or dislikes oneself, feels heartened or disheartened by what one sees in the social mirror, and is proud or ashamed of one's performances or characteristics. Self-esteem is thus the general name that social psychologists give to the evaluative aspect of self-regard.

Although self-esteem almost certainly arises at least in part out of evaluative processes, it seems more usefully conceived as the *affective* dimension of self-regard. The experience of a self invariably has an affective component: one does not merely see oneself positively or negatively, or with approval or disapproval, in a neutral cognitive sense, but responds emotionally to what one sees in the social mirror. One *feels* good or bad, cheerful or dismayed, elated or deflated. Reflexivity prompts an emotional response to self, and that is the fundamental reality to which self-esteem refers.

We can carry this analysis a step further by treating self-esteem as a socially constructed emotion grounded in *mood*. Mood involves physiological arousal (or depression) and subjective feeling along a dimension we might label dysphoria/euphoria. Dysphoria may be defined as 'an emotional state characterized by anxiety, depression, and restlessness'; euphoria is 'a feeling of great happiness or well-being' (*American Heritage Electronic Dictionary*, 1992). In regarding mood as the bodily underpinning of self-esteem (similar to what Kemper [1987] calls a primary emotion), we are asserting that it is a universal human experience and not exclusively a cultural construction. Because we are cultural creatures whose experience and expression of emotional states is socially regulated and culturally shaped, it is impossible to observe a culturally unmediated experience or expression of dysphoria or euphoria. This fact does not, however, prevent us from postulating something like 'mood' as a way of depicting universal potentials in human experience. Indeed, we argue it is nearly impossible to make any warranted statements about emotion without developing such constructs.

Like other affective states, mood is experienced not directly or automatically, but in terms of culturally supplied meanings. Even such primary states as fear or anger derive the greater part of their meaning not from the underlying visceral sensations or neurological correlates, but from the way human beings interpret and talk about them. These emotions are situated, and derive their significance from the circumstances in which they are aroused and the lines of conduct they direct or encourage. It is the same with mood: it is the situational interpretation of the affect that shapes the individual's experience.

Self-esteem, we argue, is a culturally available way of interpreting mood.[7] It is not the only available interpretation, of course, and it is an important task to specify those situations or social circumstances in which this interpretation is employed in preference to others. Sometimes people who experience dysphoria or euphoria merely say they are in a 'good mood' or a 'bad mood,' or that they are having a 'good day' or a 'bad day.' Sometimes they say they are depressed, in the everyday and non-clinical sense, or blue, or sad, or elated, or euphoric. Sometimes they say they are depressed, and mean this word in a clinical and medical sense. And under some conditions, they interpret their feeling-state in terms of self-esteem or in other terms of self-reference that both lay and professional usage conceive as indicators of self-esteem.

Self-esteem (and its associated terms of self-reference) thus provides a label the person may attach to feelings aroused when he or she sees the self reflected in the social mirror. Self-reference arouses a variety of emotions: one may respond to an image of oneself with anxiety, fear, sadness, anger, love, and in countless other emotional ways. We argue that of those feelings potentially aroused by the experience of self, or associated with the experience of self, mood is of central significance. Sometimes the social mirror reveals an image that depresses mood, sometimes it reveals an object that elates it; sometimes the person associates pre-existing feelings of dysphoria or euphoria with the image he or she sees in the mirror. Whatever the case, however, mood is integral to our experience of self, and 'self-esteem' is an available social construct that enables individuals to interpret such self feelings or encourages others to interpret them on their behalf.

It is not surprising that contemporary Americans frequently experience and interpret their feeling-states in terms of self-esteem. 'Self-esteem' resonates strongly in a culture that emphasizes the centrality of the individual and that has a long tradition of discourse about the 'power of positive thinking' to help the person overcome obstacles, find success, and enjoy happiness. Moreover, in a culture that makes the self a central object and that prompts considerable discourse about it, there is not only a ready market for, but also eager suppliers of, vocabularies of self. The concept of self-esteem has been available for well over a century, and psychologists, educators, and others have accumulated and promulgated a large body of research findings. This professional discourse permeates everyday thinking about the self, and self-esteem is now the concept *du jour* of popular discourse.

The appeal of self-esteem as a term for interpreting feelings does not stem only from individualism or the conceptual entrepreneurship of psychologists, educators, and therapists. In a social world where a significant number of social relationships are not provided for the individual but are open to individual choice or initiative, 'liking' and 'disliking' are important dimensions of self-regard. Where social and personal identities are often transitory or open to choice, so are the terms and outcomes of self-evaluation. In a stratified and status-conscious society, social comparisons with the positions, possessions, performances, and attributes of others become especially important. These and other circumstances of contemporary life seem not only to produce dysphoric and euphoric affect, but to make the esteem or regard in which one holds oneself a major concern. There is, in other words, a nice fit between the circumstances that shape individual affect with respect to the self, the issues aroused by those circumstances, and the discourse of self-esteem that has been so readily available from professional sources.

If we regard self-esteem as an emotion grounded in mood, then we have a potentially better explanation of how Prozac improves self-esteem. The explanation is better not because it replaces the one we had constructed earlier, but because it strengthens and extends it. We can now explain why Prozac seems to affect self-esteem rather directly and miraculously in some people who take it, while at the same time accounting for the fact that in others it elevates self-esteem more gradually as depression remits. And, as a bonus, we get a better grasp of the relationship between self-esteem and depression and of the nature of depression as a social construct and a form of mental illness.

Prozac directly affects mood. Indeed, it is sometimes called a 'mood-brightener' because of this effect. Those who are depressed and for whom Prozac is a successful treatment will often report that they experience a gradual 'lifting' of the depression, or that they feel like a cloud or a fog has been dispelled. Things seem brighter; life seems more hopeful; darkness gives way to light. If someone who has been experiencing dysphoria and interpreting it in terms of low self-esteem experiences this brightening, it seems natural to expect that this person would describe the change as an increase of self-esteem, and find it rather a miracle that a pill should have such an effect on self-regard. A therapist who has been treating a depressed patient and who has been interpreting the patient's depression partially by linking it to self-esteem may employ and perhaps also communicate self-esteem as a way of interpreting the change the patient has undergone. In short, Prozac changes an underlying condition of mood, and where this condition has been interpreted by the person or by mental health professionals in terms of self-esteem, the change in mood is likely to be interpreted as a change in self-esteem.

This formulation suggests that self-esteem and depression are alternative ways of labeling and experiencing the same underlying affective reality. Under some conditions we say we are depressed, under others that we have low self-esteem, and under still others we speak of both conditions. Such an inference is only partially warranted, however, and it is important to understand its limits as well as its implications.

We make no claim here that depression is not a clinical illness. It is clear that the mental health industry has succeeded in defining depression as an illness and in having this definition far more widely accepted in recent years. However, to say this is not to argue that 'depression' *merely* constitutes one of several alternative vocabularies for experiencing dysphoria. There is enough stability of symptoms both within and across cultures to convince us that there is an underlying 'reality' to which the term 'depression' applies; what clinicians call depression is a disturbance of mood that may be appropriately addressed from within a medical framework. The disturbance has a complex of biological and social causes, and it has measurable biological consequences and efficacious medical treatment. And even if depression were a social construction confined to contemporary Western culture, its construction as a medical problem would confer upon it a reality that would be likely to yield only to medical treatment.

To argue that there is an underlying condition[8] that we may label as 'depression' is not, however, to assert that it is encompassed by any single social construct, including that of 'clinical depression.' Mood is a fundamental aspect of the human experience of self, and it is arguably possible for mood to be disordered at a fundamental biological or neurological level. People experience changes of mood that seem inappropriate in light of circumstances not only to others but also to themselves. They are dysphoric or euphoric at times or under conditions that do not seem sensible or rational to others or to themselves. They find it difficult to improve their mood when they want to or when the culture expects them to; they find it hard to temper or regulate mood when they want to or the culture expects them to. Still, no matter how it may be disordered, mood must be *interpreted* in order to be experienced. Such affective states are open to a variety of interpretations, depending upon the vocabularies available to the person or pressed upon the person by others. Once applied, the terms – for example, 'depression,' 'self-esteem,' 'sadness' – used to interpret feelings have a further impact upon feelings. They shape, and do not merely express, affect. Thus, the biological reality of disordered mood may be expressed in a variety of social constructions.

Depression and self-esteem are connected not only because both are rooted in mood but also because contemporary psychiatric and psychological thinking links depression and self-esteem. Part of this linkage lies in the way psychiatrists and therapists conceive of and diagnose clinical depression: in the eyes of the clinician low self-esteem is a sign of major depression. Lack of self-worth, a tendency to blame oneself for everything that goes wrong and self-hatred are among the symptoms of a major depression.[9] Thus, a connection between the socially constructed experience of self-esteem and the clinical construction of depression is built into the very structure of our thinking about this aspect of the person.

Another major part of the linkage between depression and self-esteem lies in the fact that both are particularly useful cultural constructs in the contemporary world, and perhaps especially in American society. Depressed mood, lack of interest in or the motivation to undertake ordinary activities, and lowered self-esteem are not only among the significant symptoms of depression but also serious indicators of failure to meet the expectations of contemporary American culture. Our cultural expectation is that people have the right to pursue happiness – indeed, not only to pursue it but to get it. People are supposed to be in a positive mood except on some defined social occasions, such as mourning, and even then only for a limited period of time. They are supposed to be energetic in life, to take a healthy and avid interest in the people around them and in their vocational and avocational pursuits. And they are supposed to be liked by others and to like themselves. The constellation of symptoms we associate with depression, in other words, looks very much like a specification of how individuals may fall short of what their culture expects of them. Moreover, high self-esteem seems to be a requirement of many social roles and not merely the psychological trait constructed by psychologists and clinicians.

This way of looking at the symptoms of depression as measures of the degree to which the person falls short of cultural requirements does not imply that the depression is any less real or that it does not have a biological component. But whatever the underlying neurological processes associated with what clinicians call 'depression,' the specific form this condition takes in the contemporary world seems linked both to cultural definitions of the ideal person and to the existential conditions of contemporary life. American culture seems to demand a bright mood, to make happiness an important and valuable condition and to make evidence of happiness a significant item of personal display. We should be happy and act it. Contemporary sociability entails a considerable measure of choice of significant others, dependence upon the good feeling of others for one's participation in social life, and capacity to respond positively to social overtures. We should be prepared to manifest good feeling toward others and to encourage them to manifest it toward us. We say that people are 'depressed' when they are not functioning in the way we feel they should – that is, when they cannot manage emotions within culturally prescribed limits or in a socially advantageous way.

The success of Prozac thus seems to lie in the fact that it produces an actor capable of role-making and role-taking in a way that is culturally preferred and even practically necessary in the contemporary world. It produces an actor who can sustain a good mood and interpret himself or herself as having the requisite amount of self-esteem. It makes the person receptive to others and favorably disposed toward them in a way the culture defines as appropriate. It produces an actor capable of role performances that others will reward and that the person can imagine others approving. It influences a culturally significant dimension of personal experience – mood – for which there is an available, culturally legitimate and more or less coherent means of interpretation supplied by a professional and popular discourse that links depression and self-esteem and authorizes medical treatment to restore the person to health.

Prozac and the Real Self

In the wake of Prozac's success in treating depression there arises the question of where this development leaves the self. Much is made of Peter Kramer's observation that those whose lives have been enhanced by Prozac sometimes feel they are 'not themselves' after they stop taking the drug. If they were themselves while taking the drug, then who were they before they took it? And who are they now? Those who are grateful for Prozac's impact may, nonetheless, feel at a loss to account for the change in their feelings and behavior. Their experience of changes may well raise questions in their minds about how it is possible to undergo such a profound change of feeling, about the reality or durability of the change ('Is it me or is it Prozac?'), and about the years that may have been lost to illness. Moreover, some patients report that they are 'not themselves' while on Prozac, finding themselves uncomfortable with their newfound capacity to feel good, to be socially outgoing, or to take risks they previously would have shunned. One mother of adult children found herself unexpectedly standing up for herself in front of meddlesome in-laws and demanding children. 'I found myself arguing, saying no, and even bringing up issues I long thought dead.' She said such boldness wasn't 'really her.' Another patient, an actor, said he suddenly found himself attending auditions that he had previously passed up. He felt 'braver' without having 'accomplished any of the lesser hurdles.' He felt Prozac was causing him to 'get ahead of himself,' and he now wondered which was the 'real' self – the one with or without Prozac.

The symbolic interactionist approach to the self helps settle some of the questions popular discourse and clinical experience raise about Prozac and 'the real self.' It also focuses more precisely our understanding of the social and theoretical implications of Prozac and other psychoactive drugs. We begin with some observations about how to assimilate the success of Prozac and other antidepressives into our theory of the self.

Sociologists are resistant to biological theories of human behavior, and perhaps especially to those that appear to lodge the self in the processes of neurotransmission rather than in the social world. There are good intellectual and historical reasons for this resistance, for biological explanations do lend themselves readily to the ideological defense of existing social arrangements and thus to the continuing exploitation of those whom those arrangements oppress. Whether in matters of race, gender, or class, the belief that biology is destiny typically supports an unjust status quo. And there is a special concern about psychoactive medications that arises from the fear that they may be too readily used to 'adjust' personality to fit cultural requirements. In their response to the biological turn in psychiatry, social scientists must continue to be alert to such problems and to the seductive appeal of biological reductions.

At the same time, however, social psychologists should also be alert to opportunities to specify more precisely the parameters within which their generalizations hold true and the organic conditions on which they depend. The social psychologist interested in the self is concerned primarily with 'the mind' – that is, with the ways in which human beings are able to take themselves into account and thus achieve the reflexivity we think a hallmark of our species. But the self is minded by a creature whose body includes a brain, whose every act is accomplished by muscles, organs of speech, vision, smell, and touch, and ultimately by processes of neurotransmission. The complex social object we call the self cannot be reduced to those processes; but its existence is not possible without them.

One of the ways we can profitably take the brain into account in our understanding of the self is by using what psychopharmacology learns about human behavior to inform our grasp of that aspect of the self that George Herbert Mead and others called the 'I.' In Mead's still-useful model of mind, self-consciousness arises when conduct meets an obstacle of some kind and the person must inspect his or her ongoing act in order to redirect it in a way that is more likely to meet success (Mead, 1934: 173–8, 192–213). Acts begin without self-consciousness when a stimulus of some kind initiates the process of releasing an impulse. The sight and smell of food, for example, provides the stimulus that permits one to experience and to begin to act on one's hunger. Likewise, another's smile provides the stimulus to our own incipient sociable response. Consciousness of self arises from the inhibition of impulse, as when the experience of hunger reminds the individual that he or she is on a diet and so must wait to eat until dinner, or one interprets another's smile as insincere and so shapes one's own attitude to fit that interpretation.

Mood is a crucial aspect of the self because it profoundly shapes both the impulses that lie within the organism awaiting release and the process in which we see our own incipient acts from the imagined perspectives of others and then permit them to continue or select others to take their place. Here we are particularly interested in the latter, that is, the profound effect of mood upon role-taking, that process in which we attribute a social role to the other and then impute motives, sentiments, and definitions of the situation. The place where the person's mood falls on the spectrum of dysphoria or euphoria – whether it is elevated or depressed – has an impact on role-taking and hence also upon the self.

Earlier we discussed the impact of mood largely with reference to self-esteem, arguing that elevated mood tended to make the person not only less sensitive to the opinions of others but also more likely to impute positive sentiments to them. Now we can generalize this position by arguing that mood shapes the role-taking process in an even more fundamental way.

At the heart of role-taking lies the cognitive mapping of the social situation into what sociologists call roles (Turner, 1962, 1985). To engage in role-taking, the social actor must hypothesize or assume a definition of a situation and on the basis of it map the participants into named and recognized social roles. In other words, in order to secure one's own goals as well as to cooperate with others, one must identify them and identify oneself, mapping the flesh-and-blood human beings with whom one is confronted into some known pattern of interlocking actions. One must know who is physician and who is patient, who is pursuer and who pursued, who is a friend and who is an enemy. Although in many situations this mapping is closely regulated by social arrangements (one generally has little room for choice, though perhaps some room for making mistakes, for example, in deciding who is the patient, who the nurse, and who the physician), in other circumstances the mapping of persons into roles is a loose and even volatile matter. Colleagues can readily be transmogrified into enemies through real or imagined acts of treachery; likewise, friends become lovers and siblings become rivals. As people imagine one another in differing ways, imputing different purposes or goals to them and different definitions to the situations that contain them, they become different persons to one another. Whoever the persons they are or become, it is the imagination of them on the basis of some cognitive map of the situation that permits action to unfold.

Mood is significant to role-taking not only because it shapes our interpretations of others' actions but also because it shapes our mapping of the social situation that confronts us at any given time. When one is in a 'good' mood – that is, feeling closer to euphoria than to dysphoria – one is likely to map others into roles somewhat differently than one would in a 'bad' mood. In a 'good' mood one sees potential friends or allies, convivial companions, fellow human beings upon whose good will one may possibly rely. In a more 'level' mood one is perhaps more likely to map others into rather conventional role terms – student and teacher, patient and physician – and to suspend judgment about possible other bases of interaction, such as friendship or enmity. And in a 'bad' mood one is more apt to see potential enemies or persecutors, or at least to consider these possibilities even as one acts toward others primarily on the basis of their conventional role relationships. Holding circumstances constant, mood is apt to influence the way actors define a situation and engage in role-taking and role-making within it.

Mood shapes the self, in other words, because it affects the way we imagine the social world and hence ourselves as participants in it. More precisely, mood has an impact on identity, the person's sense of location relative to others in the situation or the wider social world. Dysphoria, whether it is interpreted by self or others in terms of 'bad mood,' 'depression,' 'low self-esteem,' or some other social construct, influences identity by making it more likely that the person will imagine situational definitions and role structures that constitute him or her as rejected, unwanted, or unworthy. Dysphoria encourages the perception of hostile motives in others and so also the imagination of one's own lot as the target of hostility. It prompts the imagination of a self at risk, a self located in relationships of enmity or exploitation rather than of friendship or support.[10] Likewise, we argue, a position closer to the midpoint or even the positive side of the spectrum of mood frees the person to draw upon a range of socially conventional ways of cognitively mapping a situation and so establish a self free of the heavy load of negative inferences about others that dysphoria imposes. And, by the same token, euphoria may have a range of distorting effects not unlike those of dysphoria, since an excessively 'good' mood may interfere with the perception of others' actions in a way that makes it difficult to impute ill intentions to them, even when the latter are manifestly present in the eyes of others.

The impact of Prozac and other antidepressants upon the self is thus in part a result of the apparent fact that such medications directly influence mood and so shape the imagination of others and of the self. But there is more to the matter than this, for the self is made of discourse and not merely of the situated imagination of its appearance to others. Prozac does not appear on the scene free of implications, but comes with a load of medical and psychiatric meanings that shape its impact on the self. And if mood is an important – and perhaps even an increasingly important – influence on the self, it is as much because of particular cultural emphases as because of the universal constitution of human beings. Thus, to grasp the impact of Prozac on 'the real self,' we must examine these matters.

Depression, the Self, and Postmodernity

There is nothing new in the observation that drugs can profoundly affect the sense of self, for alcohol, cocaine, heroin, caffeine, and nicotine have long had such acknowledged effects. We know that alcohol is capable of reducing social inhibitions, for example, or that cocaine can induce a powerful self-confidence. And it seems reasonable to argue that these drugs have their effects through mechanisms not unlike those we have posited for Prozac. That is, drugs shape the perception of the social world and so also the experience of self.

Prozac is different from such drugs, of course, because it is a medically sanctioned drug whose use is associated with psychiatric (or other medical) prescription and whose effects on the person have some of the credibility of scientific truth. Prozac comes wrapped in the promise of medical treatment, and so is apt to be viewed by those who accept its promise not as producing an artificial self, but as restoring or uncovering a self that had heretofore been damaged or concealed. There is some of this sense of the uncovering or liberation of a true self in the use of alcohol or other drugs to relieve anxiety or inhibition and thereby to make the person feel more confident and at ease with others. But these drugs carry with them the heavy stigma of addiction and personal damage and thus a powerful set of social definitions that run counter to their users' belief in their powers to reveal a new self. Prozac, notwithstanding the still-relevant stigma of mental illness associated with its use, offers a more culturally legitimate view of a self that may be revealed or liberated by a drug that treats illness. Low self-esteem, rejection sensitivity, and a wide range of mood disturbances can be seen, in the light of Prozac's success, as indicators of a distorted or damaged self that medication can make whole. Prozac thus encourages the definition of the real self as the healthy self, one restored to its human potential by medical discovery and treatment.

One could argue, against this line of analysis, that Prozac has gained widespread acceptance precisely at a time when people are encouraged and enabled to develop highly malleable and adaptable selves. The currents of postmodernity seem to favor the use of Prozac and similar drugs not merely for the relief of depression or the restoration of healthy self-esteem, but as an instrument for the short-term creation and presentation of an altered self. If indeed contemporary people have considerable license to modify the self – to shift identities, modify personal displays, or be open to unexpected experiences – psychotropic medications may offer potent means of doing so. If the boundaries of the self are less definite and more permeable than in the past, Prozac and similar drugs may further these changes. Indeed, the very use of Prozac might become a basis for a social identity.

There are several reasons to be skeptical that Prozac will become widely viewed in such terms or that it will escalate the disintegration of the supposedly fixed and integral self of a generation or two ago. At least in the United States, Prozac seems to be an instrument individuals use to adjust their mood to cultural requirements rather than to experiment with the possibilities of the self. For the clinically depressed, it is a means of acquiring or re-establishing control over mood so that they can experience responses culturally defined as appropriate. For those whose set point of mood does not meet cultural expectations, it is a way of adjusting the set point upwards. In either case, it is an existing set of cultural conditions rather than postmodern opportunities that seems to have captured Prozac's meaning.

Moreover, the medical establishment seems to have maintained largely unchallenged control not only of the use of Prozac but also of its cultural meaning. This fact reflects not simply the legal status of the drug (which is available only by prescription and likely to remain so) but also its pharmacological effects. It is widely held that Prozac has little or no effect on those who are not depressed; it lifts mood only for those who display at least some of the clinical symptoms of depression. Statements to this effect may, of course, be a means of safeguarding the medical definition of Prozac and the construction of depression as an illness, and to that extent should probably be viewed with some skepticism. But there is no reason for skepticism about another feature of Prozac and the other antidepressants: these drugs take four to six weeks to take effect; they do not yield the instant results of alcohol or the illegal drugs. Given this delayed response, as well as the fact (or merely the belief) that they help only those who are depressed, Prozac has essentially no street value. It does not commend itself as a mind-altering (or self-altering) drug of choice. Unlike appearance, behavior, musical taste, and other ways of announcing identities, Prozac requires time to take effect and its impact is often noticed by others before the user apprehends it.

Prozac thus fosters a *medicalized* self, one defined as desirable on the basis of criteria of health rather than postmodern expressivity or adaptability. Its success also seems likely to solidify the social construction of depression and perhaps other conditions as treatable illnesses, and for reasons that relate as much to the cultural view of the person as to their inherent capacity to restore the brain to a healthy state. Depression, anxiety, and obsessive-compulsive disorder – the problems for which Prozac is ordinarily prescribed – are culturally significant illnesses. In American society, the depressed individual is likely to be a misfit, since happiness is culturally enjoined as both pursuit and condition, and since there are few social worlds where dark thoughts are rewarded or supported. Whether depression arises from conditions of the brain independently of experience, or from the reaction of the brain to stress, or (more likely) from a combination of the two, it engenders conduct that runs profoundly contrary to cultural expectations. So too does anxiety, for which antidepressants are sometimes prescribed in low doses and which is treated by a growing arsenal of anxiolytic drugs, such as Xanax and Buspar (*Consumer Reports*, 1993). Contemporary American culture, perhaps especially middle-class culture, demands a readiness for interaction with strangers in unfamiliar and stressful circumstances, and thus makes excessive anxiety a particularly disabling condition. And one could likewise argue that obsessive-compulsive disorder, in addition to making life particularly unpleasant for those afflicted with it, undermines the sense of choice, autonomy, and personal control that is so culturally valued.

It thus seems likely that the development of highly specialized drugs – silver bullets for disorders of the self – will reinforce those strains in American culture that define the person as entitled to a healthy self and view the healthy self as a key basis for a desirable social order. Prozac medicalizes the definition of the 'real self,' but in doing so it relies upon an existing set of beliefs about the person. Where once the depressed or the unhappy may have sought solace and support in talking therapies, they may now be inclined to look to small green- and cream-colored capsules.

Conclusion

The challenge of Prozac is two-fold. First, sociological and social psychological theories of the self cannot ignore the fact that medications have powerful effects on behavior and can help restore human beings to functioning where other approaches have failed. We cannot explain why or how these drugs work (neither as yet can psychopharmacologists), but we can and must explore possible ways in which their obvious impact on the brain shapes the self and its social world. To engage in this project we need not reduce the self to the brain, nor regard the self as merely an entity to be manipulated with chemical precision. Rather, as we have suggested here, we need to think more carefully about connections between self and brain, and to posit ways in which the latter may affect the former in a social context. We have tried to do so here by viewing mood as a fundamental aspect of the experience of both self and society, something that arises out of both brain chemistry and social experience, and shapes the way we perceive and respond to the social world. In simplest terms, mood shapes the imagination of others and hence also the experience of self.

The second challenge of psychotropic drugs lies in their capacity to shape the way we in the modern world view and discourse about the self. As Peter Kramer (1993a: 97–101) points out, the fact that we can use specific drugs to identify and remedy medical conditions tends to reify those conditions. If psychiatrists and the public come to believe that 'low self-esteem' or 'rejection sensitivity' are medical conditions that can be treated with Prozac, just as 'depression' can be so treated, then the effect is to give these conditions a solid reality in our experience. But something more than these particular conditions is reified in this process, for the success of drug therapy tends to support the idea of a 'healthy self.' Psychotherapy has always promised a healthy self – not a perfect self, certainly, but at least one capable of understanding its origins and to that extent shaping its own destiny – though it has delivered on that promise, at best, in an uncertain way. What psychiatry in its older manifestations could not deliver, psychopharmacology may; and if it does, it is likely to have a profound impact on cultural discourse about the self. Prozac offers a view of human nature as well as relief for depression, not only a tonic for unhappiness but support for the idea that happiness is something to which human beings are entitled and can expect to achieve. Though the roots of this idea are already well nourished in American culture, and Prozac's promise may well prove false, this new drug and others like it are almost sure to have a profound impact on who we think we are and what we think is changeable and what immutable about ourselves.

Notes

1. We use the term 'depression' here to cover several distinct conditions identified in *Diagnostic and Statistical Manual of Mental Disorders*, Fourth Edition (*DSM-IV*) (American Psychiatric Association, 1994). It includes not only major depression, either in unipolar or bipolar form, but also such conditions as dysthymia, which involve depressed mood and some of the other manifestations of major depression but fall short of the criteria for major depression. Depression is both a clinical entity and a more diffuse psychological state of being or general label for mood or feeling; the clinical and popular uses of the term are closely related, each informing and shaping the other.

2. There has been extensive mass-media coverage of Prozac, both pro and con. See, for example, Ablow (1992); Angier (1993); Begley (1994); Brink (1993); Brown (1993); Burton (1991); Cowley (1994); Cowley et al. (1990, 1991); Gates (1993); Gelman (1990); Lasch (1992); McGrath (1994); Mauro (1994); Rimer (1993); Styron 1993; Toufexis (1993); Toufexis and Purvis (1990). Recently psychiatrists Peter and Ginger Ross Breggin have written a sustained attack on Prozac in their *Talking Back to Prozac* (1994). Accounts of the legal issues associated with Prozac can be found in Lewis (1990); Marcus (1991a, 1991b);

Sargeant (1991); Schwartz and Cohn (1991). There has been considerable medical research on the relationship between fluoxetine and aggressive or suicidal behavior, reported in Ashleigh and Fesler (1992); Ioannou (1992); Masica et al. (1992); Rosenbaum et al. (1993); Selzer (1992); Tollefson (1990). Not surprisingly, Prozac has attracted devoted followers, committed opponents, and a degree of publicity that threatens to overshadow its use in the treatment of clinical depression.

3. The widespread use of Prozac will perhaps give rise to a process of 'becoming a Prozac user' that in some respects resembles the classic process of 'becoming a marijuana user' charted by Howard Becker (1953, 1967). Prozac's impact is gradual and subtle, however, and it remains an open question as to how much and in what ways the experience of this drug is learned and socially shared. David Karp (1993, 1996) has examined the meaning of anti-depressants to depressed people and describes the 'career' of depression in relation to such drugs.

4. Not only is there no research on the effects of Prozac on the self, but there is less research overall than one might expect given the drug's widespread use. In addition to Kramer (1993a), whose book and other articles (1990, 1993b, 1993c) provide a more balanced view than his critics (see Breggin and Breggin, 1994) have alleged, we have consulted a number of sources as well as clinical experience in building a picture of the effects of Prozac and other antidepressants. These include Beal et al. (1991); Dunlop et al. (1990); Eisenberg (1992); Fava et al. (1993); Fichtner et al. (1992); Franklin (1991); Grady (1990); Hellerstein et al. (1993); Hierholzer (1990); Joyce (1988); Kendler et al. (1992); Potter et al. (1991); Reimherr et al. (1984); Stewart et al. (1988); Wender and Kline (1981).

5. Unless otherwise indicated, patient reports and descriptions are drawn from the clinical files of one of the authors.

6. This view is confirmed indirectly even by one of Prozac's most fervent opponents, Peter Breggin, who, with Ginger Ross Breggin (1994), reports several clinical anecdotes in which a chief negative effect of Prozac is its alleged tendency to make some users insensitive or uncaring about significant others. Perhaps a drug capable of reducing an excess of social sensitivity produces an insufficiency in those who are not suffering from an excess.

7. The assertion that self-esteem is a way of interpreting mood glosses a complex set of linkages between the dimension of mood and a variety of social actors who supply and employ terms that shape its meaning. Self-esteem has become a term of popular discourse, and to allege that self-esteem is interpreted mood is in this respect to say that the term has entered common usage and refers to the euphoria/dysphoria dimension. It is not to say, however, that the popular use of the term is confined to this dimension, since self-esteem appears to have multiple referents in contemporary discourse. Likewise, self-esteem has long been in use as a psychological and social psychological term, and there it generally means something other than interpreted mood. However, our analysis recommends shifting its scientific definition in the direction of common usage. What we social psychologists intuitively have in mind when we refer to self-esteem seems closer to interpreted mood than to any other theoretical anchorage we may give the term. The contemporary uses of 'self-esteem' are explored in Hewitt (1998).

8. It is more accurate to say there are several underlying conditions. The several forms of depression identified in *DSM-IV* may be viewed as approximations – and probably very rough approximations – of several underlying conditions. Given the fact that individuals whose symptoms appear similar do not necessarily respond similarly to the same drug therapy, and given that a particular drug, such as Prozac, may successfully treat several different conditions, it is clear that we must be very cautious about assuming any one-to-one correspondence between psychiatric labels and underlying neurological realities. But it would be equally foolhardy to assume there are no connections at all.

9. *DSM-IV* defines a major depressive episode as occurring when the person has experienced either depressed mood or loss of interest and pleasure during a two-week period, along with at least four other symptoms drawn from a list of seven. One of these is characterized as 'feelings of worthlessness or excessive or inappropriate guilt . . . nearly every day.' In addition, to qualify as a major depressive episode, the symptoms should not be mixed with those of mania or be better attributable to bereavement, and they must 'cause clinically

significant distress or impairment in social, occupational, or other important areas of functioning' (American Psychiatric Association, 1994: 327).

10. It should go without saying that these assertions hold 'other things being equal.' That is, to argue that dysphoria prompts the imagination of a hostile social world is not to say that the social world is never 'really' hostile, for of course it is. To say that evil is sometimes a product of our imagination of it is not to say that it always is. Moreover, the malleability or volatility of our cognitive mapping of the social world exists only where there are some degrees of freedom to choose how one will interpret others' actions and how one will respond to them.

References

Ablow, K.R. (1992) 'Prozac: What Kind of Cure?,' *Health*, a supplement to the *Washington Post*, February 11. p.9.

American Heritage Electronic Dictionary (1992) Boston: Houghton-Mifflin.

American Psychiatric Association (1994) *Diagnostic and Statistical Manual of Mental Disorders*. 4th edn. Washington, DC: American Psychiatric Association.

Angier, N. (1993) 'Drug Works, But Questions Remain,' *New York Times*, December 13. p. B8.

Ashleigh, E.A. and Fesler, F.A. (1992) 'Fluoxetine and Suicidal Preoccupation,' *American Journal of Psychiatry*, 149 (12): 1750.

Beal, D.M., Harris, D., Bartos, M., Korsak, C., Splane, G., Quant, R. and Starke, J. (1991) 'Safety and Efficacy of Fluoxetine,' *American Journal of Psychiatry*, 148 (12): 1751.

Becker, H. (1953) 'Becoming a Marijuana User,' *American Journal of Sociology*, 59: 235–42.

Becker, H. (1967) 'History, Culture, and Subjective Experience: An Exploration of the Social Bases of Drug-Induced Experiences,' *Journal of Health and Social Behavior*, 8 (3): 163–76.

Begley, S. (1994) 'One Pill Makes You Larger, and One Pill Makes You Small,' *Newsweek*, February 7. pp. 37–40.

Breggin, P.R. and Breggin, G.R. (1994) *Talking Back to Prozac*. New York: St Martin's Press.

Brink, S. (1993) 'Singing the Prozac Blues,' *US News & World Report*, November 8. pp. 76ff.

Brown, A.S. (1993) 'Miracle Worker (an Interview with Peter D. Kramer),' *People Weekly*, 40 (November): 153–5.

Burton, T.M. (1991) 'Panel Finds No Credible Evidence to Tie Prozac to Suicides and Violent Behavior,' *Wall Street Journal*, September 23. p. B4.

Consumer Reports (1993) 'Halicon and Prozac,' *Consumer Reports*, January.

Cowley, G. (1994) 'The Culture of Prozac,' *Newsweek*, February 7. pp. 41–3.

Cowley, G., Springen, K., Leonard, E.A., Robbins, K., and Gordon, J. (1990) 'The Promise of Prozac,' *Newsweek*, March 26. pp. 39–41.

Cowley, G., Springen, K., Gordon, J., and Koehl, C. (1991) 'A Prozac Backlash,' *Newsweek*, April 1. pp. 64–7.

Dunlop, S.R., Dornseif, B.E., Wernicke, J.F., and Potvin, J.H. (1990) 'Pattern Analysis Shows Beneficial Effect of Fluoxetine Treatment in Mild Depression,' *Psychopharmacology Bulletin*, 26 (2): 173–80.

Eisenberg, L. (1992) 'Treating Depression and Anxiety in Primary Care,' *New England Journal of Medicine*, 326: 1080–4.

Eli Lilly and Company (1993) 'Prozac Facts,' *Informational Brochure*. Indianapolis, IN: Eli Lilly and Company.

Eli Lilly and Company (1993b) 'Prozac (Fluoxetine Hydrochloride),' *Informational Brochure*. Indianapolis, IN: Eli Lilly and Company.

Fava, M., Rosenbaum, J.F., Pava, J.A., McCarthy, M.K., Steingard, R.J., and Bouffides, E. (1993) 'Anger Attacks in Unipolar Depression, Part 1: Clinical Correlates and Response to Fluoxetine Treatment,' *American Journal of Psychiatry*, 150 (8): 1158–63.

Fichtner, C.G., Horovitz, R.P., and Braun, B.G. (1992) 'Fluoxetine in Depersonalization Disorder,' *American Journal of Psychiatry*, 149 (12): 1750–1.

Franklin, D. (1991) 'The Ups and Downs of Prozac,' *In Health*, January/February: 24ff.

Gates, D. (1993) 'The Case of Dr Strangedrug,' *Newsweek*, June 14. p. 71.

Gecas, V. and Schwalbe, M.L. (1983) 'Beyond the Looking-Glass Self: Social Structure and Efficacy-Based Self-Esteem,' *Social Psychology Quarterly*, 46: 77–88.

Gelman, D. (1990) 'Drugs vs. the Couch,' *Newsweek*, March 26. pp. 42–3.

Grady, D. (1990) 'Wonder Drug,' *American Health*, October: 60–5.

Hellerstein, D.J., Yanowitch, P., Rosenthal, J., Samstag, L.W., Maurer, M., Kasch, K., Burrows, L., Poster, M., Cantillon, M., and Winston, A. (1993) 'A Randomized Double-Blind Study of Fluoxetine versus Placebo in the Treatment of Dysthymia,' *American Journal of Psychiatry*, 150 (8): 1169–75.

Hewitt, J.P. (1994) *Self and Society: A Symbolic Interactionist Social Psychology*. Boston: Allyn & Bacon.

Hewitt, J.P. (1998) *The Myth of Self-Esteem*. New York: St Martin's Press.

Hierholzer, R. (1990) 'Limitations of Fluoxetine,' *American Journal of Psychiatry*, 147 (12): 1691.

Ioannou, C. (1992) 'Media Coverage versus Fluoxetine as the Cause of Suicidal Ideation,' *American Journal of Psychiatry*, 149 (4): 572.

Joyce, C. (1988) 'Drug Banishes Blues and Bulges,' *New Scientist*, 26 (May): 43.

Karp, D.A. (1993) 'Taking Anti-Depressant Medications: Resistance, Trial Commitment, Conversion, Disenchantment,' *Qualitative Sociology*, 16 (4): 337–59.

Karp, D.A. (1996) *Speaking of Sadness*. New York: Oxford University Press.

Kemper, T. (1987) 'How Many Emotions Are There? Wedding the Social and Autonomic Components,' *American Journal of Sociology*, 93 (June): 263–89.

Kendler, K.S., Neale, M.C., Kessler, R.C., Heath, A.C., and Eaves, L.J. (1992) 'Major Depression and Generalized Anxiety Disorder: Same Genes, (Partly) Different Environments?,' *Archives of General Psychiatry*, 49: 716–22.

Kramer, P.D. (1990) 'Is Everybody Happy?,' *Good Health*, a supplement to the *Boston Sunday Globe*, October 7. pp. 15ff.

Kramer, P.D. (1993a) *Listening to Prozac*. New York: Viking.

Kramer, P.D. (1993b) 'Behind Prozac's Rising Popularity Lurk Our Cultural Fears,' *Los Angeles Times*, June 13. p. M3.

Kramer, P.D. (1993c) 'The Transformation of Personality,' *Psychology Today*, 26 (July/August): 42ff.

Lasch, C. (1992) 'For Shame: Why Americans Should Be Wary of Self-Esteem,' *The New Republic*, August 10. pp. 29–34.

Lewis, J. (1990) 'Prozac: Dark Side of a Wonder Drug,' *Trial*, August: 62ff.

McGrath, D.G. (1994) 'The Happy Dane: Hamlet on Prozac,' *The New Republic*, 24 (January): 9.

Marcus, A.D. (1991a) 'Prozac Firm Fights Drug's Use as a Defense,' *Wall Street Journal*, April 9. p. B8.

Marcus, A.D. (1991b) 'Murder Trials Introduce Prozac Defense,' *Wall Street Journal*, February 7. p. B1.

Masica, D.N., Kotsantos, J.G., Beasley, C.M., Jr, and Potvin, J.H. (1992) 'Trend in Suicide Rates Since Fluoxetine Introduction,' *American Journal of Public Health*, 82 (9): 1295.

Mauro, J. (1994) 'And Prozac for All,' *Psychology Today*, 27 (July/August): 44ff.

Mead, G.H. (1934) *Mind, Self and Society*. Chicago: University of Chicago Press.

Potter, W.Z., Rudorfer, M.V., and Manji, H. (1991) 'The Pharmacologic Treatment of Depression,' *New England Journal of Medicine*, 325: 633–42.

Reimherr, F.W., Wood, D.R., Byerley, B., Brainard, J., and Grosser, B.I. (1984) 'Characteristics of Responders to Fluoxetine,' *Psychopharmacology Bulletin*, 20 (1): 70–2.

Rimer, S. (1993) 'With Millions Taking Prozac, a Legal Drug Culture Arises,' *New York Times*, December 13. pp. A1ff.

Rosenbaum, J.F., Fava, M., Pava, J.A., McCarthy, M.K., Steingard, R.J., and Bouffides, E. (1993) 'Anger Attacks in Unipolar Depression, Part 2: Neuroendocrine Correlates and Changes Following Fluoxetine Treatment,' *American Journal of Psychiatry*, 150 (8): 1164–8.

Rosenberg, M. (1981) 'The Self-Concept: Social Produce and Social Force,' in M. Rosenberg and R.H. Turner (eds), *Social Psychology: Sociological Perspectives*. New York: Basic Books. pp. 593–624.

Sargeant, G. (1991) 'Prozac on Trial,' *Trial*, May: 101–2.

Schwartz, J. and Cohn, B. (1991) ' "The Drug Did It": A Tough Sell in Court,' *Newsweek*, April 1. p. 66.

Selzer, J.A. (1992) 'Fluoxetine, Suicidal Ideation, and Aggressive Behavior,' *American Journal of Psychiatry*, 149 (5): 708–9.

Stewart, J.W., Quitkin, F.M., McGrath, P.J., Rabkin, J.G., Markowitz, J.S., Tricamo, E., and Klein, D.F. (1988) 'Social Functioning in Chronic Depression: Effect of 6 Weeks of Anti-depressant Treatment,' *Psychiatry Research*, 25: 213–22.

Styron, W. (1993) 'Prozac Days, Halcion Nights,' *The Nation*, January 4/11. pp. 1ff.

Tollefson, G.D. (1990) 'Fluoxetine and Suicidal Ideation,' *American Journal of Psychiatry*, 147 (12): 1691–2.

Toufexis, A. (1993) 'The Personality Pill,' *Time*, October 11. pp. 61–2.

Toufexis, A. and Purvis, A. (1990) 'Warnings About a Miracle Drug,' *Time*, July 30. p. 54.

Turner, R.H. (1962) 'Role-Taking: Process versus Conformity,' in A. Rose (ed.), *Human Behavior and Social Process*. Boston: Houghton-Mifflin. pp. 20–40.

Turner, R.H. (1985) 'Unanswered Questions in the Convergence Between Structuralist and Interactionist Role Theory,' in H.J. Helle and S.N. Eisenstadt (eds), *Microsociological Theory, Vol. 2*. Thousand Oaks, CA: Sage. pp. 23–36.

Wender, P.H. and Kline, D. (1981) *Mind, Mood and Medicine*. New York: Farrar, Strauss & Giroux.

PART IV TOWARD NEW APPROACHES: EPISTEMOLOGY, RESEARCH, POLITICS

9

Psychological Distress and Postmodern Thought

Vivien Burr and Trevor Butt

In recent times, we have witnessed a marked rise in the discovery of numerous psychopathologies and syndromes. A wide variety of psychological difficulties and problems are now recognized as constituting identifiable symptoms or characteristics of syndromes previously unheard of. Premenstrual syndrome (PMS), battered woman syndrome, and attention-deficit disorder are just some of the disorders lately 'discovered' and offered up for public attention. Alongside this increase in the discovery and categorization of these types of problems is a parallel rise in the provision of counseling and therapy. Of course, if these syndromes are indeed unmitigated discoveries, the rise in therapy provision is an unambiguous blessing. However, it can be argued that the therapy industry, like any other, creates as well as serves a need.

The proliferation of named syndromes and pathologies, we argue, is part of the more general phenomenon of the *pathologization of everyday life*. More and more aspects of our lives are becoming problematic. We are now used to feeling and expressing doubt about our performance as parents, as lovers, as workers, and we scrutinize our thoughts and feelings for signs of some developmental flaw, perversion, or personal inadequacy. In turn, the problems we reveal to ourselves are viewed as the proper concern of therapists and counselors.

An important feature of this process of pathologizing is its inherent 'psychologization' – that is, the casting of difficulties and problems into psychological frameworks and therefore locating them at the level of the individual. Once this is achieved, the onus for change and the moral responsibility for the problem are placed upon the person. For example, despite the availability of alternative, more social, explanations (e.g. Parton, 1985), child abuse continues to be seen as rooted in the pathology of the individual abuser, and not in social and political contexts. Furthermore, dyslexia and some learning disabilities may be seen as socially constructed outcomes of inegalitarian educational systems. Anorexia nervosa, too, may be fruitfully seen as the product of the common, gendered patterns of cultural life. A variety of women's problems in particular may be regarded as constructions that shore up patriarchal society. In each case, locating the problem at the level of the individual draws attention away from the social conditions – poverty, capitalism, patriarchy – which might provide the contextual backdrop that is intrinsic to individual experience. In addition, this psychologization is often implicitly reductionist, frequently appealing to biological elements as the 'real' underlying causes. For example, in disparate circles, genetic coding has recently been suggested as the cause of schizophrenia, alcoholism, criminality, and, once again, homosexuality. Such reductionism has considerable implications for the individual, who is often caught in various contradictions and double binds when conceptualizing and treating his or her condition.

It is not our intention to suggest that the problems and distress experienced by people are illusory. We may be doing no more than recognizing as patterned and systematic the problems and distress that have always been experienced by people. Or it may really be the case that psychological difficulties of one kind or another are on the increase in contemporary Western societies. After all, a social causation view of mental illness has been convincingly argued. Social isolation and poverty have long been found to predict greater incidence of schizophrenia (Faris and Dunham, 1939), and Brown and Harris (1978) have shown how poverty can lead to depressive illness. Perhaps intense stress and illness do result from the particularly complicated lives we lead within contemporary social structures.

Nevertheless, regardless of whether and why psychological distress might be on the increase, it is our contention that social constructionism can go beyond the question of causation through examining the conditions under which experiences themselves become constructed as 'problems' in particular instances. Such analysis places the psychologization and pathologization of everyday life into a broader historical analysis of cultural change and social control. Furthermore, it invites us to see counseling and therapy as possibly complicit in the construction of the psychological problems that they have been called upon to address.

Social constructionists are of course not the first to question psychological and medical accounts of distress. Those associated with labeling theory (Goffman, 1961; Rosenhan, 1973; Scheff, 1966) maintained that, under certain social conditions, non-normative or deviant behavior comes to be seen as a symptom of mental illness. The person is thus labeled as 'mentally ill' – a label that then determines how future behavior will be perceived and addressed. This label is internalized by the person, whose identity and behavior become defined by his or her illness – a process Wilkins (1971) refers to as 'deviancy amplification.'

Furthermore, mental health industries have previously come under attack from various directions. Proponents of the anti-psychiatry movement in Britain and North America such as Laing (1959, 1967) and Szasz (1961, 1970, 1971) were highly critical of the personal and political intrusiveness of psychiatry. Szasz argues that psychiatry inappropriately adopted the metaphor of illness as a way of framing unacceptable behavior. He draws a distinction between real, physical illness (disease) and mental illness, which he regards as simply deviations from moral and ethical norms. Szasz, however, has no specific objection to contractual psychotherapy – that is, therapy undertaken by people freely and volitionally. Sedgwick (1982), on the other hand, is in some ways nearer to contemporary social constructionist views, since he regards all illness, whether physical or mental, as social constructions having no objectively definable ontological basis. However, he regards the illness metaphor, or the 'sick role,' as a facilitative one for the person suffering psychological distress.

Current social constructionist attention to mental health and psychotherapy issues (e.g. Parker et al., 1995) has often been heavily influenced by Foucault, and has involved a renewed radical questioning of the values and practice of the mental health professions. We believe that a broadly Foucauldian framework can fruitfully be used to understand the increasing psychologization and pathologization of everyday life just described. However, we shall argue that such an understanding demands that we do more than simply question the desirability of therapy and counseling. It requires that we both reassess the status of individual distress, and strive to develop more appropriate conceptions of therapy and counseling.

Therapy and Disciplinary Power

Foucauldian analyses of mental illness and the contemporary mental health professions have often drawn upon the historical account given by Foucault in *Madness and Civilization* (1965). However, in our argument we will draw directly upon Foucault's later work (1976, 1977) and upon Rose (1989, 1990), who uses a similar style of analysis. These perspectives are organized around the concepts of discipline, supervision, confession, normalization, and the individual.

The Rise of Discipline

Foucault argues that demographic change and changes in the mode of production in the eighteenth century brought about a radical shift in the organization and management of the population, especially at work. First, there was an increase in the size of the population, with consequent problems in housing and public health and, more specifically, an increase in the floating population, those persons who in various ways were pursuing a nomadic existence. Second, there was the growth and development of the capitalist mode of production, which was becoming more difficult and more costly to manage. Foucault argues that these two problems – the population changes, and the need to organize production more efficiently and profitably – could not be addressed by the existing cumbersome feudal arrangements. Instead, they were effectively managed by the broad adoption of *discipline* as a form of social organization and practice.

'Discipline' organizes, structures, and categorizes human activity by the use of timetables and hierarchies; increases the differentiation of tasks (divisions of labour); and makes specific use of supervision and surveillance to ensure the smooth running of the whole. Through these means, the factory, the military, the school, and the hospital alike ensured the docility, control, and productivity of individuals within them. In addition, the use of hierarchical structures with clear distinctions between one category of person and another, for example by rank or job status, ensured that the opportunities for solidarity among individuals were minimal, thus reducing the risk of resistance or revolt:

> That is why discipline fixes; it arrests or regulates movements; it clears up confusion; it dissipates compact groupings of individuals wandering about the country in unpredictable ways; it establishes calculated distributions. It must also master all the forces that are formed from the very constitution of an organized multiplicity; it must neutralize the effects of counterpower that spring from them and which form a resistance to the power that wishes to dominate it: agitations, revolts, spontaneous organizations, coalitions – anything that may establish horizontal conjunctions. (Foucault, 1977: 219)

Disciplinary Power

The supervisory and surveillance features of discipline mark an important shift in the exercise of power and in social control for Foucault. He sees this shift as a move away from the use of what he calls 'sovereign power' to the much more effective and efficient 'disciplinary power.' Sovereign power operated through the threat of what the sovereign (or the sovereign's representative) could do to the person who infringed the law, but as a form of social control it was inadequate to deal with the increasing size and complexity of the changing Western societies of the eighteenth century. By contrast, disciplinary power operates through the voluntary subjection of people to the regulations and norms of the hierarchical institutions that they inhabit; it is literally self-discipline.

The control and regulation of persons, whether in the factory, the army, or the school, is characterized by a proliferation of rules governing required behavior and their reciprocal punishments and rewards. But the effects of surveillance make the person effectively self-regulatory. This is epitomized by the invention of Bentham's Panopticon, a circular prison which houses the prisoners in cells around the periphery, where they can be watched by a single guard placed at the center. The Panopitcon's efficiency and innovation is that prisoners – who live with the constant knowledge that their behavior might at any moment be scrutinized – come to internalize 'the gaze' of the guard and thus incorporate this monitoring and control into their own selves. Disciplinary power is therefore a feature not only of prisons but of all institutions and organizations which control their members through hierarchies, divisions, norms, and surveillance. It could be argued that disciplinary power has infiltrated modern societies to such an extent that no one is beyond its reach. Some writers (Parker et al., 1995; Sarup, 1988) even see Panopticism at work in the organization of cyberspace and the computer monitoring of individuals.

Confession

This self-surveillance and self-discipline develops and is perpetuated through various practices that can essentially be seen as 'confession.' In the Middle Ages, monks were required to control their sinful desires by confession – a detailed recollection and description of sinful deeds, words, and thoughts. At this time, confession was not widespread among the general population, but during the seventeenth century it expanded greatly in the Catholic Church, and ordinary people were required to regularly examine their behavior and desires – especially those of a sexual nature – and to confess them.

In the context of the increasing need to regulate the population, the confessional played a central role in the construction and emergence of numerous categories of sexual abnormality and perversion. Self-scrutiny and surveillance through the confessional could channel the sexual behavior and desires of the population along lines favorable to the effective management and regulation of society. Thus, birth rates, age of marriage, legitimacy or illegitimacy of births, and so on, could be effectively controlled through self-discipline and confession. Rose (1989) points out that with the rise of Protestantism, the confessional came to be replaced by *self*-inspection, since the person has the right to make him- or herself accountable to God, without the mediating actions or directions of priests or confessors.

The trend toward categorization, scrutiny, surveillance, and self-inspection continued and expanded, so that in the nineteenth century it takes the form of a burgeoning sexology literature. This represented a proliferation in the classifications and divisions of sexual normality and abnormality, the detailing of perversions, and the endless dividing and sub-dividing of categories of sexual dysfunction. Foucault argues that the modern-day gatekeepers of this knowledge are no longer the clergy, but doctors, psychiatrists, psychologists, therapists, and other mental health practitioners. These are the people for whom we are now required to inspect and scrutinize our actions, wants, and secrets, and to whom we confess them. Confession has thus become a way of life:

> The confession has spread its effects far and wide. It plays a part in justice, medicine, education, family relationships, and love relations, in the most ordinary affairs of everyday life, and in the most solemn rites; one confesses one's crimes, one's sins, one's thoughts and desires, one's illnesses and troubles; one goes about telling, with the greatest precision, whatever is most difficult to tell. One

> confesses in public and in private, to one's parents, one's educators, one's doctor, to those one loves; one admits to oneself, in pleasure and in pain, things it would be impossible to tell to anyone else, the things people write books about. . . . Western man has become a confessing animal. (Foucault, 1976: 59)

Normalization

The effectiveness of disciplinary power lies in the fact that it relies not upon coercion but on the willingness – even desire – of people to submit to it. It is invisible in its workings, since signs of conflict or resistances do not betray it. The rewards for submitting oneself to disciplinary power are inherent in the system of hierarchical organization and regulation itself. The different ranks, statuses, and divisions of inmates in the military, schools, hospitals, and prisons form the conditions for an extensive set of rules, norms, and expectations attached to each position. As a member of a category or holder of a particular status, one becomes subject to a set of normative expectations of conduct, thought, dress, and so on. Adherence to these brings acceptance and validation from others, as well as, importantly, confirming to the person that he or she is reassuringly average or normal:

> Like surveillance and with it, normalization becomes one of the great instruments of power at the end of the classical age. For the marks that once indicated status, privilege and affiliation were increasingly replaced – or at least supplemented – by a whole range of degrees of normality indicating membership of a homogeneous social body but also playing a part in classification, hierarchy, and the distribution of rank. In a sense, the power of normalization imposes homogeneity; but it individualizes by making it possible to measure gaps, to determine levels, to fix specialties, and to render the differences useful by fitting them one to another. (Foucault, 1977: 184)

The 'examination' is a key concept for Foucault. It captures all the factors of scrutiny, surveillance, judgment, and normalization that he sees as central to modern disciplinary power, and demonstrates – through its use in widely differing contexts such as the doctor's consulting room and the schoolroom – the degree of infiltration of such practices into everyday life.

Such normalizing practices are not only the preserve of institutions such as schools and the military. Disciplines such as psychology have had a major role to play in extending this normalization to more and more areas of life. A great part of the business of psychologists has explicitly involved developing measures of various human capacities, generating the means or 'technologies' through which individuals can be compared with one another and with the average or norm. This began with the development of tests of intelligence, but psychometrics soon included a multitude of aspects of personality, masculinity and femininity, attitudes, and so on:

> The power of psychology lay in its promise to provide inscription devices that would individualize such troublesome subjects, rendering the human soul into thought in the form of calculable traces. Its contribution lay in the invention of diagnostic categories, evaluations, assessments, and tests that constructed the subjective in a form in which it could be represented in classifications, in figures and quotients. The psychological test was the first such device. (Rose, 1990: 109)

Furthermore, this trend has not stopped at the boundaries of academic psychology. The appeal of the normal distribution is such that it has reached a wide audience through media, such as magazines which often feature quizzes and questionnaires inviting readers to assess their own personalities in some way.

The Individual

The rise of the modern individual is intimately connected with the processes of normalization and confession. Rose (1989) argues that the act of confession – whether to doctors, therapists, teachers, parents, or lovers – produces the subjectivity and sense of self that is fundamental to our concept of the individual. The person *becomes* an individual through this process. We confess, and the other consoles, understands, and judges: more than being subjectified by the other, we become subjects for ourselves. The very act of describing and speaking of the self simultaneously *creates* it as an object for inspection. 'In the act of speaking, through the obligation to produce words that are true to an inner reality, through the self-examination that precedes and accompanies speech, one becomes a subject for oneself' (Rose, 1989: 240).

Rose argues that confession also involves an incitement to self-regulation according to some moral code. The self must be monitored, tested, and improved. In terms of psychotherapy specifically, Rose states that 'psychotherapeutics is linked at a profound level to the socio-political obligations of the modern self. The self it seeks to liberate or restore is the entity able to steer its individual path through life by means of the act of personal decision and the assumption of personal responsibility' (1989: 253–4). So, through the combined forces of discipline, normalization, and confession, the modern individual emerges as a person having a sense of self, a sense of difference from other selves, and a conviction of moral responsibility for that selfhood.

The Social Construction of Everyday Pathology

The argument here is that the 'discovery' and isolating of syndromes and pathologies – and the provision of therapy and counseling as a response – is the latest phase in a long process of the development of disciplinary power in Western societies that has been going on at least since the eighteenth century. The practice of confession has been passed down to those experts and professionals – psychiatrists, psychologists, psychotherapists, counselors, among others – who are thought to be the appropriate monitors of our psychological well-being. Foucault (1977) referred to all the sciences having the prefix psy-or psycho- as the 'psy-complex,' and argued that they all are fundamentally concerned with the supervision, monitoring, and regulation of individual functioning. Through the constant incitement to confess, our sense of ourselves as individuals is to some degree created and maintained. Images of normal sexuality, relationships, parenting, family life, social adjustment, and so on, surround us; and the social sciences have provided us with every means of inspecting and assessing ourselves – of comparing ourselves to others and to the norm, and of finding ourselves wanting.

The moral obligations to inspect, regulate, and improve one's self set us on a path to a goal we can perhaps never achieve. As Rose says, 'the self that is liberated is obliged to live its life tied to the project of its own identity' (1989: 254). This project – this search for the truth about ourselves, the search for the autonomous self – is carried out in what Rose calls the 'passage through the therapeutic.' He argues that many popular therapies have this search at their root, in one form or another. The client-centered therapy of Rogers exhorts the person to drop façades, to accept his or her own feelings, to cherish close relationships, and to move toward more intimacy and openness. Gestalt therapy seeks to recover wholeness, to find growth and maturity, to develop the person, to become oneself, while self-direction and self-control are the aims of transactional analysis. The task is to discover who we 'really are,' and to believe that the attainment of that goal is in our own hands.

This passage through the therapeutic, however, is not confined to the private consulting room. Many encounters may take alternative therapeutic forms, such as the interview with the personnel officer, the ward group of the psychiatric hospital, or even the radio phone-in:

> Psychotherapeutic language and advice extends beyond the consultation, the interview, the appointment; it has become a part of the staple fare of the mass media of communication, in the magazine advice column and in documentaries and discussions on television. No financial exchange need be involved, for on live radio phone-in programs we may confess our most intimate problems for free and have them instantly analyzed – or eavesdrop on the difficulties that so many of our fellow citizens appear to have conducting the business of their lives (Rose, 1989: 214).

Psychotherapy has thus extended its gaze into hitherto unexplored corners of our lives, which Rose describes by four processes: the subjectification of work, whereby our working lives have become suffused with issues of identity and personal fulfillment; the psychologization of the mundane, whereby routine daily life has been transformed into a series of life events which need to be analyzed, understood, managed; a therapeutics of finitude, whereby all kinds of loss and frustration become reframed as healthy or potentially pathological; and a 'neuroticization' of social intercourse, in which our relationships (and in particular their deficits) are seen as the roots of many personal and social ills.

The rise in the therapy and counseling industries, then, can be seen as an expansion of the activities of the psy-complex, and the problems and pathologies to which these industries are being addressed are part of that very expansion. Confessor and confessant together – through surveillance, psychologization, and normalization – ensure the voluntary regulation and social control of the population. As more areas of our lives become psychologized

– framed in terms of our private skills, capabilities, traits, desires, repressions, attitudes – there is a correspondingly greater potential for dissatisfaction and distress in our lives. We want to be 'normal' – a term that has latterly acquired a meaning more akin to 'healthy.' Thus, in recent times, the desire to be normal is utilized as a claim to psychological health and well-being.

Social Constructions, Personal Lives

Although the power of such social constructionist arguments may be convincing, they leave us in a problematic position. We may agree that the myriad of syndromes, pathologies, and neuroses affecting us are socially constructed, and that the therapists and counselors to whom we appeal for help are the, albeit unwitting, figureheads of an extensive system of social control through disciplinary power. Nevertheless, the distress and misery experienced by people, framed though it is in terms of personal inadequacy and pathology, cannot, morally or empirically, be ignored.

Although providing often brilliant historical analyses of contemporary life, writers such as Foucault and Rose have not broached the issue of what our response, if any, should be at the level of the individual. Indeed, poststructuralist analyses have tended to regard the level of the social or of 'discourse' as the only appropriate one. These approaches have described the 'death of the subject' and have invalidated attempts to analyze phenomena at the level of the individual, which is itself revealed as a social construction (Kitzinger, 1992; Sampson, 1990). The 'strong' constructionist approach of Foucault suggests that all this psychopathology is a production of society. Indeed, the individual agent is an invention of the Enlightenment. Through the medium of language, we have invented the self and encouraged introspection by developing a vocabulary of confession.

The writings of Foucault have been criticized by Sedgwick (1982) and Habermas (1986) on the grounds of their anti-humanism. Walzer (1986) adds that it is impossible to see what Foucault envisages as an alternative to the rise in disciplinary power he attacks. On the face of it, he appears to advocate any local resistance that neutralizes discipline, but elsewhere criticizes those prison reformers who follow the implications of his argument. In fact he is unimpressed with any alternatives at all. He believes that to envisage any alternatives is merely to participate in the present system along with its disciplinary power that he abhors.

Rorty (1989) endorses these criticisms. Like Habermas and Walzer, he wants to give more credit to democratic societies, and sees disciplinary power as better for humankind than sovereign power. His view is that the rise in disciplinary power, with all its restraints, is more than compensated for by the decrease in pain and suffering that ensues. But, unlike modernist critics, he applauds what he terms Foucault's 'ironism.' The ironist is a person who accepts that all his or her views and beliefs – including his or her most cherished values – are in the end constructions, and who accepts that his or her starting point is always historically and socially contingent. There is nothing deep inside us except that which is laid down through social processes. There is no intrinsic human nature; the self and subject are indeed social productions. Unlike Foucault, Rorty thinks that the modern subject, encumbered as s/he is with self-examination and self-criticism, is better off than the pre-modern one. He agrees with much of Foucault's analysis, but believes that it leaves us paralyzed and without hope. What is needed, perhaps, is an understanding of how people are constructed as sufferers and recoverers, and what can be done to help them.

Our argument here is that therapy and counseling do not in any simple way create problems, as a Foucault-inspired analysis might claim. Disciplinary power may, as Rorty asserts, have produced better citizens. The self-reflective person should be more aware of the rights of both him or herself and others. However, therapeutic vocabularies have over-sensitized people to their faults and misfortunes – and helped them to be defined as such – and this must be addressed. In order to do so, we need a psychology which takes a broadly social constructionist theoretical framework, but which at the same time allows us to legitimately address the experience of the contemporary individual. However, this examination of psychological experience must be done without sliding back into a modernist search for essentialist truths.

A Postmodern Psychology

Rorty (1989) generally equates a postmodern position with an ironical stance. He identifies two strands of ironists in philosophy: American pragmatists like James and Dewey, and European existentialists like Nietzsche and Heidegger. In the sketch of a postmodern psychology that follows, we will draw on a number of psychologists who reflect these two traditions in some way, and we have found the ideas of personal construct theorists and existentialists to be particularly rich. Our aim is to outline the main features of a postmodern psychology and to show how it can conceptualize the experience of psychopathology in helpful ways. We will contrast modernist and postmodernist understandings of psychopathology using the four interrelated themes that Polkinghorne (1992) identifies as characterizing postmodern thought.

Foundationlessness

Modernist approaches presuppose an objective world that we come to know through the expansion of scientific knowledge. Academic psychology seeks indisputable truths about humankind that often transcend time and culture. Rorty (1982a) applauds the aims of the Enlightenment project, with its intention to free humankind of the prevailing religious dogma and to replace it with a humanist ethic and scientific inquiry. But science, too, can enshrine a dogma, and people come to expect it to rescue them in the same way that God was once supposed to.

In contrast, postmodern thought emphasizes the local and contextual nature of knowledge. There is no universal human nature to be discovered. We have no original sin, nor are we basically good beings who violate their basic nature when cruel to others. Our values are laid down by society, and the nuggets of truth psychologists have collected, like Oedipal feelings and actualizing tendencies, only reflect local moral orders, and not human essences. Accordingly, language is no longer seen as a transparent medium used to describe the objective world. Indeed, even the term 'medium' is seen as misleading. It is not something used to express the thoughts and feelings of some deep, inner self, but a tool with which we constitute the world. Rorty (1989) cautions us that we should never assume we have reached a final description of the world; we can never speak 'nature's own language.' The world may be 'out there,' but truth is not. 'Truth' comprises descriptions of the world, and anything can be redescribed; everything is changed through redescription, and can be made to look either good or bad.

Earlier concepts of mental illness saw constitutional factors and individual temperament as reasons for illness. In the redescriptions of life offered by the current objective, reality-oriented, scientific knowledges of stress and abuse, blame is shifted to the environment. To define one's self as 'abused' or 'neurotic' is not to arrive at a value-free description. It is to take a new perspective on events, to reconstrue them. To 'get in touch with your feelings' today is not a matter of discovering a truth that was not clear yesterday. In the therapeutic encounter, Kelly (1969b) contends that 'insights' occur when the client adopts the perspective or story of the therapist. Indeed, he was suspicious of insight and of the truth it was supposed to herald, and claimed that it is what the client is left with when stripped of his or her imagination (Kelly, 1969b: 347).

Fragmentariness

The Enlightenment project encouraged a search for an ordered and unified view of the world. In psychology, this has led to the metaphor of 'depth' of a person. In psychoanalysis, by and large a structural and modernist approach, 'deeper' and invisible layers of the person are seen as incorporating more truthful statements about him or her. Surface behaviors are caused by deeper unconscious motives. When 'in touch with our feelings,' we have discovered the causes of our affects and behaviors. A postmodern approach to psychology sees depth as merely a spatial metaphor applied to the person. The attribution of causality to deeper layers is seen as misleading.

Modernist thought penetrates our everyday thinking when we 'discover' how we 'really feel' about someone or something. Perhaps we find that we are in love with someone, or that there is something fundamentally wrong with our current relationship. Object-relations theory (see Bott-Spillius,

1988), a dominant variant of psychoanalysis, sees ambivalence toward our objects as resulting in 'splitting,' a defensive maneuver to avoid anxiety. Although used to some extent by everyone, it carries overtones of psychopathology. 'Splitting' implies an ego that was naturally whole to begin with, and 'defense' assumes a deep or core self that is being defended, presumably, at some cost.

Postmodern thought accepts and even celebrates plurality. The spirit of 'both/and' rather than 'either/or' predominates, without a need to reconcile what we really think or feel. The rhetorical model of humankind proposed by Billig (1991) shows how we take up positions in argument in response to the positions adopted by others. We may appear as radicals to our parents and conservatives to our friends as we position ourselves in discursive space. Potter and Wetherell (1987) demonstrate how the same person can produce both apparently racist and anti-racist opinions, and thus how the concept of 'attitude' lying somehow behind our behavior does not explain our deeds and actions.

Similarly, persons take up different positions with respect to their own lives: 'Are you *really* happy in your marriage?' 'Is your life empty?' The meaning of such questions becomes unstable and contingent, as there is no static, fundamental layer of experience to be contacted. From an existentialist perspective, Spinelli (1995) suggests that we think of consciousness as having vertical splits in it rather than horizontal ones. Psychoanalysis proposed horizontal splitting, with conscious material at a surface level repressed into deeper unconscious levels where it motivates surface behavior. Following Sartre (1958), Spinelli proposes that we do not need the concept of repression, that unconscious material was never conscious in the first place. Our action in the world is naturally pre-reflective, or unconscious, and is only made conscious through reflection and the use of language. Like Fingarette (1969), he sees consciousness as a skill, an ability to spell things out. However, a person may be not only unable but also unwilling to spell something out, since doing so may produce a conflict of feelings or interests. This is dissociation rather than repression. Vertical schisms in consciousness endow no single fragment with inherent importance. In narrative terms, we could see this process as an ability or willingness to elaborate a particular story-line. Coaxers and available media may facilitate the telling of a certain story: 'Once I loved my parents, but now I realize they abused me'; 'I thought I was happy in my marriage, but now I realize I am unfulfilled.' Alternative stories lead parallel lives, and there is no final and truthful story or account of our selves or our experience.

Once we have spelled out and committed ourselves to a new story, it often acquires the status of an insight, and yesterday's tale seems like a self-deception. The theme of foundationlessness insists that there is no story that ever captures the whole truth. Perhaps we are never so dangerous – both to others and ourselves – as when we are certain, when we crusade, when we are utterly convinced by our own case.

Constructivism

Modernist psychologies posit an objective world that is revealed to us through our senses. There is a split between this objective world and our subjective reality, which mirrors the objective world in consciousness. Postmodern thought proposes that we will never be able to penetrate 'the real' with our imperfect perceptions and constructions. Although we have no basic human nature in terms of content, we are naturally sense-making beings, who interpret events and confer meanings upon things. The perceived world is not a more or less perfect replica of objective reality; we produce constructions that serve our purposes and help us in our projects.

This stance echoes the work of the existential phenomenologists, who prefer to talk of 'the lived world' rather than the objective world and subjective representations of it. Merleau-Ponty's *Phenomenology of Perception* (1962) is an attempt to show that neither empiricism nor intellectualism – the research programs of realism and idealism, respectively – can succeed in understanding human beings. Although radically different from each other, they both commit the error of positing an objective world that is entirely separate from a disembodied *cogito* that attempts to represent it in consciousness. We cannot understand the lived world through this dualism. The world we experience is *between* subject and object. It is both made and found. Similarly, here there is an emphasis on the interpersonal rather than the *intra*personal; it is the interaction between people – the conversations, the gestures and symbols, and the negotiated accounts – that should be psychology's starting point. Kvale (1992) comments that Merleau-Ponty's psychology was in many ways a forerunner of postmodern thought, and for fifty years was marginalized within mainstream psychology.

Shotter (1992), building on Merleau-Ponty's analysis, addresses the realism/constructionism issue in comparing empirical and hermeneutic methodologies. On the one hand, realism has produced an empirical method of investigation; it is affordances in the world that allow us to talk about that world in certain ways. Our ways of representing it are grounded in nature. On the other, idealism, in its current guise of textualism (see Rorty, 1982b), advocates a hermeneutic method. Here, our ways of talking about the world determine what we will find there. Shotter argues that, paradoxically, we must assert that both of these competing claims are true. We are limited both by events in the world and by our constructions of them. Indeed, following Derrida (1978), he claims that each approach – couched as it is within a systematic discourse – gives credibility to the other through its absent presence.

So we make our worlds, but what we can make is always regulated by what the world affords, which exerts a resistance to our constructions. Individual psychopathologies are both found and made. An interesting illustration might come from the perception of body odor. We can imagine that a century ago, most people smelled strongly. Now, with the advent of plumbing, central heating, and, moreover, an industry devoted to clean, fresh fragrances, we have the opportunity and the motivation to present ourselves as odor-free. We readily identify and are repelled by body smells. This has been accompanied by a general sensitization to smells. Just a decade or two ago, the smell of cigarette smoke was everywhere. Now it is seen not only as a threat, but also as offensive and associated with disease and ill health. This sensitization surely represents both the making and the finding of a problem; the smells are there, but they always have been. Like a palate becoming educated to the taste of fine wine through a language rich with metaphor, the language of smells becomes elaborated to pick out what was once merely background. Similarly, we have become sensitized to our feelings, our inner lives, our psychological states. The discourse in which it is elaborated is primarily psychiatric/psychological. The modernist framework of psychoanalysis has been exported into everyday life, with its notion of a deep unconscious and early hidden traumas that are responsible for current unhappiness.

Polkinghorne (1992) makes the point that these three themes together – foundationlessness, fragmentation, constructivism – comprise a negative epistemology. They appear to call into doubt – even to scorn – humanitarian advances occasioned by the Enlightenment. The charge of relativism or perspectivism, where, in the absence of a truth standard, one perspective seems as valid as any other, has been made against postmodern approaches (Burman, 1990; Parker, 1992; also see Hollinger, 1994). It is Polkinghorne's fourth theme, 'neo-pragmatism,' which makes for an affirmative aspect to postmodern thought. If the three themes leave us with no criteria for action in the world, pragmatism provides this purchase.

Pragmatism

Following James, Rorty (1989) defines truth in terms of 'what is good by way of belief.' In our imperfect construction of reality, we can never assume that we have arrived at a final and definitive description of it. We can never use nature's own vocabulary. It is a mistake to think that the world will constrain us into speaking the truth. A real world exists independent of us, but constructions of it are our property, our responsibility.

Kelly (1955) built his psychology of personal constructs on what he called the philosophical position of 'constructive alternativism.' This holds that there is no ultimately correct way of construing anything. Constructions cannot be evaluated in terms of their truth. Yet one perspective is *not* as good as another. Some ways are certainly more useful than others. What makes them more or less useful is their ability to help us to anticipate the world, to beat the world to the punch. This pragmatic principle accepts that any construing has to take into account a 'real world' of events; you cannot whimsically make anything you want of things. Yet events in the world are never perceived in the raw, so to speak; they are always served up, 'cooked' by our constructions.

Our constructions, then, are to be judged not in terms of their truth, against some answer in the back of nature's book, but in terms of their usefulness. Does a particular vocabulary help us in our project, or is a new one called for? Is an atom best conceived as a particle or a wave when we have a particular aim in view? It does not matter that two incompatible pictures of reality result from these conceptions. From a pragmatist stance, we should not ask whether a particular theory is correct. A more interesting question is: does this theory do its job?

Too often, the dominant stories of psychopathology do not do the job. For one, they can reduce people to helpless victims. Van Deurzen-Smith (1994) points out that the concept of sexual abuse is now used so widely that it makes it more difficult to focus on those real and dreadful cases of abuse that need urgent attention. If it is true, she says, that one-third of women have been sexually abused by the age of eighteen, then 'abuse' has been defined so broadly as to become meaningless. Certainly, people who feel abused need understanding and recognition for the distress caused to them. But this is only part of the therapeutic task. The pragmatic approach would pay less attention to syndrome-criteria, and – emphasizing the practical context of action – more to the meanings that would allow the individual to create new action-possibilities.

Kelly (1969a) recommends that we apply Vaihinger's 'as if' philosophy in psychology. The indicative mood in our language shapes our thinking and leads us to confuse things in the world with our constructions of them. For example, I conclude that I am an introvert, suffering from stress, unable to form close intimate relationships. Instead, Kelly advocates the use of an 'invitational mood' that makes our constructions explicit and highlights their pragmatic value. Suppose I construe myself as if I were oppressed, abused, or stressed – or, perhaps, as resilient, able to resist, or empathize with others under oppression. The casting of language in the invitational mood leaves people open to extend themselves – elaborating possibilities, instead of being stuck in unhelpful definitions that make them impermeable to change. The over-emphasis on *definition* is what Sartre (1958) criticizes as living in bad faith. His insistence that we must recognize our freedom is, of course, not a denial of how circumstances in the world force limits on us. But, following from Kelly, we are free to reconfigure that which we cannot deny.

We will now return to the issue of the experience of psychopathology, and show how narrative psychology – which broadly draws upon the four features outlined above – can be used to understand the proliferation in psychopathology as it is manifested at the level of the individual.

Narrative and the Appropriation of Psychopathology by Individuals

We naturally story our experience. The constructivist approach sees the person as putting together events in a way that makes sense to him or her.

So, in remembering the past, we do not simply recall events as they happened; rather, we selectively recall, narrating a story of the past that makes sense to us. The 'facts' of the past are not like mushrooms, waiting to be collected; they are picked out within shifting narrative searchlights. When a new story emerges, new facts are remembered. Sarbin (1986) has made a convincing case that narrative 'emplotment' is ordinarily used by people to read meaning into events confronting them. Once we have adopted the tales of, say, abuse, events from the past suddenly make sense within this story. Memory is thus not a simple matter of accuracy, but one of construing afresh in the present. As Kelly (1955) contended, the person is not determined by his or her autobiography, but rather by the way he or she writes it.

But story-telling is not a simple individual-level phenomenon. The stories we inhabit belong to a particular time and social context. Plummer (1995) considers the proliferation of 'sexual stories' in late modernity, and why it is that a particular type of story appears to 'have its time.' Following the symbolic interactionism of Blumer (1969), he argues that stories are good examples of 'joint action' – they are not principally individual productions. Though they require a basis in the lives of tellers, they also need encouragement and the articulation of others to produce them. It is also necessary to have audiences willing to accept them, and perhaps recognize their own experiences within them. The psychopathological stories of stress, abuse, and survival tell not only of lived experience – the traces in individuals' lives that are woven into narratives – but also of therapists who 'coax' them, and 'readers' who accept them as plausible.

White and Epston (1990) point out that in 'storying' our experience, we have to draw on the discourses available to us. Following Foucault (1980), they suggest that these discourses will reflect those 'objective,' scientific knowledges that make universal truth-claims. Here, White and Epston are referring to the power/knowledge coupling, a site where the therapy industry now figures prominently. The complaints presented to therapists are, expectedly, couched in therapeutic languages (often before any tangible encounter), validating and reproducing therapeutic discourses – a process similar to what Gergen (1989) calls the 'warranting voice of therapy.'

Therapy is the child of Enlightenment-based psychiatry and psychology, and its stories often reflect interventionist narratives of illness and passivity. The very term 'patient' means one who passively suffers. The 'patient's' experience is one of discovery rather than invention. He or she 'now realizes' that he or she has been abused, suffers from stress, has this or that syndrome. From the modern, realist worldview, one would evaluate memories and realizations in terms of their truth-value: 'Was she really abused by her father?' 'Am I really suffering from depression?'

A constructivist account, by contrast, would see these revelations as constructed narratives, an inseparable mixture of construction and event. They have been subject to what Spence (1986) terms 'narrative smoothing' – facts that fit the new theory or story emerge and are reinterpreted, those that do not are forgotten. Accounts must therefore be judged in terms of narrative truth rather than historical truth. Within narrative theory, mental illness becomes a framework in which to interpret experience, rather than the surface expression of real underlying disease entities. The 'patients' have used the prevailing vocabulary of illness to weave together their stories. From our standpoint, to ask about the truth of these stories is to ask a silly question. Rather, one should ask whether these stories make sense. Do they do justice to the person's experience? And are they helpful to people? Can going over the past, examining their relationships, wondering what is wrong with them, lead to their living their lives in a more satisfactory way?

Many modernist tales, with their assumptions of progress and emancipation through scientific discovery, see therapy as empowering in this way. Where there was id there shall be ego; where once we were driven, we shall take up the reins of our lives. Through insight and reflection, we will become the masters of our own ships. Although notoriously difficult to evaluate, meta-studies of therapy effectiveness show a definite therapeutic effect (Smith and Glass, 1977). But there seems to be a high price to pay. We have a proliferation of syndromes from which we are suffering. In the view of Hillman and Ventura (1992), we are a 'society of recoverers.' Individuals, sensitized to their suffering, feel helplessness, rage, and despair. The modernist faith in cures and progress has led to a blurring of Freud's distinction between 'common unhappiness and neurotic misery.' Kovel (1976) notes that whereas the aim of therapy – initially a short-term enterprise – was to relieve neurosis, to reduce it to common unhappiness, the therapeutic target is now discontent and unhappiness at large. 'Growth' is the promise of many humanistic therapies – developing the self, perhaps even creating a new self. Discussing psychology's 'sanction for selfishness,' Kvale comments that, with modernity, the soul has evolved into the self or psyche, an entity cut off from its social and historical context, and bent on its own 'actualization' (1992: 43). It is worth asking whether or not this has ironically led to – at least in part – an apparent increase in unhappiness.

The Implications of a Postmodern Psychology for Therapy and Counseling

The implications of postmodern thought, as it has been outlined here, are quite radical in terms of the status, practices, and purposes of psychotherapy and counseling.

First, the status of the therapist or counselor as 'in possession' of expert knowledge is questioned under a postmodern psychology – and thus the therapist–client relationship comes under new scrutiny. Traditional, modern forms of clinical practice connote oppression, signifying power relations that operate to the disadvantage of the pathologized client.

The status and power of the mental health professions has already been challenged by a number of initiatives in the US, Britain, and Italy (see Parker et al., 1995) which have attempted to empower mental health service users. In the practice of therapy and counseling, attempts should be made to deal with the power differential between client and therapist. As Bannister (1983) argues, a differential in power is inevitable in the therapy situation, but the nature of therapeutic expertise should be more clearly defined. Within a postmodern framework, the therapist does not have, in mystified form, an enclosed view of what is natural or good for clients. He or she does not speak from any position of essential knowledge, and does not see things in terms of skills that the client ought to acquire. He or she does not have a patent on what is rational, and does not encourage any sort of therapeutic dependency. For Bannister, there are various metaphors of the therapeutic relationship that he rejects as inappropriate. These include doctor/patient, priest/penitent, trainer/trainee, and friend/friend. He follows Kelly in advocating a research supervisor/research student model. This positions the client as a researcher who always knows most about his or her project, and who takes ultimate responsibility for it. The therapist or supervisor has a general eye for how different sorts of projects might be approached.

Second, practitioners need to examine the way that the prevailing constructions of sanity and insanity, normality and deviance, pathological and healthy inform interactions between themselves and their clients in ways that actively construct their clients as particular kinds of people. Harper (1995) describes how, in his own clinical interview with a client, his questions subtly construct the client as 'paranoid.' Practitioners might actively seek to offer their clients new and more liberatory ways of constructing experience. For example, the Hearing Voices Network aims to help people to redefine their experience in ways which do not reduce their status to that of victimized patient (see Parker et al., 1995; Romme and Escher, 1993).

Third, practitioners must therefore question their usual normative framework and recognize the extent of human diversity in experience and behavior. This diversity exists not only between people, but also in the apparent inconsistency and fragmentary quality of individual experience. Social constructionism rejects the unitary, consistent self of liberal humanism. There is no deep, real self to be mined, no true inner feelings to be contacted. Social constructionism exhorts us to recognize the truly situated and relational nature of human experience and conduct. If we do not possess true selves, we must learn to live with and, further, see opportunities in our fragmentation. Mair (1989) has put forward a model of self as a community, and suggested that one task of therapy is to allow the different voices of this community to be heard.

Fourth, language is not primarily a medium through which we express ourselves; rather, language speaks through and constitutes us. There is nothing inside us that is isolated from social practices and language, but there is no reason to believe that our 'vocabulary' of self cannot be changed. Seemingly indisputable accounts of others and us are, in fact, disputable. We can encourage the elaboration of 'subjugated knowledges' that might better reflect our lived experience than the dominant discourses. We are not determined by our past – we write and rewrite it. Just as history may be written from many perspectives, so many personal autobiographies are equally possible. It is the *way* we construct the histories that is important. We must experiment with different narratives, in search for those that best empower us in dealing with our circumstances. A postmodern psychology can help construct new vocabularies through which to construct new worlds of meaning and relationship (Gergen, 1992).

Fifth, we are pre-reflective beings, whose action and experience arise jointly out of interaction with others. We cannot always expect to find individual causes and reasons for our conduct. Traditional psychology individualizes problems and locates them in intrapsychic processes, but this is already being questioned by the rise of such approaches as family therapy, which, even with its own epistemological difficulties, privileges the social system in which individuals are enmeshed. Many of the problems that people experience may be better understood as products of the identities that they are unable to resist within the context of their family, social group, or society. Accordingly, our attempts to help should focus on providing effective strategies for resisting the debilitating constructions of themselves and their discursive positions (Burr and Butt, 1993).

Conclusion

We have argued that a social constructionist analysis of the current rise in therapy and counseling offers a penetrating account of how through surveillance and disciplinary power, they may serve social control. However, we have argued that such analyses often stop short of making recommendations for change, particularly at the level of individual subjectivity. We believe that a postmodern psychology is capable of doing so without abandoning a social constructionist framework, and believe that there is much that can be done to address these needs within the current framework of therapy and counseling.

Rorty (1982c) argues that the aim of the social sciences should be to act as interpreter for those who, for one reason or another, cannot speak for themselves. Like the novelist, the psychologist, faced with conflict and cruelty, makes lives intelligible to others, thereby enlarging the human community. A specifically postmodern psychology, we think, can also make people more intelligible to themselves – without the search for any foundational self. Rather, they might be enabled to produce self-narratives which allow them to live at peace with themselves.

References

Bannister, D. (1983) 'The Internal Politics of Psychotherapy,' in D. Pilgrim (ed.), *Psychology and Psychotherapy*. London and New York: Routledge. pp. 139–50.
Billig, M. (1991) *Ideology and Opinions*. London and Thousand Oaks, CA: Sage.
Blumer, H. (1969) *Symbolic Interactionism*. Englewood Cliffs, NJ: Prentice Hall.
Bott-Spillius, E. (ed.) (1988) *Melanie Klein Today*. London and New York: Routledge.

Brown, G. and Harris, T. (1978) *The Social Origins of Depression*. London: Tavistock.

Burman, E. (1990) 'Differing with Deconstruction,' in I. Parker and J. Shotter (eds), *Deconstructing Social Psychology*. London and New York: Routledge. pp. 208–20.

Burr, V. and Butt, T.W. (1993) 'Personal and Social Constructionism.' Unpublished paper, University of Huddersfield.

Derrida, J. (1978) *Writing and Difference*. Chicago: University of Chicago Press.

Faris, R. and Dunham, H. (1939) *Mental Disorders in Urban Areas*. Chicago: University of Chicago Press.

Fingarette, H. (1969) *Self Deception*. London and New York: Routledge.

Foucault, M. (1965) *Madness and Civilization: A History of Insanity in the Age of Reason*. New York: Vintage.

Foucault, M. (1976) *The History of Sexuality, Vol. 1*. Harmondsworth: Penguin.

Foucault, M. (1977) *Discipline and Punish: The Birth of the Prison*. London: Allen Lane.

Foucault, M. (1980) *Power/Knowledge: Selected Interviews and Other Writings 1972–1977* (C. Gordon, ed.). New York: Pantheon.

Gergen, K. (1989) 'Warranting Voice and the Elaboration of Self,' in J. Shotter and K. Gergen (eds), *Texts of Identity*. London and Thousand Oaks, CA: Sage. pp. 70–81.

Gergen, K. (1992) 'Towards a Postmodern Psychology,' in S. Kvale (ed.), *Psychology and Postmodernism*. London and Thousand Oaks, CA: Sage. pp. 17–30.

Goffman, E. (1961) *Asylums*. Harmondsworth: Penguin.

Habermas, J. (1986) 'Taking Aim at the Heart of the Present,' in D. Couzens Hoy (ed.), *Foucault: A Critical Reader*. Oxford: Basil Blackwell. pp. 103–8.

Harper, D.J. (1995) 'Discourse Analysis and Mental Health,' *Journal of Mental Health*, 4: 347–57.

Hillman, J. and Ventura. M. (1992) *We've Had a Hundred Years of Psychotherapy and the World is Getting Worse*. New York: HarperCollins.

Hollinger, R. (1994) *Postmodernism and the Social Sciences: A Thematic Approach*. London and Thousand Oaks, CA: Sage.

Kelly, G.A. (1955) *The Psychology of Personal Constructs*. New York: Norton.

Kelly, G.A. (1969a) The Language of Hypothesis: Man's Psychological Instrument,' in B. Maher (ed.), *Clinical Psychology and Personality: The Selected Papers of George Kelly*. New York and London: Wiley. pp. 147–62.

Kelly, G.A. (1969b) 'Epilogue: Don Juan,' in B. Maher (ed.), *Clinical Psychology and Personality: The Selected Papers of George Kelly*. New York and London: Wiley. pp. 333–52.

Kitzinger, C. (1992) 'The Individuated Self-Concept: A Critical Analysis of Social Constructionist Writing on Individualism,' in G. Breakwell (ed.), *Social Psychology of Identity and the Self Concept*. London: Surrey University Press (in association with Academic Press). pp. 221–50.

Kovel, J. (1976) *A Complete Guide to Therapy*. Harmondsworth: Penguin.

Kvale, S. (1992) 'Postmodern Psychology: A Contradiction in Terms?,' in S. Kvale (ed.), *Psychology and Postmodernism*. London and Thousand Oaks, CA: Sage. pp. 31–57.

Laing, R.D. (1959) *The Divided Self*. London: Tavistock.

Laing, R.D. (1967) *The Politics of Experience*. Harmondsworth: Penguin.

Mair, J.M. (1989) *Between Psychology and Psychotherapy: A Poetics of Experience*. London and New York: Routledge.

Merleau-Ponty, M. (1962) *Phenomenology of Perception*. London and New York: Routledge.

Parker, I. (1992) *Discourse Dynamics: Critical Analysis for Social and Personal Psychology*. London and New York: Routledge.

Parker, I., Georgaca, E., Harper, D., McLaughlin, T., and Stowell-Smith, M. (1995) *Deconstructing Psychopathology*. London and Thousand Oaks, CA: Sage.

Parton, N. (1985) *The Politics of Child Abuse*. London: Macmillan.

Plummer, K. (1995) *Telling Sexual Stories: Power, Change, and Social Worlds*. London and New York: Routledge.

Polkinghorne, D. (1992) 'Postmodern Epistemology of Practice,' in S. Kvale (ed.), *Psychology and Postmodernism*. London and Thousand Oaks, CA: Sage. pp. 146–65.

Potter, J. and Wetherell, M. (1987) *Discourse and Social Psychology*. London and Thousand Oaks, CA: Sage.

Romme, M. and Escher, S. (eds) (1993) *Accepting Voices*. London: MIND.

Rorty, R. (1982a) 'The World Well Lost,' in R. Rorty (ed.), *Consequences of Pragmatism*. Hemel Hempstead: Harvester Wheatsheaf. pp. 3–16.

Rorty, R. (1982b) 'Nineteenth Century Idealism and Twentieth Century Textualism,' in R. Rorty (ed.), *Consequences of Pragmatism*. Hemel Hempstead: Harvester Wheatsheaf. pp. 139–59.

Rorty, R. (1982c) 'Method, Social Science and Social Hope,' in R. Rorty (ed.), *Consequences of Pragmatism*. Hemel Hempstead: Harvester Wheatsheaf. pp. 191–210.

Rorty, R. (1989) *Contingency, Irony and Solidarity*. Cambridge: Cambridge University Press.

Rose, N. (1989) *Governing the Soul: The Shaping of the Private Self*. London and New York: Routledge.

Rose, N. (1990) 'Psychology as a Social Science,' in I. Parker and J. Shotter (eds), *Deconstructing Social Psychology*. London and New York: Routledge. pp. 103–16.

Rosenhan, D. (1973) 'On Being Sane in Insane Places,' *Science*, 179: 250–7.

Sampson, E.E. (1990) 'Social Psychology and Social Control,' in I. Parker and J. Shotter (eds), *Deconstructing Social Psychology*. London and New York: Routledge. pp. 117–26.

Sarbin, T. (1986) 'The Narrative as a Root Metaphor in Psychology,' in T. Sarbin (ed.), *Narrative Psychology: The Storied Nature of Human Conduct*. New York: Praeger. pp. 3–21.

Sartre, J.-P. (1958) *Being and Nothingness*. London: Methuen.

Sarup, M. (1988) *An Introductory Guide to Post-Structuralism and Postmodernism*. Hemel Hempstead: Harvester Wheatsheaf.

Scheff, T. (1966) *Being Mentally Ill: A Sociological Theory*. Chicago: Aldine.

Sedgwick, P. (1982) *Psycho Politics*. London: Pluto.

Shotter, J. (1992) 'Getting in Touch,' in S. Kvale (ed.), *Psychology and Postmodernism*. London and Thousand Oaks, CA: Sage. pp. 58–73.

Smith, M. and Glass, G. (1977) 'Meta-Analysis of Psychotherapy Outcome Studies,' *American Psychologist*, 132: 152–70.

Spence, D. (1986) 'Narrative Smoothing and Clinical Wisdom,' in T. Sarbin (ed.), *Narrative Psychology: The Storied Nature of Human Conduct*. New York: Praeger. pp. 211–32.

Spinelli, E. (1995) 'The Unconscious: An Idea Whose Time Has Gone?,' in H. Cohn and S. Du Plock (eds), *Existential Challenges to Psychotherapeutic Theory and Practice*. London: The Society for Existential Analysis. pp. 217–47.

Szasz, T.S. (1961) 'The Myth of Mental Illness,' *American Psychologist*, 15 (February): 113–18.

Szasz, T.S. (1970) *Ideology and Insanity: Essays on the Psychiatric Dehumanization of Man*. New York: Doubleday.

Szasz, T.S. (1971) *The Manufacture of Madness*. London: Routledge & Kegan Paul.

van Deurzen-Smith, E. (1994) 'Questioning the Power of Psychotherapy: Is Jeffrey Masson onto Something?,' *Journal of the Society for Existential Analysis*, 5: 37–44.

Walzer, M. (1986) 'The Politics of Michel Foucault,' in D. Couzens Hoy (ed.), *Foucault: A Critical Reader*. Oxford: Basil Blackwell. pp. 51–68.

White, M. and Epston, D. (1990) *Narrative Means to Therapeutic Ends*. New York: Norton.

Wilkins, L. (1971) 'The Deviance-Amplifying System,' in W. Carson and P. Wiles (eds), *The Sociology of Crime and Delinquency in Britain. Vol. 1: The British Tradition*. London: Robertson & Co. pp. 252–60.

10

Women's Madness: A Material-Discursive-Intrapsychic Approach

Jane Ussher

Women's madness is a subject that has fascinated artists, poets, playwrights, and novelists for centuries. Representations of woman as mad range from the dangerous harridan in the attic to the melancholic maiden languishing helplessly on her bed; all stand as reminders of the potential mysteries and dangers lurking beneath the external signifiers of 'woman.' But making madness synonymous with femininity isn't merely a matter of misogynist fantasy or fear. Mental health statistics still attest to the preponderance of women deemed 'mad,'[1] and in need of statutory regulation (Bebbington, 1996; Busfield, 1996). Community surveys, hospital admissions, and statistics on outpatient treatment, both medical and psychological, all concur: adult women report more mental health problems than men, and are more likely to be diagnosed and treated for madness.

For decades now, researchers have pursued the factors underlying this gender difference, claiming that if we can explain it, we will have the key to a general understanding of mental health problems (e.g. Bebbington, 1996). Numerous competing biological, psychological, and social etiological theories have been put forward from the fields of psychiatry and psychology, and clinicians of all varieties are working to dispense expert knowledge and care in attempting to ameliorate or prevent such problems. Lay texts, too, proliferate, offering myriad self-help suggestions and 'alternative' treatments. Women's madness has clearly moved from mythology to mass industry. No longer so alluring and enigmatic, at least on the surface, its categorization, containment, and cure seem to be assured.

Yet, as we know, these institutionalized investigations and interventions have not gone unquestioned. A range of critics, including anti-psychiatrists, postmodernists, and feminists from a number of different ideological camps, have subjected expert analyses of women's madness to critical deconstruction. Much of what has been for decades – perhaps centuries – taken for granted has been dissected and discarded as biased, misconceived, or misogynist. However, in mainstream research and clinical practice, very little has changed. Madness as an illness remains basically unchallenged. Science categorizes symptoms into syndromes that are operationally defined and analyzed in objective research. Individual women are offered reductionist explanations and often biomedical cures for their symptomatologies. Psychological interventions may not blame the body, but they still mainly focus on the subjectivity of the *individual* woman. The gap between critical analysis and the institutionalized regulation or treatment of madness seems impossible to bridge.

Why is this the case? And what can be done to effect change? In this essay, I will address these two questions, reviewing both mainstream and critical approaches to the phenomenon of women's madness, as well as the relationship between the two. I will argue that a material-discursive-intrapsychic perspective should replace the current positivist, and closely aligned realist, epistemological perspectives underlying mainstream research and clinical intervention. This approach would recognize the 'materiality' of mental health problems as they are experienced by women, intrapsychic pain and defenses, and the discursive construction of madness and femininity – all without privileging one level of analysis above the others.

A Reflexive Pause

Before I embark upon this analysis I would outline the reasons why I have arrived at this particular position. My interest in women's madness was first inspired by my own mother's mental health problems and her subsequent treatment at the hands of myriad professionals when I was an adolescent, described elsewhere (Ussher, 1991). Thus, I discovered the stigma of 'madness' very early in life. It was a subject that could not be discussed, inspiring fear and dread. I learned to live with my mother's mental health problems without ever naming as 'madness' the problems she experienced, either to her or to anyone else. Naming them now is only possible because of the twenty-five-year distance which has since elapsed – and also because she is now no longer deemed 'mad.' My training as a psychologist now equips me not only to name, but to research, diagnose, and treat other women who suffer similarly. I have spent many years doing so.

Yet there was a time, for a number of years, when I stopped; I could no longer reconcile my academic and professional training with my knowledge of feminist and social constructionist thinking on the subject of women's madness. I felt that I could only take part in critical analysis or deconstructionist debate. However, I no longer believe that this is enough, for myself at least. Critical thinking is essential; deconstruction of madness as a concept must be done. Yet we cannot ignore the pain and suffering experienced by the women – and men – who are deemed mad. We cannot dismiss mental health problems as linguistic constructions or mere justifications for regulatory control; we need to offer something more concrete than critique for women who come forward for help. At the same time, we need to address the fact that postmodern and feminist thinking is not having the impact it should on mainstream research and clinical practice; the fact that it is invariably dismissed or ignored. Rather than wringing our hands at the injustice of this situation, we need to offer a way forward. This is what I want to try to contribute to here.

Explaining Women's Madness: Mainstream Accounts

The focus of this essay will be largely on epistemology, rather than on the arguments which unravel the relationship between gender and madness, outlined elsewhere (Ussher, 1991). I take this approach because virtually all researchers and clinicians have adopted the *realist/positivist* epistemology that has dominated science since the seventeenth century. Therefore, while mainstream biomedical and psychosocial theories and interventions for women's madness may appear to have little in common – or even to stand in opposition to each other – what is often overlooked is the fact that researchers in both fields share the same epistemological assumptions,[2] and, as a consequence, adopt the same methods in investigating women's madness. Arguably, it is the particular nature of the positivist/realist standpoint that translates into a refusal to engage postmodern and feminist debates, resulting in the standard reductionism and marginalization of historical and cultural factors.

As the term 'positivism' has often been used in a loose and general manner, it may be helpful to outline a definition at this point. Keat (1979) identified two major elements within the positivist position. The first element is 'methodological naturalism,' the demand for homogeneous methods and approaches in both the social and natural sciences, with the latter providing the model for the former. Second, science follows realist logic: knowledge is only possible as the result of observation, and the only things that can be observed are those which are accessible to the senses. Causality is understood in terms of antecedent conditions and general laws governing phenomena; facts and theories, moreover, are clearly separated from values, with only the former being the legitimate focus of scientific interest (O'Brien, 1994: 9). The fundamental premise of a scientific-realist perspective is that objects have real existence independent of any perceiver, knowledge system, or practice.

Methodological Naturalism in the Analysis of Women's Madness

The adoption of methodological naturalism is clearly evident in mainstream analyses of women's madness. First, in both biomedical and psychosocial study, the models of research that are adopted clearly mimic those adopted in the natural sciences. This has resulted in the emphasis on the homogeneous use of *hypothetico-deductive* methodologies, and on standardized, validated measures of both dependent and independent variables – that is, mental health problems and their causes – through an emphasis on objectivity, reliability, and research replicability.

The limitations of hypothetico-deductive methodologies have been well documented elsewhere (e.g. Harré and Secord, 1972; Henriques et al., 1984;

Hollway, 1989; Ingleby, 1982; Shotter, 1975), and attention is often drawn to such problems as: the artificiality of controlled studies; the limited number of variables able to be studied at any one time; the limitations of quantitative analysis; the assumption that the individual can and should be studied separately from cultural and historical factors; the assumption that the individual should be the sole focus of attention at all; the notion that objectivity is at all possible; and the liabilities of predictive models of cause and effect. Each of these critiques will be explored in more detail below.

Categorization and Consensus Definitions of Mental Illness: Knowledge Through Observation

Following a thesis of methodological naturalism, the desire for valid and reliable comparison across epidemiological and treatment studies – and the need to facilitate research into etiological mechanisms – has precipitated the desire to establish 'consensus definitions' of mental health problems: the archetypal case being the American Psychiatric Association's *Diagnostic and Statistical Manual of Mental Disorders* (*DSM*; American Psychiatric Association, 1994). The desire for uniform definitions of mental health problems may appear on the surface to be a necessary first step for both research and clinical intervention. However, the very notion of categorization of madness into psychiatric syndromes has been criticized from many different angles.

The focus on diagnostic categories reifies notions of madness as discrete, consistent, and homogeneous clinical entities, which further have an identifiable etiology, and *cause* the symptoms women report. This acts to deny the social and discursive context of women's lives, as well as the gendered nature of science, which defines how women's bodies and lives are studied (Keller, 1985). In contrast, as many critics have argued, madness can be conceptualized as a social category created by a process of expert definition (Ingleby, 1982; Littlewood and Lipsedge, 1982; Szasz, 1961; Ussher, 1991). In this view, madness is a socially constructed label, based on value-laden definitions of normality. Parallel arguments have been made about many other 'disorders,' both physical and psychological (Foucault, 1967; Sedgwick, 1987), leading to a deconstruction of expert diagnosis, and to a questioning of the existence of many 'syndromes.'

If a phenomenon cannot be objectively observed and measured using reliable, standardized techniques, then it cannot be 'known' within a positivist paradigm. This has resulted in a methodology-driven, rather than a theory-driven, analysis of women's madness and its possible etiology. For example, the role of unconscious factors cannot be easily assessed within a hypothetico-deductive frame, and so they are not included in the majority of mainstream analyses (e.g. see Bebbington, 1996). Accordingly, as historical, political, and wider societal factors are not easily operationalized and assessed, they are only addressed within social constructionist or feminist critiques (e.g. Chesler, 1995; Ingleby, 1982; Showalter, 1987; Ussher, 1991). According to a positivist paradigm, madness is construed as an individual problem – a disorder affecting an individual woman, on whom biomedical or psychosocial factors impact and produce symptomatology.

The woman who presents herself with problems is implicitly positioned as passive within the discourse of positivism, since agency is not easy (if at all possible) to observe. So it is inevitable that it is her body – or her symptoms – that are the entire focus of attention. Yet women are not passive objects either in relation to interpretation of physical or psychological symptoms, or in relation to the symbolic construction of madness. Seeking treatment for mental health problems is a process of active, reflexive negotiation with symptomatology, current life events and life-style, and cultural, medical, or psychological ideas about madness. Many women make sense of their experiences through positioning themselves as suffering from depression, anxiety, or problems such as premenstrual syndrome (PMS); others may experience symptoms but not make ascriptions of any of these problems. To position these women as 'false negatives,' as they are in the case of PMS research (Hamilton and Gallant, 1990), is to misinterpret the active negotiation and resistance with/in the dominant discourses (Ussher, 1997a).

As psychological symptoms are not always visibly apparent, they have to be observed through the interface of subjective accounts. As these accounts may fall outside the required standards of objectivity and replicability, in empiricist research they are collected through the use of standardized instruments. This is why there has been an inordinate amount of attention given to developing reliable and valid standardized questionnaire measures for assessing the incidence of specific mental health problems. Thus, the complexity and contradictions evident within women's subjective accounts are negated, and a qualitatively rich source of data is left uncollected and unexamined.

Within a positivist/realist frame, women are made to fit the researcher's model of specific syndromes. This is in direct contrast to grounded methods of data collection and analysis, where the constraints of a priori assumptions are not imposed upon participants' accounts, which are collected in a more open, inductive manner (Henwood and Pidgeon, 1994; Potter and Wetherell, 1986). The use of questionnaires also assumes that 'symptoms' can be categorized and classified in a dichotomous manner, as existing or not – with the only added complexity being the notion of a *degree* of symptomatology. That a woman might reply that she sometimes has a symptom and sometimes does not – that it depends on what is happening in her life – is not acknowledged at all. Inside this strict framework, it is forgotten, as is her overall assessment of the meaning of her symptoms.

Focusing Within the Person: Biology or Cognitions

Within a positivist/realist paradigm, the body is implicitly considered to be fundamental or more 'real' than psychosocial variables. This has led to the disparity between the number of biomedical and psychosocial etiological theories and therapies for women's mental health problems, as women's 'abnormality,' discontent, anger, or illness has historically been attributed to the body, or to the vagaries of reproduction (Ussher, 1989). This focus on the physical body is a direct result of the assumption that it is biomedical factors that can be observed and measured in the most 'objective' manner, removing the potentially confounding interface of the woman's subjective interpretation. In what is a totally reductionist viewpoint, the body or biology is conceptualized in terms of physical processes – the action of hormones, neurotransmitters, or ovarian function, considered separately from any meaning or cultural context.

There have been many critiques of the notion of the body, or biology, as objective entities which can be understood as separate from sociohistorical knowledge, experience or subjectivity (see Foucault, 1979; Henriques et al., 1984; Stainton-Rogers, 1991). Individuals do not experience symptoms in a sociocultural vacuum. The bodily functions we understand as a sign of 'illness' vary across culture and across time (Littlewood and Lipsedge, 1982; Payer, 1988; Sedgwick, 1987). Women's recognition or interpretation of physical and psychological changes cannot be understood outside of the social and historical context in which they live (Martin, 1987; Ussher, 1991). For example, there is much evidence now of cultural differences both in women's reporting of premenstrual symptoms, and their perception of these as signs of 'PMS' (Chandra and Chaturvedi, 1989; Dan and Mongale, 1994). Equally, definitions of sexuality as a sign of madness differ greatly between the nineteenth century and today. In the nineteenth century it was arguably the 'sexual woman' who was at risk of being defined as mad; today it is the *a*sexual woman (Ussher, 1997a).

It was in the context of the 'discovery' of sex hormones in 1905 (Oudshoorn, 1990) that hormonal theories of women's madness evolved. Rather than accepting the body as something which exists above and beyond the measurement tools and definitions of science, it can be argued that the aspects of biology and the body we are allowed to 'know' are those which meet the criteria of the measurement tools currently in use. The development of new technology for calibrating the body will undoubtedly lead to a new set of meta-theories for women's madness. In psychological models of madness, the emphasis on cognitions is arguably equally reductionist; the focus may be on biology, but it is still an essentialist view of madness, looking within the woman for the problem and following a simple model of cause and effect.

The Adoption of Unilinear Models of Cause and Effect

Within the existing research on women's madness, each of the variables which appear in the biomedical, psychosocial, or multifactorial models is clearly operationally defined, reinforcing the assumption that they are discrete antecedent entities which exert independent causal influence in the etiology of specific syndromes. Within this framework, both mental health problems and the resulting symptoms are positioned as independent variables invariably conceptualized in a dichotomous way (Walker, 1995).

Biomedical accounts dominate the field and provide the basis for the widespread use of medical interventions, in particular, psychotropic drug use. The attribution of symptomatology to 'synaptic events,' such as noradrenaline, 5-HT, serotonin, dopamine, and acetetycholine neurotransmitters (de Fonseca, 1989), can obviously be applied equally to men and women. Yet here it is that sex differences – and not those of gender – become salient. One perspective, of course, implicates female hormones (Paykel, 1991), particularly oestrogen and progesterone, that are manifested in 'reproductive syndromes': PMS, postnatal depression (PND), or menopausal problems. Another view emphasizes genetics. For example, Slater and Cowie (1971) claimed that the gene for depression was located in the X chromosome, and thus women, having two X chromosomes, would be more liable to suffer from it.[3]

Social or environmental factors which have been reported to be associated with more frequent reporting of mental health problems include: marital status, with married women reporting higher rates of problems than single women or married men (Bebbington, 1996); caring roles, with women looking after small children (Brown and Harris, 1978) or elderly relatives (Brody and Schoonover, 1986) being at higher risk; employment status, with work generally providing a protective factor, particularly for working-class women (Parry, 1986); absence of social support and economic or social power; (Chesler, 1995); and, gendered role socialization, which leads to depressogenic attributional styles (Wierzbicki and Carver, 1989). Other factors addressed have emphasized heterosexual relationships as the perceived fulfillment of life (Ussher, 1997a), and an emphasis on affiliation rather than achievement, leading to vulnerability when relationships are under threat (Kessler and MacLeod, 1985). In addition, representations of femininity, which position woman as labile or as Madonna/whore (Ussher, 1997a), are also of importance, as feminine qualities and roles are generally devaluated (Bebbington, 1996). Lastly, sexual violence and abuse in adulthood or childhood are clearly central in environmental accounts (Browne and Finkelhor, 1986; Koss, 1990).

Psychological theories which have been put forward to account for these elements include 'cognitive vulnerability,' specifically the greater likelihood of women to attribute problems to internal, stable, and global factors (Calicchia and Pardine, 1984); 'coping styles' (Sowa and Lustman, 1984); and 'perceptions of control' (Martin et al., 1984). Psychodynamic theories, including object relations theory (Chodorow, 1978; Dinnerstein, 1976), Kleinian theory (Klein, 1984), and Freudian theory (Mitchell, 1975), have been particularly influential in psychotherapeutic circles – as well as in many recent feminist critiques – but have had less impact on mainstream research and practice.

The need to test the influence of these antecedent variables within a hypothetico-deductive model has led to the almost universal adoption of unilinear models in both biomedical and psychosocial research, where the reporting of symptoms is correlated with a single predictive factor. Given the predominance of these unilinear models of etiology, it is not surprising to find that unidimensional approaches also dominate research on the effectiveness of both biomedical and psychosocial treatment. One worrying consequence of adopting a unilinear approach is that causal assumptions are often made on the basis of treatment effectiveness. For example, in a study which reported the positive benefits of fluoxetine for treating premenstrual complaints, Menkes et al. concluded 'these findings thus support the proposed role of serotonergic hypoactivity in the aetiology of PMS' (1993: 101). Similarly, in a study of oestradiol patches, Watson et al. argue that their positive result 'supports the earlier observation of a link between premenstrual syndrome and ovarian function' (1989: 731). However, the finding that a particular treatment reduces premenstrual symptoms does not necessarily have implications for etiology. Aspirin is an effective cure for headache, and inhalation of CO_2 an effective treatment for panic attacks, yet we would not propose that either aspirin or CO_2 are implicated in the etiology of either disorder.

The very premise of a causal relationship is also flawed, as the discovery of a *correlation* between reported symptoms and a particular biomedical or psychosocial substrate does not mean that the substrate *caused* the symptoms. Each may be related to a third variable, or not related at all. Indeed, as Bebbington (1996) pointed out, correlations between scores of neuroticism on personality questionnaires and measures of depression may reflect the fact that similar questions are used on both, rather than any association between neuroticism and depression. Thus, the search for general laws underlying gender differences in mental health problems is potentially blinding us to the complexity of the phenomenon, and to the complexity of women's experience.

Multifactorial Models: Away from Linear Models?

A number of suggestions have been offered in an attempt to resolve the contradictions and inconsistencies in mainstream research and theory. Many researchers still continue to search for the Holy Grail – the single underlying cause or treatment for mental health problems. Others have focused on the disciplinary divide between medical and psychological approaches, and as a result have suggested the adoption of multifactorial models, where biological and psychosocial vulnerability can be addressed within a framework that acknowledges the interaction between the two (e.g. Bancroft, 1993). Alternatively, there have been suggestions of an interaction between cognitive and social vulnerability (Brown and Harris, 1978), where certain women are more prone to depression or anxiety as a result of the interaction of environmental factors – such as loss or stress – and cognitive factors, such as the overvaluation of one goal at the expense of others.

While these multifactorial models have provided a lead in moving away from narrow unidimensional thinking about women's madness, they only offer a partial answer, and arguably operate almost solely at the level of theory, having had little influence on research practice, which continues to be conducted in a unidimensional vein. For example, Paul Bebbington, in acknowledging the etiological complexity of women's depression, concludes:

> Clinical experience suggests that depression arises because of a complex cascade, whereby for instance external circumstances interact with cognitive sets and induce physiological responses that in turn change the way circumstances are appraised. This may then change cognitions and physiological status, leading to a further spiral. . . . I feel this is actually how depression develops, *it becomes extremely hard to research*, and progress has to fall back on the integration of piecemeal approaches. (Bebbington, 1996: 299, my emphasis)

It is only 'extremely hard to research' within the constraints of methodological naturalism, outlined above. It is only researchers who adopt this epistemological stance (myself included, until recently) who feel constrained to remain within their own professional boundaries, only able to pay lip service to the notion of a multifactorial model at the conceptual level. There are a number of reasons why this is so: the practical difficulties of crossing professional boundaries (which include professional rivalries); differences in epistemological or methodological training; and the pressure to locate research funding in one institution as a result of research assessment exercises. Within a positivist paradigm, moreover, to measure the influence of myriad multilayered factors simultaneously could be seen as a sign of poor research design, perhaps introducing 'type 1 errors,' where significant relationships between symptomatology and putative predictive variables are found by chance.

Objectivity: The Separation of Facts from Values

Underpinning the whole of the positivist/realist endeavor is the commitment to scientific objectivity. The goal of the scientific enterprise is to remove the possibility of bias or of values, and to examine research questions or test hypotheses in a precise and replicable manner. Thus any information on symptomatology is collected in a systematic and objective fashion, and any inconsistencies found are used as confirmatory evidence for the unreliability of women's subjective accounts.

The fact that women's accounts of mental health problems is considered to be biased or 'subjective' – yet researcher's are not – illustrates the absence of reflexivity in positivist/realist research. Yet, as has been argued elsewhere (e.g. Billig, 1991; Harding, 1987; Hollway, 1989), the ideological stance of researchers affects the research questions they ask, the epistemological stance and methodologies they adopt, and the interpretations of the data collected. Research or theory-building that is explicitly conducted within a feminist framework, specifically challenging the dominance of biomedical models by directing attention to the social-political context of illness diagnoses (i.e. Chesler, 1995; Ussher, 1991), is often dismissed by positivist/realist researchers as not meeting the criteria for 'good science';

rather, it is deemed biased or political (see Koeske, 1983, for an example of this in relation to PMS research). However, it is clearly 'political' and ideological to elevate the researcher or the clinician to a position of power, implying that he or she is the only one qualified to 'know' (Foucault, 1989). Put bluntly, it is equally ideological to reify the notion of madness as an illness (see Ingleby, 1982). The emphasis on objectivity does not strengthen positivist/realist research; it weakens it, as it can so easily be undermined.

Scores of mainstream researchers are aware of many of these critiques. However, while researchers or reviewers are happy to acknowledge the importance of social or psychological etiological factors (i.e. Bancroft, 1993; Bebbington, 1996; Busfield, 1996), they are less comfortable with including any mention of the historical or cultural construction of madness, or of gender. Furthermore, they rarely question the right of experts to intervene. This is because women's madness is still conceptualized within an objectified positivist/realist frame. Social constructionism, of course, is seen as incompatible with positivist/realist research and theory, largely because it contravenes many of the assumptions of this particular model of science. A further reason for the lack of impact of these critiques is the fact that, as Mary Parlee has commented about feminist research, 'very few feminist researchers have over the last few decades gone to the scientific heart of the matter by outlining or carrying out *doable* alternatives in research' (1991: 29). This, in my view, is the challenge to critical theorists, whatever their persuasion.

Social Constructionist and Feminist Critiques: A Move Away from Positivism

Social Constructionism and Feminism

Positivist/realist approaches have been challenged in many areas of health and illness (e.g. Foucault, 1967, 1989; Ingleby, 1982; Nicolson, 1986; Stainton-Rogers, 1991; Tiefer, 1986; Ussher, 1997c; Yardley, 1997). These critiques are not unique to women's madness. Alternative models of conceptualizing, researching, and treating symptoms have been developed from within a broadly social constructionist perspective, as outlined by the other contributions to this volume. As is evident from these accounts, social constructionist approaches take a critical stance towards taken-for-granted knowledge; they acknowledge cultural and historical specificity, and hold that knowledge is sustained by social practices (Burr, 1995). Social constructionists challenge the realist assumptions of traditional biomedical and psychological research, arguing that subjectivity, behavior, and the very meanings of 'health' and 'illness' are constructed within practice, language, relationships, and roles. Science is part of this constructive process, and, as a consequence, research or clinical intervention can never be seen as objective or neutral. This does not mean that scientific research is pointless, but merely that reflexivity in theory and practice is an essential part of the scientific enterprise.

Social constructionist critiques have been used to 'dethrone' experts in many arenas, and to challenge the underlying assumptions of science. But social constructionism has also been used as the epistemological basis of much research and clinical practice (e.g. McNamee and Gergen, 1992; Shotter and Gergen, 1989), where 'the gaze' of the researcher is on the 'social' rather than on the individual, and where methodological naturalism is explicitly rejected.

For example, there has recently been a move towards the use of discursive theories and methods, which focus specifically on the role of language and its relation to cultural practices. These approaches draw upon principles from ethnomethodology, (Garfinkel, 1967), conversational analysis, linguistics and poststructuralism (Henriques, et al., 1984) in viewing discourse as constructive of reality and action-oriented (Potter and Wetherell, 1986). The term 'discourse,' refers to a set of shared cultural beliefs and practices, which are utilized in everyday life in order to construct meaning and interpretation about the world (Parker, 1992). It is also often argued that discourses are constitutive of subjectivity (Foucault, 1979; Potter and Wetherell, 1986). This stands in direct contrast to traditional psychosocial research that conceptualizes factors such as 'cognitions' as fixed entities that can be reliably measured. Here, the very notion of *a* cognitive style is dismissed, as interpretation and meaning are continuously negotiated within discourse. From a methodological point of view, this leads to the use of qualitative methods, and again to reflexivity in research practice (for examples, see Ussher, 1997b; Wilkinson and Kitzinger, 1995).

Many of the now numerous feminist critiques of women's madness, and of the treatment of women within the mental health professions, could also be placed under a broad social constructionist umbrella. Feminist critics have argued that misogynist assumptions about gender roles and normal femininity are used in diagnosing 'deviant' women. They argue that assumptions about the proper position of women within the institution of heterosexuality, furthermore, are used to prescribe notions of normality. Also, strategies of locating distress or deviancy in the womb – or, more recently, in reproductive hormones – reinforces notions that women are more animalistic or biologically driven than men. Obviously, this view also dismisses all legitimate anger or discontent as the result of 'raging hormones' while ignoring the social and political inequalities implicated in symptoms of distress (see Chesler, 1995; Penfold and Walker, 1984; Ussher, 1991). This has led to critical feminist analyses of mental health research and treatment and to the development of women-centered approaches in theory and therapy – but also to the deconstruction of the very concept of women's madness.

The Limitations of Social Constructionism

Despite the welcome addition of many such constructionist-inclined critiques, there are many issues that potentially remain unaccounted for within a social constructionist epistemological frame. One of the main problems is that in adopting a radically social constructionist perspective – or in arguing that 'madness' exists entirely at a discursive level – we are implicitly denying the influence of biology or genetics, and diminishing the meaning ascribed to the body in general (Turner, 1984; Yardley, 1996). Whilst the emphasis on social and discursive phenomena is understandable as a reaction against biological reductionism, positioning the body as irrelevant in the etiology, interpretation, or meaning of madness or psychological symptomatology is clearly inappropriate. Other material aspects of women's lives may also be negated in a discursive analysis: the influence of age, social class, power, economic factors, ethnicity, sexual identity, personal relationships and social support, or a prior history of sexual abuse, among other factors.

Thus, within a social constructionist or discursive approach, the 'reality' of mental health problems may appear to be denied; madness can appear to be conceptualized as merely a social label or category. One of the conundrums facing feminist critics is the contradiction between the social or cultural construction of madness, which pathologizes and dismisses women, and the increasing number of women who seek treatment for mental health problems, as they perceive them to have a significant influence on their lives. As Parlee notes, 'what is strategically difficult for feminists, is that many women now derive genuine benefits in their personal lives from an ideology that functions to explain and obscure social contradictions in their lives and those of other women' (1989: 20). Ironically, many women adopt a biological narrative in explaining their psychological symptoms; therefore, social constructionist analyses may seem to have little to say to these women. Reconciling a deconstructionist critique at a macro-level with the needs of individuals at a micro-level is a problem facing all those who would put forward a radical critique of mental illness (Ussher, 1991).

In addition, it is not clear how a social constructionist critique which 'normalizes' madness and denies its status as pathology would impact clinical intervention. Whilst social constructionist and feminist therapy have been developed in a number of areas, they are notably absent from mainstream clinical training, as well as in articles in refereed academic journals. If we are to deconstruct the very notion of madness, how can we offer women treatment without being accused of reifying its existence? Moreover, does this not reify the notion of madness as an individual illness, to be solved by the woman herself? If we are rejecting realism, does that mean we are embracing 'relativism,' with all the problems that entails?

Moving Forward: A Material-Discursive-Intrapsychic Analysis

Moving to a hard-line social constructionist position clearly leaves us with questions unanswered. I suggest a move toward a position where material, discursive, and intrapsychic aspects of experience can be examined without privileging one level of analysis above the other, and within an epistemological and methodological framework that does not make a priori assumptions about causality and objectivity. 'Material-discursive' approaches have recently been developed and applied to a number of areas within psychology, such as sexuality, reproduction, and health (see Ussher, 1997a, 1997b; Yardley, 1997). This is a result of both frustrations with traditional psychology, which has tended to adopt a solely materialist standpoint, and dissatisfaction with the neglect of material aspects in many discursive accounts. This integrated material-discursive approach is to be welcomed, yet arguably does not always go far enough, as the intrapsychic is often still left out, ostensibly because it is seen as individualistic or reductionist, or not easily accessible to empirical investigation. When intrapsychic factors are considered – for example, in psychoanalytic or cognitive theorizing – they are invariably conceptualized separately from either material or discursive factors.[4] It is time that all three levels together are incorporated into theory and practice.

The Level of Materiality

To talk of materiality is to talk of factors that exist at a corporeal, societal, or institutional level – factors that are traditionally at the center of biomedical or sociological accounts. This would include biological factors associated with psychological symptomatology, material factors which institutionalize the diagnosis and treatment of mental health problems, and gender inequalities, specifically in heterosexual relationships. The latter would encapsulate economic conditions facing women (often fostering dependence on men) and structural, legal, and emotional support for women. It would also include issues of social class which lead to expectations of 'normal' behavior for women and men, which are implicated in educational or employment opportunities available to both, as well as in the way individuals are treated by institutions such as social services or mental health professions. Whether and how children are present in the relationship, and the tangible consequences of being married (or not), are also part of this level of analysis. Previous history of abuse or of bereavement is partly a material event, as is family history – the number of siblings, parental relationships, and factors such as parental divorce or separation from parents in childhood. There are also many material consequences of experiencing or being treated for mental health problems in terms of physical or psychological vulnerability in a context of relative structural and economic powerlessness. Sex, ethnicity, and sexuality are also associated with materiality, with respect to the reproductive body, gendered or sexual behavior, and with physical appearance.

The Level of the Discursive

To focus on the 'discursive' is to consider social and linguistic domains – talk, visual representation, ideology, culture, and power. What is arguably of most relevance in analyses of women's madness is the discursive construction of madness, particularly medical or psychological expertise (see Foucault, 1967), as well as the analysis of the relationship between representations of 'woman' and 'man' and the actual social roles adopted by individual women and men.

For example, within a discursive account, rather than 'femininity' being seen as pre-given or innate, it is seen as something that is performed or acquired. In the process of becoming 'woman,' women follow the various scripts of femininity which are taught to them through family, school, and through the myriad representations of 'normal' gender roles in popular and high culture, as well as in science and the law (see Ussher, 1997a). They have to negotiate the contradictory representations of femininity which are available at any point (Ussher, 1997a). The fact that many women take up the archetypal position of 'woman' – always positioned as secondary to 'man' – is attributed to the dominance of patriarchy, and to the fact that gender is constructed within a 'heterosexual matrix' (Butler, 1990).

Within a heterosexual matrix, the traditional script of femininity tells us that women live their lives through a man. To have a man, and keep him, is the goal of every girl's life. Girls are weaned on fairytales and stories that reinforce this narrative and remind them of the terrible fate of women who fail: Cinderella and her ugly sisters or Snow White and her wicked stepmother. In adulthood, women are again reminded of it through romantic fiction, women's magazines, television soap operas, or Hollywood films. The 'good girl' is invariably self-sacrificing, but she always gets her man. In the late twentieth century, 'getting' still means monogamy, and usually marriage. *Not* 'getting' means being positioned as sad or bad – the spinster on the shelf or the shameful whore. Furthermore, the sexual woman is always deemed to deserve all the condemnation that she gets.

This isn't merely an analysis of the outmoded script of heterosexual femininity that many women have rejected in their quest for a more autonomous or agentic life. It is one of the explanations put forward for why women stay in unhappy, neglectful, or violent relationships with men (Dobash and Dobash, 1979), and is arguably one explanation for why women blame themselves marital or family difficulties as depression (Ussher, 1997d). Women are taught to gain happiness through relationships, invariably with men. They are also taught that it is their fault if these fail.

The Level of the Intrapsychic

Intrapsychic factors are those which operate at the level of the individual and the psychological – factors which are traditionally the central focus of psychological analyses of women's madness. This would include analyses of the way in which women blame themselves for problems in relationships, and the psychological explanations for why this is so. It would include an analysis of psychological defenses, such as repression, denial, projection, or splitting, as mechanisms for dealing with abuse, difficulty, and psychological pain. Specifically, the focus is on the way women often blame themselves, or their bodies, for problems that they experience. It would also include women's internalization of the idealized fantasy of motherhood, and of the expectations of being 'woman' in a heterosexual social sphere.

Integrating Critical Realism and Feminist Standpoints

A number of methodologies and research strategies have recently been developed within a material-discursive framework. In this context I will briefly outline two compatible epistemological standpoints which will potentially allow us to move forward in research on women's madness: critical realism and feminist standpoint theory. I will then outline how a material-discursive-intrapsychic analysis can be applied in clinical practice.

Critical Realism Critical realism is one example of a material-discursive-intrapsychic approach that can reconcile both the biomedical and psychosocial aspects of experience, as well as incorporate the cultural and historical context in which the meaning about experience is created. Critical realism (Bhaskar, 1989) affirms the existence of 'reality,' both physical and environmental, but at the same time recognizes that its representations are characterized and mediated by culture, language, and political interests rooted in factors such as race, gender, or social class (Pilgrim and Rogers, 1997). Thus, the role of hormones, the endocrine system, or physiological arousal, as well as the influence of social stressors, age, or economic factors, can be acknowledged and studied as 'real' in analyses of the etiology of mental health problems. The existence of authentic symptoms would also be acknowledged, whether they be psychological or physical. However, these symptoms are not conceptualized as independent entities that exist separately from the historical or cultural context in which women live. They are always positioned within discourse, within culture. 'Madness' is therefore always a product of the symbiotic relationship between material, discursive, and intrapsychic factors; one level of analysis cannot be considered without the other.

The anti-empiricism and apparent relativism of much of social constructionist and poststructuralist theory is rejected by those positioned within a critical realist epistemology (Pilgrim and Rogers, 1997; Ussher, 1997c). But the positivist/realist position that 'reality' can be observed or measured through systematic scientific methods that are objective or value-free becomes suspect. Critical realism does not limit methodological inquiry to the hypothetico-deductive methods used by positivist/realist researchers, or the qualitative methodologies used by discursive researchers. A variety of *skeptical* approaches are suggested (Bhaskar, 1989), meaning that multiple methodologies can potentially be used, either simultaneously, or in succession. Thus the whole spectrum of methods, ranging from experimentation, questionnaires, qualitative interviews, to participant observation, might be used if they were appropriate to the research question being asked. This approach implicitly accepts as legitimate all the questions that the researchers might set out to answer, rather than limiting the research questions because of epistemological or methodological constraints. The results of individual studies could then be seen as pieces within a complex jigsaw that has to be fitted together to make sense. The 'integration of piecemeal approaches' – which Bebbington concludes is inevitable (1996: 299) – would not be considered problematic here.

Furthermore, the findings of existing research on women's madness could be reinterpreted within a critical realist frame; we could legitimately incorporate the results of biomedical experimental research on causation, questionnaire studies, the subjective accounts of women, and deconstruction of wider discursive constructions of madness into one framework. However, in doing so we would have to reject many of the epistemological assumptions underlying individual studies, and the status given to many existing accounts. For example, critical realism explicitly rejects what have been described as the 'predictive pretensions' of natural science: we are dealing with open and not closed systems, and therefore can only explain and describe – not predict. The assumption is that the complexity and fluidity of human agency and the influence of continuously shifting cultural and historical contexts exclude any possibility of accurate prediction in the social sciences (Pilgrim and Rogers, 1997).

This suggests that we should abandon all attempts to accurately predict single factors that precipitate the onset of symptomatology, or the effectiveness of one treatment over all others, within mental health research – an enterprise which has, in any case, been fruitless. Instead, we should be aiming to describe, explain, and understand the symptomatology women experience: what it means to women, the factors which may be implicated in both the timing and degree of symptoms, and the ways in which women cope with perceived difficulty.

The combination of the move away from meta-theory or generalizable laws and the abandonment of prediction does not mean that we cannot or should not develop effective interventions for women who seek help for mental health problems. We may still want to systematically examine the effectiveness of a particular treatment option in treating symptomatology; we may still want to compare treatments. Within a critical realist framework, we can utilize whatever methodologies are appropriate to address these research questions. However, we cannot make causal assumptions about the etiology of mental health problems on the basis of treatment effectiveness. If we find that a treatment for a particular diagnostic category (such as depression or anxiety) is effective for a significant proportion of women, we cannot assume that this is *the* cure, as is often implied in the current research literature. Or, conversely, if only a minority of women are helped, we should not reject this as a treatment for all women. As mental health problems are fluid and multifaceted phenomena with many possible etiological routes, we should expect to find myriad means of prevention and intervention.

This approach confirms the increasingly common clinical observation that individual symptom-based approaches are most appropriate for helping women, and that a range of treatments should be available in clinical practice, tailored to the individual women within her particular social context. While clinicians may specialize in one type of treatment due to their own professional training and arena of expertise, there needs to be an acceptance of multidisciplinary approaches, where biological, psychosocial, and discursive factors are acknowledged and integrated into interventions offered to individual women seeking help.

The final and perhaps most radical premise behind a critical realist approach is the acceptance of the legitimacy of lay knowledge, which is invariably viewed as having equal, although not superior, status to expert knowledge (Bhaskar, 1989; Pilgrim and Rogers, 1997). This allows for the voice and views of women deemed 'mad' to be a legitimate part of the research agenda; it explicitly welcomes an acknowledgment of subjectivity, hitherto marginalized or ignored in mental health research. For example, the way in which women construct their understanding of mental health problems in relation to both medical and media accounts of madness and 'normal' femininity can be seen as a fruitful avenue of research. Critical realism explicitly provides acceptance of the fact that lay knowledge may occasionally be superior to that of the experts (Pilgrim and Rogers, 1997). This does not mean an unquestioned acceptance of lay knowledge as 'truth,' for both lay and expert knowledge are open to scrutiny and deconstruction. What it does mean is that 'expert' knowledge is not automatically accepted as superior or 'true.'

Feminist Standpoint Theory A second epistemological stance that is applicable in researching women's madness is feminist standpoint theory. Arguably a sub-type of the critical realist approach, feminist standpoint theorists also assume that knowledge is grounded in social reality, and emphasize the importance of lay knowledge. Escaping an emphasis on observation and prediction, as well as the separation of facts from values, standpoint theorists underscore reflexivity, and recognize both the 'material' and constructed attributes of the body and personal experience (Harding, 1993; Smith, 1987).

Feminist standpoint theory differs from other critical realist approaches in its specific emphasis on gender at both a material and a discursive level. For its adherents argue that positivist/realist epistemologies have provided a distorted accounts of women's experience, partly because science itself is gendered (Keller, 1985). It is argued that a less distorted view can emerge by attempting to view the world 'through our participants' eyes' (Harding, 1991, 1993), thereby valorizing the accounts of women. It is also argued that the distinctive features of women's social situations in a gender-stratified society may be directly utilized as theoretical and research resources (Harding, 1993).

Feminist standpoint epistemology also emphasizes the role of research as an impetus for social change, and encourages the use of the research process for women's empowerment. Because this standpoint presumes the individual to be 'agentic' (see Henriques et al., 1984), women are positioned as instrumental in the process of political and personal change. So, feminist standpoint theory is concerned with research *for* rather than *on* women, moving away from traditional science-based accounts of women's experience, and generating new theoretical accounts through which to bring about social change (Harding, 1993).

In the arena of women's madness, feminist standpoint epistemology could specifically harness the feminist critiques of madness and yet still provide a framework for 'do-able' research on women's experience of mental health problems, within a material-discursive-intrapsychic framework. In clinical intervention, feminist standpoint theory would follow the principles of a critical realist approach in the assessment of problems, as well as in the design and implementation of intervention, but would include a specific focus on gender issues as central to the agenda, as is common in feminist therapy.

In order to give a concrete illustration of how both women's madness and mental health symptoms can be conceptualized in this framework, I will provide a brief description of a case of an individual woman positioned as 'mad.' This is a composite case based on my own clinical work with women, with significant details changed in order to protect anonymity and confidentiality.

Clare

Clare is forty-three years old and lives with her husband of twenty-two years. She has three children, aged seventeen, nineteen, and twenty-one. She has been referred for psychological help in order to address her symptoms of depression. These include frequent tearfulness, lethargy, loss of appetite, difficulties in concentration, and early morning wakening. Clare describes her life as empty and without purpose. Some days she feels as if she can't go on any more. Other days she feels angry and is worried she might lose control. She describes her family as 'wonderful,' and says she is lucky that her husband still 'puts up with' her after all these years. The problems she experiences are seen by her to be all her own fault.

Clare came forward for help at the present moment for two reasons. First, her husband had told her she should 'sort herself out,' because he was getting fed up with her 'mooning about the house.' He was also annoyed about having to occasionally help with the shopping or cooking, as on some days Clare could not function at all. The second reason was because a friend had told her that she was ill, and should get treatment from her doctor. Clare had always had a fear of 'going mad,' because her mother had a history of depression. She could accept the notion that there was something physically wrong with her, but would not accept that she had a psychological problem. So, her friend telling her that she was ill offered her a positive way forward. On her first visit to the doctor she told him she thought that she must have a

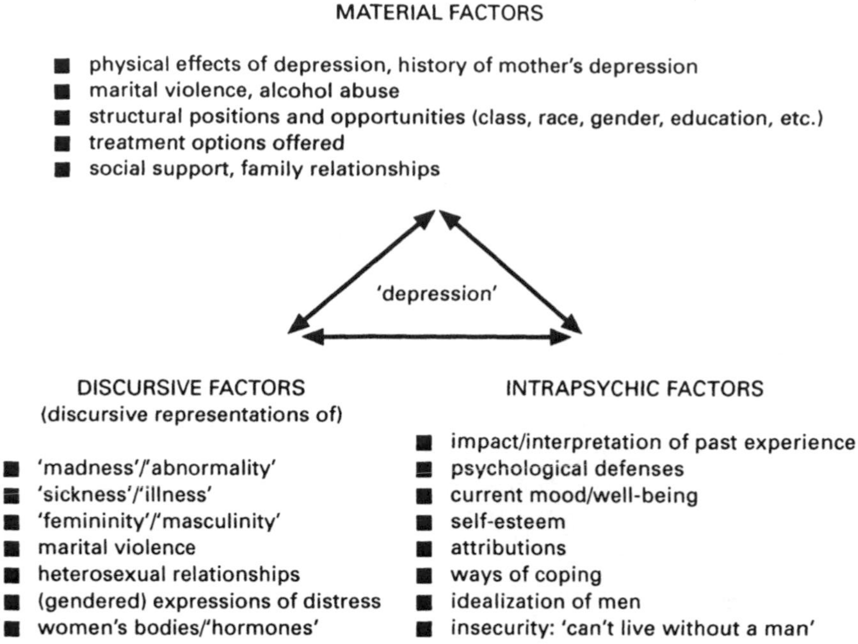
MATERIAL FACTORS
physical effects of depression, history of mother's depression
marital violence, alcohol abuse
structural positions and opportunities (class, race, gender, education, etc.)
treatment options offered
social support, family relationships
'depression'
DISCURSIVE FACTORS
(discursive representations of)
'madness'/'abnormality'
'sickness'/'illness'
'femininity'/'masculinity'
marital violence
heterosexual relationships
(gendered) expressions of distress
women's bodies/'hormones'
INTRAPSYCHIC FACTORS
impact/interpretation of past experience
psychological defenses
current mood/well-being
self-esteem
attributions
ways of coping
idealization of men
insecurity: 'can't live without a man'

Figure 10.1 *A material-discursive-intrapsychic approach*

hormonal imbalance. She only agreed to see a psychologist for assessment because it was part of a multidisciplinary treatment package, and a physician was also seeing her.

The interrelationship between material, discursive, and intrapsychic factors in the etiology and presentation of Clare's difficulties is presented graphically in Figure 10.1.

The material factors here could include: the length of her marriage, which was associated with feelings of boredom, frustration, and absence of desire; the demands of her children and husband, on both an emotional and a practical level; the fact she had no independent income, and thus no independent economic power; her lack of academic or professional training, due to having left school and started a family early in life; the fact that her husband drank heavily, and as a result was frequently violent toward her; the fact also that she had very little social support, as the family had recently moved into the area and her family and friends were all living many miles away; and the physical symptoms she experienced, as well as possible changes in her body.

Next, discursive factors might include: the specific conceptualization of women's distress or discontent as an individual problem, leading to Clare's being described as both 'mad' and 'ill'; the discursive construction of reproduction as cause of her lability, leading to Clare blaming her hormones for her distress; the emphasis on heterosexual relationships and motherhood as the center of a woman's existence, leading to pathologization of the woman who is not thus 'fulfilled'; the discursive construction of femininity and of the woman's marital role, which leads to expectations of female passivity, service of the family, and the absence of expressive anger in women; and the acceptance of male alcohol misuse and violence as 'normal' masculinity.

Intrapsychic factors, finally, may involve: Clare blaming herself (or her body) for her problems, in contrast with the exoneration of her husband and family; her fear of madness, resulting from her mother's experience, leading to a sensitivity to any change in her psychological state; her low self-esteem, which was a product of both her past and her present life; her patterns of thinking, which increased her feelings of hopelessness; her ways of coping (through withdrawal and self-punishment); and the psychic pain she experienced, which was labeled 'depression.'

While each level of analysis can be described separately, Clare's 'depression' can only be understood as an interaction of all three; they are irrevocably interlinked. Her symptoms, which were undoubtedly real to her, resulted from the continuous interaction of all of these factors. And given these circumstances, very few individuals would not be 'depressed.' However, Clare is not 'mad.' She is not deviant, deficient, or, in this case, necessarily in need of 'expert' intervention. However, there are a number of ways to address her problems. Unfortunately, hers is not an atypical case history, so suggestions made in this context can arguably be applied more broadly in this sphere.

For one, intervention could take place at a number of different levels: in individual, couple, family, or group therapy which allowed for the acknowledgment of these three interrelated levels of analysis; psychological intervention with her husband, to deal with the issue of violence and his feelings about their relationship; community intervention which focuses on the social environment in which Clare lives; facilitation of training, education, or employment, to address her economic and psychological powerlessness; provision of alternative housing, if marital break-up is her preferred solution; as well as the facilitation of self-help strategies or support from wider social networks. Taking this approach to intervention does not blame Clare for her problems, or locate the cause of her symptomatology within 'her.' This is, of course, an implicitly multidisciplinary undertaking – no one person could attempt all of this. However, Clare may have a preference about what type of support or help *she* wants; this should be a guiding factor in what is offered, if anything is offered at all. A different form of 'intervention' would be a deconstruction of discursive constructions of gender and madness, changing the meaning of Clare's experience from pathology to understandable response.

Conclusion

'Madness' is a phenomenon experienced by individual women at material, discursive, and intrapsychic levels; we cannot disentangle one from the others. An epistemological shift to material-discursive-intrapsychic analyses allows us to incorporate these different layers of women's subjective experience, and the different types of expert knowledge about both 'madness' and mental health problems, into one framework. What may appear to be contradictions or irrevocable disagreements within a positivist/realist frame are then transformed into different parts of the complex picture – one that only makes sense when all the different parts are considered together. The shift from a positivist/realist approach to a material-discursive-intrapsychic approach is analogous to the shift from capturing the world through a pinhole camera to capturing it on moving film. Neither provides a more 'true' vision of reality; the camera is merely more simplistic, limited, and can only show one fragment of the world at any one time, while a whole range of experiences can be captured – in all of their fluid complexity – with the more sophisticated medium of moving film. A shift from positivism/realism to a material-discursive-intrapsychic epistemology and practice will serve the same purpose in exploring women's madness, both as discursive construct and as a set of symptoms experienced by individual women.

All of this may seem a utopian analysis, and it certainly requires greater resources than are often available in the field of women's health. But there is no reason why it should be utopian. If we look outwards from our own ideological and professional boundaries, we may surprise ourselves at what can be achieved.

Notes

1. I will use the term 'madness' to refer to the discursively constructed category which effectively defines individuals so categorized as 'Other,' as fearful or fragile, and 'mental health problems/symptoms' to refer to the symptoms women report.

2. In a critical analysis of the epistemological assumptions of science and social science, Sandra Harding (1987) has defined epistemology as a theory of knowledge which sets out who may legitimately be deemed a 'knower,' what requirements information or beliefs must meet in order to be legitimated as 'knowledge,' and what kinds of 'facts' may be known. Epistemology therefore determines both methodology – the 'theory and analysis of how research does or should proceed' (Harding, 1987: 3) – and research methods – the techniques deemed legitimate or appropriate for gathering evidence or information.

3. Both of these levels of explanation have been subjected to a barrage of critical analysis. Suffice it to say that there is no evidence for the biological root of reproductive disorders, if indeed such disorders exist (see Bancroft, 1993; Ussher 1989; Walker, 1997), and the argument for an X-linked genetic hypothesis has been convincingly overturned (Bebbington, 1996: 319–20).

4. There are exceptions. For example, the feminist psychoanalyst Karen Horney (1967; originally 1931) developed theories of sexuality and gender relationships that encapsulated material, discursive, and intrapsychic levels of experience.

References

American Psychiatric Association (1994) *Diagnostic and Statistical Manual of Mental Disorders*. 4th edn. Washington, DC: American Psychiatric Association.

Bancroft, J. (1993) 'The Premenstrual Syndrome – A Reappraisal of the Concept and the Evidence,' *Psychological Medicine, Monograph Supplement, 24*. Cambridge: Cambridge University Press.

Bebbington, P. (1996) 'The Origins of Sex Differences in Depression: Bridging the Gap,' *International Review of Psychiatry*, 8: 295–332.

Bhaskar, R. (1989) *Reclaiming Reality: A Critical Introduction to Contemporary Philosophy*. London: Verso.

Billig, M. (1991) *Ideologies and Beliefs*. London and Thousand Oaks, CA: Sage.

Brody, E.M. and Schoonover, C.B. (1986) 'Patterns of Parent Care When Adult Daughters Work and When They Don't,' *The Gerontologist*, 26: 372–82.

Brown, G. and Harris, T. (1978) *Social Origins of Depression*. London: Tavistock.

Browne, A. and Finkelhor, D. (1986) 'Impact of Child Sexual Abuse: A Review of the Research,' *Psychological Bulletin*, 99 (1): 66–77.

Burr, V. (1995) *An Introduction to Social Constructionism*. London and New York: Routledge.

Busfield, J. (1996) *Men, Women and Madness: Understanding Gender and Mental Disorder*. New York: New York University Press.

Butler, J. (1990) *Gender Trouble*. London and New York: Routledge.

Calicchia, J.P. and Pardine, P. (1984) 'Attributional Style: Degree of Depression, Respondent's Sex, and Nature of the Attributional Event,' *Journal of Psychology*, 117, 789–95.

Chandra, P.S. and Chaturvedi, S.K. (1989) 'Cultural Variations of Premenstrual Experience,' *International Journal of Social Psychiatry*, 35: 343–9.

Chesler, P. (1995) *Women and Madness*. New York: Doubleday.

Chodorow, N. (1978) *The Reproduction of Mothering: Psychoanalysis and the Sociology of Gender*. Berkeley: University of California Press.

Dan, A.J. and Mongale, L. (1994) 'Socio-Cultural Influences on Women's Experiences of Premenstrual Symptoms,' in J. Gold and S. Severino (eds), *Premenstrual Dysphoria: Myths and Realities*. Washington, DC: American Psychiatric Press.

de Fonseca, A.F. (1989) 'Psychiatry in the 1990's,' in I. Hindmarsh and P. Stoner (eds), *Human Psychopharmacy: Measures and Methods, Vol. 2*. New York: Wiley.

Dinnerstein, D. (1976) *The Mermaid and the Minotaur: Social Arrangements and the Human Malaise*. New York: Harper.

Dobash, R. and Dobash, R.E. (1979) *Violence Against Wives: A Case Against the Patriarchy*. New York: Free Press.

Foucault, M. (1967) *Madness and Civilization: A History of Insanity in the Age of Reason*. London: Tavistock.

Foucault, M. (1989) *Birth of the Clinic*. London: Penguin.

Foucault, M. (1979) *The History of Sexuality, Vol. 1*. London: Penguin.

Garfinkel, H. (1967) *Studies in Ethnomethodology*. New York: Prentice Hall.

Hamilton, J.A. and Gallant, S. (1990) 'Problematic Aspects of Diagnosing Premenstrual Phase Dysphoria: Recommendations for Psychological Research and Practice,' *Professional Psychology: Research and Practice*, 21 (1): 60–8.

Harding, S. (ed.) (1987) *Feminism and Methodology*. Indianapolis: Indiana University Press.

Harding, S. (1991) *Whose Science? Whose Knowledge?* Milton Keynes: Open University Press.

Harding, S. (1993) 'Rethinking Standpoint Epistemology: "What is Strong Objectivity?",' in L. Alcoff and E. Potter (eds), *Feminist Epistemologies*. London and New York: Routledge.

Harré, R. and Secord, P.F. (1972) *The Explanation of Social Behavior*. Oxford: Basil Blackwell.

Henriques, J., Hollway, W., Urwin, C., Venn, C., and Walkerdine, V. (1984) *Changing the Subject: Psychology, Social Regulation and Subjectivity*. London: Methuen.

Henwood, K. and Pidgeon, N. (1994) 'Beyond the Qualitative Paradigm: A Framework for Introducing Diversity within Qualitative Psychology,' *Journal of Community and Applied Psychology*, 4: 225–38.

Hollway, W. (1989) *Subjectivity and Method in Psychology: Gender, Meaning and Science*. London and Thousand Oaks, CA: Sage.

Horney, K. (1931) 'Die Prämenstruellen Verstimmungen,' *Zeitschrift für Psychoanalytische Pädagogik*, 5: 1–7. 'Premenstrual Tension' in K. Horney (1967) *Feminine Psychology*. New York and London: Norton. pp. 99–106.

Ingleby, D. (ed.) (1982) *Critical Psychiatry: The Politics of Mental Health*. London: Penguin.

Keat, R. (1979) 'Positivism and Statistics in Social Science,' in J. Irvine, I. Miles, and J. Evans (eds), *Demystifying Social Statistics*. London and New York: Routledge.

Keller, E.F. (1985) *Reflections on Gender and Science*. New Haven, CT, and London: Yale University Press.

Kessler, R.C. and MacLeod, J. (1985) 'Social Support and Mental Health in Community Samples,' in S. Cohen and L. Syme (eds), *Social Support and Health*. New York: Academic Press.

Klein, M. (1984) *Envy and Gratitude, and other works, 1946–1963*. New York: Free Press.

Koeske, R. (1983) 'Sociocultural Factors in Premenstrual Syndrome: Review, Critiques and Future Directions.' Paper presented at the Premenstrual Syndrome Workshop, National Institute of Mental Health, Rockville, MD, April 14–15.

Koss, M. (1990) 'The Women's Mental Health Research Agenda: Violence Against Women,' *American Psychologist*, 45 (3): 374–80.

Littlewood, R. and Lipsedge, M. (1982) *Aliens and Alienists: Ethnic Minorities and Psychiatry*. Harmondsworth: Penguin.

Martin, D.J., Abramson, L.Y., and Alloy, L.B. (1984) 'Illusion of Control for Self and Others in Depressed and Non-Depressed College Students,' *Journal of Personality and Social Psychology*, 46: 125–36.

Martin, E. (1987) *The Woman in the Body: A Cultural Analysis of Reproduction*. Milton Keynes: Open University Press.

McNamee, S. and Gergen, K. (eds) (1992) *Therapy as Social Construction*. London and Thousand Oaks, CA: Sage.

Menkes, D.B., Taghavi, E., Mason, P.A., and Howard, R.C. (1993) 'Fluoxetine's Spectrum of Action in Premenstrual Syndrome,' *International Clinical Psychopharmacology*, 8: 92–102.

Mitchell, J. (1975) *Psychoanalysis and Feminism*. London: Allen Lane.

Nicolson, P. (1986) 'Developing a Feminist Approach to Depression Following Childbirth,' in S. Wilkinson (ed.), *Feminist Social Psychology*. Milton Keynes: Open University Press.

O'Brien, P. (1994) 'A Critique of Epidemiology: Towards a Model of Disease.' Unpublished paper.

Oudshoorn, N. (1990) 'On Measuring Sex Hormones: The Role of Biological Assays in Sexualizing Chemical Substances,' *Bulletin of History of Medicine*, 64: 243–61.

Parker, I. (1992) *Discourse Dynamics: Critical Analysis for Social and Individual Psychology*. London and Thousand Oaks, CA: Sage.

Parlee, M. (1989) 'The Science and Politics of PMS Research.' Paper presented at the annual research conference of the Association for Women in Psychology, Newport, RI.

Parlee, M. (1991) 'The Social Construction of PMS: A Case Study of Scientific Discourse as Cultural Contestation.' Paper presented at the conference 'The Good Body: Asceticism in Contemporary Culture,' Institute for the Medical Humanities, University of Texas, Galveston, TX, April 12–13.

Parry, G. (1986) 'Paid Employment, Life Events, Social Support, and Mental Health in Working-Class Mothers,' *Journal of Health and Social Behavior*, 27: 193–208.

Payer, L. (1988) *Medicine and Culture*. New York: Henry Holt & Company.

Paykel, E.S. (1991) 'Depression in Women,' *British Journal of Psychiatry*, 10: 22–9.

Penfold, S. and Walker, G. (1984) *Women and the Psychiatric Paradox*. Milton Keynes: Open University Press.

Pilgrim, D. and Rogers, A. (1997) 'Mental Health, Critical Realism and Lay Knowledge,' in J. Ussher (ed.), *Body Talk: The Material and Discursive Regulation of Sexuality, Madness and Reproduction*. London and New York: Routledge. pp. 67–82.

Potter, J. and Wetherell, M. (1986) *Discourse and Social Psychology*. London and Thousand Oaks, CA: Sage.

Sedgwick, P. (1987) *Psycho Politics*. London: Pluto Press.

Shotter, J. (1975) *Images of Man in Psychological Research*. London: Methuen.

Shotter, K. and Gergen, K.J. (eds) (1989) *Texts of Identity*. London and Thousand Oaks, CA: Sage.

Showalter, E. (1987) *The Female Malady: Women, Madness, and English Culture, 1830–1980*. London: Virago.

Slater, E. and Cowie, V. (1971) *The Genetics of Mental Disorders* (Oxford Monographs in Mental Disorders). Oxford: Oxford University Press.

Smith, D. (1987) *The Everyday World as Problematic: A Feminist Sociology*. Toronto: University of Toronto Press.

Sowa, C.J. and Lustman, P.J. (1984) 'Gender Differences in Rating Stressful Events, Depression, and Depressive Cognition,' *Journal of Clinical Psychology*, 40: 1334–7.

Stainton-Rogers, W. (1991) *Explaining Health and Illness*. Hemel Hempstead: Harvester Wheatsheaf.

Szasz, T. (1961) *The Myth of Mental Illness*. London: Secker.

Tiefer, L. (1986) 'In Pursuit of the Perfect Penis: The Medicalization of Male Sexuality,' *American Behavioral Scientist*, 29 (5): 579–99.

Turner, B.S. (1984) *The Body and Society*. Oxford: Basil Blackwell.

Ussher, J. (1989) *The Psychology of the Female Body*. London and New York: Routledge.

Ussher, J. (1991) *Women's Madness: Misogyny or Mental Illness?* Hemel Hempstead: Harvester Wheatsheaf. (Also published by the University of Massachusetts Press.)

Ussher, J. (1997a) *Fantasies of Femininity: Reframing the Boundaries of Sex*. London: Penguin.

Ussher, J. (ed.) (1997b) *Body Talk: The Material and Discursive Regulation of Sexuality, Madness and Reproduction*. London and New York: Routledge.

Ussher, J. (1997c) 'Premenstrual Syndrome: Reconciling Disciplinary Divides Through the Adoption of a Material-Discursive Epistemological Standpoint,' *Annual Review of Sex Research*, 7: 218–52.

Ussher, J. (1997d) 'Living with Drink from a Feminist Perspective: A Material-Discursive-Intrapsychic Standpoint,' in R. Velleman, A. Copello, and J. Maslin (eds), *Living with Drink: Women who Live with Problem Drinkers*. New York and London: Longman. pp. 150–61.

Walker, A. (1995). 'Theory and Methodology in Premenstrual Syndrome Research,' *Social Science and Medicine*, 41 (6): 793–800.

Walker, A. (1997) *The Menstrual Cycle*. London and New York: Routledge.

Watson, N.R., Studd, J.W., Savvas, M. and Garnett, T. (1989) 'Treatments of Severe Premenstrual Syndrome with Oestradiol Patches and Cyclical Oral Norethisterone,' *British Medical Journal*, 297: 900–1.

Wierzbicki, M. and Carver, D. (1989) 'Children's Engagement in Antidepressive Activities,' *Journal of Genetic Research*, 150: 163–74.

Wilkinson, S. and Kitzinger, C. (1995) *Gender and Discourse*. London and Thousand Oaks, CA: Sage.

Yardley, L. (1996) 'Reconciling Discursive and Materialist Perspectives on Health and Illness: A Reconstruction of the Biopsychosocial Approach,' *Theory & Psychology*, 6 (3): 485–508.

Yardley, L. (1997) *Material Discourses in Health and Illness*. London and New York: Routledge.

11

Grammar and the Brain

Steven R. Sabat and Rom Harré

Alzheimer's Disease, or, as we prefer to call it, Alzheimer's Condition (hereafter AC), is a progressive and irreversible neuropathological disorder which affects millions of people throughout the world. It strikes the middle-aged and the elderly. The incidence of this condition is expected to triple in the next forty years. It reduces life expectancy by as much as 50 percent (Katzman, 1976). The condition arises through the degeneration of neurons in the cerebral cortex and subcortical structures such as the hippocampus and the nucleus Basalis of Meynert. It results in the depletion in a number of neurotransmitters. The cortical damage occurs mostly in the parietal, occipital, and temporal association areas, leaving the primary sensory and motor regions, as well as the frontal association areas, relatively unaffected (Brun, 1983). The effects of such damage on cognitive function include problems with explicit memory, with organizing sequences of coherent movement, and with word-finding. It also results in an inability to focus attention for sustained periods of time, and in difficulties in reading, writing, and calculating. As the degree and locus of degeneration in the brain vary greatly from person to person through the course of the disease, variations are often found in the degree and type of cognitive deficits found from person to person.

A great deal of what we know about the cognitive effects of the disease derives from the performance of the afflicted on standardized tests of cognitive function such as WAIS, the Boston Diagnostic Aphasia Examination, the Boston Naming Test, the Mini-Mental State Test, to mention but a few. Due to the profound changes in the afflicted person's cognitive functions, some authors (Cohen and Eisdorfer, 1986) have referred to one of the effects of the condition as a 'loss of self.' Even though the results of standardized tests indicate a variety of defects of cognitive function in the afflicted as compared to age-matched control subjects, there are reasons to believe that the same afflicted persons are still in possession of a variety of intact cognitive functions well into the course of the disease.

Studies of the conversational capacities of sufferers in moderate to later stages in the development of AC have shown that many of their higher order cognitive functions are intact, though this is often either missed due to the limitations of standard tests or masked by the difficulties of sustaining a conversation in the face of the sufferer's word-finding problems (Sabat and Harré, 1992, 1994). In this essay we explore the relation between the brain damage characteristic of AC and the particular kinds of cognitive skills that a close study of the discourse of the sufferer from AC shows to be intact. Since frontal lobe damage is relatively minimal in this condition, so we would expect a high level of surviving cognitive functions, if we can find a way of bringing it to light behind the screen of word-finding deficits. We believe we have found just such a way in the study of how well AC sufferers manage the first and second person pronouns. As we shall show, the variety of functions that the first person pronouns are used for matches the variety of functions that the relatively undamaged frontal lobes allow people to accomplish. We believe that insufficient attention has been paid to the fine structure of the speech of AC sufferers, leading to the overlooking of surviving functions of great importance for the sufferers themselves.

The Grammar of First and Second Person Pronouns

Where would we expect to find expression of the sense of self, the sense one has of one's own singularity? The obvious place to look is in the grammar of the personal pronouns, particularly the first person and to a lesser degree the second. The grammar of the third person has little relevance in this discussion since it is almost always used to report some fact or make some comment about someone with whom the speaker is not, at that moment, in a dialogical relation. Interestingly, first and second person pronouns fall into one group grammatically while those of the third person are in another.

A third person pronoun is, literally, a pro-noun, and can, with preservation of sense, be substituted for and by a proper name or other referring expression. Such pronouns are said to be anaphoric. We can understand this distinction through the following examples. In 'Jim fell off his bike and broke his collarbone,' the successive uses of 'his' carry forward the same referential role as does the proper name 'Jim.' We know whose bike and whose collarbone only by back connection to the proper name 'Jim.' Similarly, the sense of 'he' in the following is anaphoric, fixed by the earlier occurrence in the sentence of the proper name 'Bill': 'Bill took up his saxophone and he played it to the surprise of his guests.' Third person pronouns stand in place of proper names but need proper names to fix their reference.

First and second person pronouns belong to a different word class. They are *indexicals*, having grammatical properties like 'this,' 'here,' and 'now.' For example, 'this' means 'near the speaker' or 'near me' while 'now' means 'at the same time as this act of speaking.' The meaning of indexical words is fixed by the very act of speaking.

The indexical properties of a word can be seen in the fact that the meaning of an indexical expression is completed on each occasion of use by what is known about the conditions under which each particular utterance is produced. For example, the meaning of 'I will open the door' is completed on a particular occasion of use by the listener's knowledge of the location of the body of the speaker in space and in relation to other material bodies. The utterance is also a sort of promise or undertaking. So there is a second level of meaning, the degree of commitment of the speaker to what he or she has undertaken. Again the moral force of what has been said is filled out by the listener's knowledge or beliefs about the speaker's moral character, reliability, and so on. So the role of indexical expressions, particularly 'I,' is to mark or index what has been said with the spatial location of the embodied speaker, and to qualify its moral force with what is known or believed about the speaker's character and history. The grammar of 'you' is also indexical, since it is used to index the content of a statement with the spatial location of the addressee ('It's right by you!'), and the moral standing of that person relative to that of the speaker ('You can pick up the broken glass'). We only know to whom 'I' and 'you' refer if we are present at and attentive to the unfolding conversation.

For all sorts of historical reasons, the English pronoun system is impoverished in expressive capacities, particularly in the second person and the first person plural. For instance, English does not express the difference between 'we' = 'us two' and 'we' of indefinite number, nor is there a grammatical expression of the difference between 'we' as referring to those present from 'we' referring to some such reference class as family or profession, the members of which do not need to be present on the occasion of the use of the word. The socially expressive distinction between intimate and formal forms of the second person has been lost from English long since.

An indexical expression marks the sense of an utterance with the relevant location of the speaker in space in an array of material things amongst which the body of the speaker has a place. There is also presupposed an array of embodied persons with whom a speaker has certain 'moral' relations, expressible in terms of obligations, duties, and rights. We shall call locations in this array, following recent writings on the subject, 'positions.' One always acts from a position, that is, in the light of and with the force of the duties, rights, and obligations one has to those with whom one is currently interacting. 'Positions' are contestable and often contested. Speaking in the first person singular is authoritative in tone but that presumed authority may be challenged.

English does not have grammatical resources for indexing what is said with the multiple patterns of social status relations in which speakers stand to other members of their local hierarchy. These must be expressed in other ways. Whereas a French speaker can and must choose between 'tu' and 'vous' in addressing someone, and so express intimacy or respect (and distance), English speakers must use other devices such as tone of voice and terms of formal address.

Drawing on a wide range of languages, we can assemble the following as a kind of generic grammar of first person usages. Some pronoun systems may exhibit all four, others various combinations of them. We must remind ourselves that the main personal indexical expressions in some language are not pronominal but carried by inflexions of the verb.

1 The descriptive content of a first person utterance is indexed with the spatial location of the embodied speaker as a thing amongst things. If someone uses the first person in a report of what he or she can see, feel, hear, and so on, we understand that what is reported is seen, heard, or felt from the spatial location of the speaker at that moment. For instance, in hearing 'I can feel a draft,' we know where the draft can be felt, namely where the speaker's body is located. The use of demonstratives is also a first person use, since the sense of 'this' and 'that' or 'here' and 'there' depends on the location of the speaker on the occasion of utterance. Perceptual reports in the first person express the organization of perceptual experience relative to the embodied location of the speaker.

2 First and second person pronouns index the moral force of an utterance with the 'position' of the speaker and interlocutor in the local moral order, an array of persons ordered by relations of obligation, duty, and trust. For instance, the use of 'I' commits the speaker to what has been promised, undertaken, or otherwise prefigured in what has been said. This commitment is understood by others by reference to their knowledge of the speaker's moral character (reliable, dishonest, and so on) with respect to the matter in hand. When someone has said 'I'll do the dishes,' we generally expect that the dishes will be done by that person.[1] Similarly when an order, request, or exhortation is addressed to a second person, singular or plural, the efficacy of the order is determined by the position of the addressee in the local moral order. This is expressed in the indexical force of 'you.' So 'You do the dishes' is effective as an order just in so far as the speaker and addressee take themselves to be standing in such a relationship that the speaker can issue orders to the other person. Most people live their lives in many moral orders, so the phenomenon of positioning is both complex and ephemeral.

3 First and second person pronouns of many oriental languages index the illocutionary force of an utterance with the 'social status' of the speaker and interlocutor in the local social order, the array of persons ordered by relations of social class, respect, and so on. English pronouns do not serve this indexical function, but in most European languages it is strongly present in second person uses, the 'tu/vous' distinction in its various manifestations, in both pronoun use and in verb inflexions (Brown and Gillman, 1960). The Japanese first person forms have strong indexical implications for the relative standings of speakers and addressees in local social orders. For example, in Japanese the choice of 'watakushi' rather than 'watashi' as the first person expression displays or expresses the respect due to addressee and at the same time expresses the high standing of both. It would be interesting to collect examples of pronominal use by speakers of Japanese who are AC sufferers, and to compare these with the cognitive capacities that we can infer from the way such people manage their lives.

4 Indo-European languages use verb inflexions rather than pronoun variants to mark the time of occurrence of what is talked about relative to the act of speaking about it. In 'I went to a great party last night,' the tense of the verb expresses the fact that the party occurred before the uttering of the remark. 'I,' in our Western way of story-telling, indexes personal anecdotes with the personal identity of the speaker throughout a life course. It does not change to mark the fact that what is being described is past, present, or future with respect to the telling of the tale. In some Indonesian languages, notably Kawi, the classical language of the region (Becker and Oka, 1974), the forms of pronouns, including first and second person, are sensitive to time. For example, the locative particle 'Nga-' (roughly 'then'), when prefixed to the deictic formative '-k-' (roughly 'there'), and to one of the person particles '-i,' '-a,' or '-u,' yields an inflected pronoun, 'Nga-k-i,' for example, meaning 'I-at-some-other-place-at-some-past-time.' English uses of tense and the temporal indexicals 'now' and 'then' (the latter indexing the content only with a time other than the present) leave the 'I' as indexical of a continuing and self-identical person throughout a narrative. Kawi story-telling is not under the demand that tends to constrain much story-telling in Indo-European languages. Unless otherwise indicated we assume a picaresque unfolding of events in the order in which they are mentioned in the story. English 'and' often means 'then.' An Indonesian story can be ordered by virtue of the importance of the events narrated, since the broad temporal structure is expressed by the tense of the indexical pronouns.

In the light of these observations on the significance of grammatical forms, where would one look for an expression of the seemingly elusive sense of personal identity? Presumably, we would examine the uses of the first person, in pronouns and verb inflexions, demonstratives, and tenses. Somewhere in the grammar of these devices the conventions for the expression of the sense of self might be found. In so far as certain cognitive functions such as forming intentions, taking responsibility, making plans, and so on, are expressed in language, they will find expression in forms which make essential use of first and second person indexicals.

Discursive Productions of Self and Locus of Brain Injury in Alzheimer's Sufferers

As has been described in recent research, AC sufferers with a moderate degree of deterioration in word-finding ability, and even toward the latter stages of the disease's progression, continue to manifest an intact sense of personal identity, of a sense of their own singularity as having a continuous point of view in space and time, as demonstrated by their continued competence in the use of first person pronouns. The various manifestations of social selves, as reliable, honest, and so on, appear in discursive properties of their conversations with others (Sabat and Harré, 1992, 1994), for instance in all sorts of indices of respect and condescension. The former are appreciated and the latter resented. The relationship between such discursive productions and the areas of the brain which are affected primarily by the disease, as well as those which are relatively spared from insult, may provide clues for the further understanding of the subtle relations between presentations of selfhood and brain function. This is because the common belief is that different parts of the brain are implicated in different aspects of cognition and its linguistic expression. To test out this idea we need to spell out in some detail how AC affects the brain itself.

The General Pattern of Brain Damage in AC

Although the pattern of degeneration in cortical and subcortical areas is not exactly the same for each person, it is possible to appreciate the areas of the brain most generally damaged by examining the pattern of degeneration in a large number of cases. The cortical areas damaged most severely include the association areas of the occipital, parietal, and temporal lobes' lateral surfaces, and the inferior and medial surfaces of the temporal lobes (Brun, 1983). Such damage would account for a variety of symptoms such as apraxia (the inability to carry out sequences of coherent movement such as tying one's shoe-laces or dialling a telephone call), sensory-motor problems (discriminating correctly between right and left) due to parietal association area damage, visual agnosia (the inability to identify objects correctly though the objects can be seen in all their detail) due to occipital association area damage, and aspects of aphasia (linguistic problems of understanding or producing spoken or written words), araphasias (the production of unintended syllables or phrases while speaking), and problems in the naming of objects due to damage to areas surrounding and including Wernicke's area.

On the subcortical level, there is severe damage to the hippocampal complex, including the entorhinal cortex, of the Limbic System which affects aspects of declarative or explicit memory functions, especially recall of recent events from memory, and to the nucleus Basalis of Meynert, adversely affecting the levels of the neurotransmitter substance acetylcholine. In addition, there are marked changes in other transmitter systems, including reductions of dopamine, norepinephrine, and serotonin. AC sufferers show marked reductions in two or more of these systems. At the cellular level, according to Scheibel (1983), the disease results in changes that begin with a loss of dendritic spines, followed by a loss of small dendrites and then of larger dendrites. In more advanced stages, the triangle-shaped pattern of the cell becomes pear-shaped. The entire pattern of degeneration seems to be the reverse of the maturational pattern that occurs during development.

Cortical areas that show less degeneration, relative to those outlined above, are the primary projection areas of the occipital, temporal, and parietal lobes, and the classic motor strip of the precentral gyrus in the frontal lobe. Thus primary sensory function and aspects of volitional movement can remain relatively intact. Perhaps most important for the present discussion, another cortical area that shows relatively less degeneration than do those named in the preceding paragraph is the prefrontal cortex. It is this area which has been implicated in many functions which appear to be critical to the discursive manifestation of self, and which will be the focus of the balance of this section.

Prefrontal Cortex Function

Fuster (1995) has discussed what he calls the 'temporal perspective' of frontal lobe function in which he asserts that the associative areas of the frontal lobe, or the prefrontal cortex, 'support the cognitive functions that are indispensable' for the temporal organization of behavior to occur. One such cognitive function that Fuster identifies is that of *planning*, or representation of action for the immediate future. Another is that of recent, or working, memory. After outlining the reasons for implicating the prefrontal cortex in such functions, we will advance a theoretical position wherein it may be possible, as a result of the relatively small amount of damage to this area in AC sufferers, to dissociate the planning aspect from that of aspects of explicit memory.

Among the effects of damage to the prefrontal cortex, Fuster cites the generally impoverished speech of the person, in which there is a lack of spontaneity, fluidity, and dependent clauses, wherein the person lives in the here and now to the exclusion of the future. This characteristic is not true of some AC sufferers at moderately severe stages of the disease, as appears in the structure and content of their conversations with sympathetically inclined interlocutors. Dr M., discussed by Sabat and Harré (1994), for example, asks her physician, 'How long is this going to continue?' referring to the disease itself. Such a question implies an understanding of time beyond the present moment. Dr B. similarly asks, 'When are we going to get my mind back?' and, in so doing, indicates that he believes that his mental functioning at the present time is lacking from his point of view but also, by the phrasing of the question, implies that he is aware of some such time in the future when it may be possible to make some sort of restitution of those same functions.

A second function of the prefrontal cortex, according to Fuster, involves what can be termed 'anticipation' or 'expectancy,' which is correlated with the appearance of a unique neuroelectric signature that can be recorded from the scalp of human subjects, the 'contingent negative variation' or *Bereitschaftspotential*. Such electrical activity is recorded most prominently over the motor and premotor areas of the frontal cortex, but Fuster argues that such activity reflects an effect that stems from a downflow from the dorsolateral prefrontal cortex. It is clear in the behavior of some AC sufferers (Sabat, 1991; Sabat and Harré, 1992) that the ability to anticipate situations is present. Thus, the relative sparing of dorsolateral areas of the prefrontal cortex in AC may be significant in supporting the ability to engage in behavior that involves an anticipatory, or expectational, ability.

The role of the prefrontal lobe in the temporal organization of behavior has also been supported by the analysis offered by Milner (1995), who cites a number of studies in which the authors conclude that the left frontal lobe plays a major contribution in the programming of voluntary actions. Such studies involved patients with damage to the left anterior and others with damage to the right anterior frontal areas. The former were slower in developing strategies for problem-solving tasks than were the latter, who were unimpaired on the same tasks. As Milner states, 'Their failure did not appear to be attributable to either verbal or spatial difficulties but rather to an inability to plan a few moves ahead' (1995: 74–5). To the extent that the prefrontal lobe is involved in planning ahead so as to achieve goals, there is evidence that some AC sufferers in moderate stages of the disease are, in fact, able to formulate and carry out strategies whereby goals can be achieved.

For example, Dr M. was dissatisfied with the way in which the support group she attended was organized. Although as a PhD and a trained social worker, she knew exactly what needed to be done to make the group function more effectively, she could not do those things herself for two reasons: (1) she had significant word-finding problems which, she felt, compromised her ability to communicate effectively and caused her great frustration and embarrassment; and (2) to interfere with the leaders of the group 'is not my role' as a member of the group. Thus, she spoke to S.R.S., engaging him to come to speak to the group so as to help organize it more to her liking. Specifically, one of her qualms involved the fact that the members were not introduced to one another and so she said, 'We should see that everybody has names, or something like that,' implying that when S.R.S. did come to the group meeting, which was scheduled for the following week, one thing that should happen at that future time is that proper introductions should be made. Furthermore, when the day of that meeting arrived, Dr M. told S.R.S. that 'this was the time when we, uh, I, I, was looking forward [to],' indicating that during the previous days, she was keenly anticipating the present moments. Such behavior would fall into the category of what Milner describes as the frontal lobe's role in the temporal organization of behavior, specifically in the 'prospective aspect of organizing a sequence of responses to be executed' (1995: 74).

Another common disturbance of cognitive function following frontal lobe damage involves apathy, or lack of concern, in which the patient will admit the evidence of disability, but show a distinct lack of interest that borders on disdain (Stuss and Benson, 1984), suggesting by action and verbal production that the problem is of little importance. There is a distinct lack of self-criticism in such cases that has been described by Luria and Homskaya (1964) as a problem involving a general loss of feedback mechanism or an inadequate evaluation of the person's own action. This symptom has been shown not to be true in the case of many Alzheimer's sufferers (Sabat and Harré, 1994) in moderate to severe stages of the disease.

Closely connected to the discursive presentation of self is the use of language in planning actions and anticipating the future, as described in the previous section. One common dysfunction following frontal lobe pathology, specifically to the posterior inferior aspect of the dominant hemisphere in most people, is Broca's aphasia. This disorder, primarily an expressive disturbance, is characterized by a nonfluent production of words – that is, sparse, agrammatic, dysprosodic output (Stuss and Benson, 1984). Another feature of frontal lobe dysfunction, transcortical motor aphasia, is due to pathology of cortical areas anterior to or superior to Broca's area, and involves an inability to initiate spontaneous speech. Also termed frontal dynamic aphasia, this problem was viewed by Luria (1966) as a frontal lobe language disturbance. Other disturbances in language output have been shown to result from damage to the Supplementary Motor Area of the frontal lobe (Penfield and Roberts, 1959) involving initiation of speech and also the inability to maintain a sequence, which affects comprehension (Albert, 1972). The person thus affected will comprehend individual words, but not sequences of words, or grammatical structures of spoken or written language (Samuels and Benson, 1979). Stuss and Benson (1984) argue that there is a strong suggestion that syntactical language functions are primarily a left frontal lobe function.

It is clear from previous research (Sabat, 1991; Sabat and Harré, 1992, 1994) that the discursive productions of Alzheimer's sufferers indicate the *absence* of symptoms such as those described above, and such an absence may be a result of the relatively small amount of damage to the frontal lobe in cases of AC. In fact, the ability of Alzheimer's sufferers to engage in conversation may indicate that some degree of working memory is intact, for if it were not, there could be no normal give and take in the continuous manner that characterizes a conversation.

Finally, going back to the nineteenth century, one of the most widely accepted changes that accompany frontal lobe damage involves the all-too-obvious changes in personality that have been variously described as tactless behavior, puerile joking (*Witzelsucht*), sexually disinhibited humor, inappropriate and near total self-indulgence with a corresponding lack of concern for others, grandiosity, and blunted feelings. Also, a vacancy of facial expression has often been observed along with indifference and dullness. Pathology in the orbital aspect of the cerebral cortex has been associated with the former, whereas pathology in the dorsal-lateral aspect has been implicated in the latter manifestations (Stuss and Benson, 1984). Although there have been reports in which caregivers of Alzheimer's sufferers have noticed changes in the sufferer's personality, such changes have not included the types described above.

The fact that there is some damage to the prefrontal cortex of Alzheimer's sufferers may be at the root of the problem of keeping the connection between intact intentions and the ability to comment verbally on the nature of those intentions when asked. For example, there are instances in which the afflicted person, a participant in an adult day care program, is observed time and again to be walking toward the building's exit. It must be made clear that the person in question seems not to be engaged in some 'random walking behaviour,' because when he leaves the room in which the activities are taking place, he always walks to the exit. The fact that he walks to the exit may be seen as indicating the presence of implicit memory of relatively recently learned information, for example where the exit is relative to the activity room. A number of studies have shown that such forms of implicit memory are intact in Alzheimer's sufferers. When asked, 'Where are you going?' the person cannot say, and responds with 'I don't know.' In such a case, the person's intention or desire to leave the building is intact, yet the ability to translate that intention into words, which would require some aspects of explicit memory function, is not.

In the above case, it can be appreciated that the person described has, by the use of the locution 'I don't know,' an intact sense of him or herself as a singularity, living a particular and definite trajectory in space and time, as well as, implicit in his behavior, an intact intention. In the next section we will explore, in finer detail, this relationship between the grammar of selfhood, responsibility, and intentionality and the behavior of Alzheimer's sufferers.

Selfhood, Responsibility, and Intentionality as Displayed in the Discourse of Alzheimer's Sufferers

The discourse of Alzheimer's sufferers reported herein shows that the sense of personal identity, the sense of singularity – as well as the taking of responsibility and the expression of intentions – can remain intact despite the advancing deterioration of brain function due to the disease. We will present samples of such taped and transcribed discourse in the pages to follow. No attempt was made to correct mispronunciations of words. However, it must be kept in mind that this is an idiographic study. We present what follows as a pair of cases that could be typified as the basis of an ongoing intensive design. Further empirical research is required to establish the degree of generality that can be attributed to our observations and their analysis.

Case 1

Dr B., who had been diagnosed years before our association, and whose history has been reported elsewhere (Sabat and Harré, 1994), revealed in his discourse an intact sense of personal singularity as well as a story of the taking of personal responsibility. The following extract, from the beginning of our association, serves as the first example. At this time, Dr B.'s cooperation was being enlisted and it was explained to him that it would be helpful for us to have some background information regarding his family relationships. He was reluctant to divulge any information before discussing the idea with his wife (S.R.S. had discussed this with his wife by letter and by phone conversation shortly before):

Dr B.: Let me do this, um, first I want to think about what this is about and secondly have my wife if she thinks it's uh, doesn't dest, des, destroy the family. So look, bear with me, bear with me, my wife is the, uh, and I will have to talk about that. Okay, uh, I'd like to, I like to see what my wife does. That's the linch, the linchpin. I don't want to give out, do the uh, to give out personal family and . . . Right now I have to chew out a lot of things um, and uh, let's see how the lay of the land is because we have a very strong family any which one of them could knock the socks off.

In this extract, Dr B. indicates that he wants to bring his wife into the decision-making process regarding the issue of divulging information about his family. Here we can see that he is taking responsibility as a husband, as a partner, and as one who is aware of his own limitations. He refuses, provisionally, to give out any information that might be private, without first consulting with his wife, because he doesn't want to do anything that will 'destroy the family.' He is also indicating a sense of the future and his intentions, his plans, in that 'my wife is the, uh, and I will have to talk about that.' In addition, he is indicating his sense of singularity as an embodied being among others in speaking of 'my wife' and 'we have a very strong family any which one of them could knock the socks off.'

In the next extract, we find Dr B. referring to his reaction to having Alzheimer's:

Dr B.: Well, I uh, oh but my everything that dominates me now is Alzheimer's. No question about it.
S.R.S.: What is it that you think about?
Dr B.: What do I think about?
S.R.S.: Um hum.
Dr B.: I think about, uh, the delumition [diminution] of what I've been able to do and what I may never do.

In the last sentence, Dr B. indicates a sense of the future in that he has considered the fact that there are things that he may never be able to do – things that he could have done if not for the disease. Thus, he can see a future far different from that which he had anticipated in the past. Additionally, we can see that he locates the sense of that diminished capacity with himself in psychological space and that he must cope with the sense of future losses.

There came a time in our association when Dr B. apparently wondered whether or not the research, of which he was an integral part, would continue. That is, given what he saw as his own diminished ability, he brought up the subject of his being able to stay at work on what he called 'The Project':

Dr B.: So – are you gonna throw me out of the shed?
S.R.S.: Not me. Not for a minute. Are you kidding?[2]
Dr B.: What keeps you going about me?
S.R.S.: What keeps me going about you? Now there's a question. You mean why do I keep coming and talking with you and doing this?
Dr B.: Um hum.
S.R.S.: I think that you have a lot to teach about the effects of Alzheimer's, especially in terms of the things you can still do. The person who has the

disease is not, in my opinion, well understood. I want to change that with your help. It's a matter of human dignity.
Dr B.: Well, I got a lot of dignity.
S.R.S.: You certainly do . . .
Dr B.: Um hum. What I want I think I've got. I've got that you have stayed with me. I have a lot of feeling for my family and uh, so I'm hoping that you will stay with me.
S.R.S.: I'm here and I will be.
Dr B.: You're here, cause that gives me what I need for Alzheimer's but it also gives me, you know, other things.
S.R.S.: I will be here and I will work with you.
Dr B.: I will never say that I am going to give up.
S.R.S.: You'll never say you're going to give up?
Dr B.: I'm never going to give up . . . You stay with me, I stay with you and we're gonna help each other.

In this extract, Dr B. indicates again his sense of singularity or personal identity through the use of personal pronouns, his ability to plan ahead in terms of what he will do, his intention to follow through on his plan not to give up, and that he understands that our work together had benefits for all concerned. This idea of mutuality, or reciprocity, indicates his sense of the need to be of help to others and of taking responsibility to achieve that end. His use of the first person pronoun locates the sense of dignity with his unique embodiment, something he owns.

On numerous occasions, Dr B. indicated his sense of moral relations that are expressed in terms of obligations, duties, and rights in various acts of positioning. As examples from his remarks we select the following occasioned by a specific personal context. He was clearly aware that S.R.S. had obligations beyond working with him, one of which was to drive his daughter home from school directly after the meetings. Consequently, Dr B. learned this 'routine' and often expressed his awareness of such: 'Now are we constrained here in terms of, do you have to run off?' Another example is evident in his gratitude for being able to discuss his anxieties openly:

Dr B.: Well I sure do . . . really glad, you know, you let me ventilate. Were you here in the time? I mean did, did you come out purposely for you, for me to work?
S.R.S.: Yes.
Dr B.: That's very good, very kind.
S.R.S.: You're very important to me.
Dr B.: I'm delighted to keep talking, but you have your own.
S.R.S.: Well, I still have time.

His sensitivity to behaving in accord with the local moral order was also evident in the way he responded in a situation involving the daughter (D.J.S.) of S.R.S. At the time, she was ten years old and had come to the Day Care Center where Dr B. spent two days each week. In this particular situation, she was playing in the room where the conversation was taking place and Dr B. was commenting on the fact that he wished that one of his sons (J.) would find a nice woman to marry.

S.R.S.: J. was really nice. He and I spoke for a while. He's such a bright guy.
Dr B.: Ya, so where's a nice woman for him?
S.R.S.: Maybe nice women don't have such good taste these days.
D.J.S.: Hey! [*Taking 'offense'*]
S.R.S.: Well, you're not there yet! [*Laughing*]
Dr B.: [*Chuckling*] Don't listen!
D.J.S.: Thanks!
S.R.S.: We're teasing!
Dr B.: It's only a fun thing, it's a fun thing.

The last line was spoken in a soothing, reassuring way in an obvious attempt to prevent the ten-year-old girl from taking seriously what was only meant in jest. Here, Dr B.'s sensitivity to the situation and to the child's sensibilities was clear, for he certainly didn't want to leave her with hurt feelings.

Finally, with regard to the idea of 'positioning' as it relates to the expression of aspects of the social self (self 2), we find Dr B. extremely desirous to be seen, or positioned, as being different from the other participants in the day care program. He was, after all, an accomplished academician for decades and that aspect of his social being was very important to maintaining his social identity. Thus, he reacted negatively to being treated in a way that did not recognize his 'standing' in the local social order:

S.R.S.: Are you saying that you feel that you have no status with the rest of the day care people?
Dr B.: Oh, absolutely. Absolutely. There, there should be some here, hierarty.
S.R.S.: So you feel that you're a pretty bright guy, but that you're not really treated differently than people who aren't as bright?
Dr B.: Ya, that's, that's forces me to do something like this. And I, I say that. Remember when you put the thing, when you gave me the letter?[3] It was a very strong statement that I am something above, or something like that.
S.R.S.: You feel that you are not treated with as much deference as you think you deserve? Is that accurate?
Dr B.: Honestly, yes.

Case 2

Dr M. had been experiencing word-finding problems for seven years before she began her association with the project. She had been diagnosed initially as suffering from Alzheimer's two years before the first meeting. At age seventy-five, she could look back on a life of academic distinction having earned two advanced degrees and spent decades teaching at university level. During the time of these conversations, her word-finding problems grew worse. She was unable to write her name, found reading to be very problematic, had difficulty dressing and with using eating utensils.

Despite her many difficulties, it was apparent from her discourse that she maintained a sense of her own singularity as a person, her identity as one among others. This could be seen clearly in her use of first person pronouns. Likewise, she recognized that she did not want to be positioned as an Alzheimer's sufferer with all the defects that such an identity would connote. In this sense, she refused to cooperate with others who would attempt to position her in such a way, thus indicating her own intentions insofar as her social self was concerned, as the following comment shows:

Dr M.: Sure, I uh, I can handle myself when I try not to let myself be presented as, as Alcazheimer's, I'm very different.

Here she is locating herself, in social psychological space, as an individual capable of taking command of her situation. The four occurrences of the first person – three of 'I' and one of 'myself' – that appear in this passage index the content of the three propositions they qualify with her commitment to self-management and a refusal of positioning as the helpless victim of disease. As was true in the previous case, Dr M. also displays a sense of fairness – an aspect of one's duties and obligations in the local moral order.

Dr M.: Now then – I want to tell you something uh, that has some – I hope you're getting something out of this.
S.R.S.: Oh yes! Oh yes! No question about it!
Dr M.: Because I, I feel I, I don't want to, to use your time.

It was clear by this time in the development of the association between Dr M. and S.R.S. that Dr M. was deriving a great deal from the weekly two-hour meetings. She eagerly awaited the scheduled day and believed that she could not continue, in good conscience, to enjoy the meetings if the benefit were not mutual. She would not want to 'use' or waste the time of her interlocutor if he were not deriving benefit from the meetings as well.

Her intentionality and planning ability, as well as her sense of personal responsibility, were also manifested on many occasions. Just previous to the following extract, she had been discussing the fact that anxiety and nervousness can impede performance of such things as recalling information, speaking, ordering words, and that it might be useful to find a way to restore calm when she felt anxiety was heightened. Almost at the end of the meeting, referring to her imminent holiday, she said:

Dr M.: Now what do, do you want to give me a, a uh, I'm going to be away. I appreciate learning about what I could do without you.
S.R.S.: Oh – oh, you want homework.
Dr M.: Yes! Yes! Yes! [*Laughing heartily*]

Here she knew that she was going to be on holiday, understood the relationship between lowered anxiety and enhanced performance, and wanted to be able to achieve a sense of relaxation on her own while she was away. In this case, she was assuming responsibility for her own future emotional state.

Another example of her ability to think ahead and plan also occurred toward the end of the meetings, when she would say something such as:

Dr M.: All right! Now let's, let's think in terms of uh, getting some cl, cloat, closure for this day.
S.R.S.: Um hum.
Dr M.: And what's going to happen for the next day.

Getting 'closure' on a meeting was very much in the spirit of the trained social worker that she was, and by engaging in such discourse, she was also showing the continuing existence of that social self.

She also revealed the ability to take responsibility with regard to what priorities she needed to establish in her life:

Dr M.: Now that I know where, where . . . I, I, I need to find for myself what are the real important things in uh, one person's life and see how that . . . we have to see how it works out.
S.R.S.: One thing we can do is, we can set goals.
Dr M.: I was going to say exactly that . . .

Still another instance of taking responsibility and planning future action was revealed in her reaction to the support group that she had been attending. As a professor and a social worker, she knew how groups should be organized and found the organization of the support group lacking. One problem that she identified was that the members were not properly introduced to one another and were not aware of the nature of each other's problems. In discussing her reaction she came to the decision that she would address the group at the next meeting:

Dr M.: So we had all these people getting together and so here's what I'm going to say for this thing. Something like this: What I'd like to say, uh, for my, me as a member of the group, uh, where uh, uh, I, I wanted to tell you about myself . . . I was a person who has spent all my life as a professor, all about talking. But in the last two and three years I've have much decreased ability. My big plo, problems is words. [*Now she says as an aside*] I don't have these people knowing.
S.R.S.: Oh, I see, they don't realize what your problem is.
Dr M.: They don't – no, and that's, that's crazy . . . So I, I had prepared, I just thought that what I need, uh, what the group needs, to introduce themselves to each other . . . so we should take a little bit of time to help each other relating problems.

Of course, the above extract once again shows that Dr M. has located her problems as well as her desire to improve the group with her own singularity, as seen in her use of first person pronouns.

Commentary and Conclusion

We have demarcated both realms of phenomena into two broad and fuzzily bounded classes, the anatomical-neurological and the cognitive-discursive. Brain studies reveal a pattern of damage to some parts more than to others. Roughly speaking the cerebral cortex is undamaged relative to the deterioration in Broca's and Wernicke's areas. Conversation studies reveal a pattern of deficits in 'word-work' that is greater for some discursive skills than others. Roughly speaking, pronominal and self-referential talk is competently performed within the constraints that come from problems with word-finding. While searching for particular words, a grammatical 'I-frame' had already been put in place. In this our two participants displayed, each in their own way, an intact sense of self, as a 'semiotic subject,' capable of discerning meanings and planning and executing (within constraints) behavior that depended on those meanings.

Matching the upshots of studies of the brain that demarcate relatively damaged and undamaged areas with studies of cognition as displayed discursively, showing relatively defective and relatively intact cognitive functioning reveals a striking correlation. It seems to show that self-reference, as displayed in mastery of the grammar of indexical devices such as the personal pronouns, and the functional capacity of the cerebral cortex are related. It is not too extravagant a conclusion to draw, we believe, that the site of the neurological mechanisms with which people manage at least one important part of intentional thinking is to be found in that part of the brain that is relatively undamaged in sufferers from AC.[4]

Notes

1. Autistic children are reported to be unreliable in commitments, and uncertain in their use of the first person.
2. S.R.S. took this question to mean, 'Are you going to stop me working on the Project?'
3. In recognition of his contribution to research on AC, Dr B. had received a letter of commendation from the Dean of Arts and Sciences at Georgetown University.
4. In studies of the relation between brain function or dysfunction and cognition only individual brains can be investigated. Most studies are based on a methodology in which $N = 1$. A person is set a cognitive task while his or her brain undergoes a PET scan. There is no room for a statistical analysis of the results of a population of similar experiments. In our studies we have examined the cognitive performances of two individuals, as these performances are expressed in conversation. Our work is based on two cases, in each we have $N = 1$. Technically each is an idiographic study of the life situation and cognitive skills of a person, and between these two situations and performances there are both similarities and differences.

However, generalizing from $N = 1$ case histories is possible. Generalizing is accomplished in two ways in the sciences. The extensive design pre-selects a population each member of which is subjected to some treatment and the results analyzed by some statistical method – it may be as simple as averaging. The wider the class, the narrower is the information that is obtained. The intensive design is based on a thorough study of one or a few cases, which are defined as typical. The results of the study of the typical individual are said to hold of every individual sufficiently similar to it. The richer the information obtained from the typical case, the narrower the population to which it can safely be extrapolated may be. Anatomy and physiology use the intensive design, while agricultural science tends to use the extensive. Each has its place in a fully developed science. The transition from an idiographic study to an intensive design is simple. One merely declares one's individual subject to be typical of some reference class and then case by case expands that class. The studies reported in this essay could be taken as the beginnings of a broader, generalized claim, simply by the redefinition of an idiographic subject as the source of an intensive design, that is, as a typical member of class the members of which have yet to be identified. This is true of both the neurological and the cognitive components.

References

Albert, M.L. (1972) 'Auditory Sequencing and Left Cerebral Dominance for Language,' *Neuropsychologia*, 10: 245–8.

Becker, A. and Oka, G.N.I. (1974) 'Person in Kawi,' *Oceanic Linguistics*, 13: 229–55.

Brown, R.W. and Gillman, A. (1960) 'The Pronouns of Power and Solidarity,' in T. Sebeok (ed.), *Style in Language*. Cambridge, MA: MIT Press. pp. 253–76.

Brun, A. (1983) 'An Overview of Light and Electron Microscopic Changes,' in B. Reisberg (ed.), *Alzheimer's Disease*. New York: Free Press. pp. 37–44.

Cohen, D. and Eisdorfer, C. (1986) *The Loss of Self*. New York: Norton.

Fuster, J. (1995) 'Memory and Planning: Two Temporal Perspectives of Frontal Lobe Function,' in H.H. Jasper, S. Riggio, and P.S. Goldman-Rakic (eds), *Epilepsy and the Functional Anatomy of the Frontal Lobe*. New York: Raven Press. pp. 9–20.

Katzman, R. (1976) 'The Prevalence and Malignancy of Alzheimer's Disease: A Major Killer,' *Archives of Neurology*, 33: 217–18.

Luria, A.R. (1981) *Language and Cognition*. New York: Wiley.

Luria, A.R. and Homskaya, F.D. (1964) 'Disturbance in the Regulative Role of Speech with Frontal Lobe Lesions,' in J.M. Warren and K. Akert (eds), *The Frontal Granular Cortex and Behavior*. New York: McGraw-Hill. pp. 353–71.

Milner, B. (1995) 'Aspects of Human Frontal Lobe Function,' in H.H. Jasper, S. Riggio, and P.S. Goldman-Rakic (eds), *Epilepsy and the Functional Anatomy of the Frontal Lobe*. New York: Raven Press. pp. 67–84.

Penfield, W. and Roberts, L. (1959) *Speech and Brain Mechanisms*. Princeton, NJ: Princeton University Press.

Sabat, S.R. (1991) 'Facilitating Conversation via Indirect Repair: A Case Study of Alzheimer's Disease,' *The Georgetown Journal of Languages and Linguistics*, 2: 284–96.

Sabat, S.R. and Harré, R. (1992) 'The Construction and Deconstruction of Self in Alzheimer's Disease,' *Aging and Society*, 12: 443–61.

Sabat, S.R. and Harré, R. (1994) 'The Alzheimer's Disease Sufferer as a Semiotic Subject,' *Philosophy, Psychiatry, and Psychology*, 1: 145–60.

Samuels, J.A. and Benson, D.F. (1979) 'Some Aspects of Language Comprehension in Anterior Aphasia,' *Brain and Language*, 8: 275–86.

Scheibel, A.B. (1983) 'Dendritic Changes,' in B. Reisberg (ed.), *Disease*. New York: Free Press. pp. 69–73.

Stuss, D.T. and Benson, D.F. (1984) 'Neurological Studies of the Frontal Lobes,' *Psychological Bulletin*, 95: 3–28.

12

Does a Story Need a Theory? Understanding the Methodology of Narrative Therapy

Fred Newman

What's Philosophy Got to Do with It?

In his essay 'Postmodern Thinking in a Clinical Practice' (it appears in *Therapy as Social Construction*, a quite useful anthology edited by Sheila McNamee and Kenneth Gergen, 1992) William Lax writes that 'during the past 10 years the social sciences have undergone significant changes through the increasing influence and acceptance of postmodern thinking' (1992: 69). In a footnote to this statement, Lax documents some of the authors and their fields where this influence is being felt, such as: Geertz in anthropology/ethnography; Foerster in cybernetics; Flax, and Fraser and Nicholson in feminism; Ricoeur and Gadamer in hermeneutics; Barthes, Derrida, and Lyotard in literary criticism; Gergen, Sampson, and Shotter in social psychology (Lax, 1992: 82).

Narrative therapy, while not itself a social science, has likewise been influenced by postmodern thinking to the degree that it is sometimes referred to as the therapy of postmodernism. Many of the authors cited above have contributed to its development. Philosophers, however, are conspicuously absent from this noteworthy group of thinkers – particularly those philosophers in the Anglo-American tradition who over the last several decades have explored the highly complex issue of meaning.

To be sure, in recent years many postmodernists and the social scientists influenced by them (along with critics of postmodernism) have been studying the work of Ludwig Wittgenstein. But the relevant semantic, analytical writings by Wittgenstein's followers and his critics, in my opinion, have been largely unexamined or ill examined. The result is that the philosophical sensibility of much of postmodern thinking within psychology is determined by social scientists who have no formal training in philosophy and, consequently, are unfamiliar with the subtleties of the philosophical study of meaning and the other epistemological topics it has produced. Instead, these social scientists have tended to borrow formulations from Wittgenstein that they use to authorize their analytically-philosophically uninformed statements.

That social scientists such as Gergen (1982, 1991, 1994), Shotter (1990, 1991, 1992, 1993a, 1993b), and others, including Morss (1993, 1996) and Parker (1992, 1996), attend to philosophical matters at all is both noteworthy and commendable. After all, there is a long tradition of social scientists having no use whatsoever for philosophical inquiry. Still, the results are troublesome. Postmodernism is, arguably, the contemporary form of a very old philosophical debate, and lack of knowledge of the history and nuances of that debate puts postmodernism and narrative therapy at a great disadvantage. It leaves their principal defenders at the theoretical level, as well as the practitioners, vulnerable to critiques based on their own ignorance rather than on the astuteness or validity of the pro-scientific, pro-modernist position. Why is this problematic? Because, in my opinion, narrative therapy – like postmodernism broadly speaking – is a great post-philosophical advance currently under severe attack by an establishment with both an ideological and a pragmatic (sometimes vulgarly pragmatic) commitment to preserving the increasingly conservative status quo of modernism.

This essay is designed to make some modest addition to the philosophical sophistication of postmodern *thought* and, at the same time, to make some practical contributions (which might grow out of a greater degree of philosophical sophistication) to the *practice* of narrative and other forms of postmodern therapy.

Meaning Is No Simple Idea

> The simple idea from which the narrative approach developed is that people make meaning, meaning is not made for us. This simple statement contains a wealth of implications. For one thing, it puts people in the driving seat of their lives: we produce the meanings of our lives. Certainly, the ways we speak and the things we speak about are part of our cultural heritage; they are handed down to us, and they are our tools for making sense. The argument of this book is that these ways of making sense are susceptible to change. We can change the ways we speak. In doing so, we can also change much about the way we organize and understand our worlds. Language is not simply a representation of our thoughts, feelings, and lives. It is part of a multilayered interaction: the words we use influence the ways we think and feel about the world. In turn, the ways we think and feel influence what we speak about. How we speak is an important determinant of how we can be in the world.
>
> So what we say, and how we say it, matter. As will be explained below, we can apply this idea not only to objects in the world but also to ourselves and to our relationships. This grounding idea about the relation of words to reality has far-reaching consequences that are now being harnessed for therapeutic ends.
>
> (Winslade and Drewery, 1997: 33–4)

Even a cursory glance at this opening paragraph of Winslade and Drewery's 'The Theoretical Story of Narrative Therapy' would leave almost anyone trained in philosophical analysis puzzled and prompted to ask questions like the following.

First, the contrasting of 'people make meaning' with 'meaning is not made for us' is confusing in several different ways. Why is there a contrast at all? People making meaning does not preclude other people making meaning for us. At a minimum, it might be more reasonable to say that people make meaning *and* that meaning is made for us.

Second, what do 'people make meaning' and 'meaning is made for us' mean? Are the authors speaking here of the fact that people create all the sociocultural artifacts of the world, including language and meaning? Or are they rather pointing to the self-conscious production of specific meaning-making conventions (defining or the making up of terms) by scientists, logicians, sports announcers, poets, and others in the activity of creating particular cultural products? How are we to understand, even *prima facie* (what is 'the picture'), the process by which the meaning of language is passed along from parents (and others) to children (and others)?

Third, in what way does 'people make meaning' imply that they are in 'the driving seat of their lives'? What if the meaning that people make puts someone else in the driver's seat? In telling us that we produce the meanings of our lives, the authors make an abrupt and apparently unself-conscious shift from what is traditionally understood in philosophical semantics as 'the meaning of language' to 'the meaning of life.'

Fourth, why identify the ways we speak and the things we speak about as tools for making sense rather than, let's say, for communicating? Indeed, why is language identified as a representation at all? Do the words we use influence the way we think and feel simply by virtue of the former representing the latter? What do the authors mean when they speak of 'how we speak'? Standing up? Sitting down? Having an accent? Using a 'second language'? Talking too loud?

Fifth, when the authors say 'we can apply this idea not only to objects in the world but also to ourselves and to our relationships,' do they mean to imply that 'ourselves and our relationships' are not in the world? And if we and our relationships are not in the world, where are they? It seems to me that it is the *negation* of what they call the 'grounding idea about the relation of words to reality' that has had 'far-reaching consequences' for therapeutic ends.

It is not simply that the authors' formulations are philosophically confusing. What Winslade and Drewery offer up as the 'simple' grounding idea for understanding narrative therapy is something which (at least on my reading) is thoroughly inconsistent with what narrative therapy seems to be. For as far as I can tell, narrative therapy (which I formulate somewhat imprecisely as the activity of making up ever-changing stories about ourselves and our relationship to other features of the world) is based on our species' ability to create an infinitude of stories *without* changing the meaning of language, or life, at all. This is not to say that we human beings cannot or do not change the meaning of language, but rather that our unlimited capacity to create new stories (seemingly at will) requires that meanings themselves do not transform willy-nilly in the activity of creating new stories. Otherwise we would never know if we had in fact changed the story, since the meaning might have changed in such a way as to make us think it the same old story. The point here is in some ways analogous (and obviously related) to that quite special feature of language, namely that with a finite number of letters (an alphabet) and words (a basic vocabulary) we can create an infinitude of words and well-formed sentences. It is precisely this dialectical feature of our culture and the understanding of it that seems to me to be the not so simple idea that gives rise to narrative therapy.

I have no wish to engage in semantic logic-chopping or analytic criticism for their own sake. Rather I want to point out some of the ambiguities and confusions which diminish the capacity of narrative therapy and/or other postmodern therapies to liberate people from the modernist straitjacket – the problems that, in Wittgenstein's sense, we can help our clients make vanish. The making up and the playing out – the performing, if you will – of new stories will, like Wittgensteinian language-games (1953), ultimately make new meaning (if nothing else, a new meaning for what language is and perhaps for what stories are). But language-games are not designed to make new meanings or new languages. Rather, their purpose is to expose to us the metaphysical character of the old meanings (including the meaning of meaning): 'When we look at such simple forms of language the mental mist which seems to enshroud our ordinary use of language disappears. We see activities, reactions, which are clear-cut and transparent' (Wittgenstein, 1965: 17). Likewise, narrative-making or story-making is not designed (or shouldn't be) to make new meanings or even new stories, but to expose the limitations and constraints of the old meanings and the old stories.

In the Beginning Was the Story

> And any theory not founded on the nature of being human is a lie and a betrayal of man. An inhuman theory will inevitably lead to inhuman consequences – if the therapist is consistent. Fortunately, many therapists have the gift of inconsistency. This, however endearing, cannot be regarded as ideal.
>
> (Laing, 1967)

The 'simple' idea that Winslade and Drewery introduce at the beginning of their essay is actually, it seems to me, a rather deep-rooted, outdated, and inhuman theory of meaning. In its representationalism it goes back at least to Plato and the Greeks. In its understanding of learning it goes back at least to St Augustine. (See the quote from Augustine's *Confessions* cited at the beginning of Wittgenstein's *Philosophical Investigations.*) And, in its commitment to the hegemony of the explanatory as the primary mode of human understanding, it goes back to the evolution of modern science.

The scientific model, a key element of an extraordinary story that has been of unprecedented value in assisting us to understand the nature of so-called 'physical reality,' has come to be more than just a way of understanding the physical world. Over the last hundred or so years it has achieved its paramount status as the universal definition of understanding itself (see, e.g., Hempel and Oppenheim, 1953). Given its staggering successes, that the scientific model should have achieved such ascendance in Western culture, and thereby in world culture, is not surprising. Yet this cultural phenomenon has also produced serious misunderstandings, and all sorts of harm(s) deriving from such misunderstandings. Modern psychology is the name of one of these misunderstandings. Indeed, the uncritical imposition of the scientific model of explanation onto conscious life activities (the subject matter of psychology) is – following Laing's observation above – as good an example as any of a 'theory not founded on the nature of being human,' that is, therefore, a 'betrayal.'

This remarkable historical phenomenon – the scientizing of all human understanding – has been written about extensively and both applauded and deplored (Winch, 1958). What troubles me is that so many of the post-modern social scientists and narrative therapists who explicitly oppose the traditional scientific model persist in locating their understanding of under-standing within an explanatory framework. Here I merely wish to make a few remarks about what I take to be the most significant methodological differences between the modernist conception of understanding and what I would like to think is the postmodernist break with that mode of under-standing.

The explanatory and/or predictive mode that has come to dominate science and, over time, all understanding is methodologically rooted in the capacity to derive, deductively (or at least inductively-logically), a character-ization – a definite description – of a specific phenomenon from some specifically characterized set of universal or general or statistical laws and a specifically characterized and empirically verified set of preconditions. This explanatory or deductive model of explanation is inseparable (scientifically speaking) from a roughly agreed upon vocabulary (taxonomy) for the science and the relevant phenomenon in question. After all, the 'deducibility' of the event (its definite description) to be explained from the laws and precondi-tions (their descriptions) fully depends – logically – on how those laws, preconditions, and conclusions are characterized. Thus, the system of describ-ing the phenomena of physics, chemistry, or any other science is altogether critical in a scientific-theoretical systemization: without it we cannot satisfy the deducibility (the 'follows from') criteria. The historical fact of science is that this feat – the creation of systemized ways of characterizing (describing) the phenomena belonging to a particular area of study – was accomplished without fundamentally 'betraying' the object of study (whether stars, physical forces, bodily organs, chemical reactions, or subatomic particles).

The discovery of a systematic (theoretic) method for describing the movement of stars or physical phenomena in general does not, however, prove the correspondence theory of truth or representationalism. It is merely historical evidence of a profoundly creative and valuable story (system-ization) called physics. There has never been, nor could there be, evidence that the systematic language of physics – taken description by description –

corresponds to any phenomena at all. However, the creation of that particular story (system) has been of enormous value for that form of human life that we call explaining. In other words, there is no requirement, nor has there ever been, that scientific descriptions 'correspond' to 'reality.' All that has ever been required by scientists or ordinary human beings is that these descriptions fit into an overall deductively acceptable system or science that accounts for what it says it accounts for. To put the matter bluntly – it has to work!

Indeed, it could be argued that modern science grew out of, and at the same time established, such a correspondence that was both impossible to establish and unnecessary. Few could, or would wish to, deny the success of the science story. But the science story does not in any way imply the correctness of the correspondence theory or so-called 'representationalism.' It is not correspondence *per se* that postmodernism need discredit, but the imperialistic imposition of science – explanation, truth, self, and all the other critical elements of the science story, including epistemology itself – on other areas of life. This is the 'betrayal' that postmodernism in general and narrative therapy in particular must redress.

Science never needed, wanted, nor made much use of modern philosophy of science. It was far too successful – indeed, gloating – to take an interest in what made it possible. (Postmodernism, by contrast, has understandably turned its attention to philosophy.) Science gives us a unique way of describing both particular phenomena and general patterns of the world that makes empirical evidence relevant and deducibility possible. But human (conscious) activity does not have those characteristics; or, at the very least, they are not essential to it. It is a fundamental betrayal, carried out in the name of science, to insist that it must.

The point I am making is not that science could not possibly have explained human life activity; what I am saying is that it hasn't and doesn't. From its hegemonic position, of course, modernist science can insist that it has and does; its practitioners and defenders have the institutional locations and power to make their insistence stick. Moreover, they can explain (away) their ongoing failure by saying that they just need more time. Or – since they control, by and large, the meanings of success and failure – they can within certain limits name their failures 'successes.' But any examination – indeed, any scientific study – of how well science has done by imposing the scientific model on human life would be likely to show little or no evidence, indeed, no scientific evidence, that it has worked.

Still, that will not suffice. Ultimately postmodernism, including narrative therapy, must create an approach which is rooted not in the inhumanity of the scientific model as imposed on life activity, but in a specific mode of understanding for understanding (not explaining) human life activities. Story-telling should not be turned into a kind of explanation. It is, rather, an alternative to explanation – a non-explanatory mode of understanding the phenomenon of human life activity that is consciousness (DeBerry, 1991; Newman and Holzman, 1997; Searle, 1992).

As a mode of understanding, story-telling predates the age of science and the hegemony of explaining as the only valid mode of human understanding. The mythic mode of understanding (meta-narratives) reigned supreme in many cultures in many different parts of the world for thousands and thousands of years before Western science and the deductive/predictive model of explanation became dominant. In retrospect, it seems to have been the Greeks – particularly Plato and his student Aristotle – who effected the transition from the former to the latter. Beginning with Thales, the philosophers known as the pre-Socratics (including some who were actually contemporaries of Socrates) introduced to Western culture the question of what everything is made of (water, air, atoms, etc.). The resolution of these pre-Socratic debates about the relationship between how the world is and its connection to human beings was accomplished with the creation of methodology by Socrates and Plato, and with Plato's creation of epistemology. But it was Aristotle who returned explicitly to the pre-Socratic initiative, creating the varied systems comprising what has come to be known as ancient science; it would dominate Western understanding until the advent of modern science.

Not only did Aristotle create the systematic (if not substantially correct, at least formally valid) taxonomy necessary to science, but he also introduced both the principles of logic and the principles of teleology (the notion of causality) that permanently shaped the explanatory scientific mode. For hundreds of years after the rediscovery of Aristotle's writings, which underwent a Catholic 'reformation' at the hands of Thomas Aquinas, 'scientific' explanation and the religious/mythic understanding of human activity uneasily co-existed to make matters comprehensible (if contradictory). But as modernism came to dominate in the sixteenth, seventeenth, and eighteenth centuries through the accomplishments of science and technology, coupled with the emergence of mercantile and then industrial capitalism, the ever-growing bias in favor of explanation as the most effective – indeed, the only truly valid – mode of understanding increasingly took hold in Western culture and society.

Discovery

An extraordinary cultural artifact of Western civilization is the enduring debate over whether or not certain features of the world, which virtually everyone knows to exist, do or do not exist 'in reality.' This philosophical conundrum goes back at least to the pre-Socratic Heraclitus the Obscure and his commentaries on the continuousness of change ('the flux'). For thousands of years, philosophers, and occasionally anti-philosophers, have been arguing the matter. The debates have been so heated as to give rise to a philosophical taxonomy for classifying the various protagonists as idealists, realists, conceptualists, materialists, and so on.

First-year students of academic philosophy are frequently astounded to discover that some people actually take such matters seriously. Indeed, no small part of what is presented as the philosophical puzzle is that no *ordinary* person does. But while questions having to do with whether or not things exist and/or whether or not claims that things do or don't exist can be rationally justified have little or no significance to the man or woman in the street, they do have their value for those (opportunistically) inclined to make use of them. More importantly, these questions tend to distract attention from related matters that *are* important.

The emergence of modernism can be examined in many different areas, including technology, science, and commodity production. In the area of methodology (the understanding of understanding), modernism brings into focus the activity of discovery. Among other things, discovery is a process by which our species comes to know the nature of what there is. One example is the 'discovery' of America in 1492, a defining moment in the history of mercantilism. Frequently distorted in children's history books as a mission to discover if the Earth came to an end, Columbus' historic expedition was in fact propelled by the recognition that indeed there was something beyond the horizon. It was an effort to find out not whether anything was there, but what it was that was there. In other words, discovery as a mode of investigation presupposes that something or another, from the furthest stars to the nearest falling objects, from the movement of blood to the movement of cannon shot, exists. That is, discovery in the new age was not about searching for unicorns or the end of the rainbow; it was about finding things that were obviously there in order to understand them better.

The age of discovery produced astounding and invaluable results in every domain. In the real world (in history), what there is, and whether there is anything at all, are not abstract philosophical questions of any serious interest to anybody. What is discoverable, and the accompanying epistemological question of what can be known, dominated modernist (scientific) thought even as, within the academy, some of the more traditional idealistic questions were being raised and raised again. And in this case, I would submit, the realists and/or the materialists (aka the Marxists) were no less guilty than the idealists. For it is the question itself, not the side taken, that is abstract and irrelevant. The question of real significance for ordinary people in the modern world is (as it always has been) what can be discovered, what can be known, and how this knowledge can effectively be used for various purposes. Nowhere does the abstract argument from illusion deter anyone from their efforts at discovery.

But the hegemony of discovery, of knowing, of science and modern epistemology, has had a rather bizarre and, in my opinion, very undesirable consequence. Over time, the success of discovery produced a cultural-methodological bias in opposition to all that which cannot be discovered. The remarkable yields of discovery in so many domains turned discovery (discoverability) itself into a criterion for existence. Yet, as I have already suggested, 'existence' needs no criteria; it is neither predicate nor property. Furthermore, existence is – quite correctly and reasonably – *presumed* as a precondition *for* the activity of discovery. But the preeminence of discovery and its gradual positivist transformation into a criterion for existence itself has led to the rather curious and paradoxical situation in which imaginary things are created in order that they might subsequently be discovered! Psychology, while not the only example of this most peculiar historical phenomenon, is certainly a good example (Danziger, 1993, 1997; Gergen, 1994; Newman and Holzman, 1996).

The creation of imaginary things for the purpose of discovering them is troublesome. Among other things, it leads to a universe glutted with such imaginary objects whose existence is justified on the grounds that they are in the process of being discovered (putting-the-cart-before-the-horse-ism). Far from negating the quite valuable scientific activity of hypothesizing entities that are then empirically or mathematically further investigated, I am speaking here of the arbitrary creation of constructs for no other purpose than to render 'imposable' the model of deductive explanation.

Lest you suspect that what I am saying here is itself imaginary – or if you are too close to the pseudoscience of traditional (modernist) clinical psychology to see that *DSM-IV* (American Psychiatric Association, 1994) is not at all comparable to the systemized taxonomy of physics or chemistry but is, judged scientifically, a scam and a fraud (Newman and Gergen, 1999) – let us briefly consider what I am talking about in a closely related area of study: history.

History is of great value for the current consideration of the nature of psychology. The question of how to understand history – as a scientific explanatory mode of understanding, or as something else – has been debated intermittently for centuries. The efforts of twentieth-century positivism to scientize history, to make it fully explanatory, reached their apotheosis in an important essay by the distinguished logical positivist Carl Hempel (1965, first published in 1942). (The many reactions to this seminal essay are useful to examine as well, e.g. Dray, 1957; Newman, 1968; Scriven, 1959.) Hempel purports to show that even though history, for a variety of reasons, might not have a systematically theoretically consistent frame of reference as do physics, chemistry, and the other natural sciences, the deductive model must be implicitly employed for historical analyses of given events to be explanatory at all. The so-called 'covering-law' model of history takes actual accountings – for example, of Cortés' invasion of Mexico – as incomplete sketches which must be filled out. To fill them out properly, to arrive at a full-blown explanation, one must not only introduce additional preconditions required for the *explanans* (the invasion) to be useable for deducing the event of Cortés' victory (the *explanandum*), but one must also articulate and/or discover implicit general laws 'governing' its occurrence. However, Hempel's laws, which turn out to look like universal statements about Cortés-like people and invasion-type events, are transparently imaginary; they have no scientific justification other than that they are required for the model to be applied. There is no verifiability possible: 'Cortés-like people' implies a universe of discourse that includes only Cortés.

Hempel's position, although trivial, is to some extent true: if all understanding is necessarily explanatory, then the imposition of the deductive model in the absence of any independent existential evidence is defensible. But how do we justify the claim that history must be explanatory? We might be perfectly ready to acknowledge the extent to which history leads to a greater understanding of the world without needing to equate that understanding with explanation.

By analogy, the characterizations in *DSM-IV* can be of substantial value. But their value is thoroughly undermined, in my opinion, by the a priori demand that they be part of a scientific explanatory system. Hempel's essay was especially vulnerable to the charge that the deduction in question (the sketch filled out) was either tautological (and therefore trivial) or false. Explanations using *DSM-IV* are similarly vulnerable. I am not arguing that human beings – our history, our psychology – could not have been scientifically understood (explained). But so far as can be told, it simply did not happen. The science story doesn't work.

Most historians, even those sympathetic to an objectivist standard, have found that efforts to create theoretically sound systemizations ultimately betray history – the subject matter of History (e.g. Scriven, 1959). The imposition of the explanatory model is, therefore, a betrayal not merely of moral significance, but of human beings' ever-evolving developmental concern with understanding. The insistence that everything can be explained, that everything can be known, effectively undermines a most important area of study: the study of the unknowable, of that which cannot be known or explained. Is this to advocate on behalf of pre-scientific mysticism? Quite the contrary. It is the uncritical imposition of the deductive model on phenomenona which, by their nature, cannot be subsumed by science that generates the unicorns and centaurs (and gods) of modernism.

Don't Explain!

On one wall of my therapy office is a lovely poster of the late African American jazz singer Billie Holiday. It constantly reminds me of the title of one of her most beautiful songs, 'Don't Explain.' (On another wall is a poster of Che Guevara, reminding me that revolutionaries are guided by great feelings of love.) On my bookshelves sit, among others, the writings of Ludwig Wittgenstein and Lev Vygotsky. Each in his own way – Wittgenstein in the philosophy of language and related topics, Vygotsky in the area of human development – recognized the need to create a method other than the scientific one for studying becoming. Wittgenstein made language-games the centerpiece of his therapeutic method for better understanding the unsystematic, unexplainable, nuanced activity that is language in use (1953, 1965, 1980). Vygotsky employed tool-and-result methodology (as opposed to the tool for result, instrumentalist method of science) and his most significant practical-critical discovery, the zone of proximal development (zpd), to better understand human development as fundamentally a cultural phenomenon (Newman and Holzman, 1993; Vygotsky, 1978, 1987, 1993). Wittgenstein and Vygotsky were, in my view, the two late-modernist thinkers who set the stage for postmodernism and for narrative therapy.

I prefer to think of narrative therapy as one among many new therapeutic approaches identifiable more generally as postmodern. Social therapy, the term I use to describe the clinical work I have been doing along with my many colleagues for almost twenty years, is another postmodern approach (Holzman and Newman, 1979; Newman, 1991, 1994, 1996; Newman and Holzman, 1996, 1997). What seems to me to be characteristic of this family of new therapies (or at least should be if they are to be consistent with what motivates them) is that they jettison the methodological paraphernalia of the scientific model. Postmodern therapies must eliminate truth. They must eliminate explanation. They must eliminate the use of *DSM-IV* as anything other than a perhaps poetic glossary, a compendium of the usual characterizations of human emotionality, but surely not analogous to the systematic theoretical taxonomy of the sciences. The understanding of becoming that is narrative therapy – the creating and the telling of stories that capture, without betraying, the ever-changing reality of human consciousness and, hopefully, of human development – must make a clean break with epistemology. While I think they are of great significance, efforts to create a postmodern epistemology, such as Gergen's 'social epistemology' (1995) or Shotter's 'knowing of the third kind' (1990, 1993b), do not go all the way in eliminating many of the epistemological conceptions which these authors themselves acknowledge are pernicious.

As Lois Holzman and I discuss in *The End of Knowing* (Newman and Holzman, 1997), epistemology is best recognized (knowing is best understood) as a sociocultural phenomenon, one that has dominated Western civilization from the Greeks until the current century. Its most important product, science, is and will continue to be, without doubt, a lasting contribution to human development. But like all great cultural developments, it is not universal in its usefulness. Indeed, in its declining years the scientific method, imposed on areas to which it has no relevance – and, as such, imposed inhumanely – has effectively paralyzed human development. Modern psychology, in my opinion, embodies that paralysis. It seems to me that narrative therapy in particular, and postmodern therapy in general, is not and must not be related to as a kind of explanation but as an entirely different mode of understanding. Not only can it help people with their emotional problems, it can help us better understand what emotional problems, cognitive problems – indeed what human consciousness – are all about.

For only in the sense that it fully exposes, in practice, the painful constraints of modernistically overdefined emotionality can it serve to liberate us. Like Wittgenstein's language-games and Vygotsky's zone of proximal development, the creating and telling of stories produce in their activity a sensuous understanding of the individualistic fly bottle in which we reside. It is postmodern story-telling, rather than pre-modern meta-narrative myth, which helps us to see the limitations of the modernist understanding of conscious human life activity. The last thing narrative therapy needs is to explain.

Winslade and Drewery's essay (1997) purporting to tell the 'theoretical story of narrative therapy' does more harm, in my opinion, than the seen-at-a-glance problems I spoke of at the beginning of this essay. Taken together, the title of their essay and the various confusions about the issues of meaning imply either that there is or that there should be a theoretical story for narrative therapy. In this I believe they are seriously mistaken. I would urge not only that narrative therapy needs no theory but that in having one it is inhumanly disfigured. For the having of a theory, obviously critical to an explanatory science, fundamentally distorts story-telling as an alternative mode of understanding. The story created in the narrative session (or the new life activity, the new play, the new performance created in the social therapeutic session) is not designed to create new fictions. Rather, its purpose is to expose the fictional nature of what is presented by both ordinary language and ordinary psychology in their explanatory mode as 'the truth.'

As Gergen (1994) points out so eloquently in his recent writings on identity politics, it is a sad irony that individuals and groupings of people in our culture who have had less than their fair share rapidly become as dogmatically insistent on the truthfulness of their separate identity-based stories as the dominant culture is dogmatic about the truthfulness of the official, oppressive story. (It is sadly ironic because, as Gergen argues, all those competing alternative stories end up being used to undermine the justifiable claims of such individuals and groups for a fair share.) Narrative therapists must be concerned that the new story created for or by the client not become as dogmatically accepted as was the old, more societally pre-determined story. The emancipation that postmodern therapies provide comes from people recognizing, discovering, and transforming their life activity based on a new post-scientific understanding of the 'storiedness,' the cultural mythicality, the human authorship, of human consciousness.

To transform this activity into an explanation is, in my opinion, simultaneously to misunderstand what science as a (modernist) mode of understanding is and is likely to go on being, and to misunderstand what non-scientific (postmodernist) modes of understanding are and must continue to be created. Stories do not need theories any more than works of fiction do: we do not and need not ask which is a truer story, *Moby Dick* or *Les Misérables*, although surely there is much to say about these two creative masterpieces.

Much can be said about the *practice of method* (Holzman and Newman, 1979) that is narrative therapy and/or social therapy and/or other modes of postmodern therapies. But they require no theoretical backup. They must not be true. If we do not recognize this, I fear that those who come to us for help will be locked into their new stories in as problematic a manner as they were locked into their old ones. The sign on the wall of the postmodern therapist's office must read: 'Don't Explain.'

Author's Note

Thanks to my long-time collaborator Lois Holzman for valuable discussions of the ideas expressed in this chapter.

References

American Psychiatric Association (1994) *Diagnostic and Statistical Manual of Mental Disorders*. 4th edn. Washington, DC: American Psychiatric Association.

Danziger, K. (1993) *Constructing the Subject: Historical Origins of Psychological Research*. Cambridge: Cambridge University Press.

Danziger, K. (1997) *Naming the Mind: How Psychology Found Its Language*. London and Thousand Oaks, CA: Sage.

DeBerry, S.T. (1991) *The Externalization of Consciousness and the Psychopathology of Everyday Life*. Westport, CT: Greenwood Press.

Dray, W. (1957) *Laws and Explanation in History*. Oxford: Oxford University Press.

Gergen, K.J. (1982) *Toward Transformation in Social Knowledge*. London and Thousand Oaks, CA: Sage.

Gergen, K.J. (1991) *The Saturated Self: Dilemmas of Identity in Contemporary Life*. New York: Basic Books.

Gergen, K.J. (1994) *Realities and Relationships: Soundings in Social Construction*. London and Cambridge, MA: Harvard University Press.

Gergen, K.J. (1995) 'Social Construction and the Transformation of Identity Politics.' Presented at the New School for Social Research, New York City.

Hempel, C. (1965) *Aspects of Scientific Explanation and Other Essays in the Philosophy of Science*. New York: Free Press.

Hempel, C. and Oppenheim, P. (1953) 'The Logic of Explanation,' in H. Feigl and M. Brodbeck (eds), *Readings in the Philosophy of Science*. New York: Appleton-Century-Crofts. pp. 319–52.

Holzman, L. and Newman, F. (1979) *The Practice of Method: An Introduction to the Foundations of Social Therapy*. New York: Practice Press.

Laing, R.D. (1967) *The Politics of Experience*. New York: Ballantine.

Lax, W.D. (1992) 'Postmodern Thinking in Clinical Practice,' in S. McNamee and K. Gergen (eds), *Therapy as Social Construction*. London and Thousand Oaks, CA: Sage. pp. 69–85.

McNamee, S. and Gergen, K. (eds) (1992) *Therapy as Social Construction*. London and Thousand Oaks, CA: Sage.

Monk, G., Winslade, J., Crocket, K., and Epston, D. (eds) (1997) *Narrative Therapy in Practice: The Archeology of Hope*. San Francisco: Jossey-Bass Publishers.

Morss, J. (1993) 'Spirited Away: A Consideration of the Anti-Developmental Zeitgeist,' *Practice: The Magazine of Psychology and Political Economy*, 9 (2): 22–8.

Morss, J. (1996) *Growing Critical: Alternatives to Developmental Psychology*. London and New York: Routledge.

Newman, F. (1968) *Explanation by Description: An Essay on Historical Methodology*. The Hague: Mouton.

Newman, F. (1991) *The Myth of Psychology*. New York: Castillo International.

Newman, F. (1994) *Let's Develop! A Guide to Continuous Personal Growth*. New York: Castillo International.

Newman, F. (1996) *Performance of a Lifetime: A Practical-Philosophical Guide to the Joyous Life*. New York: Castillo International.

Newman, F. and Gergen, K.J. (1999) 'Diagnosis: The Human Cost of the Rage to Order,' in L. Holzman (ed), *Performing Psychology: A Postmodern Culture of the Mind*. New York: Routledge. pp. 73–86.

Newman, F. and Holzman, L. (1993) *Lev Vygotsky: Revolutionary Scientist*. London and New York: Routledge.

Newman, F. and Holzman, L. (1996) *Unscientific Psychology: A Cultural-Performatory Approach to Understanding Human Life*. Westport, CT: Praeger.

Newman, F. and Holzman, L. (1997) *The End of Knowing: A New Developmental Way of Learning*. London and New York: Routledge.

Parker, I. (1992) *Discourse Dynamics: Critical Analysis for Social and Individual Psychology*. London: Routledge.

Parker, I. (1996) 'Against Wittgenstein: Materialist Reflections on Language in Psychology,' *Theory & Psychology*, 6 (3): 363–84.

Scriven, M. (1959) 'Truisms as the Grounds for Historical Explanation,' in R. Gardiner (ed.), *Theories of History*. Glencoe, IL: Free Press.

Searle, J. (1992) *The Rediscovery of Mind*. Cambridge, MA: MIT Press.

Shotter, J. (1990) *Knowing of the Third Kind: Selected Writings on Psychology, Rhetoric, and the Culture of Everyday Social Life*. Utrecht: ISOR.

Shotter, J. (1991) 'Wittgenstein and Psychology: On Our "Hook Up" to Reality,' in A. Phillips-Griffiths (ed.), *Wittgenstein: Centenary Essays*. Cambridge: Cambridge University Press. pp. 193–208.

Shotter, J. (1992) ' "Getting in Touch": The Meta-Methodology of a Postmodern Science of Mental Life,' in S. Kvale (ed.), *Psychology and Postmodernism*. London and Thousand Oaks, CA: Sage. pp. 58–73.

Shotter, J. (1993a) *Conversational Realities: Studies in Social Constructionism*. London and Thousand Oaks, CA: Sage.

Shotter, J. (1993b) *Cultural Politics of Everyday Life: Social Constructionism, Rhetoric and Knowing of the Third Kind*. Toronto: University of Toronto Press.

Vygotsky, L.S. (1978) *Mind in Society*. London and Cambridge, MA: Harvard University Press.

Vygotsky, L.S. (1987) *The Collected Works of L.S. Vygotsky, Vol. 1*. New York: Plenum.

Vygotsky, L.S. (1993) *The Collected Works of L.S. Vygotsky, Vol. 2*. New York: Plenum.

Winch, P. (1958) *The Idea of a Social Science*. New York: Routledge & Kegan Paul.

Winslade, J. and Drewery, W. (1997) 'The Theoretical Story of Narrative Therapy,' in G. Monk, J. Winslade, K. Crocket, and D. Epston (eds), *Narrative Therapy in Practice: The Archeology of Hope*. San Francisco: Jossey-Bass. pp. 32–52.

Wittgenstein, L. (1953) *Philosophical Investigations*. Oxford: Basil Blackwell.

Wittgenstein, L. (1965) *The Blue and Brown Books*. New York: Harper Torchbooks.

Wittgenstein, L. (1980) *Remarks on the Philosophy of Psychology, Vol. 1*. Oxford: Basil Blackwell.

Index

The letter n *following a page number indicates a reference in the notes*

Printed in the United Kingdom by
Lightning Source UK Ltd., Milton Keynes
136858UK00003B/156/A

9 780761 952534